Mrs. Sherlock
Holmes

Also by Brad Ricca

•

Super Boys:
The Amazing Adventures of Jerry Siegel and Joe Shuster—
the Creators of Superman

MRS. SHERLOCK HOLMES

The True Story of New York City's Greatest

Female Detective and the 1917 Missing Girl Case

That Captivated a Nation

Brad Ricca

St. Martin's Griffin

New York

www.stmartins.com

Designed by Kathryn Parise

The Library of Congress has cataloged the hardcover edition as follows:

Names: Ricca, Brad, author.
Title: Mrs. Sherlock Holmes : the true story of New York City's greatest female detective and the 1917 missing girl case that captivated a nation / Brad Ricca.
Description: First Edition. | New York : St. Martin's Press, 2016. | Includes bibliographical references and index.
Identifiers: LCCN 2016036711 | ISBN 9781250072245 (hardcover) | ISBN 9781466883659 (ebook)
Subjects: LCSH: Humiston, Grace (Mary Grace), 1869–1948. | Women private investigators—New York (State)—New York—Case studies. | Women lawyers—New York (State)—New York—Case studies. | Missing persons—Investigation—New York (State)—New York—Case studies.
Classification: LCC HV8083.H86 R53 2016 | DDC 362.82/9765097471—dc23
LC record available at https://lccn.loc.gov/2016036711

ISBN 978-1-250-16083-6 (trade paperback)

Our books may be purchased in bulk for promotional, educational, or business use. Please contact your local bookseller or the Macmillan Corporate and Premium Sales Department at 1-800-221-7945, extension 5442, or by email at MacmillanSpecialMarkets@macmillan.com.

First St. Martin's Griffin Edition: January 2018

10   9

For my mom

CONTENTS

CAVEAT EMPTOR

This story is intended for three classes of readers, and no more. It is intended for those who have to bring up children, for those who have to bring up themselves, and for those who, in order that they may think of bettering the weaker, are, on their own part, strong enough to begin that task by bearing a knowledge of the truth.

For it is the truth only that I have told. Throughout this narrative there is no incident that is not a daily commonplace in the life of the underworld of every large city. If proof were needed, the newspapers have, during the last twelvemonth, proved as much. I have written only what I have myself seen and myself heard, and I set it down for none but those who may profit by it.

REGINALD WRIGHT KAUFFMAN,
preface to *The House of Bondage*
(1910)

•

If ever prayer came from the depths of a broken heart,
it was that forlorn plea for a lost sister.

EUSTACE HALE BALL, *Traffic in Souls:*
A Novel of Crime and Its Cure (1914)

Mrs. Sherlock
Holmes

Prologue

May 27, 1914

Pushing through the water, the massive steamship *Olympic*, sister of the lost *Titanic*, docked at New York City carrying passengers, thousands of sacks of mail, and the mind of the world's greatest detective. But that was only part of the truth. As a dark thunderstorm rained down, a burly man in a brown fedora watched from the dock as the four ghostly smokestacks of *Olympic* seemed to gain more height in the misty air. The man ducked his face and walked with purpose to the tent marked QUARANTINE. As he disappeared past the doors, reporters waited with their cameras, hoping for the opportunity to snap proof of the meeting between this man, William J. Burns, America's famous detective, and the *Olympic*'s special passenger that day—Sir Arthur Conan Doyle, the creator of Sherlock Holmes.

When Billy Burns and Doyle clapped hands inside, it was only the second time the two had met since Doyle's first visit to New York in 1884. Burns had a bushy mustache that readers knew from the newspaper illustrations that accompanied the accounts of his sensational encounters. Doyle's own, more traditional handlebar was bigger, longer, and framed his squinting eyes in a most natural manner. Lady Jean Doyle, Sir Arthur's younger wife, smiled at the two men, mirrors of each other's fictions. A former Secret Service agent, Burns had solved major national cases, including the sad murder of Mary Phagan in Atlanta. Burns had parlayed his fame into the William J. Burns International Detective Agency, with busy branches all across the country. He was often referred to as the American Sherlock Holmes. "There are no mysteries in crime," Burns once said. "Mysterious disappearances of men and women . . . they don't occur, for the simple reason that for every act, be it great or small, there is a motive, hidden though it may be from general knowledge."

The Doyles piled into Burns's auto as he drove them to the Plaza, accompanied by a police escort. As the rain drummed on the roof, Doyle, who was over six feet tall and weighed over two hundred pounds, looked out into the rising lights of the city. He saw a bright sign for Morton Salt that featured a man with a top hat—and nearly gasped when the hat actually tipped forward. The streets of separate houses had been replaced by buildings with similar signs advertising Blackstone Cigars and Heinz 57 India Relish that were taller than the churches. Doyle heard very few whips, only the grinding of cars. Out of the corner of his eye, he saw a dark motorcycle. New York unfolded before him, uncaring of his astonishment, but at the same time thriving on it. Doyle tried to take in all the wide streets and tall buildings. Some, like the Woolworth Building, were over fifty stories high. At the top of all those floors was a gilded apex meant to create the illusion of even greater height. Doyle sat back in his seat and said, half to himself, "I am amazed, fairly paralyzed at the sight of New York."

In the warmly lit Plaza, the party moved past walls of Flemish oak decorated with pictures of Bavarian castles. There, under a chandelier made of iron grapes topped by a barmaid hoisting a foamy stein, reporters asked Doyle for his opinions on a myriad of topics. Doyle, who knew he was much loved here, put his hands in his waistcoat and happily obliged the reporters. He said he was looking forward to his few days in New York, before he and his wife would head off to the Selkirk range in Canada for a wilderness adventure. When the questions turned political, Doyle said he admired Colonel Roosevelt a great deal, calling him a superman. The author also had great praise for the New York police—and, of course, his good friend Billy "Hot Tabasco" Burns. Doyle embraced him with laughter. Finally, someone asked about the real news that day, from Doyle's home, England, where there had been fifty-eight arrests at Buckingham Palace during a suffragist rally. The radicals were attempting to deliver a petition to the royals when fifteen hundred police broke up the demonstration and arrested the group's leaders. Doyle listened to the question, anxious to answer.

"Something drastic is sure to happen," Doyle replied, "and to happen speedily." Doyle spoke with a sliding, elegant speech that worked its way across the old Scots vowels. "There will be a wholesale lynching bee, I fancy. For the English mob when thoroughly aroused is not a respector of sex, and the woman will have brought down the thunder on their own heads." The reporters wrote swiftly in their notepads.

The next day, Doyle and his wife were driven up the river to visit the famous Sing Sing prison. Doyle insisted that he be locked in a solitary cell for five full minutes. Everyone else waited outside. Afterward, he walked down the tight corridor where they kept the prisoners waiting to be executed. In the circular room past that hallway, Doyle raised a pudgy leg and lifted himself into the electric chair itself. Doyle closed his eyes and tried to feel something. Afterward, Doyle laughingly proclaimed that the black chair—"Old Sparky"—had a good-bottomed seat despite its "sinister wires." Doyle said, slyly, that "it was the most restful time I have had since I had arrived in New York."

When they got back to the Plaza, Doyle took a look at some of New York's famous newspapers. His face turned red as he read them. He was furious that his previous comments on suffragists had not gone over well with the Americans. To clarify his words, Doyle agreed to an interview with Marguerite Mooers Marshall of the *New York Evening World*.

"I never said such a thing!" exploded Doyle, once Marshall asked about his quote about a lynch mob supposedly hunting suffragettes. "I am anti-suffrage," admitted Doyle. "All I meant was that I should not be surprised to hear of a lynching."

Lady Doyle, pretty and thin and dressed in pink, leaned in to stop her husband from saying one more word.

"Please," Lady Doyle begged Marshall, "don't say he thinks it would be a good plan to lynch those women." Marshall looked at Lady Doyle and wondered if she was his actual Watson. Marshall reworded the question in her head and asked Sir Arthur again. "Surely this is just a manifestation of a widespread feminine restlessness and revolt," Marshall said. "You are not an opponent of Woman's Progress?"

"Certainly not," retorted Doyle. "I would have women enjoy the best educational opportunities. I would have them enter the arts and the professions they choose." He thought a moment, before putting what he wanted to say into different words.

"I like to see a woman with brains who uses them," gruffed Doyle. "I love and honor women as wives and mothers. But I cannot approve of a campaign of destruction."

Lady Doyle added that since Great Britain boasts so many women, if they got the vote they would indeed manage the country. "Who would want to live under the rule of woman?" she asked. She laughed a high sound.

"Suffragist that I am, I confess I wouldn't!" agreed Marshall.

In the piece that followed, Marshall called Doyle the "biggest, blondest, breeziest Englishman we have seen in many a long day. He has that physical fitness kept by so few Americans in late middle life; that erectness and absence of superfluous tissue which mean just one thing— regular outdoor exercise. He played in a hard game of football at the age of forty-two." Alongside the story ran a cartoon of a lynch mob going after an old woman labeled "suffragette."

Later that day, Doyle visited the Tombs, the new eight-story prison located in lower Manhattan. Doyle desperately wanted to meet Charles Becker, the New York City police officer who had been convicted and sentenced to die for the murder of a small-time bookmaker named

Herman Rosenthal. The sensational case had held the attention of newspaper readers for months. "It's against the rules," said the warden, shaking his head. Instead, Doyle was allowed an extensive private tour. They started on the lowest level, in the furnace room, and worked their way up through closets, coal bins, the cramped exercise yard, and the shadowy grates in the doors that separated murderers from the open world. Doyle searched every corner, according to the *Evening World*, "just as if they were looking for a clue to some enthralling mystery."

Doyle pronounced it "a most superior prison." "Do you think it would do for the incarceration of suffragettes?" a reporter asked.

"It would make an excellent place for that," Doyle replied, with a wink.

The next day, young suffrage activist Inez Milholland Boissevain read Doyle's quote. She was angry at it, but she still laughed. She wrote off a response to the papers.

Sir Arthur is one of the minor novelists, and still more, he is one of the minor prophets. Englishmen of Sir Arthur's chuckle-headed type say exasperating things like that about the militants one minute, and the next minute beseech them to bury the hatchet. Well, they'll bury it.

Doyle read this and harrumphed. This was getting out of hand. The Doyles were leaving for their long vacation soon, but they had a few days left in Gotham to fix this. Doyle knew that his best defense was to fall back on his old practical detective. So the next time he spoke with reporters, Doyle went to his bread and butter. Sherlock Holmes had been his breakthrough as a writer, but, though Doyle was certainly grateful to the old chap, he had retired him in 1893 in "The Adventure of the Final Problem," where Holmes fell to his apparent death at Reichenbach Falls, locked in combat with his mortal enemy, Professor Moriarty. The irony, Doyle knew, is that it was the frustrating mysteries surrounding Holmes himself that was part of the great draw of his stories. But he was not about to tell his readers that. Sherlock Holmes stories were sellouts whenever they appeared in *The Strand, Collier's*, and *The American Magazine.*

In truth, Doyle just wanted to write different sorts of books, having articulated Holmes since 1887. But the public was always restless, and perhaps Doyle was too, so he returned to the detective in 1901, resurrecting him outright in 1903.

"A Cornish fisherman was the worse critic I had," Doyle told the reporters. "He told me, 'Well, sur, Sherlock Holmes may not have killed himself falling over that cliff. But he did injure himself something terrible. He's never been the same since!'" The crowd clapped. Doyle, basking again in the adoration of his readers, couldn't resist adding that, given the amount of crime he was hearing about in New York, "the history of America would be better if you could get a shipload of Sherlocks over here." He pronounced it *Shrrlock.*

Before he left New York, Arthur Conan Doyle took the time to film brief cameos in several motion pictures. He and his wife appeared for a moment in episode 22 of *Our Mutual Girl*, a comedic serial detailing the adventures of a young woman in New York. In the short episode, Doyle confers with Burns on a case. Doyle also appeared as himself in both *The $5,000,000 Counterfeiting Plot*, a dramatic serial about a Burns case, and in *Universal Animated Weekly* number 117, a more traditional newsreel that covered his arrival in America.

After filming completed and they said good-bye to Burns, the Doyles left New York. They made their way to Alberta in a private train car—complete with their own parlor—where they sat in chairs and watched as the wilderness rolled out beside them like an endless painting. When they returned home to England, the First World War had begun. By the first of July 1916, the Somme River in France, normally full of rich, flowing water, ran red with blood. The Battle of the Somme cost twenty thousand British soldiers in a single day. One of the men on the edge of these impossible numbers was Kingsley Doyle, Sir Arthur's son, who was gravely wounded but miraculously survived. He was still recovering from his injuries when the flu came sweeping across Europe in 1918. Kingsley, who was twenty-five, became ill and died. The Doyles were devastated.

The papers said that Sir Arthur Conan Doyle had been, off and on, a proponent and practitioner of spiritualism—that is, the practice of so-called psychical research to communicate with the dead. After his son's tragic passing, Doyle told friends that he turned back to spiritualism because "the war has shown us the breakdown of nearly every social and religious system we held dear." He turned out lights, lit candles, and spoke words into the air.

"Some time ago," continued Doyle, "I said I knew of thirteen mothers—thirteen—who were receiving direct messages from sons who passed away. Doubt was expressed—gentle doubt—by a newspaper, which asked: 'Who are the mothers? What are their names?' Well, I know thirty mothers now who are receiving these messages.

"Millions of men and women are looking," Doyle said, "as they never have done before for a sign and a consolation." The war, and sickness, had brought death to every doorstep at a quicker pace than usual. Parents were looking for their children everywhere they could, even in the corners beyond death. What Doyle was describing was an older, deeper mystery.

Doyle often quoted Dr. James Hyslop, a psychologist who was active in psychic research through scientific means and logic. Hyslop said that in attempting to communicate with the dead, "all that interests me is that it comes, and that it corresponds with evidence in this world."

"There is no death," claimed the author of Sherlock Holmes. "Only a veil."

1

True Detective Mysteries

A single electric bulb looped down from the uneven ceiling. It sparked hot white. A man with dark features stepped into the bright circle below it, which lit up a scar near his left eye.

The dark man palmed his hat and crunched his unlit cigar. He surveyed the entire room, fixing his eyes into its soft, webby corners.

Hello? he asked. His accent started from a growl and slid upward.

The room smelled of damp cement, wood, and oil. Two other men followed him in. One was enormous. The other was short and wore overalls. That one looked at everything with keen, moving eyes. He was looking for shiny nails. The fat man perspired. As the dark man searched, the short man knocked on the walls with his knuckles. He listened to the walls as if they were speaking to him.

He held up a hand and they all stopped.

There were pipes and a tin sign and some saws on the floor, but otherwise the room was more or less empty, except for a large bench against the wall. In the corner of the room was a bag that they were all staying away from. After a moment, the dark man began stepping in slow circles on the planked flooring. The others followed him into a corner, where exposed brick lay against the bottom half of the wall. The fat man took off his coat, then his vest.

The short man in overalls examined the large table. He motioned, and everyone helped him move it. They pushed it to the side and stared downward. The floorboards were missing. Instead, in the cement floor, they saw a door, set into the ground like a gate to hell.

The dark man dropped to a knee. He pulled back the door and stared down into a black hole in the ground. They listened again for voices. There was no telling where it went.

Call her, the man said, as he jumped in.

2

The Missing Skater

February 13, 1917

From the front window of her family's second-floor apartment, Christina Cruger pressed her face against the glass, looking out on the street below. There was the usual mix of afternoon people in hats and coats on the sidewalk. They were walking with their bags and babies in the bitter February cold. The sun flashed through the clouds over the Hudson and onto Harlem. The snow fell when it wanted to.

Twenty-year-old Christina wiped away the steam and scraped at the spidery frost on the window. Her lungs strained this close to the cold air, a side effect of her illness. But her worry was growing elsewhere. She could feel it in her stomach.

When her little sister Ruth had left two hours ago, she was wearing layers of old winter clothes and a floppy hat. She had to run an errand, Ruth told her. So Christina, who was named after her mother, watched her sister leave, as she always did, from the same window: Ruth walked briskly up the hill on Claremont Avenue before she turned east, then crossed Broadway before disappearing behind the wooden buildings. Christina watched those same corners now, looking for her sister's blue coat, swinging into the scene, framed by the peeling paint of the window frame. But the coat never appeared. This wasn't like her, thought Christina. Not Ruth, who had just graduated high school with good grades and taught Sunday school. She would just be a minute, Ruth had assured her, with that smile of hers.

Just a minute.

Looking out on the falling snow, it occurred to Christina that her sister might have gone ice-skating. A huge sense of relief filled her. That made sense. Christina scolded herself for not seeing it sooner. Ruth loved skating more than anything and had said her errands included picking up her ice skates from getting sharpened. And Ruth had let it slip that there was a new boy from Columbia University whom she liked. That made Christina feel better. With their parents up in Boston, now would be a good day for ice-skating. Ruth could keep secrets; Christina knew that. At the same time, her sister wouldn't let her worry like this, either. And Ruth wasn't dressed for ice-skating, certainly not with someone from Columbia. Christina couldn't remember his name.

Christina coughed, steaming up the window again. What if Ruth had become sick again herself? What if she was in a hospital somewhere? Christina shuddered; she had just left the hospital herself not that long ago. Or, worse yet, was Ruth passed out on a frigid sidewalk somewhere down there? Christina watched the clock. It clicked and whirred in the still room. What if she had been run down by one of those filthy automobiles on Broadway? Christina looked down. The shadows of the streetlamps were getting longer, like candles. She could see Ruth in her mind, smiling. Everyone thought of Ruth that way. Christina could not picture where her sister might be.

Christina picked up the receiver on the phone and pushed twice on the switch to call down to the operator. As she waited for her voice, Christina saw the people who had left their homes hours ago now returning, their shoes finding their earlier footprints. Christina was finally connected on the phone to her other sister, Helen. She worked as a bookkeeper at the Mexican Petroleum Company on Broadway and was three years older. Helen listened intently through

the small black cone she held up to her ear. Like her father, Helen
was very businesslike. She asked Christina to remember everything
that Ruth had told her before she left. Christina recited that Ruth
had left just after eleven o'clock to do some marketing for their
mother. She then went to a store to cash a check for twenty-five dollars. After paying some bills, Ruth had come back home to give her
sister the receipts and to have lunch. Ruth then said she was going to
the bank at 125th Street and Eighth Avenue. Then she was going
to pick up her sharpened skates, which she had dropped off in the
morning.

Ruth had gone ice-skating, Helen said quickly, instantly arriving
at the same conclusion as her sister. Probably at Notlek, Van Cortlandt, or the indoor rink at Saint Nicholas. This reassurance made
Christina feel better.

But once Helen hung up, she packed up her things and left work.
The air was chilling. There was a bit of snow on the ground. Helen
finally reached the neighborhood and began retracing her little sister's
steps. The family's bank, the United States Mortgage and Trust Company, was a big building on the corner with dark glass doors. It was
closed. Helen looked around. Could someone have seen Ruth come
in with the money she was going to deposit? Had she been the victim
of a robbery? Helen glanced around at the people lost in coats around
her. Helen tried to see inside the bank. The footprints by the door
made one, uneven shape.

Helen then made a round of the shops along Eighth Avenue near
125th Street. She went to Soames Dry Goods, but no one had seen
Ruth there. She saw a neighbor, John Gerbige, and quizzed him, right
there on the street.

"I haven't seen her since she made a stop at Gardella's stationery
store," John said, shaking his head. He estimated that was sometime
past two, but not much after. Helen went over to Gardella's, but no
one could remember her being there. No one at the Keysone Department store had seen her, either. Helen was puzzled.

Three blocks over, Helen went to the Metropolitan Motorcycles shop at 542 West 127th Street, one of those strange Harlem roads that came out of nowhere to cut across another at a sharp, sudden angle. It lay across the map like a broken stitch. Helen looked up. She was only about two and a half blocks northeast from home. Up close, the store was big and inviting, with a door in the center of two long windows. Helen saw black metal motorcycles poised behind the plate glass, which was covered with painted lettering. The store had a sign that read SKATES SHARPENED, so Helen knocked on the door, shaking the thin glass. She shivered. The sun had already set. The store was closed, which she sort of expected, so Helen turned back down the street, passing a candy store on the corner. They had conversation hearts for sale in the window.

There were cabbies in stands and people up in windows, who all seemed to watch her. Helen talked to a few other people here and there. Someone on the street told her that they did see a girl in a blue coat leave the motorcycle shop and head east. Helen's eyes lit up. But why would Ruth be walking in the opposite direction from home? That didn't make sense. Then it hit her that Ruth had probably headed for the ice.

Helen walked swiftly to the Notlek outdoor ice rink on 119th Street and Riverside. She knew they still had an evening session going on. Helen circled the low fence and peered at all the people in mackinaw coats pushing and twirling around. Her eyes focused. She saw hands that were held tight across the cold, white ice. Helen's eyes watched spinning, moving figures, visible against the white, but she couldn't—or didn't think—she saw her sister. She cursed herself for not coming here first.

The skies were dark now, and almost everyone had gone back to their homes, high or low in the clear, cold air. Helen knew she had to go home, too. Ruth had probably been at the rink, she told herself, but had probably left before her arrival. Helen walked home with speed. She imagined walking into the apartment and seeing Ruth there, nursing a purple ankle. Helen would scold her sister, and they would all laugh, agreeing never to tell their father about any of it. As she made her way home, quicker now, her boots cracking the icy crust, the street was lit by a moon that was split in half between light and darkness.

When Helen returned home, Christina was crying. So Helen, age twenty-three, who had her father in her, picked up the telephone receiver and asked to be connected to Mr. Alfred Brown, a lawyer who was the corporation counsel of Mount Vernon and her father's partner in an oil concern. Henry had told his daughters that if anything untoward happened at home, they should ring Mr. Brown straightaway. Helen filled him in, and the two immediately agreed to summon her parents back home.

On the way to the apartment, Mr. Brown sent a telegram to their father. It read:

COME HOME QUICKLY, RUTH HAS DISAPPEARED.

At the apartment, Mr. Brown tried to calm the girls down. He called the police, relating the details as Helen and Christina watched. By the time their parents came home, early the next morning, it was Valentine's Day, 1917. And pretty Ruth Cruger, eighteen years old, was lost.

Somewhere out in the snow.

＊

Ruth Cruger was smiling from under a deep pompadour of pulled-back hair, her mouth spread into an easy smile. She was wearing a soft white dress and had a great bow in her hair. Her hands were clasped on her lap. Her dark eyes were made up of tiny black dots. As she looked out, unmoving, from the front page of the *New York Evening World,* over the crease and with a handwritten "Ruth Cruger" beneath her photograph, she seemed closed in by the hand-drawn, curlicue frame. She looked positively happy. In fact, the photo seemed purposefully cropped to show only her face. Henry Cruger, her father, stared at the photo even though he had a hard time doing so. He had not imagined that everyone would see her so soon, in the evening edition on February 14, amid reports of Germany and war.

Henry was a short, unassuming man. The top of his head was bald, framed by two clumps of black hair. He wore dark, circular eyeglasses and had a mustache shot with gray. Henry was a public accountant of some renown and had offices at Grand Central Terminal. The night before, he had been eating dinner in Boston at the Grand Hotel with his wife when he was told that he had a long-distance call from his friend Mr. Brown. As Henry put the receiver to his ear and tried to hear over the clinking of silverware, Mr. Brown said words that made no sense to him. Henry found himself nodding and agreeing anyway. He and his wife left the restaurant immediately and got on a train at twelve thirty in the morning, bound for New York.

Later that morning, from home, Henry called the police himself. After he was transferred to the Fourth Branch detective house, Henry told the story of his daughter's disappearance. He could almost hear the detective on the other end of the line skritching out words on his notepad like *blue coat* and *tam-o'-shanter hat*. When Henry was done, the detective said that the police would be back in touch soon. When the detective hung up, Henry thought he must have forgotten to tell him everything.

Henry stayed home that day as his family watched the door and the phone. Henry had to focus. When the mail came, he went through each square envelope very carefully, fearful of what he might find. There was nothing. Henry had to be strong for his family. So he said good, hopeful things. Henry finally decided that he should hire a private detective. As Henry reached for his worn New York City directory, his daughter Helen slipped away from the small apartment.

Henry had already given the police a list of Ruth's destinations, including the bank, the motorcycle shop, and the stationery store, whose purpose on Ruth's excursion was still mysterious. So when he talked to the detective agency, he told them the same things. Henry also tried to explain what kind of girl she was, how she was bright, helped at church, and watched over her sister when Christina was sick, but he felt the words came out all wrong. So he stuck to numbers and facts. She went here, then there, and then disappeared. Henry hung up. That afternoon, two police detectives came by the apartment. Detective Lagarenne was tall and had brown hair. His partner, McGee, had dark hair and looked like Fatty Arbuckle. When they came to the door, Henry's heart was in his mouth.

Helen was still gone when the detectives arrived. She wanted to check the bank and the other stores that were closed the night before. Helen first went to the motorcycle store at ten thirty in the morning, but it was still closed. As Helen approached the door, she saw something new. There was a movable sign with a small black hand pointing downward. She followed the direction with her eyes and saw a small stairway under the sidewalk that led to a cellar, but it was locked up. Helen tried the bank next. It was busy, but no one had reported a robbery or had seen her sister. She returned to the motorcycle store at 12:45, but it was still closed. The pointed little hand was gone.

When Helen went back to the motorcycle store at 2:30 in the afternoon, it was finally open, and Helen walked in through the glass doors. She saw a man kneeling by a bicycle, turning a heavy wrench. When he saw her, he stood up. He was dressed in khaki. He smiled at her with a warm, dopey grin.

"Yes?" the man asked. He spoke with an accent.

Helen explained that she was looking for her sister, who had her skates sharpened the day before. She described her, with her funny hat and blue coat.

"Yes," the man said, nodding. His voice seemed like it was starting and stopping as he figured out the right words. "She left her skates here in the morning and came for them in the afternoon, paid me, and went on."

Helen's heart lifted and fell in an instant.

"What kind of shoes did she have?" asked Helen. The man looked down at her feet.

"Like yours," he said, cheerily, raising his eyes back to hers.

Helen then asked if he had seen which way she had gone. He thought for a moment, trying to remember.

"At 1:20. She went east," he said, his hand pointing out the direction. He wanted to help more, but Helen excused herself, thanking him for his kindness. She ran home to tell her father. When she walked in, Henry had a twinge of alarm. The two detectives—Lagarenne and McGee—had just left. They had told Henry that they had so far found nothing. But Helen did have something. A direction.

Helen told her father about the motorcycle shop. Henry immediately called Fourth Branch to leave a message. Henry stared at his strong daughter. She had the right idea. As she retired to her room, exhausted, Henry went out himself to search the empty, ramshackle buildings around 123rd and 124th. Theirs was a nice neighborhood, but the buildings in the shadows, wedged between alleys and streets, were still there, still occupying space. Henry could hear crying children and parents screaming in strange languages. Henry stared up into the dark windows of the tenements, sometimes catching someone's eye. There were so many occupied places here, known and not, all throughout the city. Parents and children and dogs and babies seemed to fill every invisible corner, pushing out against the city's uneven seams. As the afternoon sank into night, Henry made his way home. He paused at the stairs of his own building, his eyes drawn downward to the closed cellar door. He descended the steps down and entered the basement. He looked tensely into every black corner, where the walls met each other in shadow. He could almost hear his heart beating, the sound reverberating against the cool walls.

The next day, Henry put on his coat and went down to the Fourth Branch detective house at West 123rd Street near Manhattan Avenue. Mr. Brown accompanied him. Henry told Detectives Lagarenne and

McGee that he wanted his whole neighborhood checked and everything possible done in terms of publicity. "I want the property searched all around," Henry demanded.

Henry then asked the detectives about the man his daughter had talked to. The motorcycle man with the accent. The detectives said he was an immigrant named Alfredo Cocchi. Lagarenne assured Henry that he had personally searched the store the day before—through and through—and found nothing. They even searched the basement and the closets. Henry insisted that they put this Italian man under surveillance anyway, but Lagarenne calmly assured him that there was no reason to do so. Cocchi was respectable; he had been in business there for a year and a half and had a wife and children. Lagarenne said that Cocchi's wife was a little troublesome, but that was all. Henry asked about the bank, too—if there could have been criminals in the area, looking for easy targets who had money in their pockets. The police said they would look into it.

There was a pause as the detectives looked at each other. Lagarenne fixed his gaze back on Henry and asked if his daughter had been involved in any kind of romantic affair. Henry stared right through the two detectives as if they were made of glass. They suggested that she was perhaps on some youthful love affair and nothing more. Henry, asked them, in so many words, how they could ask him about his daughter like that. Henry Cruger saw things in absolutes. The thought of his daughter running away with a man was an utter impossibility to him.

Lagarenne then revealed that they had their first clue and pulled out his notebook. In their canvass of the area, a cab driver said that he had driven that night to 127th and Claremont Avenue, which was no more than a block from the Cruger apartment. There, he picked up a man and a young woman who matched the newspaper description of Ruth Cruger. Henry froze. The cabbie said he picked them up near Ruth's home and dropped them off near a subway entrance.

Henry put his head in his hands, reeling. The detectives cautioned him against talking to the newspapers. If the cabbie's story was true, and they warned him that the account was uncorroborated, it suggested an elopement rather than a kidnapping. They had to proceed carefully. They didn't even have the cab driver's name yet, the detectives explained. Henry didn't believe them.

Henry was furious that the detectives had not told him this immediately. So when a reporter called later that day, he didn't heed the detectives' request for silence. This was his daughter, after all.

"She is very attractive in appearance," Henry told the reporter. "She cared more for her studies than for social life. She was happy and contented at home and, I am sure, had no love affair. She was endeavoring to recuperate from the slight overexertion to which she subjected herself in passing the examinations that enabled her to graduate from the high school early this month. She taught Sunday School." He took a breath.

"She is not the kind of girl who would stay away from home without letting us know of her whereabouts," Henry said. She had just gone out to get "a pair of skates attached to a pair of tanned shoes," he said. "She wore a long velour coat." Repeating it acted as a tonic on his unquiet mind. As he read it, he wondered what man out there might help him.

By Friday afternoon, anyone who read the papers—or even looked at the front page on the cold city streets, layered with streetcars and motorcars—knew that Ruth Cruger was the Harlem girl who had disappeared. The *New York Times* headline on February 16 read PRETTY GIRL SKATER STRANGELY MISSING. People all over the city read the story and shook their heads. The photograph spoke for itself. When Henry finally got home that night from walking the streets, looking and studying every face he could, he heard his wife crying in the other room. He had to find this driver.

The next day, Saturday, a short dark-haired woman walked up to the Fourth Branch detective house. She walked quickly, her body set against the cold as she led a small boy in a heavy coat that covered everything but his wide eyes. The woman carried a bundle of something in her arms. It was noon. She entered the building and proceeded to the main desk. She uncovered her head to reveal medium-length hair. She then announced that her name was Maria Cocchi and that her husband, Alfredo, who owned a motorcycle shop in Harlem, was missing.

3

The Coroner's Cabinet

March 4, 1905

Apoliceman and a doctor approached the wooden building that tilted off the corner of the street. They crouched as they moved forward in a half run. There was a general store on the first floor, its door shut. There were jars in the windows. They saw the stairs leading up the side to the second floor. As they got closer, they could see the white paint curling down the sides. The steps rattled as they walked up.

The door was half open, so the men pushed their way in. They stepped into a small apartment consisting of two rooms filled with only a few sticks of furniture. In an old rocking chair beside the living room window, a man sat with his back to them. His legs were crossed and a briar pipe dangled in his right hand. The men walked around to get a better look. His chin rested on his chest. A dark line of blood ran down his forehead and onto his white shirt.

"Sonta," the cop said.

Everyone knew that name in Kingsland, New Jersey, in 1905. Joseph Sonta was one of the small town's first settlers and its richest citizen, though no one really knew what he did. Sonta had nine children who rolled over him like water whenever he came home from his long days spent playing cards and drinking wine in a back room somewhere. At the same time, he seemed to protect a single coal of anger burning in him at all times. He was a *padron* with a belly laugh that everyone recognized. Kingsland had been his domain for ten years. Now, he was dead in a rocking chair after someone had shot him twice in the head.

The policeman looked around as the doctor's hands floated over Sonta's body. This was not Sonta's home; it belonged to an immigrant named Giovanni Tolla. Like many Kingsland residents, Tolla had come to America by writing to Sonta from Italy and enclosing some money. A year later, Tolla; his wife, Antoinette; and their two small daughters, Catherine and Mary, arrived in New Jersey on the promise of work. The young couple, both only twenty-four, were very poor but were well liked in the little town. Antoinette, a good mother and wife, was very religious. She had brown eyes and dark brown hair and was very beautiful.

After leaving the apartment, the men approached the small crowd gathered outside and asked them questions. The crowd smelled like cigarettes. Everyone had the same story: They had seen a woman running down the middle of the street from Tolla's house with a gun in her hand, shouting, *"Gli ho sparato!"*

When the cop asked about those words, someone told him it meant, "I shot him."

"I shot him," Antoinette Tolla had said, as she had run down the street.

She didn't get far. They found her with friends, collapsed and hysterical. Sheriff James Mercer, of Bergen County, took her into custody and locked her in the Hackensack jail, since Kingsland didn't have one. It was March 4, 1905, the day of Teddy Roosevelt's second inauguration. A few days later, as Antoinette sat in her cell, the spring term of the grand jury heard the facts of her case.

"The first case of homicide of which I will speak," said Justice Garretson, "is that of the woman alleged to have shot a man while sitting in her home. The evidence shows that she came into the room behind him, secured a pistol and shot him in the head. If these facts be proven, you must indict for murder."

Within three hours, the grand jury indicted Antoinette Tolla for first-degree murder. Two weeks later, she faced trial before the exact same judge. The prosecution's job was fairly easy. Sonta's son Rocco, age six, claimed to have been there and was brought forward as a witness. He said that his father and Mr. Tolla had been talking quietly when Mrs. Tolla crept up behind him and killed his poppa. Several of Antoinette's neighbors testified on her behalf. Some reached the stand only to start sobbing. Others just shrugged their shoulders. None of them spoke English. A local student served as their interpreter, but many feared that the young man didn't seem to know what he was doing. After a witness would become animated and flash their hands for several minutes, the interpreter would deliver a few sentences in dull, uninspired tones. He fumbled over words and tenses, facts and beliefs.

When it came time for Antoinette's defense, she took the stand and faced the court. She said that she was sad that she had shot Sonta. She told the interpreter that she had only shot him because he had threatened her honor. Sonta had been hounding her for months, Antoinette said, even in front of her husband. But since Sonta had brought them here to America, her husband was afraid to defend her. Antoinette looked down at her lap. She said that she had appealed to Mrs. Sonta for help, and she told Antoinette to buy a gun.

"To frighten him," Antoinette said.

At about 1:30 on the afternoon of March 4, Sonta had arrived at the Tolla household unannounced—as usual. Antoinette's husband was half asleep on a trunk in the living room. At the sight of Sonta barging in, big and drunk, Mr. Tolla jumped up and left in a fit of anger. Antoinette watched her husband leave.

"Why does Giovanni always leave when I come in?" Sonta bellowed, jokingly upset as he collapsed into his favorite rocking chair.

"It's on account of your coming," Antoinette said, facing him. She told the interpreter that Sonta then seized her and pulled her into his arms. He held her against him and kissed her. But she bit his hand and managed to escape to the other side of the room.

"I'm going to have you even if I have to kill your husband," said Sonta. His eyes were devoured by drink. "I've got a gun here in my pocket," he said, "and I mean to have you this afternoon."

"Maybe I'll kill you," he said.

Antoinette fled into the kitchen. Her own little gun was hidden in the pocket of her apron. She grabbed it, then waited for an opportunity to run to the door and outside. Antoinette stood, breathing heavily, waiting for the signal of Sonta's deep snore. Once she heard it, she left in haste.

About a half hour later, Antoinette returned home to find Sonta asleep, still sitting in the rocking chair. She could see her husband asleep in the bedroom. As she tried to sneak past Sonta, he grabbed her arm, pulled his gun, and again attempted to pull her down into the chair with him. His breath and hands were on top of her. She pulled out her gun and shot him in the head.

"You have done me," Sonta said, dying, "what I intended to have done you."

In the courtroom, Antoinette waited patiently for the strange sounds of the translation to end. When it did, the prosecutor asked how Sonta could have said anything with a bullet in his head. Antoinette became confused. She started to cry.

On the afternoon of April 26, the case went to the jury. Two hours later, Antoinette Tolla was pronounced guilty of murder. When her sentence was translated, she collapsed in her seat, before being taken back to the Hackensack jail.

The next week, as the trees began to bloom, the judge sentenced Antoinette Tolla to be hanged the following month, on June 9, 1905. After an appeal, the Supreme Court of New Jersey sustained her conviction and resentenced her execution for January 12, 1906. There were a few personal petitions from some of Tolla's friends, but Governor Edward C. Stokes was not swayed by any of them. As

Christmastime came, fast and cold, they began building gallows in the prison yard.

⁂

The woman who was rapidly taking the stairs of the Essex County courthouse was tall, thin, and dressed almost completely in black. Those who turned to stare saw just a touch of white at her sleeves and neck. She wore a magnificent hat that swept behind her like a great black bird. From the back of her hat flowed short folds of what looked like mourning veils. As she sped by, someone thought she was a nun and called her "sister." When her hat tilted forward, the woman's mouth lit up with a twitch of amusement.

Inside the courtroom, all the seats were taken. So when the woman opened the back door and walked in, courteous men in the back row stood and offered their chairs. But she kept walking, straight as an arrow. Halfway down the aisle, another man stepped out to offer her his place. As she raised her head to politely refuse, people noticed that she was young and pretty, with jet-black eyes and hair. She kept walking all the way to the front of the courtroom. When she reached the first row, the confused prosecutor even offered her his seat, but she declined. She set her bag on the table and addressed the judge with a bright glance.

"Mrs. Mary Grace Quackenbos," the woman said. "For the defense."

⁂

Four years earlier, a man stopped talking in front of a small lecture hall on Washington Square in New York City. He was in his late forties, with a full brown beard and soft eyes. His paisley cravat was loose under his dark wool suit coat.

"Think for yourself," he said, his eyes searching for the ones in the room who might actually be paying attention to him. "Be an inquirer—make no assertion unless you can support it by reason."

This was the signature lesson of William Clarence D. Ashley, dean of the New York University School of Law, and every student sitting before him who expected to graduate knew it by heart. When he moved across the front of the room, he would sometimes disappear behind the oddly placed Doric column that was stuck right in the middle of the room. Ashley would eventually reappear on the other side, his voice still going. When he lectured during the day, the rows of wooden seats were filled with stalwart, earnest young men.

But here, in the night class, the spaces between students was greater. So were the differences. There was a Chinese man, a black man, even a professional baseball player who couldn't help yawning. There were Russians, Germans, and Jews. There were women, too, though never more than a handful. The night class was its own creature; it wasn't easier, it was just different. And on this night, seated in the front row, was a woman in white clothing.

Mrs. Mary Grace Quackenbos was a mysterious figure, even for the night class. There were whispers that she was actually a rich heiress who was only slumming as a law student because she wanted to figure out how best to protect her family's millions. She was supposedly married to some kind of doctor. There was even talk that she had once been a singer and had taken up the law only as a punishment by her father, who was some big name. And everyone knew she was often late to class because she was always out shopping. In the night session, there was always this kind of gossip. The long hours encouraged it.

Part of the truth was that Grace was at NYU because the more prestigious Columbia Law School didn't admit women. NYU had, in fact, been admitting women to its law school since 1890, a full sixty years before Harvard. There was no better choice in the city. But that didn't mean that NYU was without its pitfalls. Another female law student named Clarice Baright was in a property law class when a pocket of snickering classmates opened the skylight, dumping her with heaps of cold snow, even though she was already sick with fever. After that, the girls all decided to sit up front.

On this night, Grace was indeed in the front row, but not because she was afraid of a little weather. Not that anyone would have the guts to dump snow on her, anyway. She sat in the front to be closer to the source. She wanted to give Dean Ashley her full attention. He taught the law in a way that made infinite sense to her. He always started with facts. In his view, there was no correct solution, only the logic of a good defense. He valued opinions but made his bacon in the argument itself. He taught the importance of contracts and hated recitation. Famous names and cases didn't matter to him. Ashley's students were taught to analyze the facts of a case, select the important points, and reason correctly in order to deduce principles from such facts. It was in this crucible of ideas that not only the lawyer but the detective was born.

"Many a good street car conductor has been spoiled by a foolish idea that he could become a lawyer," Ashley would often say. Grace heard this curious phrase many times in class and often wondered if his words were meant for her. Ashley believed that a law degree might be beneficial to society women but only so that they could know what a deed or power of attorney was. The rest of her classmates probably thought this was Grace's interest as well.

And it might have been, at some point. But somewhere along the way, that changed. What Grace found particularly fascinating was Ashley's view on cases. Ashley would walk in, tip his beard up, and speak on how cases could be used to illustrate a particular set of learning objectives; as in real life, rarely were there precise answers to the issue at hand. For the final decision of a case, Ashley cared nothing. It was only the process that he taught and stood by. The first principle was his shrine. In class, he built his cases on interviews, public sources, and even personal experience. He built stories out of fragments. Ashley would then lead his students to an "aha" moment, during which conventional wisdom was trumped by deeper, more seasoned insights. This great connection to life—real life—intrigued Grace deeply. Ashley began to notice this student in the front.

One night in class, students looked around and realized that Grace was missing from her familiar spot in the first row. Whispers cut through the classroom. Had she given up? Dropped out? Or was it something even worse?

She's in the day class now, someone piped up.

With the personal aid of Dean Ashley, Grace Quackenbos had been moved to the regular program. She completed a three-year law degree in two short years, graduating in 1903, one of only twelve women in her class. She immediately received a clerkship with the Legal Aid Society of New York, which offered low-cost legal help to the poor. Grace was admitted to the bar in the state of New York in 1905, becoming one of only a thousand female lawyers in the whole United States.

⚙

Grace was going through her mail one afternoon when she opened a letter from a group of Wellesley College girls. Their letter told the sad story of a woman in New Jersey named Antoinette Tolla who was doomed to hang for defending herself against a man who had threatened her. The papers had not reported on her case. Grace had never heard of her. Mrs. Tolla was innocent, the girls said. They begged Grace to help her.

Grace felt a strange connection to the woman she was reading about, this Antoinette Tolla. Grace was twenty-six years old, just like Mrs. Tolla, and had passed the bar just as Antoinette was being shown her jail cell.

The next morning, Grace set out bright and early for New Jersey, feeling very young and inexperienced, and without the faintest notion of what she might do when she got there. Grace was a full-fledged lawyer and had been for two months, but she had never argued a case. And she had taken to dressing completely in black.

Grace went to see Sheriff Mercer at the Trenton jail, where they were now holding Mrs. Tolla. The sheriff told Grace that he had no authority to let her see the prisoner. Grace wandered about the shadows of the jail, wondering what to do next. As she tried to guess what

Dean Ashley would do, she was approached by a man who suggested she call on Father Lambert, a nearby priest who ministered at the jail. The priest welcomed her in and told her everything he knew about Antoinette Tolla. Father Lambert believed strongly in Antoinette's innocence. He advised her to go straight to the governor since there was so little time left. The priest confessed little hope for Antoinette's earthly future, but he prayed for it anyway.

That afternoon, Grace took the train to see the governor. As Grace watched the rectangular glimpses of a gray-and-black landscape pass by her, she didn't like her chances. When Grace arrived, she waited an hour before the governor received her. Governor Stokes listened patiently as Grace went on about a woman she had never even met. When Grace had finished, the governor took a deep breath and replied slowly.

"My dear young lady," he said, looking down on her. "Your efforts are useless. The woman is guilty, and I can't do anything about the sentence. The law must take its course.

"However," he added, after a long pause. He reached for a thick book on a shelf above his desk. "Here is the Record on Appeal. If you care to take it with you and read it, you may have it."

Grace left his office carrying the heavy book. As Grace boarded a late train bound for New York, she knew that, according to the edict of the law, there were only two days left in Antoinette Tolla's life. But there wasn't a ghost of a chance to save her, especially here on a train. Settling back into her seat, Grace opened the law book and paged through it until she found the appeal of Tolla's conviction to the Supreme Court of New Jersey. There on the nighttime train, Grace read the ruling that refused Antoinette a new trial, her eyes stopping on this section:

No pistol seems to have been found other than the one used by the defendant. Her account of Sonta's exhibiting a pistol, as well as her statement of his remark after he was shot through the brain, is manifestly fanciful.

Grace sat upright. Why did it say "No pistol *seems* to have been found"? Why "seems?" If there was no pistol on Sonta, then no wonder Antoinette was convicted—there could be no argument for self-defense. But Antoinette was clear in her explanation that there was a gun. Grace hurriedly gathered her things together and left the train at Trenton, eager to follow up on the tiny lead.

By the time Grace got back, it was already midnight. She phoned Governor Stokes, asking him to let the prosecutor give her access to the case records. The governor obliged, and Grace got a room in a local hotel. She tried to fall asleep but could only stare at the small clock in her room. The hands seemed light and fast. Antoinette Tolla had less than forty-eight hours to live.

The next day was Sunday. Grace spoke with Mr. Koester, the original prosecutor of the case, but he said there was no gun in evidence. The trail was cold again. After thinking for a moment, Grace brightened up with an idea. After getting an address, she went to see the county coroner, an older man named Morgan. When she got to his house at five that afternoon, he was seated at an old-fashioned organ playing "Nearer My God to Thee." Morgan silently offered Grace a chair. She listened politely, in the very bright room, shifting in her seat as Morgan pushed the keys and pumps. When Morgan was done playing, Grace told him who she was. He looked her up and down.

Grace decided not to waste time bluffing. She told Morgan that she was here to see the gun taken from Sonta's dead body.

Morgan hesitated. But then, to Grace's surprise, he nodded.

After rummaging about in another room, he laid out an envelope that held the contents of Sonta's pockets when he died, including some money. He also clunked down what sounded to be a fully loaded pistol. It lay there, heavy on the table. Grace asked if she might use the telephone.

As she walked into the hallway, she was trembling. She called the governor to tell him that Sonta *did* have a gun and that the appeal had been wrongfully considered! The governor asked to speak to Morgan immediately. Grace gave him the phone and tried not to listen as they exchanged low, mumbling words. Morgan handed Grace the phone again. Governor Stokes instructed Grace to secure an affidavit from Morgan and come before the court of pardons the very next day.

On January 11, Grace appeared before a panel that consisted of the governor, the chancellor, and the six lay judges of the court of appeals. Grace wasn't the only one fighting for Antoinette. A few states over, the *Cincinnati Enquirer* had gathered two hundred thousand signatures in her favor from Cincinnati, Cleveland, and Pittsburgh after an incendiary editorial. Various counts and countesses from the Italian consulate were also present. And an anonymous letter had been sent to the county saying the jail would be blown to smithereens by dynamite if Antoinette was not released. Another letter said that if the hangman left his Newark home for Hackensack on the day of Antoinette's execution, he would be killed before his arrival. The Italians didn't mess around. But it was only when Grace showed the court the gun that they ordered an immediate thirty-day reprieve for Antoinette Tolla.

Grace was elated. At the same time, she knew that she still had lots of work to do. She now had to disprove that Antoinette Tolla had shot Sonta in the back of the head in cold blood, as had been initially stated in the case. Grace went straightaways from the capitol to the jail. As she turned the corner with an interpreter, Grace saw Antoinette Tolla in person for the very first time in her life.

When Grace told Antoinette Tolla the unbelievable news, it was several minutes before the pretty woman with long black hair regained enough composure to hear the particulars. Then, as considerately as possible, Grace urged her to tell the details of her story. Grace was sure her translator was better than the court-appointed one.

"Sonta's overtures toward me began some five months before the tragedy," Antoinette explained. "I had been making daily trips along the railroad tracks just south of town, collecting bits of wood and half-burned coal for use as fuel. We were too poor to get it in the regular way. Sonta began following me there every day, and annoying me with persistent advances. Finally, I denounced him angrily and threatened to tell my husband. Sonta only laughed at this, and when I stopped going to the tracks to avoid him, he began coming to my home and annoying me even in the presence of my husband. My husband became bitterly resentful of these visits, but he was afraid of the influential Sonta and his vengeance, and dared not oppose him too openly.

"On the afternoon of March 4, after my husband flounced out in anger leaving us alone, Sonta again attempted to force himself upon me, I quarreled violently with him, and it was then that he threatened my life. He had been drinking and was in a reckless mood. Taking a revolver from his pocket, he waved it before me and told me he would kill me, my husband Tolla, his wife, or all of us, but that he was determined to have his way, and that I could not escape him. I was badly frightened. I tried to reason with him but he would not listen. Then, still holding the pistol in his right hand, Sonta removed a large roll of bills from his pocket with the other, and offered me a choice. Either I could accept the money and submit to him, he said, or he would kill me, do as he wished, and then shoot himself, too." Grace winced. The translator for the first trial had gotten much of this wrong.

"At that moment, Sonta's six-year-old son Rocco, who had been playing in the street, appeared at the door. He became frightened when Sonta turned on him, reproving him in a loud voice, and the boy began to cry. I then fled into the kitchen, where I secured my pistol, and placed it in the pocket of my apron. At the first opportunity, I ran to the outside door, where I met my husband coming in. I continued to Sonta's home, where I remained about a half-hour pleading with Sonta's wife and his oldest daughter, Annie, to do something to help me.

"When I returned to my own home, Sonta was sitting in the rocker, smoking his pipe. My husband had fallen asleep in the bedroom, he reached out and drew me to him roughly. His face was flushed, there was a strange, fixed look in his eyes.

"I struggled to free myself. Terrified, and scarcely realizing what I was doing, I grasped the pistol in my apron pocket and fired twice. Both shots struck Sonta in the head, one penetrating the skull near the right temple."

As Grace prepared to leave, Antoinette's eyes filled with tears again, and she clung to Grace's hands as if she would never let go. Then, turning to the interpreter, Antoinette laughingly asked him to tell Grace that she reminded her of a bunch of black grapes. In Italy, Antoinette explained, black grapes meant good fortune. Seeing Antoinette up close, Grace noticed that she had a scar on her forehead and one under her lower lip.

The next day, Grace spent some time investigating the records of the autopsy surgeon in the coroner's office. When she finally found the actual report, it showed that Sonta had four superficial wounds, two where a bullet had entered the right temple, gone through the brain, and exited under the left jaw. Here was Grace's proof that the first and fatal bullet had not been fired at Sonta from the back. She grabbed the report and stuffed it in her bag.

Grace was again not alone. The Susan B. Anthony Club of Cincinnati appealed to President Roosevelt himself to pardon Antoinette. His response was that "he has no authority to interfere in this case, and he will not do so." At a time when Italians all across the United States began to mobilize their newfound political power, an Italian priest, Father Pozzi, wondered, "has America become the woman-killing country?" Governor Stokes remained immobile. "There is no evidence of any kind to show that Sonta ever attempted to assault the woman," he stated. A bullet in the back was never self-defense. It was murder. Grace had to change the minds of Stokes and those who shared his opinion.

On February 9, when Antoinette's reprieve was almost at an end, Grace was granted another hearing before the court of pardons in Trenton. Grace submitted all the new affidavits she had collected. Most important was the doctor's report on the autopsy. After her presentation in the big courtroom in the State Building, Grace retired to the corridor outside the chamber. She paced nervously up and down for almost an hour, awaiting the court's fateful decision.

When Grace was summoned back into the chamber, the court had decided to give her a choice. They would, right then and there, agree to commute Mrs. Tolla's death sentence to life imprisonment—which was all they really had the authority to do—or they would grant an additional reprieve of thirty days to give Grace an opportunity to petition before the court of errors and appeals for a new trial altogether. The governor and his board had ruled that Grace had introduced sufficient new evidence to justify a retrial, but they did not have the authority to grant one. They were asking the new lawyer to make a very difficult choice.

And she had to make it immediately.

If Grace accepted Antoinette's sentence of life imprisonment, she would be condemning her young client to a penalty tragically severe for a woman who had acted in defense of her own life and honor. But if Grace sought a new trial and failed to secure one, there would be no more reprieves, and Antoinette would die. It was a gamble with the highest of stakes. Dean Ashley had not covered this in law school.

Grace asked for a short recess. When it was granted, she returned to the corridor. Antoinette's husband, Giovanni Tolla, was waiting there anxiously and misinterpreted Grace's grave attitude to mean the worst of outcomes. He pleaded with Grace to ask the court that he be allowed to die in his wife's place.

After reassuring him that such a sacrifice would not be required, Grace walked down the hall to the office of the attorney general, Robert McCarter. She did not know the older attorney, but she was hoping that he might be able to give her the kind of advice that Dean Ashley used to. McArthur beckoned her into his office, small but filled with large books. He was cordial but said that her problem was an individual responsibility. He did not feel free to interfere. Grace felt the sting of his words as he shut his door. But she recognized their truth.

Grace returned to the pardon board and accepted the thirty-day reprieve to try for a new trial. She prayed she had made the right decision. Grace was only licensed to practice law in New York, so she hired a local Newark attorney named Samuel Kalisch to aid in the presentation of the case before the court of errors and appeals. That night, Grace again went back to the jail to tell Antoinette Tolla that her agony was not yet over.

The day before, an immigrant named Jerry Rosa was hanged in the jail yard. A few hours before his scheduled execution, the terrified man had somehow eluded his guard and barricaded himself in a closet. No threat or inducement could get him out, and it had finally been necessary to break through the wall and spray a powerful hose on him until he was exhausted. They pulled him out of the closet, half-conscious and soaked to the bone. When his time finally arrived, Rosa absentmindedly marched to his death, less than a hundred feet from Antoinette's cell window.

⁂

With three days left to Antoinette's reprieve, there was still no decision from the Supreme Court. Grace had presented her case weeks before and grew so uneasy that she called on each of the judges separately to remind them. This was not something she had learned at NYU, but she had run out of options. She was thinking of unreported guns and poorly translated testimony. Grace begged them to render a prompt decision.

Grace was also having difficulty even seeing Antoinette Tolla. Since her initial lawyer was court-appointed, the sheriff of the jail didn't officially recognize Grace as Antoinette's attorney. This was the stupidest thing Grace had ever heard.

On the penultimate day of the reprieve, the court ruled that sufficient new evidence had been presented to warrant a new trial for Antoinette Tolla. But in the same breath, it declared that it had no jurisdiction to reopen the case at this late date. Grace was angry, but would not give up. The March term of the court of pardons was to begin its session the following day. Grace was determined to be heard in that session, for that would be the final day of Antoinette's reprieve. Grace also proceeded to get out a writ of error for the United States Supreme Court, as a final, wild gesture to stay the hanging. The writ required Antoinette's signature, so Grace made the trip once more to the jail. Antoinette signed her name numbly, and Grace left again.

An East Coast snowstorm was falling as Grace boarded a late train to return to Trenton. Grace sat down, exhausted. As she looked around the train, she was surprised to see Governor Stokes sitting across the aisle, reading an evening newspaper. Grace stared at him to make sure she wasn't seeing things as the train shook. When the train stopped, he came toward Grace with a smile.

"Are you still working to save Mrs. Tolla?" he asked.

"I would not give up as long as there was hope," Grace responded.

The following afternoon, Grace was granted a ten-minute hearing before the governor and his board. She knew it was her—and her client's—very last chance. Grace told them that this time she had come not for mercy, but for justice. The Supreme Court had ruled that the evidence justified a new trial, but the Court was powerless to grant it. Grace quoted the opinion of one of the justices:

Her (Mrs. Tolla's) state of mind on that occasion was one evincing deliberation and premeditation: but had the excluded testimony (as to antecedent sexual assaults and indignities) been admitted, the verdict upon this vital point might have been different, A prolonged and persistent course of efforts to debauch a woman have a different effect on her mind than a single solicitation. A strong element of premeditation was shown in the purchase of the pistol. I cannot agree, however, that if the pistol was not used in self-defense it may not have been purchased with that object, and if it was, the strong element of premeditation drops out of the case or, at least, is rendered doubtful.

Grace concluded her plea with the contention that, since the courts of law declared themselves powerless to right the wrong done to this woman, it was the duty of the court of pardons to pass on the evidence as a trial court and jury and consider a full pardon based on its contents.

This was a bold interpretation of the law. It was also Grace's last-ditch effort. She hoped that her legal reasoning was more persuasive than the lateness of the moment. Her ten minutes were up.

When Grace was recalled to the room, it was to hear that the governor, after a vote of six to two by the board, had commuted Antoinette Tolla's death sentence to seven-and-a-half years' imprisonment. It was the only time in the history of the state of New Jersey that the court of pardons had commuted a death sentence. Allowing for the time Antoinette had already spent in jail, and with good behavior, her actual term might be about five years.

When Grace, the woman in black, finally told Antoinette, she screamed with happiness, promising that she would devote her time in jail to getting home to her little family.

As Grace left the jail, she felt enormous satisfaction. Somehow, it had all worked out—not exactly as she wished, but better than she had feared. This whole experience had been one surprise after another. At times, the law had almost totally failed her; it was only by applying creative hard work to a small window of luck that Grace had managed to save Antoinette's life. This was astonishing to Grace. Facts were important—the discovery of the gun had saved Antoinette's life—but it was quick thinking and imagination that had brought about the happy resolution. Grace took note of that. As she passed the courtyard on her way out, she saw the wooden gallows, high and empty, towering in the night sky.

4

The Heatherbloom Girl

February 1917

The New York City detectives sat Maria Cocchi down right away. The little boy, released from the clutches of his woolen coat, sat quietly next to her, his eyes staring at the men. Mrs. Cocchi spoke quickly, in Italian. Her hair was all different places at once. Once she calmed down, she told the detectives about her husband's actions in the hours before his disappearance.

"He came in about 12:20," Maria said. "He wanted his lunch as soon as possible. He seemed nervous and irritable, but I thought little of it." The Cocchis lived not in the motorcycle shop but in a small apartment nearby, at 75 Manhattan.

"He has been working hard of late and is very nervous, anyway," Maria said. The little boy stared as the detectives took notes. The other bundle in Maria's arms moved; it was a newborn girl. Maria slipped her baby back under the folds of her coat and continued.

"He ate without saying anything," she continued rapidly, "and then got up and played with the baby awhile. Then he asked me for $10, saying he wanted to pay the electric light bill. I gave it to him, and he said 'goodbye' and left. He did not pay the light bill sometimes," his wife admitted. But he was "an expert mechanic who always made money." And "business was good."

"I thought he would go right to the shop, but about half an hour later a man called up and said the shop was locked and he wanted his motorcycle. I called up all the hospitals in the neighborhood and all of our friends trying to find Alfred, but no one had seen him." The detectives were writing everything down.

"I can take care of my babies," Maria kept saying, "I will take care of my babies. I can take care for myself."

The detectives told Maria Cocchi how they had questioned her husband and searched his shop just before noon on Thursday.

"That's funny," Mrs. Cocchi said. "My husband had made no mention of this."

After she finished speaking, the detectives went down to the motorcycle shop again. It was padlocked, so they took a pair of pincers and twisted the steel until it bent into ribbons. People gathered outside and watched as Lagarenne and McGee walked in slowly. They went over everything for a second time. There was very little that anyone from the street could see, other than the big black machines through the glass. It was all the same grimy New York building, for the most part. The detectives left after a short time. They took a few papers they found, but that was all.

The detectives started knocking on doors in the neighborhood again. The newspapermen who had started to show up began to do the same. From neighbors, customers, and friends, the papers began to cobble together a profile of Alfredo Cocchi, the man already cleared by the police but now queerly missing. They started filling him out with numbers: he was thirty-five years old, about five foot seven in height, and weighed 135 pounds. Cocchi did not wear a beard, and he had pale skin, which was unusual for an Italian. When he disappeared, he was wearing a green cap, a dark brown sweater, and a gray silk shirt. He wore black shoes and socks. He was now classified, like Ruth, as a missing person.

On the sly, neighborhood friends of Cocchi also told the detectives what everyone was thinking. Cocchi was terrified when the police came to his door on Wednesday. Not because he was guilty of anything having to do with some Harlem girl, but because of his Italian heritage. It seemed like everyone blamed the hot-blooded Italians for everything these days, especially the police. Especially after Petrosino. Cocchi's disappearance was nothing sinister, his friends and neighbors said. He was just scared. He had probably gone home to his family in Italy. They had been urging him to join the army anyway. The detectives had found a letter to this effect among Cocchi's things. Everything else they saw in the store confirmed Mrs. Cocchi's claim that her husband had left quickly. His shop overalls were in the middle of the floor. A small bench was overturned. A back door was unlocked.

When a reporter asked Lagarenne about Mrs. Cocchi, he swiftly dismissed the thought of her involvement. "She knows very little of his business," he said. He explained that she was probably just jealous and mad that her husband had left home. They had been hearing rumors that she kept him on a short leash.

The detectives checked out two other motorcycle shops that Cocchi had once owned, just in case, one in the Bronx and one in New Jersey. Meanwhile, Fourth Branch detectives visited Harlem pawnshops looking for Ruth's gold wristwatch and her high school graduation ring. According to Henry Cruger, the ring had her initials inlaid in blue enamel on a smooth silver band.

That Sunday, as the police cooled their heels and the broad strokes of New York City ran in slower lines, churches all over the city said prayers for poor Ruth Cruger, either on wooden altars or in the quiet space of individual thoughts. She became a communal wish in the gray, white air. The new Washington Heights Baptist Church on 145th and Convent raised this prayer particularly loudly. Made of Hurricane Island granite and white Georgia marble, the church was the cornerstone of the neighborhood and rose from the sidewalk like the very mind of God Himself cut and hammered down into architecture. The Crugers attended every Sunday.

Known as the mother of New York churches, it could seat a thousand parishioners. When it was full, it looked like a neighborhood version of the afterlife. There was a sliding oak wall at the back of the altar that could be pulled back to reveal a shimmering wall of blue stained glass. People came from far away just to see its mechanical baptismal font, which would slowly rise from the flat floor from a secret underground chamber.

The first-floor Sunday schoolroom was one of Ruth's favorite places in the world. The Christian Endeavor Room was where Ruth could sit with the children. The double set of sliding doors concealed the infant room. Ruth would play with the littler girls, reading Bible stories, and standing and smiling when their parents came to claim them, lifting their small bodies high into the air. Ruth would smile among all the bright, white children. She would teach them about the poor widow from Luke 21: 1–4 who put only two tiny coins into the offering cup yet gave more than all the rich combined.

But on this Sunday, those same girls in dresses and ribbons came in with their heads bowed in the disbelief of early despair. They slowly gathered in the rectory and got on their knees in silence. Some were crying. Many were crying. The Reverend Pattison, a tall, handsome man, entered the room and sat among them. The reverend often commended Ruth and was sometimes seen encouraging her. He had personally baptized her a year ago last Easter. As he sat with his flock, they all prayed for Ruth's safe return.

In another part of the church, behind closed doors, the Mothers' Committee drafted an official resolution that served as their own kind of prayer. They condemned the "appalling condition of city streets where it is not safe for our girls and boys to go unprotected." The resolution was adopted with the hope that all of the "mothers of New York unite to get better protection for their children." Later, under the direction of the same committee, the girls in the church sat in long rows, preparing ten thousand circulars with a photo of Ruth to send to police commissioners and hotel managers. The com-

mittee got movie-screen projectionists all across the country to flash
her grainy picture on the screen before Charlie Chaplin's *Easy Street*.
The mothers of the committee wanted to cover the country with Ruth's
smile. They ordered her photo sent to conductors, brakemen, and
drivers. These women who met behind closed doors represented a
powerful community. Their actions were the measurement of how
much they loved Ruth Cruger. And the idea of her.

⚜

Later that night, when Henry was out, the phone rang in the apartment. His wife Christina paused, then picked up the receiver. She
heard only a faint buzz on the other end.

"I saw your daughter," the voice on the line said. It was a woman.

Mrs. Cruger listened, waiting for the woman to speak again.

"At Manhattan and 128th Street at about 4 o'clock Tuesday afternoon," the woman said. Mrs. Cruger wrote it down in the pad by the
phone that was already covered with numbers.

"She was a slender girl," the woman on the line said. "Wearing a
long brown coat such as the newspapers say your daughter wears. The
collar was turned up about her face, but I could see she seemed dazed.
She was crying." For Mrs. Cruger, who listened with doubt, this last
word still cut sharply. The woman went on: "A man about forty years
old, not at all foreign looking, had her by the arm and was urging
her along and arguing with her almost angrily. They passed out of
my sight north on Broadway. I did not think anything of the incident
until I read of the disappearance of Miss Cruger in the newspapers."

Mrs. Cruger asked for her name, but the line was already dead.

When Henry came home, his wife was shaking when she told him
about the call. Henry went to his notebook and checked the numbers. In the absence of his daughter, numbers were the only things
he could trust. He respected their complete lack of disguise. And he
was sure they could help find his daughter. The time given by the
caller was a full half hour after Ruth had supposedly left in a cab with

a mysterious stranger at 125th and Lenox, which was the story the detectives had told him. The caller didn't mention a cab, but her description of the man was eerily similar. Was it the same man?

Henry knew that finding a forty-year-old man in a coat in New York City was probably an impossible task. Henry tried to rethink his approach. If there was a connection between the two stories—if the man seen pushing Ruth along was indeed leading her toward a cab—then Henry needed to find the cab driver from the story the detectives had told him. That driver, Henry hoped, might be the only person who could determine who the mysterious man was and where he and Ruth had come from. Henry was settled. He had to find this cab driver. He had to find this chauffeur.

The next morning, Henry took a series of cab rides all across Harlem, following the route his daughter had supposedly taken. Henry sat in the back, his eyes on the street as the city passed him by, all legs and coats and hats. The jingling horses of the old days were all but gone. He saw the black girders of the elevated train frame the sky. They held up great signs for Howard Clothes ("The Gentleman of Good Taste") and Maxwell House ("Good to the Last Drop"). He passed a middle-aged woman with a chalkboard held around her neck with burlap twine. It read BEGGAR'S PERMIT BADGE 2622. BLIND. There were two horizons in the city now—the burnished steel above and the uneven brick and wood below. When Henry saw police on the sidewalk, he slumped his face down into his collars. But he watched them all, though their smiles hurt him. He was searching for form and repetition and anomaly. Henry Cruger, the accountant and father, had, of necessity, become a detective.

Ruth had not been seen in four days. Later that day, the *New York Times* reported that Police Commissioner Woods had taken a "personal interest in the case." Woods promised that "all detectives of the Fourth Branch who could be spared be sent in search of her." But every day was counting down to a worse and worse conclusion. The papers—and there were nearly twenty daily papers now—reported that

Henry Cruger had hired his own private detectives from the Martin Donnelly agency. They hit the hospitals and came up empty. Henry still kept riding in cabs. He knew that if she had reached the subway, she could be long gone. But he couldn't think about that. All he could grasp right now was Harlem.

Every paper in the city was now devoting space to Ruth Cruger. Twice a day, Henry went downstairs and purchased every rag he could get his hands on. He pressed them to his chest as he maneuvered up the stairs before unlocking, then locking the door. He read the papers, one by one, studying the different accounts. The *Evening World* had the best coverage by far, and he liked the reporter there, so he was shocked when he opened the *New York Times* and read the name of the mysterious chauffeur he had spent so much time hunting for. The *Times* identified the witness as Henry Rubien, a Turk cabdriver who had a stand at 125th and Broadway. Rubien had told the detectives that he had picked up the mysterious couple on Manhattan Street and took them uptown to the subway station at Lenox Avenue and 125th. The words replaced each other in a blur as Henry read as fast as he could.

"I had seen her often in the neighborhood," Rubien said. "But I did not know her name. When she entered the taxicab, I recognized her as a girl who had passed my stand. When I saw the pictures of Ruth Cruger in the papers, I knew it was she."

Henry Cruger hurriedly put on his cuffs, ran for the door, and found himself on the sidewalk. He passed fruit carts and newsstands to get down to Broadway to the exact same taxi stand he had been riding from. Henry asked for Rubien's cab. Someone pointed him out, and Henry had to look twice. Rubien was one of the men whose cabs he had been riding in all week. When their eyes met, Rubien looked almost relieved.

The air on the street was cold, so they got into his cab and Rubien started driving. As Henry Cruger sat in the backseat and watched the back of this familiar head, he heard a different story than the one he was hearing from the police. Rubien said that his cab was hired at 3:15 on Tuesday afternoon at 127th and Broadway. A young man, alone, stepped off the curb and hired the machine from the stand at 125th Street and Broadway.

"The man directed me to drive a block to 127th and Manhattan," Rubien said. "Right across the street from Cocchi's shop." Rubien said he then saw a girl about 150 feet away. "The man then jumped from the cab," said Rubien. "He took her by the arm and rather roughly urged her into the car, telling [me] to take them to the subway station, which he did." The girl, who looked unsure of her feet, carried a bundle with her. Rubien couldn't rightly see what it was without being nosy. He said that the girl and the man spoke to each other with great familiarity. Rubien dropped them off uptown at the Lenox Avenue subway at 125th Street.

Rubien told Henry that the girl looked just like the photos in the newspaper and that she wore "a dark coat" and a "wide black hat." When Henry asked why he never said anything to him all the times he had been riding in his cab, Rubien replied that he had been cautioned by the police to keep silent. There was silence now again.

"It looked as if she had been crying," Rubien said.

Henry was becoming increasingly certain that the suspicion in the pit of his stomach was leading him toward the truth. Henry asked if the man who had called the cab was Alfredo Cocchi, the Italian motorcycle shop owner.

The driver shook his head. It was not.

Henry asked again.

The cabbie knew Cocchi. He was a good man. It was not him.

After a pause, Rubien said that he overheard the two people talking about how the girl had been quarreling with her parents about a student from Columbia. A boy. Henry straightened in the seat. Rubien described the mysterious man as being under six feet in height and under thirty years old. He had a roundish face, was good looking, and wore nice new clothes.

Henry wondered if he was sitting on the same side that his daughter had been, barely a week ago. And he wondered, more than ever, what she was thinking about in that moment.

When Henry reached home, there were more reporters gathered at the stoop of the apartment. So he stood and talked to them, even though he was tired. After talking to Rubien, and for the first time in days, he felt as if he had some answers, ones he could build on to form a statement of fact. For the first time, Henry felt like he had something of value to say.

"My girl has been kidnapped," Henry said to the reporters. "This talk about her having gone away voluntarily is an unwarranted insult to her and to us. It is nothing more than a screen for police shirking." Henry knew that the detectives wouldn't care for his statements, but turnabout was fair play. The thought that his daughter—his lovely daughter with her smile and voice that was getting quieter in his head—had most assuredly come to harm after leaving that oily little shop was just too much to bear.

At home, Mrs. Cruger had been in no condition to talk to the press. She was shut behind her bedroom door. Every night, she would awaken everyone in the house by crying out for her missing daughter. But in hearing the news from her husband about Rubien, she finally agreed to speak. "My daughter would never go off this way unless she were drugged," she said. "I am certain that she is under restraint somewhere. If she is alive and at liberty she would have communicated with me long ago." Henry was very proud of his wife for saying this.

That night, in his chair and with his daughters and wife quiet and enclosed in their rooms, Henry watched his missing daughter stare at him from framed photographs on tables. Henry once again read the evening editions, trying to find some hope. As he read the paper, Henry was surprised to see that Mrs. Cocchi, the wife of the motorcycle man, had published a letter. It read:

> *Alfred: I believe you are innocent and all your friends do. Please come home. Remember our happy married life—nine and a half years and the children.*

Henry could sometimes be filled with hate, a killing hate—for that woman, her Italian husband, the cops, even the people he had seen on the street who weren't his daughter or didn't know who she was. This hate galvanized him. But it did not last. Henry would then try to fall asleep, waiting for that half a second when he woke, when his daughter was still in the room with him, seated in the other chair, smiling about something or other. Or even being mad at him. Henry wouldn't care. As long as she wasn't crying, like Rubien said she had been. Anything but that. All he knew was that no one could ever know or understand what it was like to have his daughter taken from him. No one. There, in that room, Henry felt as if something had been pulled from him and something else had come to take its place. He could feel it standing in the corner. He tried to ignore it, breathing hard and fast.

To Henry, this whole mystery had swept over his family like the city itself: immense but suffocating, unrestricted but demanding. Henry felt as if they were only beginning to grope their way out of the short routines they had carved out for themselves, which ran from hallways to streets to buildings. Now, the larger city in his mind was filled with impossible hope and miserable fear—with nothing in-between.

⚜

The next day, Arthur Hale Woods, the police commissioner of New York City, was reading a newspaper on the second floor of the central office. Downstairs, his men were claiming that that they might be getting close to solving the Ruth Cruger mystery. Privately, they were telling him that they were fairly sure she had just run away from home like so many others before her. Case closed, they said. But Woods saw the headline PRETTY GIRL SKATER MISSING and wasn't so sure that "case closed" would be enough.

Woods placed the newspaper back on his monumental desk. By now, Ruth had been missing for a week. The police were deploying a massive public effort to cast their net over the entire Atlantic seaboard. Some of the papers even suggested that Ruth had been kidnapped and sent into the city's serpentine underworld of white slavery. Henry Cruger believed that his daughter had been drugged with a vial needle before being forced into that cab and onto parts unknown. Mr. Cruger publicly criticized the police with great furor. "The Fourth Branch Detective Bureau is not doing the work that should be done," Henry told the *Times*. On his desk, Woods had two crystal inkpots and a black candlestick telephone that wound its way to a box on the wall. There was a brown wooden intercom for communicating with his secretary. He thought about Mr. Cruger's words.

Woods, tall and thin, straightened his tweed jacket as he rose from his chair. Even at forty-seven years old, he still kept his hair short on the sides, just like in the old days, though it was now only peppered with black. At his new bride Helen's insistence, he had finally shaved his mustache, even though he thought it just brought out the bags under his eyes. Best not to argue with the niece of J. P. Morgan, he would tell her.

On the long table next to his desk lay a street map of New York City, dimpled with push pins. Smaller maps were hung on the walls. Woods had been commissioner since 1914, after being promoted by Mayor John Purroy Mitchel, the "boy mayor" of New York who had been elected at age thirty-four. After Woods's small inauguration in his office, the mayor, tall and thin himself, pulled his new police commissioner aside and said, "You big fool." Woods promised that he would cut vice, clean up the gangsters, and kick the deadly Black Hand gangsters straight out of New York. These words were big talk from a former Groton English teacher.

The commissioner's office was located on the second floor of the police central office, located in a new white building at 240 Centre Street. They jokingly called it the White House. The building was huge, humming with electricity, and had its own dispatch center. In the basement was a gun range with special interrogation cells just for the detectives. The old Italian Squad had occupied the first floor. Sometimes, Woods would go up to the observation deck that looked out over the whole block. He could see the bar called Headquarters down on the first floor of the opposite street. Over on the other side, Woods saw the canvas tents of the Italian gun dealers who sold pistols and blackjacks to his own policemen.

Two weeks after his first day as commissioner, Woods, the mayor, and New York corporation counsel Frank Polk were walking through the lunchtime crowd in the Park Row Plaza outside City Hall. It was early spring, just past one o'clock on a sunny day, when an old man with a sunken face emerged from the shifting crowd. He pointed a pistol at the mayor. Woods was about two jumps away, but somehow made it in one. Woods slammed the old man to the ground—but not before the man's gun fired in a quick blast of smoke and fire. People scattered and screamed.

The mayor sat up and patted his suit, looking for blood. He was unscathed. But Mr. Polk had been shot in the left cheek of his mouth. As Woods held the would-be assassin down, the mayor, who had also pulled his gun, towered over him.

"Why did you try to shoot me?" he asked.

Later that day, when cops ransacked the old man's apartment, they found a steamer trunk filled with letters and anarchist pamphlets. The would-be assassin's name was Mike Mahoney. A blacksmith by trade, he had been out of work for a very long time. Before his arraignment, the cops took him into a room at Central, where 250 detectives—all of them masked—looked him over to see if they recognized him. None of them did. They feared a more insidious conspiracy.

"We are dealing with strange forces," they all agreed.

Before that moment on the plaza, Woods's voice as commissioner was almost inaudible. There were rumors that people at police headquarters didn't even know what he looked like. But now—after jumping to stop an assassin—Woods had the power to start enacting some of his more radical ideas. He could run instead of walk.

During his first year in office, Woods locked up two hundred known criminals. He went after labor strikers, Black Handers, anarchist bombers, and reinstituted the Italian Squad. He enacted new uniform regulations to ensure that every officer's brass buttons shone at a shared level of brilliance. Woods even created the first domestic bomb squad to combat foreign spies and terrorists. Everyone knew him now.

But Woods wasn't just hard-boiled. The massive city map on his table was also lined out with his play streets program, whereby traffic would shut down on certain roads so that tenement kids could play stickball without fear of being run over. The police put out signs attached to cement blocks that said DETOUR as kids in hiked-up pants and white shirts laid down grounders. At the same time, out in the blue part of the map lay Woods's controversial Harlem River Floating Station, an aquatic headquarters in the middle of the Hudson to be used in the event of emergency or terrorist attack. Woods's nimble imagination was ready for apocalypses both small and large. He even started a project in Flatbush with police dogs called the Barking Squad.

As Woods looked over the map, his shadow crossed the streets of Harlem, otherwise known as Italian territory. Woods always thought of his friend Joe when he thought of the Italians. Every time Woods walked through the front door of headquarters, he expected Joe Petrosino, the larger-than-life cop who ran the Italian Squad, to walk out of his office to the right, smiling for all the world. Woods preferred that image in his mind, instead of the other one.

In early 1909, Joe Petrosino underwent a secret mission to Italy to hunt down Lupo the Wolf, the crime lord who had left a trail of bodies behind him in the boroughs. But the New York papers leaked his whereabouts, and Petrosino was shot dead on the beautiful streets of Palermo, leaving a wife and family behind. When his body returned to New York City, over 250,000 people attended his funeral at Saint Patrick's Cathedral. Police Commissioner Woods, his friend, was among them.

The remaining Italian Squad vowed to avenge their leader by catching Lupo. While Petrosino's lieutenants followed more traditional means—using newly passed laws against guns and kidnapping—the youngest member of the squad, an ex–pro baseball player named

Thomas McDonough, was still involved in Petrosino's last plan. McDonough crafted a perfect disguise as a fruit grocer in Little Italy and held character for a year, waiting for Lupo to slip up and reveal his whereabouts. When Lupo finally appeared on the street, the Irish kid, with the help of the Secret Service, caught the Wolf on a counterfeiting ring, finally ending his long campaign of murder.

What happened to Petrosino wasn't the only black mark on Woods's record. A year earlier, on July 30, explosions lit up the early-morning sky on Black Tom Island off Jersey City. The explosion was so massive that the Brooklyn Bridge began to sway back and forth in the sky. The island was an ammunitions dump, blown to smithereens by German agents seeking to keep the munitions from being supplied to the Allies. Woods did his best to clean it up and find out who did it. But it had happened under his watch.

The papers said that Woods was the kind of man who stayed in the shadows. But that wasn't true. Standing over that map, watching his own long shadow engulf Harlem, he knew how this missing-girl case would go. Before joining the force, Woods had been a reporter for the *Evening Sun*. He still had friends there. That's how he knew how fast this story would light up and go. He knew he was sitting on a firecracker. So a day later, Woods assumed personal charge of the Ruth Cruger case.

Unbeknownst to Woods, other armies stood ready to help him. At Wadleigh High School, one hundred girls volunteered to help in the search for their onetime classmate. Like the church, they decided to conduct a mail and telephone investigation of all surrounding towns. They reached out as far as Saint Louis and Atlanta. When the girls called these places on the phone, they said they were searching for their missing sister.

The neighborhood around Wadleigh was not without its own controversies. Located on 114th Street between Seventh and Eighth Avenues, the school enrolled around 2,700 students, who were taught by eighty or so teachers. The morning session met from morning until two; the afternoon from one to five. The teachers and students knew those times well. They weren't the only ones. When school was dismissed, long arms of departing students reached out from every side of the school and out into the frontier that was Lenox Avenue in Harlem. Just three blocks away, between 110th and 112th, a string of vaudeville joints and places called merry-go-rounds started to get going just about the same time that school let out. The girls, walking home, could hear pianos banging away on Dixieland jazz music. Women in dried-up makeup smiled at the children from dark doorways. But worse—much worse—was the group of boys who appeared from these pleasure palaces every day at exactly five o'clock to watch the girls walk home. Parents complained to the police when these boys started to brush elbows with the girls, giving them insults, mashing on them, and engaging in "low talk."

"Our responsibility ends when the children pass into the streets," said Wadleigh assistant principal Miss Speirs when confronted with the problem. "What happens there is the affair of the parents. We have a police officer in the building . . . but he cannot watch each pupil all the way home.

"Let us hope they make the trip in safety," she added.

"It is enough to watch the girls in school," said Miss Goodrich, another teacher. "How funny!" added another teacher, Miss Conant. "No one ever insulted me in the street."

The police were privately calling this area the New Tenderloin, a wellborn successor to the old red-light district in the heart of Manhattan. The cops said the gang who was bothering the girls got together four years ago. The police didn't know what they were calling themselves yet, only that they had come up from the dumps of the east side and spoke a coded jargon and used secret hand signs.

⚜

The people huddled on the subway platform stared up at the flickering terra-cotta ceiling. The lights lit the mosaic tiles on the wall that spelled out 157th Street. The crowd, bundled up in coats and hats, pressed back against the wall. They had come in down the slate stairs under the rotunda, passing the white tiled columns. When the subways opened, Mayor McClellan said that "without rapid transit Greater New York would be little more than a geographical expression." Everyone was intrigued by the labyrinth.

A young woman, her motion stopped in frames of interrupted light, staggered out past the line of people. She was moving toward the electrified rail line. A man in a suit saw her. He raced toward her and grabbed her hand. The train was getting louder and the overhead lamps began to rattle. As the train sped out of the black tunnel, the woman pitched and began to fall off the platform itself, just as the man pulled her back. The man yelled for help, and the ticket man ran over to help her back up. As the train washed them all in light, sound, and force, they all held her back. She struggled, then screamed.

A couple, older and calm, stooped over to comfort her. The lights dimmed again.

"I've been away from home two nights," the girl cried. "Something terrible has happened, and I'm afraid to go home." The couple offered to take her to their apartment to calm her down.

When they had gone, it struck the man that the girl was the one from the papers, so he hurried to tell the cops. Detectives began a slow house-to-house search near the subway station, looking for the couple who had rescued her. When she was finally found, the girl was positively identified. She wasn't Ruth; she was a married woman who had angered her husband.

Similar stories were appearing all over the city. A boy in scruffy clothing made his way across Times Square, dodging the people who were looking up at the electric signs. A few years ago, it was the Heatherbloom petticoats girl who stole everyone's attention. Every night, crowds gathered and fuddy-duddies snorted as the sign sparked to life and the figure of a young girl skipped across the slashes of electric rain. The twinkling wind began to swirl, whipping up her flashing white skirts. The Heatherbloom girl was thirty feet tall and was hailed as the most realistic depiction of a woman ever seen. The sign was gone now, replaced by one for Omega Oil. People still stared. As the boy weaved in and out, his shoe brushed against a crumpled-up piece of paper. He stopped in the middle of the pulsing crowd to pick it up. The boy looked at it, dumbfounded. In a single line, the writer said they were being detained on Riverside Drive. It was signed Ruth Cruger.

The stunned boy stuffed the note in his pocket and ran to the nearest police station. He rang the bell under the green lamp. Fourth Branch was alerted, and they sent a squad to the address on the note. The cops nearly knocked the door down, but no one lived there. They pronounced it a joker's fake. The detectives returned back to the Fourth Branch, grumbling. This was only one of hundreds of false leads.

There were now forty full detectives assigned to the Cruger case. They all reported to Captain Alonzo Cooper, the pug-faced head of the Fourth Branch gumshoes. As leads came in, Cooper shoved them off in groups of two in a coordinated hunt across the city. They tracked down every clue, as janitors, neighbors, and passersby saw Ruth Cruger everywhere they looked. She was with foreign men, on steamships, and in movie theaters all across the city. There were young women with clothes and hair like Ruth's living in apartments across the hall from the nineties to Hackensack—yet none of them were really Ruth; they were just different mirrored images of the same face. In the city, during those weeks, if you were a girl with dark hair or if you carried ice skates, you were given a second look—or a hard glance to the ground.

By now, detectives had counted 699 tips that had come in about Ruth Cruger. They blamed Mr. Cruger's own public bravado for causing this tidal wave of clues. No one still expected to see Ruth at the doorstep with a sheepish look on her face and an engagement ring on her finger. Her mother knew that Ruth would at least have called by now. That simple thought, if given enough room, was insurmountable.

A few years earlier, Woods had completely revamped the way detectives worked in the city. When Woods agreed to take the job of fourth assistant deputy police commissioner, he insisted that he travel to

London to study the inner workings of the famed Scotland Yard. Woods privileged the detective—the thinker, the intelligentsia—more so than the average beat cop, whom he saw as more of a useful brawler. Woods had been head of the detective bureau himself and watched as interdepartmental infighting got case after case dismissed. When Woods returned from touring Scotland Yard, he had civility and organization on his mind.

Once in charge, Woods took his detectives out of the police houses and put them in their own nests, called branches, after the English way. They had single buildings with a head captain in charge of each branch. They looked like everyday New York houses, lacking even the signature green lamps that marked the more obvious police buildings. These places were different on the inside as well. Some of the detective branches had dorms and lounge areas. Third Branch had its own jail in the basement. The Fifth in the Bronx had a garden with arbors and vines. The branches were all interconnected by a sophisticated direct phone system.

Fourth Branch was a three-story house located at 342 West 123rd Street near Manhattan Avenue. Its territory covered Fifty-ninth Street on the south and Fifth Avenue on the east, all bound up by the meandering Hudson on the west. Fourth Branch was especially known for their cooking. When crime hid itself away, detectives would don aprons instead of guns and work the new gas oven. The *Washington Times* sent a reporter over for a feature piece on this new breed of sophisticated lawman. The reporter was surprised to see a detective on a bench reading Victor Hugo's *Les Misérables*.

"This," the detective said, tapping his finger to the book, "is the only story of a criminal really worth reading. It is the third time I have accompanied Jean Valjean through his amazing sad adventures. I'm reading the story to the men, and we are getting a lot of enjoyment out of the experience."

New York was impressed by Woods and his crime fighters. The *Evening News* even called him "an American Sherlock Holmes." Woods liked that.

By February 28, two weeks after her disappearance, the *Times* issued an editorial on Ruth Cruger. "It is one of the impenetrable mysteries of recent times," they wrote. "It is still too early to despair about Miss Cruger. She may be found, and we trust that she will, but it is the simple fact that, in spite of all the confident reports, all the misleading clues, all the neighborhood gossip, which seems to be utterly vapid and without foundation, nobody knows where she is, why she went away. Even in the complex life of crowded modern cities there are a few such mysteries." There were now fifty detectives on the case, all reporting to Captain Alonzo Cooper of Fourth Branch.

⚜

The ice of winter finally began to melt and New Yorkers welcomed a world they thought had been lost to them forever. Coats came off, and rain washed the filthy streets. Captain Cooper ordered a launch from Harbor B to troll through the newly splashing waters. Even at night, a police boat pushed through Pelham Bay, flashing its lights over the floating white ice. The temperature was still cold enough that all of the inlets were still frozen into blocks. There were still places that resisted them.

Outside the city, the world was also changing. The leading news item of the day was the Zimmerman telegram, an intercepted, coded page in which Germany seemed to promise parts of the American Southwest to Mexico if it would invade the United States to distract it. Austria was massing troops along the Serbian frontier, and Germany, Italy, Russia, France, and even England were in a turmoil, with panics in their capitals. On March 5, Woodrow Wilson began his second term as president, and the prospects of war seemed less dim. In gray Atlantic waters, fifty more submarines were added to the American fleet to purr under the waters, "to send enemy vessels to the bottom."

Ruth Cruger, though still lost, was transforming, too. The photograph of her that was being shared across the country had expanded from a portrait to include her full, buxom upper body. In an interview with the *Sun*, her mother revealed that Ruth had suffered through typhoid fever the previous August. Her illness had left her with a slightly weakened heart, though she otherwise had recovered well.

"We thought, perhaps, the weakened heart had caused her to collapse on the street," Mrs. Cruger said. "But we've searched every hospital without learning anything about her."

"We have tried many methods," Henry Cruger said, "and nothing has resulted so we have decided to use publicity. I hope to make the face of my daughter familiar to people, that every father and mother in America can be a detective."

By March 1, a new assistant district attorney, John T. Dooling, had been assigned to the investigation. Dooling, a young-looking man with thick black hair parted on the side, had uncovered several new pieces of information that had the potential to jump-start the case. Dooling had discovered that Ruth had gone ice-skating—alone—at Van Cortlandt Park and Central Park more frequently than anyone knew. This was in direct opposition to what Henry Cruger was telling the press. Dooling, who was convinced that Cocchi had just gone to ground to avoid anti-Italian sentiment, sent an open letter to him through the press. Dooling promised Cocchi that if he ever came back, he would be treated fairly by the police.

These stories that were coming out of the district attorney's office began to fray the edges of that smiling photograph of Ruth. Dooling had uncovered another story: several Sundays before she had disappeared, Ruth had an incident on her way to church. As she walked alone to Sunday school, Ruth kept tight to the sidewalk. At the intersection of 127th Street and Riverside, she saw a man sitting on the steps of a walk-up. He was very well dressed. He had a black mechanical car, gurgling at the curb. As she passed, the man smiled at Ruth.

"Would you like to go for a ride in my motorcar?" he asked.

Ruth didn't say anything and kept walking, even faster now, but she felt his eyes on her. She told her father and her best friend about it that night, after supper, but she couldn't remember much. She couldn't remember anything about his face. She just knew that his clothes were rich and he had a smooth voice.

Dooling was also looking for the "young man," as he was called, who was seen by Rubien, the taxicab driver. Dooling said that an informant, who wished to remain anonymous, had placed this man's information in the hands of the Fourth Branch. This was the clue that had always been the most provocative. The readers of the papers knew that "young man" had always been code for "suitor." There was another story of a similar young man who apparently hung around Teachers College at night and who had accosted two women. He would approach women and ask them to dinner. "He would say, 'How do you do, Miss Smith?' When the young woman replied that she was not Miss Smith, he said: 'You're not, well you certainly are very like her,' and thereupon attempted to strike up a conversation which ended up in an invitation to dinner."

These stories, and what they suggested, made many of Ruth's friends angry. The Crugers' pastor, Reverend Pattison, managed to get a five-minute appointment with Police Commissioner Woods. After waiting, Pattison was finally admitted to Woods's office, and they talked for over an hour. Pattison defended Ruth's reputation and tried to convince Woods that she had fallen afoul of evil. Woods didn't agree—he was 95 percent sure that Ruth had eloped. But Woods admitted that he would never dismiss the possibility of that other 5 percent. Pattison was surprised at that.

Similarly disgusted with the police and with what he was reading in the papers about Dooling's so-called discoveries, Henry met with the district attorney, a thin man named Edward Swann. With his approval, Henry then offered a $1,000 reward for information leading to his daughter's whereabouts. The district attorney's office would handle the incoming clues. Swann had been thinking about offering a reward anyway.

From then on, Mr. Cruger made a trip to Mr. Dooling's office every single night. He came armed with the letters that each day's mail had brought to his home. Henry Cruger looked noticeably older to his friends and acquaintances; his friends could see it in his eyes and cheeks. All he could do was push forward. His daughter had now been missing for over a week.

When he returned home on the night of February 22, Henry Cruger once again took a call from his favorite reporter from the *Evening World*. When the reporter asked him what he thought of the state of the investigation, Henry didn't hold back.

"The police of New York City and the reporters of police news of all the New York newspapers and news bureaus have been digging, picking, gossiping, guessing, pretending, and hinting in the chance of finding a defect in the girl's reputation on which they might put the blame for her disappearance, and they have found not one sliver of scandal; not even a surreptitious note in a Sunday School book or a wave of the hand from a window, or a meeting with a boy at which anybody and everybody was not welcome."

"It is a test," offered the reporter, writing about Henry, "with pride swelling up above his troubled grief and worry . . . to which he would not care to put any young girl's station; but he cannot help being proud to the tips of his fingers of the way Ruth's reputation has stood it."

"Even if she had not stood that test so beautiful," Henry added, "even if the meanest and nastiest guesses about her were true, she is my own dear girl and I would want her and I don't want her a bit more than her mother and sisters want her. And nothing else is going to count until we find her or know what has become of her." He felt like telling the cops to all go to thunder. But he didn't. He knew that to let yourself go was easy, but to keep hold of yourself was hard.

"My girl Ruth must not be a lost girl," Henry said. But as he looked at the black-and-white photo of his daughter, staring up from the newspapers, he couldn't help feeling like the whole city had already turned her to stone.

5

These Little Cases

June 1905

A long line of people unwound itself from the open door at 269 Madison Street. Men twirled their hats and women pulled their thin knit shawls around their shoulders. As the people slowly moved forward, their eyes lingered on a golden sign hung near the door. Those who knew English read JUSTICE FOR THOSE OF LIMITED MEANS FOR MODERATE FEES. Those who could not just marveled at the gold. Ever since the office had opened on June 1, 1905, everyone in the neighborhood knew this was the place to get good, honest legal help.

When they finally reached the waiting room inside, they saw plush chairs and inviting walls painted in soft green and white. There were gay prints on the walls and fresh curtains at the windows. When the owner of the firm was in her office, people in the waiting room could see her through the open door, seated at her desk or moving between stacks of papers in a flutter of black clothing. Her office had high-backed chairs and deep red walls. Her desk had a lamp on it and was covered in inkwells and knickknacks. Hanging heavily on the wall behind her was a painting of Mother Mary, holding a swaddled baby Jesus, her right hand pointing up to an imagined sky just above the gilded frame.

In a corner of the little office was a framed card on the wall with a quote from Kipling. It read:

> *No one shall work for money,*
> *No one shall work for fame,*
> *But each for the joy of working,*
> *And each in his separate star,*
> *Shall draw the thing as she sees it*
> *For the God of things as they are.*

As the people came in and poured their stories out to the woman in black, a young man stood and took notes behind them. When a client was finished telling his or her story, Grace would, with a flush of animation, grasp their hands to give them a feeling of hope. The next person was then beckoned in with a welcoming smile. Today, though, a small man and his associates were seated in Grace's office. She was not smiling.

"You know," said Grace, "I should not hesitate to send any of you men to jail if you don't do what is right." The man, a German, was an East Side employment bureau proprietor involved in crooked practices. Grace paused, letting her words sink in.

"But," she continued. "if you will do the best you can and work on the level, I will do everything in my power to help you." That was her standing promise to all.

Grace left the Legal Aid Society because she felt that she could do better on her own. So on her own dime, she opened the People's Law Firm. Her mission was to help the city's poor immigrants with their legal problems. Her main goal was to avoid taking cases to court. Instead, she worked toward private settlements. It was less expensive for her clients, avoided endless hours in court, and helped speed up matters when a client couldn't speak English well. Grace had seen countless of examples of how language barriers hindered the judicial process at the Legal Aid Society and seemed assured of her solution. Grace wasn't so sure that the poor needed a lawyer so much as they needed someone to plainly interpret the law for them. The convoluted phrasing and mouth-twisting Latin words spoken by lawyers were hard enough even for English speakers to understand.

As new waves of people were sifted into New York's sundry neighborhoods, the city was full of new legal problems, which were caused by everything from wicked employers to the slumlords running the city's many stylike tenements. The location of the People's Law Firm in the center of lower New York was ideal. To the east were the Hungarians; to the west, the Austrian and Russian Jews. There were Italians, Armenians, and sometimes even a Greek or an Egyptian in Grace's sitting room. She caught her cases from walk-ins or through local groups such as the New York Charity Organization Society, which sent new people to her almost every day. Her settlement fees were sometimes the whole sum of one dollar, with the time of payments made to suit the condition of the client. If people were desperate and had no money, Grace would reassure them that it would be fine. She was affectionately known as the "Portia of the East Side." Among the Italians, her card announced her as *"Prezzi Moderati per Cliente di Modeste Condizioni."* Near the Williamsburg Bridge, her cards were in Yiddish. Her most popular nicknames however, were "sister" and "mother."

The lines outside the People's Law Firm began to stretch so long that an Upper West Side branch was soon opened at 216 West Twenty-third Street, followed by a Lower East Side location at 156 Leonard Street in Little Italy. Soon, the little headquarters itself had to be moved to 10 Bible House, across from Cooper Union, the free institution of higher education whose great hall was still filled with the invisible words of presidents, including the echo of Lincoln himself.

On Monday evenings, Grace joined the heads of the East Side branch to hear the more complicated cases. In her little office after hours or sometimes on the warm front steps in the summertime, unofficial courts were convened where both parties would plead their case. Grace, her face alive with sympathy and interest, would listen carefully. Afterward, she would confer with her lawyers, and they would try to work out a fair settlement. This was the outcome Grace always strived for, but, despite all her efforts, there were some cases that defied that hope. This was New York, after all.

One such case involved a young, lost-looking boy with black hair who wandered into the People's Law Firm one night asking for the lady lawyer. He looked like he was wearing hand-me-down clothes cut from a man triple his size. Through an interpreter, Grace learned that the boy had been sent over from Russia by his relatives and put to work by a kinsman who ran a haberdashery in the city. The boy worked hard for a year and half without any wages. When he realized that his friends were getting paid at their jobs, the boy went to his boss and boldly asked for his money. The boss pulled him aside, smiled broadly, and said he would give the boy twenty-five dollars and a ticket back home to Russia instead. He knew that the boy was very homesick. Months passed by, and the boy never saw the money or a ticket. But he had heard of the woman who wore black.

Grace wrote a note to the boy's employer asking him to meet with her and the boy the following Monday. The man wrote back and agreed to come around in the evening. When the time came, Grace lurked outside the building, around the corner and out of sight. But no one showed up. Grace briskly walked up to some women who had gathered near the steps and asked if they had seen a boy. The ladies said they had seen a boy approaching from the other direction but that he had gone away with an older man. Grace had guessed that the boss might try something like this. Mad at herself, Grace stormed home. Later that night, she was summoned to the police station to attend to two little girls she knew, who were accused of stealing a hundred dollars.

At the police house, Grace was surprised to see her Russian boy in the custody of an officer. She discovered that the boy's devious employer had brought the boy in on a makeshift charge of larceny. At court the next morning, the boy's boss had seven witnesses to back up his charges that the boy stole from him. On the other side of the aisle, Grace had no witnesses. It looked as if she had already lost.

When it was finally her turn, she asked for the specific charges against the boy to be repeated. Once they were, Grace pointed out that the boy was being officially charged with stealing money from his place of employment. She then asked the judge if he knew that the boy had been working for this man the whole time without pay. How could he steal from an employer he didn't really work for? The judge dismissed the boy and ordered his boss to be brought up on charges instead.

When news of cases like this began to spread, some of the other, more unscrupulous lawyers for the lower class began to get nervous. For years, these lawyers had invented the work of filing and fee gathering to take advantage of New York's newly American, mostly illiterate community. When they heard that the People's Law Firm was growing, these shysters grumbled in saloons as they drank their long beers. Some of these lawyers, who managed long, endless cases, were not only angry at Grace's obvious success, but that she was actually getting results for her clients.

As her enemies kept their hours in bars, Grace continued to spend hers in court during the day and in her office late into the night. At Bible House, Grace paid for most everything herself. She hoped that whatever people could pay—and many could—would allow her to hire a stenographer and some more assistants. Especially women. "I will train any woman who comes to me," Grace said adamantly. "There is plenty of work for women lawyers who are womanly and do not let their brains dominate their hearts."

Many of Grace's clients were women. Mrs. Rosie Pasternack lived in a tenement house on the East Side with her tailor husband when the stork surprised them with three screaming babies. A few newspapers ran their story, and people soon began sending in donations to the newly expanded family to help with the hungry mouths. But once the money started coming in, Mr. Pasternack quit his job and started drinking full-time. Rosie sneaked out one afternoon to meet with Grace. She didn't know what to do. She needed that money for her babies, but she had no use for her husband anymore. But what could she do? Grace had an idea. She sued the embezzling father for lack of child support, and, when he couldn't pay, she sent him off to Blackwell's Island, leaving Rosie alone with her children and free from her parasitic husband. Rosie panicked, wondering who would provide for her, but Grace told her to wait. Once the new developments of Mr. Pasternack's imprisonment were reported in the papers, Rosie got even more donations than before.

A great number of Grace's cases involved marriage, especially translating European unions into American ones. One happy couple had been married by a rabbi in Austria before they came to New York. But things changed once they hit New York, and the husband left, claiming that the Austrian government never sanctioned the marriage in the first place. The woman came into Grace's office and cried her eyes out. She begged Grace to talk to her husband. Grace asked the woman if she really wanted her to do that. When the answer was finally a no, Grace sent a letter to the Austrian government instead. When she received an official reply that the match had been sanctioned, Grace sued the husband for support.

There was also the case of Mary, who had been in jail for three months before she got a message to Grace that she desperately needed help. Mary, who was tall with brown skin, held a good position in a clean, decent household but worked long hours and was homesick. One day, a new female friend invited Mary to a ball, and Mary readily accepted the invitation. She wore the best thing she owned to the ball.

After the ball, the friend left Mary alone with a man, a friend of hers, to escort Mary home. Mary was nervous but went along anyway. Her friend had assured her that the man was a gentleman.

"If you don't give me your money, I'll have you arrested," the man told Mary once they were alone in the dark.

Mary resisted. The man called a policeman and falsely charged her with larceny. When the court couldn't prove the larceny charge, the prosecutor had her arrested for violation of section 150 of the Tenement House Act: prostitution. The man lied, said Mary. Her employer testified to her good character, but it was to no avail.

"That woman saw my lady pay me," Mary told Grace, adding that she earned twenty dollars a month and that her new friend had seen how much money she had when Mary treated her to a picnic. Grace could see what had happened. Grace knew that she couldn't get charges brought against the man, so she focused on getting Mary released instead. Some of her cases were victories only in that they avoided even worse outcomes.

Grace dealt with financial predators of all stripes. Another case involved an Armenian tea merchant who arrived in New York with a hefty seven thousand dollars with which to begin his dream business. After consulting with one of the large brokerage firms on financial opportunities, the man was advised to invest his money several times over in a variety of important-sounding investments. The only problem was that, afterward, there was nothing left for him but plenty for his consultants. The tea merchant hired an attorney who was able to negotiate a settlement of only a few hundred dollars. The tea merchant turned to Grace next, who roared into court and was able to get him back a much larger portion of his money to start his business anew.

Unfortunately, there were also cases of a more pitiful nature. Grace met a poor tailor who mortgaged his precious sewing machines and household furniture for a much-needed seventy dollars. But the bankers handling the paperwork wrote up the mortgage note for $95 instead of $70. The tailor found he could no longer pay the people working for him or make his normal mortgage payment. So he flung himself into the Hudson River, leaving his wife and six little ones to struggle on alone. The little family was days away from losing everything when the widow went to the People's Law Firm. Grace took the case and threatened to sue the mortgage holders if they did not release the debt on the poor tailor's family. The bank told Grace that the family couldn't afford a lawsuit. Grace defiantly told them that she would fund it herself. The bank released the debt, and the man's widow, selling all his machines but one, was able to eventually enlarge her late husband's business and support all of their children.

"There is something deeply tragic about these little cases that are spread out before lawyers," Grace said. "The newly-made Americans are almost at the mercy of any older, cleverer citizen that wants to grind down the heel of oppression on their necks. Things are all so strange to them and the law is so curiously complicated that they awake suddenly to find themselves tangled hopelessly in muddles that seem often to choke them and blind them. It is to fight the battles of these poor and ignorant without taking all their profits that the People's Law Firm was started, to fight as eagerly for $5 as for $500."

Grace would tell the story about how a man once came to the firm, very earnest over a case but unable to pay. Grace told him that he could sue as a poor man but that he had to make out an affidavit that he had not a hundred dollars in the world.

"Is your wife worth a hundred dollars?" Grace asked, as she always did, referring to his wife's net worth.

The man looked over at his wife.

"You want to know if my wife is worth a hundred dollars?" the man gasped. "I tell you I would not sell my wife for ten thousand dollars. You don't get my wife!"

Another client, an old woman named Mrs. Glover, had no money but said she would pay with something else. Grace agreed. Once the case was over, Mrs. Glover patted Grace on the shoulder.

"Dearie," she said. "I'm going to make you something loverly."

"What are you going to make me?" Grace smiled.

"I'm going to make you a hat. A lovely hat with two white wings, so you won't have to wear that awful one you have on now."

As Grace's reputation began to grow, greater New York began to hear whispers of the indomitable woman in black. Soon, people in the nicer neighborhoods began paging through the city directory and asked to be connected to number 2659 Gramercy. Soon, Grace was representing New Yorkers in insurance trust-buster cases. One such suit lasted three years and was finally ruled in Grace's favor; she was able to return seventeen thousand dollars to twenty-three widows in Bath Beach. Regardless of her clients' income base, Grace's opponents remained similar: they were often the rich or the desirous to be, driven by that merciless presence that stood behind all the great possessions, carrying its own kind of curse.

One afternoon, a man with dark features and fashionable clothing made the trip to Bible House. His watch and cufflinks gleamed in the otherwise dreary line. When it was finally his turn, he walked in, sat in Grace's office, and announced that his name was Manuel Walls, the second secretary of the Spanish delegation to Washington. Grace closed the door. Mr. Walls, who was young and handsome, told Grace that on returning from a trip to New Brighton in August, he entered his Fifth Avenue bachelor apartment to find that his door had been forced open, his armoire broken into, and the dress suitcase in which he kept his jewels and coins missing. The total loss amounted to three thousand dollars in personal property, which Mr. Walls immediately reported to the police. After a few days, the police told him they had no leads.

Grace took his case and, after questioning Walls, escorted him out and got to work. She quickly identified a suspect: Mr. Lane, a tall New York acquaintance of Walls who had been to his apartment and had seen his coins and jewels. Grace's detective work painted Lane as a cosmopolitan young man of "good address and Tenderloin tastes." Grace even found a witness putting him in the apartment house on the day of the robbery. With plenty of circumstantial evidence on her side, Grace went before the grand jury and got Lane indicted. Now, she just had to find him.

Grace put fliers around the area of Walls's apartment asking for information. Within hours, James Matthews, a Pullman car porter, offered up Lane in exchange for twenty-five dollars. He wanted the money in advance. Grace declined but offered Mr. Matthews double the sum if he helped bring about Lane's capture. Matthews refused, so Grace had him subpoenaed to appear before the judge. But when Grace showed Matthews a photo of Lane in court, he calmly stated that he had never seen him before. They had to let him go.

As Grace boiled in frustration, District Attorney Nott told her to report to Dooling so that a detective could be placed at her disposal. That Saturday afternoon, Grace asked Detective Cooney to go to Grand Central Station to meet Matthews when he came in off his car. Grace asked Cooney, very politely, if he might get Matthews to understand how utterly complicated she might make his life if he did not tell her Lane's whereabouts.

Within hours, Matthews said he would be very happy to help.

The next day, Grace and the police detective found Lane posing as the keeper of a chop suey restaurant. The police raided the place and arrested Lane. He confessed that he had planned the heist of Walls's jewels (just as Grace thought) and that a man named Demarco had assisted him. Within twelve hours, Lane pleaded guilty before the judge. He then gave up Demarco, who led Grace to the shops where the jewelry and coins were pawned, and they were confiscated from under dirty glass. Manuel Walls kissed Grace on the cheek when she returned to his apartment with his missing riches.

"Of course, we do not bar clients with money," Grace said to the reporters who then began to call her office. "Mr. Walls is a man of means, but my idea in establishing the firm was to demonstrate that a legal bureau for the aid of the poor could be operated at a scale of prices within their reach and to their great benefit, and I think this has been done. Starting out alone, I now have four lawyers working with me, and I will have to increase the force soon on account of the press of business." She paused, wanting to get this next part right.

"We offer St. Regis law at Mills Hotel prices," said Grace, firmly, "and such other assistance as they may need in the redressing of wrongs at a cost within their means." When a reporter asked about how she had solved the case so quickly after the police had given up, Grace did not couch her words.

"To begin with, the police are no good," Grace told the reporter. "They had all the facts to start on that I had and did nothing. Even after I had made out the case against Lane it was necessary for me to find him. The police wouldn't help." The coverage of the case of Manuel Walls, sophisticated young diplomat, opened up new opportunities for the People's Law Firm. But even as more calls began to come in, it was still the "little cases" that remained the firm's bread and butter.

One such case involved Herman Romanik, a young man who recently arrived at Ellis Island from Russia. As the doctors checked him out, Herman held his breath, hoped for the best, and was rewarded with a clean bill of health and an entry into New York City. Full of hope and pride, the twenty-five-year-old Herman opened a tailor shop on Attorney Street and got to business. Through nights and into the mornings, Herman was always at the shop, mending and sewing and stitching. All the while, Herman dreamed of the day he could bring his childhood sweetheart, Lotta, over from Russia. His strong and clear image of her, full of affection, made him work all the harder.

But this story was no fairy tale; this was New York. Herman feared what might happen to Lotta at Ellis Island. Her health was not great, and many were being turned away because of the new immigration laws. So Herman saved even more money and went back to Russia to accompany her back himself. As they stood in line at Ellis Island, they were both passed as fit by the medical examiner and the Board of Special Inquiry. Herman beamed as he marched his new wife to the flat above his store in the pushcart district for their honeymoon. His wife somehow looked even more beautiful in New York than in Russia. Within a few months, the word that the couple was expecting got out to Herman's happy customers and friends, who were sure it was a son, they said, clapping each other on the back and smiling through unruly beards.

But one day, without warning, the shop closed, and the young couple disappeared from sight. Herman was finally seen leaving the flat but then returned with two doctors, who quickly went upstairs. A week later, his new bride was taken away in a car to Bellevue, and the little tailor was left to live and work alone.

"It is nothing," the bewildered Herman said to his neighbors. "She is sick. Crazy in the head, but it goes away by and by. Sure it will go away soon as the baby come. The doctors they say so. Sure it will go. She hurts nobody yet."

A few days later, Herman went to Bellevue to call for his wife. He walked up and down the wide white halls, but still he could not find her. Someone looked at the paperwork and explained to Herman that his wife had entered Bellevue as a charity case. That meant that she had been transferred to the Manhattan State Hospital for the Insane on Ward's Island. They explained to Herman that because she was a public charge, she would be deported. Herman felt as if he had been shocked with electricity. He had not been able to read the English on the Bellevue entrance card he had signed and was totally ignorant of what he had done. Herman had signed away his wife's freedom. And that of their unborn baby.

Herman went to Ward's Island and met with Dr. Dent, his wife's new doctor. Dent listened and offered to sign a bond to pay for the care of his wife but only until the baby came; then Herman's family would be deported. Herman refused. But the law was clear: "an alien who shall be found a public charge from causes existing prior to landing shall be deported, as hereinafter provided, to the country whence he came at any time within one year after arrival."

But Dr. Dent had no intention of waiting a year. He immediately notified the State Commission of Lunacy of the presence of Lotta in his institution. Dr. Dent asked that her pregnancy not be taken into consideration. She was an "alien" and insane and should be deported immediately. The commissioner general of Ellis Island, Robert Watchorn, was given the order from Washington, D.C., to deport Mrs. Lotta Romanik. Herman watched helplessly while his wife was put out on a steamer in the Hudson, due to sail at ten the following morning.

She was seven months pregnant.

Herman felt like his life was turning to sand and blowing away in the wind. A friend gave Herman a business card with Grace's name on it. The card said that she could be "consulted and retained as attorney and counsellor at law in cases involving attendance upon the courts and otherwise, especially with a view to meeting the requirements of litigants of moderate means."

Grace listened to Herman's story carefully. She knew of Dr. Dent, recalling the name from the newspaper story in which the reporter Nellie Bly falsified her own insanity to uncover the horrific conditions that existed for patients on Blackwell's Island. According to Bly's account, when the patients in the women's asylum heard Dent down the hall, they whispered, "Here is the devil coming."

First, Grace set out to procure a writ of habeas corpus to delay the deportation order. She explained to Herman that this would force the court to summon his wife before a judge and provide evidence as to why they were sending her back to Russia. The writ, if successful, would at least get her off the boat for a few days and give them some time. The problem was that it was already early evening. The boat was set to sail in the morning. They were going to have to work fast.

Rising from her chair, Grace unhooked the phone. She connected to District Judge Adams, who owed her a favor. She got him to agree to issue the writ and went over to his residence just as it was getting dark. He signed it, but the Ellis Island ferry had already docked for the day. Herman had a sleepless night, but Grace told him not to worry. There was only a small distance of choppy water separating the writ from his wife. When Grace sent the document over to the commissioner of Ellis Island the next morning via her secretary, running as she sped off the ferry and onto the pier, there was only fifteen minutes left before Lotta was set to sail. Minutes later, Lotta ran into the embrace of her husband, who was just behind Grace's envoy.

Later that day, Herman placed his wife in the New York Infirmary for Women and Children on Bleecker Street at a cost of $4.25 a day. Herman's plan, made with Grace's help, was to keep his wife institutionalized until the birth of their baby to avoid having the state seize control of her. Her full case could be heard in federal court later, and they could explain the whole misunderstanding to a judge. Grace didn't foresee any problems.

But $29.75 a week was a lot of money for a tailor on Attorney Street. After a few weeks, Herman was dead broke, and the baby was still five or six weeks away. Lotta had also become more and more violent. The infirmary was getting worried about her behavior, so they looked through her records and made a phone call. The man on the other end invited the infirmary to transfer her over to his care. The infirmary agreed, and Dr. Dent hung up the phone and immediately began the paperwork to deport Lottie under the same law as before.

Once Herman was told, he quickly called Grace. Surely, she could perform her legal magic once again. But she wasn't in her office. Her secretary told Herman that Grace had gone to Halifax with her husband for a rest and vacation. At Ellis Island, the doctors examined Lotta again and said that she was epileptic, not insane, and had been even before arriving in America.

Herman disagreed, saying that her condition was only because of her pregnancy. He begged them to show mercy. To deport her now would be dangerous and inhumane. The baby would be here in little over a month. Shaking their heads, the doctors disagreed, and Lotta was ordered to be deported. She was taken onto the steamer *Kron Prinz*, bound for Bremen.

Grace was still on vacation and unreachable, but her assistants at the People's Law Firm sprang into action. They knew that issuing a writ wouldn't work again, so they racked their brains for an alternative. Finally, someone suggested a radical solution—one that, although not a victory, might provide a compromise. What if Herman could—at the government's expense—also be deported so that he could stay with his wife? Grace's workers petitioned the court but were denied. So they got on the phones. United Hebrew Charities agreed to buy Herman passage on the steamer, and the law firm added another twenty-five dollars. If the couple had to leave America, let them at least leave together. Grace's assistants sent the order over to Ellis Island as quickly as they could. Immigration officials agreed to the concession, and the firm procured Henry's ticket to Bremen. From there, they could track back to Liverpool, where Herman's father and brother now lived.

Back on Attorney Street, Herman was swiftly trying to pack up his important belongings, including two feather beds. He well remembered the hardness of the steamer steerage bunks and wanted his dear wife to be comfortable as the boat pitched about. But no one would let him on a streetcar with such a floppy, unwieldy burden, so Herman ran to the dock himself, with the two mattresses flopped over his back.

When Herman made it to the dock, wheezing and sore and with only five minutes to spare, he was overjoyed to see his wife, Lotta. His mouth fell even further when he saw his baby son asleep in her arms. Early that morning, while Herman was scrambling with his beds, Lotta had given birth to a healthy baby boy. Herman couldn't stop staring at him. Then he realized that this changed everything. His son was only three hours old, but he was an American citizen. Herman remembered that Grace's lawyers had told him that it was unlawful to deport an American citizen. The law surely could not separate mother and child; Lady Liberty was not King Solomon. She didn't have a sword.

The steamer was held at dock while Grace's assistants tried to find a federal judge to issue another writ of habeas corpus so that Lotta's health had time to recover from childbirth. Clearly, circumstances had changed, but this was the easiest, best approach to stop the deportation. But it was noon, and all the judges in the city were away at their long lunches. The writ remained unsigned, and the ship sailed off to Germany with the new family, who left their new home and business behind.

No one was separated, which was a mercy. But Grace's lawyers couldn't shake the cruel fact that Herman and his family had been forced out of the country even though they had a legal right to stay. When Grace finally returned from vacation, she heard the story and felt sick to her stomach. The government had gotten away with something she could have easily stopped; she knew the letter of the law of this particular case in and out. But she had missed her opportunity to help. Grace tried desperately to locate the Romaniks in Germany, but to no avail.

Shaken by her experience with the little tailor, Grace seemed determined to make up for what she was sure was her fault. She immediately threw herself into more cases as she careened between her offices day and night. She became more aggressive, especially when it came to deportation. Antonio Vigiani was an Italian barber who established himself in New York and then sent for his brother's family from Italy. But they were rejected at Ellis Island and deported. According to rule II of the immigration law, when someone was ordered deported, the person could appeal to Washington; the attorney fee for such an appeal was capped at ten dollars. But some unscrupulous lawyers took advantage of the importance of this appeal and charged higher fees.

Caesar B. F. Barra was one such lawyer. Barra took Vigiani's case and undertook to have the deportation verdict reversed, but, instead of charging $10, he asked for $150. Vigiani loved his brother, so he paid the fee. After the court ruled that Vigiani's brother and family were to be deported anyway, Barra kept the money. Vigiani sought out the People's Law Firm, spitting and flailing at this gross injustice. Grace went to Barra and showed him, in print, the $10 limit of the law.

"Go ahead and crack your whip," Barra said. "I will return nothing."

Grace went before a judge, cracked her whip, and got Mr. Barra disbarred.

Grace couldn't understand how an Italian lawyer could prey on his own countrymen. In fact, one of Grace's busiest orbits was the newest branch of the People's Law Firm in the heart of Little Italy. Though her practice there was not very old, Grace was quickly learning just how much the Italians had made this part of New York City their own. There were wooden stands with fruit spilling over. Sunbleached palm crosses and tiny paintings of Christ in perfect gold ovals stood watch in nearly every window.

As the summer began, Grace was hired by an Italian named Michael Pirolla to help procure a permit from the fire department. For years, the Our Lady of Mount Carmel celebration in East Harlem was among the city's biggest religious events, running from Saturday to Monday night in the middle of July. One of its signature characteristics was the hundreds of flickering candles the local residents would string across their narrow streets to transform them into outdoor cathedrals. For years, this was accomplished using little wax candles in small glasses suspended on wires. The effect was magical, as the lights twinkled above the narrow, jagged canyons below. But setting up these lights was an arduous process, so the festival planners were hoping to switch to more modern acetylene carbide torches to light their festival instead.

When Grace explained her client's request, Fire Commissioner Hayes turned it down on the spot. There was already enough danger from the fireworks he knew the Italians had been secretly amassing for a year. Acetylene gas, though inexpensive and bright, was even more hazardous. There had just been an accident where a warehouse burned down to the street. Grace related the answer to Mr. Pirolla, who expressed his displeasure. Grace agreed and was sympathetic. She said that, given the size and scope of the project, they just couldn't do it without the blessing of Hayes. Grace advised that they respect his decision and try again next year.

A few weeks later, as the festival was about to begin, Grace was visited by Michael Pirolla again. He shut the door behind him and had his hat in his hand. In a sheepish voice, he informed Grace that after the festival planners had heard Commissioner Hayes's answer, someone had secretly done something. Grace pressed him, and Pirolla confessed that the planners had passed a resolution through the Board of Aldermen that would permit the acetylene lighting after all. They had gone over Hayes's head.

Grace went right to Hayes. She didn't like being used. The fire commissioner glowered at her and asked her to find out who did this. Hayes gathered up some men and went down to the festival, which was in the final stages of setting up. Hayes saw the new acetylene lights, clear and bright, and ordered them brought down immediately. He could sense the anger of the workers as they glared at him and slowly unwound the lights.

When the festival officially opened, booths and wagons were piled up tight against the street selling yellow wax candles that measured from six inches tall to six feet in diameter. Stray firecrackers jumped and snapped in bursts of light in the streets as children scattered under parents and horsecarts. From above, the procession, nearly five hundred Catholics strong, started to make its way through the cross-streets between 100th and 115th along First and Second Avenues. The mass of people was like some dense, moving serpent. People marched behind the banners of the Societies of Saint Antonio and of Mount Carmel. Many men and women were in their bare feet, holding the yellow candles, doing penance for their own unemployment. Frequently, the parade would stop, and men and women would run out from the crowd to pin paper money and jewelry to the banners. When the procession finally reached the Church of Our Lady at Mount Carmel, the banners, heavy with money, were donated to the church. The marchers carried their candles and left them on the altar. After one hour, the altar was so filled with waves of flickering light that the candles had to be carried to another room. The massive church on East 115th Street held Mass—in the chapel and the basement—nonstop from four in the morning until eleven at night. High Mass was celebrated at eleven o'clock.

As nightfall came, crowds of between fifty and seventy-five thousand people paraded the streets. They were singing, shouting, and banging tambourines past the cafes and stores. Hayes, Grace, and some men walked the streets to see if the Italians had complied. The display was not nearly as brilliant as it would have been with the carbide lighting, but his order had been obeyed—above him was a beautiful constellation composed entirely of candles. For the entire festival, there were only six arrests, all for the usual reasons involving drunkenness. Even the massive celebratory fireworks proceeded safely. A few days later, however, Michael Cica, an eleven-year-old boy in the neighborhood, placed a leftover firework in a tin can. He and his friends put a match to it, then turned, running at top speed and laughing. The explosion caused the tin can to be driven through his body, killing him instantly.

A few days later, the phone rang for Grace at the People's Law Firm. The voice on the other end said that if she ever appeared near the church again, she would be murdered. A few hours later, there came the same message, but in a different voice. This was repeated all day long. Later that day, while walking to court characteristically late—possibly with a shopping bag from Thurn's under her arm—Grace was startled by a dark man hiding behind a column. He whispered to her. "Don't even go to Harlem," he said, in a thick Italian accent. She could barely understand him. "Your life is in danger," he said, "and so is that of Commissioner Hayes." The man disappeared quickly, leaving Grace stunned. She knew that this was retaliation for the acetylene lanterns, but she wasn't going to let idle threats stop her, especially in Little Italy. So later that day, Grace went to see a client, Gaetaro Ligmanti, on Grand Street. An hour after, she was called to the phone. She sighed, preparing herself for the usual threat, when a new voice told her that this client's life was not worth a penny, as he had been named a victim of the Black Hand.

Grace clicked the phone and hurriedly asked to be connected to the nearest station house. She repeated what the man had said. The station cop promised her immediate police protection. A cop was stationed outside her office on 156 Leonard Street, and a plainclothes man followed her when she traveled to certain sections of the city. She had heard the three-word name that was among the most ominous in the city: the Black Hand.

⁂

Every New Yorker had read of or knew someone who had opened a letter with no return address, only to find it covered inside with primitive drawings of black crosses, daggers, and skulls, all dripping with black ink meant to look like dripping blood. There would usually be a simple, ungrammatical message asking for money—or sometimes worse: a note claiming the abduction of one's son or daughter. These letters were almost always signed the same way: with the ink-bloody imprint of a black hand.

The Black Hand was understood to be a secret criminal organization or, possibly, a loose collection of individual criminals—bombers, kidnappers, murderers, and extortionists—that the police believed was largely Italian. The public feared them. Newspapers ran accounts of the Black Hand's criminal exploits almost daily. Everyone knew the process: if you received a Black Hand letter, you were instructed to hand over money or suffer the consequences. The letters would say ominous things like, "We have you." Once you paid, you were usually left alone.

There were many stories about the origins of the Black Hand. The papers reported on a similarly named vigilante group active at the turn of the century. This group would also send strange, threatening letters, but only to people who took advantage of the weak or downtrodden. Different rumors based the origin of the organization in Sicily and claimed it had links to a centuries-old mixture of Catholicism and witchcraft. Black Handers were said to subject new members to elaborate occult rituals. Magazines ran exposés of Black Hand societies and their mysterious membership manuals, though there were clearly more mysteries than facts.

The majority of Black Hand letters asked for small sums, and they were usually targeted at successful Italian business owners. If someone didn't pay, they would usually just move on to the next mark. But sometimes their violence would escalate beyond all reason. The Black Hand frequently used dynamite, usually to blow up the doors of people who would not pay. Photographs of these ruined thresholds appeared on front pages across the city. Black Handers were also known to kidnap people, especially young children, and hold them for ransom. There were many stories of toddlers who, once their parents had finally saved enough to free them, no longer recognized their own parents. No one was immune. Some said the whole thing was just newspaper-driven nonsense. The others just locked their doors.

The Black Hand had resurfaced again around 1905, sending letters and marking doorways throughout Little Italy and Harlem. Some said they were getting even bolder. One Sunday, Father Vincent

Sorrentino, of the Church of Our Lady of Loreto, revealed that the Black Hand had threatened the church itself on Assumption Day.

"Is it not an awful thing," the father said, his voice trembling, "that a priest, the pastor of his flock, when called upon to visit the dying must carry a revolver in his pocket that the Blessed Sacrament may reach the person about to die."

The police had also discovered Black Hand strongholds on the city's outskirts, most notably in Westchester. In the quiet forest stretching into Pennsylvania, police patrols looked in the dark for the mysterious Queen of the Black Hand, who had been leading a gang that was terrorizing local merchants with letters, bombings, and even shootings. They also found, hidden in the woods, a Black Hand school filled with dummies and stiletto knives.

In East Harlem, the head of the largest Italian criminal gang was Giuseppe Morello. Known as the Clutch Hand because of his deformed right hand, Morello built a gang—a family—of notorious gangsters by sharing territory, unifying bloodlines, and being merciless to his enemies. His brother-in-law was the Wolf, Ignacio Lupo, and together they laid the foundation for bigger families to come. Morello was called the *capo di tutti capi*, the "boss of the bosses." The Wolf alone was thought to have murdered sixty people on Morello's orders. They were especially known for gruesome barrel murders, whereby the victim's body would be cut in two and folded into a barrel before being buried or shipped to an unwitting recipient. When Morello was finally busted several years later on a counterfeiting charge, agents found Black Hand letters ready to be sent, hidden in the diaper of the baby his wife was carrying on her hip. Most of the letters began with "Dear Friend," but ended with a threat of mortal violence. They all carried the same import:

> *FRIEND: The need obliges us to come to you in order to do us a favor. We request, Sunday night, 7th day, at 12 o'clock you must bring the sum of $1000. Under penalty of death for you and your dears you must*

come under the new bridge near the Grand Street ferry where you will
find the person that wants to know the time. At this word you will give
him the money. Beware of what you do and keep your mouth shut . . .

The spectre of the Black Hand—as it appeared in newspaper accounts and rumors on the streets—hung over Grace as she walked in and out of her office in Little Italy. She was steadfast, as always, but she knew that the danger she faced was real. After a few weeks, the phone calls finally subsided and the police removed Grace's protection from the Black Hand. But she still looked over her shoulder. The woman in black had been marked like a page in a book. She wondered who had that book and how long that mark might last.

⚜

One warm night at Bible House, a woman came to see Grace. She spoke very fast, and her eyes looked as if she had been crying. The translator said that the woman's husband had gone missing from the city. Grace had heard stories like this before. The woman kept shaking her head when Grace's translator said "kidnapping." Something else was going on here.

Grace questioned the woman further. Her husband's last job had been with the S. S. Schwartz Employment Agency at First Street and Bowery. After the woman left, Grace did some checking into the company but could find nothing beyond a thin line in the city directory. The husband's disappearance—and his fate—seemed, on the surface, a complete mystery.

A few weeks later, the woman returned to Bible House, accompanied by her husband, a big Russian man named Bennie. Grace was happy that the mystery had been solved, but neither the woman nor her husband, who looked ill, seemed very happy about it. The woman started speaking swiftly and loudly as she turned her husband around. As his wife started to lift up the back of his shirt, Grace modestly started to turn away. She stopped when she saw the man's bare back, marked with raised stripes.

The man's name was Bennie Wilenski, and he was fifty years old. He was impossibly thin for such a tall man. He looked like a shadow. His brow was wet with flop sweat and from the heat. He sat down on Grace's step, shivering.

"Six weeks ago," Bennie said, "I read an advertisement in an East Side paper, offering splendid work for good men." It sounded like a good idea for an out-of-work Russian Jew. The agency agreed to pay thirteen dollars for passage to Florida; the money was to be deducted from his wages at fifty cents a week. Bennie said that he and forty-one other men boarded a Clyde Line steamer for Jacksonville. The good prospect was looking worse by the moment. The men were forced to sleep on hard decks and actually refused the food because it was so bad-tasting.

After three and a half days, the dirty boat reached Jacksonville, where the heat felt like a wool coat. According to Bennie, they were met by representatives of the Hodges Milling Company and a man they called "the boss." They then took a day-and-a-half train ride to Maytown and Buffalo Bluff, their new place of employment. They were shown to their new homes: low huts that the boss called "dog houses." By now, they were all very hungry.

"Five men slept on mattresses on the floor and five on shelves higher up," said Bennie. "There was no table to eat from. The cabins were full of dirt and vermin and you put your food on your mattress and ate it there. We were all half-starved. The superintendent told us we could buy what we wanted at the grocery store. The prices were awful. A glass of ice water was five cents. The weather was very hot. It is a swampy country full of mosquitoes."

Grace looked at this big man, shaking and sweating. He continued his story.

"We were watched all night by Negroes with revolvers. At four o'clock every morning, the watchmen woke us up. We had only a few moments to eat our crackers and fish and then we had to walk for two hours into the swamp, where we handled logs all day long. When we staggered from the heat, and overwork, they dashed water on us to revive us. The foreman beat us. When we stopped to eat a few soda crackers at noon the foreman kept driving us to hurry up. If we didn't move fast enough, sometimes he would knock the cracker out of a man's hand and yell 'Hurry up!' and beat him.

"At the end of one week," Bennie said, "I was informed that I had earned $6.30, but I owed the company $7 for food. I knew this was false, but what could I do?" Bennie explained that if they stopped to rest, they were beaten on their bare backs with switches. He told of a kid named Jake Leonard from Essex Street who dropped right into the swamp from exhaustion. Wilenski grabbed some water and threw it on his face. The bosses beat both of them. No water was given to the men unless they paid for it.

"The men were always trying to escape at night," Bennie said. "We would open the only window at the back of the house and let them out. Sam Fink got away to the woods three times, but they always got him back. I hear they have put him in prison now, because down in Florida, if you owe money to a corporation and try to run away you are a criminal."

Bennie continued his story. After working for ten days, he received a $30 money order that somehow found its way to him from his wife in New York. The foreman intercepted it but let Bennie keep $10 of it because he felt bad about the water incident. But $10 was enough for Bennie to discharge himself. He paid his fee, then made his way through the swamp to Jacksonville and then borrowed more money from a Jewish Relief Society to get back home. By the time he had reached the city, he was a nervous and physical ruin. He was being seen by Dr. J. Schlansky for injuries to his back.

Grace sent some men to snoop around the S. S. Schwartz Agency, and they found a lot of activity and willing men waiting in line. Meanwhile, Grace persuaded Bennie to testify, and they got Schwartz arrested. The agent claimed that he knew nothing of the actual conditions at the turpentine camp, which was run by the Hodges, O'Hara & Russell Company. Schwartz also pointed a finger at a man named J. Francis de Lauzieres from something called the Southern Agricultural Colonization Society.

When Schwartz was finally arraigned, it was on a charge of peonage—forced human slavery through debt—in violation of section 5535 of the Revised Statutes. As the U.S. government prepared its case, Grace found several other men to corroborate Bennie's story. One such man was Edward Schoch, who worked at Buffalo Bluff and was paid ten cents for a fortnight's worth of work. He returned with a severe case of ague. As Grace was taking down his affidavit, Edward's face started burning up, and he had to be taken to the hospital.

After collecting more bits and pieces of information, Grace tracked down J. Francis, the Sunday school teacher at the Italian Episcopal Church of San Salvatore on Elizabeth Street. Schwartz had initially revealed Francis as one of the plan's masterminds. Francis said he knew nothing about the company except what he had been told by B. F. Buck, leader of the Italian-American Agricultural Society. So many societies, Grace thought. All of these people looking for ways to join together. Francis told her that Buck earned two dollars a head for recruiting workers for the camps. Francis also said, in a whisper, that Buck had the backing of Bishop Bonaventure F. Broderick, who was listed as the treasurer of the group. They had Schwartz, but Grace knew that he was only one tentacle of a larger creature, an "atrocious, bloodthirsty system." Grace needed to see it for herself. She needed to go to Florida.

Grace found an investor for her trip south to explore the conditions at the work camps. The S. S. McClure Company, the publisher of *McClure's* magazine, was the place for good, solid muckraking. They agreed to pay three hundred dollars for Grace's travel expenses. All Grace had to do was write about what she found. Grace smiled and agreed. This wasn't what she normally did, of course, but it would serve her purposes. No one could talk her out of it.

Before Grace left New York, she worked up an itinerary of the places she planned to investigate, just in case she disappeared while undercover. She took the list to her sister Jessie, who lived with her family at 9 Park Avenue. Jessie, who was fashionable and had a personality full of laughter, had married a businessman and lived the life of a New York society woman. The sisters were close, but obviously different. Jessie respected her sister's intelligence and passion for justice and helped her whenever she could. So, though she shook her head, Jessie smiled, list in hand, and told Grace that she would pray for her.

For her trip, Grace finally decided it might be time to ditch her black attire. So she paid a visit to her friend Martha Bensley Bruere to borrow a coat. Martha was entertaining her society friends, as usual, but immediately fetched a blue silk coat for her friend. Grace still wore a black hat, of course, but she borrowed one that was trimmed with a gorgeous flower instead of her traditional veils. As Martha piled clothes onto Grace's arms, she asked her what she was going south for. "Professional business," responded Grace.

"Oh, detective work!" Martha said. She was a society lady herself, unlike Grace, and was also a writer of some renown. Grace didn't know if Martha wanted more information for her gossip circle or details for a story. Not that there was a difference anymore. Grace responded in a vague, but truthful way. "Some very strange stories," Grace said. "I can't get the facts from this distance; so I've got to go."

Once Grace left Martha's apartment, her friend remarked, reaching for more tea and cookies, that such an adventure was "so like her—to feel that the wrongs of anyone within her country's gates were her concern: to treat the whole Unites States as though it was just a household and she a careful housewife dispensing domestic justice!" Martha also dispelled the notion that Grace's recent divorce had anything to do with her leaving the city.

Grace traveled through the South for seven weeks in the fall of 1906, leaving New York on a train at 12:25 and settling in for a trip that would get her into Florida by 12:10 the next day. They served chicken, roast turkey, and chicory salad on the train. Fruit, toasted crackers, and coffee were also offered in slightly shaky containers. Once Grace arrived on steady ground under the palm trees, she disappeared.

Grace made her way through Florida, Mississippi, and Arkansas by hiding in wagons or disguising herself as an old woman selling scissors. Some of the workers even reported a shabby-looking man in a hat hanging around some of the turpentine camps, sometimes taking notes in a book. Sometimes, she used her maiden name of Winterton to throw off any possible discovery. She watched from the forest, hidden, as men hacked into the tall loblolly pines with their hatchets. They fixed tin pots with curved rims onto the bare trees and cut notches on the side so that the sap seeped slowly down into the pail. A week or so later, the men lugged the full, heavy pots out to the angled still that smelled like licorice.

At some point during Grace's tour of the South—and perhaps before it even began—she stopped taking notes for an article and started gathering affidavits. In the lumber mills and the copper, coal, and phosphate mines, Grace began collecting evidence against the same evil she had heard about, and seen, at Buffalo Bluff—slavery through forced debt, or peonage. Grace was terrified about how far this practice might reach. After the Civil War, the South, rich in natural resources, needed laborers to replace the freed slaves. Unfortunately, there were still many landsmen unwilling to pay fairly for them.

When men were whipped or held against their will, Grace's work wasn't difficult—she took photos and notes. But some of the camps were more secretive. So Grace was patient and did interviews and took photographs. Grace didn't want to wade through court for the next ten years; she wanted to take down the whole system. So she got her affidavits, sent them along, and moved on to the next place the whispers in the swamps took her. In New York, Grace liked to spend her time between court cases shopping on a street filled with bobbing hats and ribbons. Now, she lurked behind branches and ate crawfish in tents. As always, Grace was relentless. One night, while she got off a train, a shot was fired from the dark and just missed her. She kept moving forward.

Grace finally returned north in October, arriving in Washington dripping with fever but carrying forty-six affidavits. She got in to see

Attorney General William Henry Moody, giving him signed letters, confessions, and photographs of men working in swamps with water reaching up to their waists. Moody, a Roosevelt trustbuster, had been trying to find proof of peonage for some time, and now he had usable evidence of the crime in the interior of the United States, hand delivered from a slightly ragged Grace Quackenbos.

Moody said that he would send Assistant Attorney General Charles W. Russell down to Florida to begin prosecuting these cases. They would need Grace as a witness, of course. When reporters asked Grace about her meeting with Moody, she "declined to discuss her trip to the South, and said that the matter being in the hands of the government it would be discourteous for her to talk about it." Meanwhile, behind closed doors, the attorney general's office realized that there was only one thing they could do with Grace besides thank her for her service to her country. They had to hire her.

Grace offered to work for free, if only her expenses were paid. Looking at her results, Moody couldn't see how they could refuse her. They appointed her through Henry L. Stimson, the U.S. attorney for the southern district of New York, the site of the original Schwartz case and Grace's base of operations. Stimson was a Yale man and new to the job, having just been appointed by President Roosevelt. He was young enough to still have black hair and a mustache that was cut close to his upper lip. In November 1906, Stimson appointed Grace to the Office of Special Assistant United States District Attorney. She was the first woman to be appointed to this office. By following the trail of one man's tears, leading from New York to Jacksonville and back again, Grace had found a new focus for her powers.

The following spring, Grace returned to the South. This time, she was allowed a small retinue of agents and lawyers. She had helped shut down several of the larger operations in Florida, drawing the ire of the local newspapers. F. J. O'Hara, a lumber magnate, alleged that one of Grace's agents had abducted one of his own workers. Grace's operative apparently charged this man with killing a witness and cutting his body to pieces. O'Hara brought a $50,000 lawsuit against

Grace, but it was dismissed. Representative Frank Clark, of Florida, also attacked Grace in the papers. He demanded to know who she was and how much she was being paid by the Department of Justice. Her inquiries into turpentine and railroad camps had the potential to stall Florida's steady march of industrial progress, charged Clark. He was angry.

"To deal with a 'muck-raker' is always unpleasant," said Clark. "It is at no time agreeable to engage in disputation with that product of our present-day civilization known as 'yellow journalism,' which, for a few pennies and an opportunity to keep in the limelight, does not hesitate to calumniate an entire community."

By April 1907, Henry Stimson was getting nervous. Public charges of murder in the newspapers, whether political rhetoric or not, were serious words. So Stimson, who had hired Grace (or at least had been asked to), wrote the attorney general to say that Grace lacked the character and skill to "deal with such an unscrupulous enemy." She was doing good work, Stimson admitted, but he worried that she was angering a whole lot of people in the process. Stimson said that "the attitude of Mrs. Quackenbos is giving me considerable difficulty and concern." Praising her investigative abilities, Stimson said that "her judgement as a lawyer in both the facts and the law was entirely untrustworthy."

Attorney General Moody had been promoted to the Supreme Court at the close of the previous year. Succeeding him as attorney general was Charles Bonaparte, a short man with a wide forehead and smile. Bonaparte said, in his unmistakably musical voice, that the contents of Grace's report were "revolting to every instinct of humanity" and are "repugnant to the enlightened opinion of modern times in all civilized countries." Our goal, emphasized Bonaparte, was to "bring those guilty of them to adequate punishment." Bonaparte reiterated that they didn't intend to "stop their spending in this area."

On the issue of Grace's pay, Bonaparte said that "her compensation amounts only to what she is obliged to pay a competent person for taking her place in the office she has established as above described her own services being rendered gratuitously." Grace returned to New York in March 1907, armed with more arrests and indictments in Florida.

Both Schwartz and other agents were eventually found guilty of peonage. But this was just the beginning: although Grace had already put a stop to a slew of turpentine farms and mines, there were still plenty of lumber camps that were guilty of peonage. While Schwartz was busy losing his company, Grace investigated the Jackson Lumber Company, whose employment agency was managed in the city by a group of Hungarians. But Grace couldn't speak Hungarian, so she asked the Department of Justice for help. They assigned a special agent named Julius J. Kron to her service.

Kron met Grace and said he would see what he could do in terms of investigating the Hungarians. He had a scar and wore wool suits set in dark plaid. After a few weeks on the job, Kron's successes had gotten him noticed. He was contacted by a man named Michael Tandlisch, who owned a restaurant on Fifth Street. Tandlisch gave Kron a long smile and told him that there was three hundred dollars for him if he could procure some court files. Kron looked puzzled. Tandlisch told Kron to meet his man, Stanley Bagg, at the Astor Hotel. Kron, five foot four and unassumingly quiet, nodded. They set the date for April 6.

When Kron walked into the Astor, he sat down and smoothed out the white tablecloth with his hands. His eyes searched the corners of the room with the barest possible movement. Bagg walked in, sat down, and proceeded to offer Kron five hundred dollars (he had raised the total) if he would give him the names of witnesses in a few cases currently before the federal grand jury. Kron knew he meant the Schwartz peonage case and that Bagg and his partner intended to bully the witnesses in order to keep their business operational. Five hundred dollars was an enormous amount of money for a private detective working for the government.

Across town, Tandlisch was at another restaurant when two federal agents moved in to arrest him. One waited outside while the other circled through the back. Tandlisch spotted him and made a mad dash through the front open window. He landed in the arms of the other agent on the street. Back at the Astor, Julius J. Kron motioned with his head and two officers stood up from nearby tables and placed Bagg under arrest.

When Kron was hired, there was some debate about his background and history. He was a bit of a rough character for government work. But when he got that first offer from Tandlisch, he went immediately to the Secret Service and set up the sting, refusing a bribe that would have made most people weak. Grace liked that, so she kept him on. She knew that there would be plenty of work for both of them. She had heard secret rumors of an even worse place down south somewhere. If only she could find it.

6

Army of the Vanished

March 1917

W hile Fourth Branch detectives looking for Ruth Cruger tracked down long-shot leads and busted down doors as far away as New Jersey, the detectives who first caught the case, Lagarenne and McGee, were still making time in the neighborhood of Cocchi's store. While standing outside the motorcycle shop, Lagarenne looked up to see STUDIO PORTRAITS lettered on the window on the second floor of the building on the opposite side of the street. After trudging to the top of the stairs and rapping on the door, they were greeted by Frank Lee, a dapper bohemian with long hair and a goatee. Lee told the detectives that he was a photographer and artist. He primarily took photos for magazines, he said. The detectives wondered if he took pictures of girls. They asked if he had seen Ruth Cruger.

"I saw a young man walking eastward on 127th Street," Lee said, "keeping pace with a taxicab which was going slowly near the curb beside her. He beckoned to her and she walked toward him. He motioned toward the cab, and she hung back for a moment, but then entered." The detectives looked at each other. This was the first corroboration of Henry Rubien's cab story. Lee didn't have any photos, which was their next, obvious question.

"I saw a girl who was under twenty years old," Lee admitted, smiling. "A red-hot looking baby doll." She was "smartly dressed in a long, dark coat, carrying a small package in her hands." He paused. "Just as she reached the corner a taxi stopped and a young fellow—maybe twenty or so—got out and tipped his hat. She looked around quickly, like she was afraid someone would see her, and then got into the cab. The fellow got in again and then the cab went north on Manhattan." Lee said that man looked rather pale.

"I don't miss much," Lee said. "Mostly I'm just looking and pretending to work." He looked down at the floor. "Business isn't so good."

The detectives asked the photographer to describe the pale man. "The man was about thirty years old," Lee told them. "Above middle height, and good-looking, with a round face. He was well dressed. His overcoat and hat were dark." The detectives listened very carefully.

Meanwhile, John T. Dooling, the district attorney, was questioning people in the relative comfort of his office. He talked to Rosalind Ware, Ruth's classmate at Wadleigh, who was escorted to his office by her mother. Rosalind and Ruth were best friends and used to walk home together after school.

"Ruth told me everything," Rosalind said.

Dooling had also brought in Miss Shelley, who worked the telephone board at the Crugers' apartment building. Miss Shelley testified that Ruth had called Rosalind only two hours before she disappeared. Rosalind said this was not true. Her mother agreed.

Looking at the handwritten phone records, Dooling saw two calls made in quick succession. The first call was indeed to Rosalind Ware's home between 1:07 and 1:09 in the afternoon. The second call was from 1:10 to 1:11 to the Kappa Sigma fraternity house in the Bronx. According to her sister, Ruth had left the apartment at 1:30.

When Rosalind left, her mother tarried, and passed Dooling a list of four names: Many, Butler, Deroka, and Ward. They were all college boys, she said, hurrying out the door. Dooling knew that interviewing these boys might be hard on the Cruger family, since it could bring up private troubles. Some of these boys belonged to socially prominent families. But Dooling didn't care. He felt that things were starting to tighten. When detectives got to the fraternity house, a student named Harold Buse said that he remembered the call. Ruth had wanted to talk to a boy named Seymour Many. He wasn't in, so Ruth hung up.

"Ruth was a mighty fine girl," said Harold. "I am sure she has not run off with any one. She came here to dances often, and was popular. She always appeared here with Seymour." The detectives looked for Seymour Many, but he was busy all day at a sports contest at Madison Square Garden. He was captain of the track team.

The next morning, Dooling arrived at his office early to find that someone was already waiting for him. The young man—athletic but stocky—couldn't have been more than twenty years old. He said that his name was Seymour Many and that he was a student at NYU. He was from Mount Vernon, Ruth Cruger's old neighborhood, and had been a good friend of hers for a long time.

They sat down in the office. Seymour told Dooling that he had taken Ruth—"Miss Cruger," as he called her—to the Wadleigh High School alumni dance on January 2. They also went ice-skating together quite frequently. Even though Ruth had moved to Harlem, they kept in touch by writing letters. "We were confidential friends," Seymour said. When Dooling asked if he could see the letters, Seymour said that he had thrown them all out.

"I always destroyed them," he said, "like I did with all letters from girls." Seymour looked away for a moment. He said that he was probably the last person in the world to talk to Ruth on the phone before she disappeared.

Seymour Many spoke of a very different Ruth Cruger than the one her father had revealed to the press. Seymour said that Ruth had a fight with her papa a couple of days before she vanished. There was a boy, Seymour said. Someone her father wouldn't let call on her. A Columbia man.

Apparently, Ruth had met this person one Sunday while skating at Van Cortlandt Park. Or was it a party at NYU? Seymour couldn't remember. Anyway, they exchanged numbers and calls and smiles. They made plans to meet again. On Sunday, February 11, Seymour said that Ruth called her new Columbia friend. She broke the news that he couldn't call on her at her home because her father had forbidden it. Ruth was furious, Seymour said. Her father said that the reason was because he didn't know anything about the young man. Seymour said that Ruth's father required that a common acquaintance introduce this boy to him. Ruth was very upset. All that studying and time at home caring for her sister had taken its toll on her. Ruth wrote Seymour and asked him to tell the Columbia man to ignore her father and to come anyway.

Seymour admitted that he had read the letter, but he claimed that he tore it up before relating its contents to its intended reader. Dooling asked why. Seymour said that he destroyed it, realizing that Ruth had been excited when she wrote it. Dooling asked Seymour to reconstruct the letter from memory, which he did.

"What day was it written?" asked Dooling.

"The Sunday before she disappeared," Seymour said.

The district attorney asked the name of this Columbia man.

"Richard Butler," said Seymour.

⁂

The next day, Richard Butler sat down across from the district attorney and a small group of detectives. Dooling eyed Butler, noting that he was athletic and handsome. Butler slid a paper across the table toward him.

The paper was titled "Alibi Schedule."

The neatly handwritten note revealed Butler's activities in precise detail—in fifteen-minute increments—on the day Ruth Cruger vanished.

Dooling quickly looked the paper over and immediately saw two places where Butler's schedule placed him close to Ruth's route. According to the schedule, Butler was at a store near 127th and Manhattan Avenue, where a man took a girl matching Ruth's description into a cab. Butler admitted being two blocks away.

As Dooling stared him down, Butler recited the relevant details of his short life. He lived at West 116th Street and was a sophomore at Columbia in the School of Mines. When asked if he knew Miss Cruger, Butler said that he indeed called on her the day she disappeared. Butler said that he set up the appointment with her by phone a few days before Ruth disappeared, on February 7. A few days later, Butler got a letter from Seymour Many telling him that Ruth's father had forbidden her to see him but that he should go anyway. This contradicted what Many had said earlier. Dooling made a note of it.

Butler then slipped his hand into his coat and produced two neatly folded letters exchanged between him and Seymour Many. One was an original; the other was a reconstruction from memory. Dooling stared across at the young man in all of his perfect brightness. Dooling, who would not reveal the contents of these letters to the press, sent them over to be tested by ink and pen experts.

Butler otherwise corroborated Many's version of events, saying that Ruth's father had strongly objected to Butler's visiting their home. Butler explained that Mr. Cruger was very cautious and that he was averse to having strangers around his daughter unless he received a formal introduction from a mutual acquaintance. Ruth was apparently mortified at her father's impossible request.

Butler told Dooling that he actually only met Miss Cruger twice in his life. The first time was in November, at the Columbia versus NYU football game. Ruth was there with Many. The second time was weeks later on a subway platform at 116th Street and Broadway. Ruth was bundled tight against the cold and talking with her friends when Butler caught her eye and she smiled. This also differed from Many's version; when pressed, he didn't seem too sure of some of the details himself.

Butler also said that Many had told him that, according to Ruth, he had passed her once or twice on the street near her home without recognizing her.

She didn't like that, said Butler.

The detectives then asked Butler about the cab and if he had a gray-belted overcoat. Butler said that he did have an overcoat like that, but he couldn't remember if he was wearing it on that particular day. That coat is "getting rather shabby," he said, laughing.

"Why did you call her up?" asked Detective Cuniffe, one of Dooling's aides.

"She looked good to me," admitted Butler. "Now don't misunderstand me; I mean she was good to look at—a pretty girl."

Butler said that they had a skating appointment on the day Ruth disappeared, but it had also been broken by letter days before. After Butler left, the district attorney told the newspapers that the handsome young man had "made a very favorable impression," though he knew there were some discrepancies. The papers also verified with the Crugers that Ruth's meeting with Butler had been canceled because of her father's objections, but it was said that Ruth had not shown any bitterness at the time.

The next day, the district attorney summoned several other Columbia and NYU students to interviews. They stood in the hallways in their sweaters and hats, shuffling their feet and slightly afraid. Dooling also called in Ruth's sister, Christina, even though he had heard she was more or less an invalid. He came away from their short interview with the impression that Ruth Cruger's home life was rather restricted and that it would have been irksome for an adolescent girl to spend so much time and attention caring for an ill sister, even though he found no evidence that Ruth had complained of it. She didn't attend dances or musical plays as much as someone her age usually did. The only activity she partook of seemed to be ice-skating. Ruth also liked riding in automobiles. She told her friends that she wished she had a car so she could take them all away. Helen Cruger, Ruth's other sister, was also questioned briefly and without friction.

Finally, Dooling summoned Rubien, the cab driver, to ask if Butler was the mysterious man in the trench coat who got in the cab with Ruth.

The driver said no, the man was not Butler.

A stenographic record was made of the stories told by Richard Butler and Seymour Many and turned over to an expert to examine for inconsistencies. The results were inconclusive. The district attorney said they had another man under surveillance for several days who was "not a college student." They said this man met Ruth several times without the knowledge of her parents. One paper reported that Ruth forsook her normal route home from school along Morningside Park—which she had followed for three years—to meet someone in secret.

Another man who said he understood ciphers claimed that a secret communication was going on in the newspapers between the men responsible for Ruth's disappearance. As police tracked down these new leads, it was revealed that Richard Butler had been on a trip to Wellesley College to see a girl he had fallen for over the Christmas holidays.

⚘

A cop in a dark blue uniform stepped cautiously onto the tar-paper floor of the rooftop. His gun was drawn. The sky was gray and spotted. Below, at the front door, a pile of policemen put their shoulders to the front door and caved it in as if it were cardboard. They ran up the carpeted stairs.

In an ornate room above, the man with the whip paused. He could hear the commotion on the stairs. In front of him, strapped to a chair, was a beautiful young woman with black hair. She was alive, but her head was rolling awkwardly to one side. The man threw the whip down and ran into the hallway. Seeing the police coming up the stairs, he pulled a pistol and fired twice. His gun, made of wood and metal, kicked back with small clouds of white smoke. The man ran up the next flight of stairs as the cops burst into the room. They freed the woman and covered her in a policeman's coat. She didn't seem to know what was happening. The police looked upward, hearing more gunfire. The slaver had been trapped and lay shot, dead, on the roof under the gray sky.

The police captain took a good look at the woman's face. She smiled as her eyes grew peaked. She had obviously been drugged. But it was really her. Her sister had been right this whole time. She—and the girl's heartbroken father—would find this welcome news, indeed. The man took the girl to the hospital in a fast-moving police car. Her father and family met her there.

The girl died in the hospital. It had all been too much for her. As her father wept over her, she looked like an angel lit by white light.

By the time the movie ended and "directed by George Loane Tucker" appeared on the screen, audience members were stunned. *Traffic in Souls* was a remarkable film, not only because of its edgy subject matter but also because it was an unprecedented ninety minutes long. When it premiered in 1913 at Joe Weber's Theatre—an eight-hundred-person venue—more than one thousand people were turned away on the first night alone. In its first week, twenty-five thousand New Yorkers saw it. The audiences who bought their tickets from the small white cupola at ten cents each were largely male, some of them seeing multiple showings per day. Sitting in the sea of chairs propped up on thin, iron legs, they watched the story of Mary Barton, a pretty girl who worked in a candy shop with her sister Lorna, who was flighty and always late to work. One day, Lorna went out to lunch with a handsome, mysterious man who drugged her and forced her into working at a brothel. The pimp worked by day as the founder of the International Purity and Reform League, campaigning against white slavery with a haranguing fist as a public cover for his unspeakable crimes. *Traffic in Souls* was such a sensation that at one point it was playing in twenty theaters in New York City alone. The film was the nation's first legitimate blockbuster.

After the lights came up and the long rows of eyes blinked back to life, people wandered out into Times Square in a daze, thinking about the dangers depicted in the film, which now felt so bracingly real. Once Ruth disappeared, newspapers reminded readers:

NEW YORK SEES FIGHT TO VANQUISH SYSTEM
THAT GOBBLES GIRLS!

Search Begun for one Thousand Girls Who have Disappeared in Three years—"Port of Missing Maidens" Combed!

Gotham, the Gobbler of Girls, is to see a great spring drive against the port of missing maidens, in which society will attempt to salvage 1000 girls who have disappeared from their homes in the past three years and never have been found!

So serious has this problem of the metropolis become police and pulpit are about to unite in a mighty effort to kill the system that is dragging young women away from their families and friends. 3500 are reported missing fully 800 never are found. Fully half those permanently missing are girls. In 1916, the DA office successfully prosecuted five white slavers.

All across the boroughs, doors closed in hallways and dead bolts clicked in wobbly locks. Fathers watched their daughters, even during the day.

What the papers called white slavery filled every parent with dread. Almost every day there were stories in the papers of girls being stolen, drugged, and sold into lives of prostitution by evil men, both local and abroad. The papers never said the word itself, the word for girls being sold and trafficked for their bodies without agency, but everyone knew what it was. Books like Reginald Wright Kaufman's *The House of Bondage*—which was an immediate bestseller in 1910 and a source for *Traffic in Souls*—were understood quite well by readers without having to be explicit. The *Times* reported that "1,000 to 1,500 Girls Disappear Yearly in New York." In the shadow of such towering numbers, it was easy for the police to say that Ruth Cruger's case was, unfortunately, not very remarkable.

In 1914 in New York, there were 4,035 people reported missing, of whom 3,240 were found and returned to their homes or otherwise accounted for. In 1915, 1,439 women and girls went lost. At the end of that year, 1,229 of this number had been accounted for. A detective who was familiar with searches for missing persons opined that most of those who disappeared were persons who "wanted to be lost." "In the case of missing girls," he said, "it has been found by the police that many of them left home after slight disagreements and went to live with relatives or friends in some other place." By "other place," he meant with men.

Henry Cruger, though of a heavy visage, refused to believe that his daughter was one of these numbers of women lost to an invisible system. But he couldn't help the thought from appearing in his mind. He could see her there, clear as day, and it filled him with great rage.

On January 4, 1910, John D. Rockefeller Jr. walked up the stairs of the Criminal Courts Building in New York City. He had been asked to head a grand jury investigation into white slavery. He hesitated in agreeing to do so but soon began the process of abandoning his post at the mighty Standard Oil, his father's company, and J. P. Morgan Steel, in an effort to "purify" his philanthropic efforts from corporate interests.

"If these stories are true," said Rockefeller, "the truth about them should be definitely known; if they are false they should be silenced." The Rockefeller Commission on White Slavery was called to investigate these crimes in the same year as the passing of the Mann Act, which was designed to prohibit the transportation of prostitutes across state lines. When the commission's final report emerged in 1913, it concluded that there was actually no vast network of slavers at work on American soil.

"We have found no evidence," the Commission declared, "of any organization or organizations, incorporated or otherwise, engaged as such in the traffic in women for immoral purposes, nor have we found evidence of an organized traffic in women for immoral purposes." All over the city, people breathed sighs or felt vindicated. But those who read further than the lede found disturbing news. The marrow of the report revealed that although there didn't seem to be a rigid organization of slavers, they still very much existed as an individualized, decentered evil:

It appears, on the other hand, from indictments found by us and from the testimony of witnesses that a trafficking in women does exist and is carried on by individuals acting for their own individual benefit, and that these persons are known to each other and are more or less informally associated.

People still stared at women who walked on certain streets, their perfume trailing out into the air behind them. On these same streets, New Yorkers heard taps on dark windows as businessmen lingered on the sidewalk. People read the papers and saw the films. They knew what was happening even if they shied away from the actual words. A man imprisoned in the Tombs named Yushe Botwin claimed that he had operated a white slavery ring with over three thousand girls over the last ten years. "Sometimes we get the girl from the school," he said. "Her parents are hard on her. She runs away." He shrugged his shoulders. "Sometimes they find her in a dance hall and there is something put in her soda water." He sat there, looking at the detectives. "The younger they are, the easier the work, and the greater the value." The papers were wondering if Ruth Cruger too had become lost to this "army of the vanished."

⁂

Ruth Cruger wasn't the only person in the case who was being spoken of in terms of white slavery. In late February, Mrs. Cocchi returned to Fourth Branch to complain that private detectives had broken into her home at 75 Manhattan Avenue at one o'clock in the morning.

"They threatened my life!" Maria Cocchi said. "They demanded I admit that my husband was a white slave agent! They wanted to know where Ruth Cruger was." The rumor was that these detectives were working for Henry Cruger. He dismissed the accusation but also said that he had no doubt that Mrs. Cocchi could aid the police a great deal if she cared to do so. He pointed out that if Alfredo Cocchi had merely been frightened away, as Mrs. Cocchi said, he would have taken the first opportunity to write and reassure her.

The district attorney disagreed. Seventeen days after Ruth Cruger disappeared, authorities announced that they were certain she had voluntarily left her home.

"Ruth Cruger will be found yet," Edward Swann, the district attorney, said. "The thoroughness of the police search indicates that she is alive. The wide publicity which has been given to the search is the thing that will eventually lead to her discovery."

That afternoon, in front of reporters, Henry stood with his two other daughters, his friend Mr. Brown, and a middle-aged woman dressed in mourning, who was standing off to the side. The reporters thought she might be the grandmother. They were surprised at her dress and immediately wondered if there was going to be an announcement about Ruth. They got ready. Henry told the reporters that, even though none of the recent clues had borne fruit, the Crugers had no intention of abandoning the search for their missing daughter. Henry reiterated that his reward of $1,000 for any information still stood and that he hoped someone would come forward. The only other news was that Henry had hired a new lawyer.

The woman stepped to the front and announced herself. She was the Crugers' new lawyer, Mrs. Grace Humiston. In a firm voice, she asked that all letters to the paper, from this point forward, be signed so as to help with their evaluation. She promised the strictest confidence. Low whispers began to course through the crowd. Why was she interested in clues? She seemed more like a detective than a lawyer. Who was this mysterious woman in black?

"Mrs. Sherlock Holmes," someone may have said.

⁂

That night, in the north Bronx, at the border of Westchester, residents noticed flashlights in the woods. They saw policemen walking in slow formation around the lakes and ponds that the young skaters favored. They kicked through underbrush and thickets still white with late snow. They looked deep into the night and feared every potential moment when they might see a girl's dead face flashing back at them. Van Cortlandt Park Lake, one of Ruth's favorite haunts, was still iced over, though authorities were being pressured to go ahead and break it up with dynamite. At night, Ruth's mother thought of the black water beneath all that shimmering ice and it turned her blood cold.

There were clues and people being followed and scrutinized like signs in the stars. There was still Butler and Many, but also the cab driver, Rubien. There was the queer photographer, Mr. Lee, and the mysterious passenger he saw get into the cab. There were also the little mysteries of scrawled notes and sightings—perhaps the police had missed something there. Perhaps Ruth was somewhere—and with someone—where she did not want to be found. Or perhaps she was already dead. They were still seeking the Italian, Cocchi, for more information on why he had run off. There was also the unsettling feeling that there was a darker, more sinister evil that they had yet to fully see.

After the initial spark of Cocchi's disappearance faded from the papers, some of the reporters remembered having heard of him before. Last winter, people had been talking about a man on Broadway who, after a mammoth snowstorm, rode a strange black machine up and down the empty, white streets. When the neighbors went to investigate, they saw a single floodlight opened and blurry on one end of the street. It sat there, as the sound behind it revved and burned. Once the spotlight began moving toward them, slowly, then swiftly, they could see it shake as the snow fell cold and quick.

As the light passed, people saw a man in goggles who looked like he was laughing as he held on to a black vehicle as it roared across the snow-covered street. Friends and neighbors stood watching and cheering, their faces hidden under layers of coats and scarves. It couldn't be a motorcycle, not in this snow, but it sounded just like one, rumbling and spitting in the dark winter night. The machine powered up and turned off, skimming across the streets. It was a motorcycle sled, one of the men said. Cocchi had invented it. He is good with machines, they said. He is smart.

Two weeks after the DA's announcement that Ruth had run away, Maria Cocchi read in the newspapers that Mrs. Cruger was confined to her room because she couldn't stop crying. Maria walked to the DA's office and sat for hours on a hard bench before someone would see her. When someone finally came up to her, she asked, through her own tears, what she could do to help.

7

The Mysterious Island of Sunny Side

July 1907

The sun was so bright that Charles Pettek could only keep one eye open as he stared up the Mississippi River as it curled out ahead of him. He turned away from the July sun and eyed the green plants on the banks, draped and dipping into the cloudy water. Even here, on the river, it was hot as the hinges of hell. Pettek knew they were somewhere close to Greenville, Mississippi, though he thought they were probably still in Arkansas. This far up, the lines between things got lazy.

As the river began to draw left, their boat creaked and headed for a rude landing on the western bank. Pettek could hear the water splashing against the dock with a hollow, wooden sound. He knew they must be at Sunny Side. On the maps he had studied, the plantation sat on a big green peninsula. But as he stepped onto the dock, it seemed more like an island, floating within the main channel of Chicot Lake. He looked again, attempting to take in the whole swell of the land. There was something white and ghostly that was slowly floating over the surface of everything.

Cotton.

Pettek then took a dummy train—a coach car that moved on its own—straight into Sunny Side. He floated his cover story to a man in coveralls and took off for the fields. As the cotton swirled around him, he saw the fields interrupted by ramshackle cabins. Farther up, he finally saw the men swinging away in the grass. Pettek saw their dark skin but knew they were not Negroes. They were thin and hot and looked like wrung-out, dirty rags. They wore clothes—white shirts and baggy pants—that made them look like peasants. Checking his watch, Pettek saw it was only ten o'clock in the morning. He walked over to talk to one of the farmers. Pettek was a translator of the Italian tongue, so they spoke of many things until the man in coveralls appeared and pointed in their direction. Another man in coveralls, who looked related, also sprang out of the crop. They approached Charles Pettek with fixed eyes. He couldn't tell who was who.

Pettek quickly reached for his credentials. The men pinned back his arms. They grabbed him and took him to the company store, located in the middle of the plantation. The men were Tom and Shelby Wright, the plantation bosses. Their behavior did not seem to surprise the farmers, who tried their best not to stare. They diverted their eyes to the green curved leaves in front of them.

Inside the store, the air was cooler, but not by much. Pettek kept trying to explain who he was, but stopped when he realized it didn't matter. The two men made Pettek sit until 4:30 that afternoon, dripping in the heat of the wooden room. Finally, the door opened and a loud man stomped in. He identified himself as C. B. Owens, the manager of Redleaf, the neighboring cotton plantation. Owens was sweating profusely through his jacket as he pointed at Pettek and formally charged him with trespassing. Owens explained that he was also the local justice of the peace.

Another man walked in, a plantation engineer, whom Owens pointed at and shouted that he was immediately deputizing him as a sheriff. This man, named Kennedy, laughed at the very action. Pettek couldn't believe his eyes. Owens drew out a warrant on an affidavit that Shelby signed and gave to Kennedy, who, on Owens's insistence, served it to Pettek, who was now officially arrested in the great state of Mississippi. Pettek, who knew he was standing squarely in Arkansas, might have felt like laughing. But he knew better because his life was still in danger.

Pettek again tried to show his identification card. He tried to explain that he had been talking to a Sunny Side farmer who owned his own land and therefore couldn't be accused of trespassing. None of it mattered to Owens, who wouldn't even look at him.

"I'm acting under the specific instructions of my superior officer, the assistant attorney general of the United States," Pettek said, with added emphasis.

Owens spat. "If the president of the United States comes down here on such an errand, we will put him in the chain gang, too!"

Tom and Shelby Wright gathered up some clerks to serve as a de facto jury. Pettek's heart was beating fast. Owens judged Pettek guilty, on-the-spot, as someone who "rides, ranges, or hunts" across the properties of others. Owens sentenced Pettek to three months in the chain gang or a fine of one hundred dollars. Pettek couldn't believe this was happening to him, but he knew these small-town justices had the power to do what they wanted. Pettek only had fifty dollars on him, but he knew that as soon as they took it, they would then charge him with vagrancy, which was very serious in Mississippi. Thinking fast, Pettek made a desperate gamble and asked if he could telegraph for the money.

For the first time, Owens looked thoughtful. After some deliberation, he allowed Pettek to telegraph for the money. Using the store machine, the sum was requested and finally sent. Pettek looked relieved. Owens said that the money should be wired directly to a justice of the peace named O'Bannon located in Greenville. This transaction was very strange, but Pettek was not in a position to ask questions. He knew that the company that owned the plantation, Crittenden & Co., had their offices in Greenville.

Once they were square, Owens let Pettek go, albeit a bit reluctantly, walking him back to the dock himself to make a show of it to the workers. When Pettek arrived back in New Orleans, he called the person who had wired him the money. He told her everything that happened and how they had to get back into Sunny Side. He had proof of nothing, but the plantation bosses obviously had something to hide. They were on the right track, Pettek said.

On the other end of the line, Grace agreed.

Grace knew that this investigation was going to be bigger than all the others. After all, she was at Sunny Side because the Italian ambassador to the United States had specifically requested her. Baron Edmondo Des Planches had been receiving strange letters from Italians living at the plantation. Concerned, Des Planches himself visited Sunny Side and was given a personal tour by the manager, LeRoy Percy. As they walked the green fields of the plantation, Percy showed the ambassador many profitable Italian farmers, most with large, smiling families. Afterward, Des Planches dined extravagantly at a restaurant called The Mirror—all at Percy's expense. Des Planches seemed pleased and promised Percy that he would encourage Italians as many as he could—to come work at Sunny Side.

But when Des Planches returned to Washington, he made an appointment to talk to Assistant Attorney General Russell. He was very much disturbed. "The Italian immigrant at Sunnyside is a human production machine," Des Planches said. He wanted Mary Grace Quackenbos, whom he had read about in the papers, to investigate immediately. Once Grace was informed of her assignment, she wrote Percy for entrance but received no assurances. Now she was stuck in New Orleans. Grace had few leads, but they all pointed to Greenville. For one, that strange payment for Pettek's release was wired there. There were also some employment agents who had offices there. In Greenville, up the river, she might get closer to the source of things.

On this trip, Grace was accompanied by Hannah Frank, her legal secretary, and Michele Berardinelli and Charles Pettek, classified as "special employees" of the U.S. government. Pettek, although understandably nervous, didn't hesitate for a second. They set out for Greenville in July 1907.

Once Grace arrived, she set up her small band at the Cowan

Hotel, a tasteful, four-story affair near the center of town. After unpacking her suitcase, Grace began to think of ways she might find leads into the shadowy plantation down the river. As Grace pondered her options, she saw a white envelope with her name on it. Of all the things she expected to read inside, a personal invitation from the man she had been writing to in vain for weeks was certainly not one of them. She looked down in disbelief at an invitation to a dinner that night in her honor hosted by LeRoy Percy and his wife.

Grace knew little of Percy himself other than that he was a man of money and land. She wondered how far back down the roll of American history that distinction went. The property filings she had pulled on Sunny Side showed that the plantation was owned by an O. B. Crittenden, though it was largely run by Percy, along with another partner named Morris Rosenstock, who handled the financial and legal part of the business. Crittenden and Percy were not the original owners of the land, nor the first to use Italians as workers there. The previous owner, Austin Corbin, contracted with Prince Ruspoli, the mayor of Rome, to use Italian workers. But this version of Sunny Side disintegrated when Corbin died in an accident and yellow fever and malaria decimated the workforce. Only the vampiric idea of using immigrants as plantation workers lingered long after the death of that other plantation.

Grace knew that Percy was fiercely dedicated to Sunny Side's success. He took trips to Italy to recruit workers and to hire labor agents. Percy and his agents had already brought several thousand Italians to the Delta. Percy boasted about his workers in southern agricultural magazines. "The Italians," he said, "were in every way superior to the Negro. . . . If the immigration of these people is encouraged, they will gradually take the place of the Negro without their being any such violent change as to paralyze for a generation the prosperity of the country."

Grace heard shadows in those words that gave her pause. And now this man had invited her to supper, deep in the heart of his southern homeland.

Percy was handsome, certainly, but also had the trait of his fellow southerners. He was a charmer, a ladies' man, and a man's man all at once and in the proper amounts. At dinner, Percy behaved as Grace expected: he smiled, bowed, and acquiesced when the moment required it. His hair was parted down the middle and longer on the sides and back than was generally accepted in the North. He wore a three-piece, light-colored suit with rounded collars. He wore his fluffy mustache like it was some kind of battlefield medal. Percy smiled easily, but his eyes were hard to interpret. He was small, though he carried himself with a perfectly straight posture. He looked, Grace thought, in between a state of glad-handing and bragging, like he was always a little tired. Grace wondered if his demeanor was a result of the heat or a general melancholic disposition. Or just a good old southern bluff.

At the same time, Grace couldn't help liking the man and, admittedly, some of his ideas. She found herself surprised by this. Opening American opportunity to immigrants was, on paper, an interesting solution to several problems. But Grace still needed to see it for herself to know if any wrongdoing was going on at Sunny Side. Luckily, Grace was capable of some charisma herself. The girl who once balked at going into a courtroom was now capable of directing an entire dinner table. She started an instant friendship with Percy's wife, Camille Bourges, who was French. Grace even said aloud that she hoped that Camille would take her on a private tour of the, according to Percy, beautiful fields of Sunny Side.

The next day, Grace wrote Percy, saying that she was looking forward to her visit. When Percy politely declined, Grace chafed in frustration. Maybe the old costumes would be necessary after all. But Grace was still convinced that this case just required more finesse. She tried to get in touch with Humberto Pierini, a local Italian travel agent who, rumor had it, had his own problems with LeRoy Percy.

Grace then tried a few more times with Percy, but to no avail. Remembering something Percy had said about the acting governor, Xenophon O. Pindall, Grace decided to write him. It was an election year, after all. The governor wrote back swiftly, granting Grace full access to Sunny Side.

A few days later, after a two-hour, somewhat shaky boat trip, Grace saw the plantation with her own eyes. She saw the same cotton grass and wooden cabins of all shapes and sizes that her man Pettck had. Helped off the landing, she was met by Percy himself, who was very welcoming despite his coldness through the post. Excusing his rudeness, he seemed determined to show her how well his plantation was doing. He looked even smaller here, and he was perspiring a great amount, but he was also quite imperial while walking on his own ground. Percy explained that Sunny Side was actually four separate plantations, held together by a rail line that ran to a central gin facility. Percy plucked profit numbers out of the warm air like they were fruit and recited them to Grace with great satisfaction.

Percy and his men took Grace to a few homesteads over near the central store, a wooden plank building stacked high above the thin road. Grace eyed the store with a bit of nervousness after Pettek's previous visit. Out in the fields, things were more horizontal. The cabins were sturdy, and the men and women were robust and smiling. This was nothing like what Pettek had described. Percy, like a proud papa, explained that these happy families were making heavy profits in cotton. They had scores of smiling children, running through the crop.

At the end of the day, Percy instructed his men to take Grace back to the boat landing. Stopping still, Grace instead insisted—politely—that she stay the night. She wanted to see more. When Percy squirmed about her request, she showed him her letter from the governor. Percy backed down in a huff and consulted with his men. He instructed one of the Wrights to give her an available cabin. Percy cautioned that it might not be to her liking, in which case they could easily transport her back to Greenville. With that, Percy said good night.

As Grace walked to her cabin, she saw the same lopsided huts that Pettek had told her about. She saw the tired men and women with sun-dark skin. She could hear that they spoke no English. When she got to her cabin, there were no screens on the windows or door. The Wright brother who had escorted her left, not even acknowledging her. She set out her notebooks. The mosquitoes came in and out as they wanted, as if they were part of the air itself. A bit later, someone brought her a metal bowl filled with water that was murky red. She knew it was only iron, but it looked a lot like blood, especially under the darkening sky. She was a long way from Fifth Avenue.

The next day, Grace woke up at five thirty in the morning to get a good look at the truth of the place, once and for all. When Grace stepped outside, all the tenement farmers were already in their fields, moving like wraiths in the stony-blue dawn. Above her, she could see faint stars.

That day, Grace realized that Sunny Side was, through and through, a real cotton plantation. Everyone she saw was working toward that purpose with abandon. Every family had their own cabin, worked their own land, and seemed to be the master of the cotton they sold. There was shared equipment for ginning on site, at the end of the rail line. There was a doctor on call from a nearby village and a priest who lived on the plantation. For the most part, these workers ignored her. They were so very busy. The fluffy flecks drifted in the air and gave everything a sweet smell.

After this first day of discovery, Grace was very impressed by Sunny Side. She knew she wasn't entirely wanted there, but that was to be expected, she supposed. These plantation owners were rude men, airs aside. Still, she found Percy to be far more upright than she had guessed, though she imagined he was behaving well because of the injuries done to Pettek. She met Crittenden, the owner of the plantation, whose ancestry stretched back to the earliest settlers of the Old South. He was cordial but dismissive. Percy's men took her to see even more successful families on the plantation. They smiled back through their black mustaches and shook her hand with vigor.

Later that afternoon, as Grace walked through the cotton, she passed a patch of high, unshorn stalks. She brushed by the brittle sleeves of green and wandered in farther. She caught a man's eye watching her. She stopped and walked up to him. He seemed as if he wanted to say something.

Through her interpreter, Grace found out that the dark-haired man was named Pasquale Georgina and that he lived on fourteen and three-quarter acres with his wife, Maria. Pasquale led Grace to his simple cabin, which consisted of a single room and a shed in the back. When the back door to the shed opened, they saw his aged mother, stooped in a chair, the skin of her wrists like paper. In the main cabin, there was another chair pulled up to a nicked-up table. The bed was wet from the leaky roof. And in a corner of the room was a small box that looked as if it had been made of old boards. It was a cradle, Pasquale said. Maria, his wife, had recently given birth. They stood and stared at the jumble of wood, almost as if they were waiting for it to move. The child died, Pasquale said quietly. The baby starved, he said, even though Maria denied herself food in an attempt to save it.

Just like the first one, he said.

Pasquale explained that under the Sunny Side system, his family was allowed $15.00 a month by the company to buy food with. But after they were charged $7.00 for their mule and $6.00 for a barrel of flour, they were left with only $2.00—a month—for any food other than bread. They had to frog gig and fish—but who had the time? Even the growing of any other vegetables on their parcels of land for meals had to be approved by the Wrights. The company—not cotton—was king.

When Grace left that hot cabin, sickness rising in her chest, she wondered about these numbers. Their cotton crop looked healthy enough—why weren't they making any money? She wrote down the few names and numbers that the farmer had told her. She was framing her case. But Grace needed more proof. She needed numbers she could point to and share. She had to see the books.

Grace had to return to New York to testify in another case, though she would only be gone for a couple of days. When she returned, she took a day in Greenville because she had finally heard back from the travel agent, Pierini, who agreed to meet with her. Pierini told her that he had worked at Sunny Side. They weren't recruiting from New York City, he said.

They were taking people directly from Italy.

With his lawyer present, Humberto Pierini showed Grace everything he had. Pierini had ties to the plantation that ran deep. Not only did he use to run the store at Sunny Side, but his father, Allessandro, was one of the watchmen on Prince Ruspoli's original estate. While at Sunny Side, Pierini amassed a European staff of twelve agents and a ship's captain named Calenda. Their job was to recruit whole families from Italy to work the cotton. They would be paid up to twenty-five dollars a family.

Pierini told Grace that they found families in Italy not only with men on the ground but also with advertisements. Pierini showed Grace a flier. It read:

> Italians!
>
> If you have parents or friends to be called to America, do not lose this great opportunity to buy the tickets from me, which tickets you can have at a great reduction.
>
> I can sell you tickets for the steamer
>
> MANILLA!
>
> Which starts from Italy in the month of August, for $45.30 with railroad fare paid to Greenville, Miss.; but I will give you two dollars commission for each full ticket.
>
> As you well know I can sell you the tickets for any steamship company at lower prices and guarantee the protection of your passages
>
> Yours truly.
>
> Humberto Pierini
>
> P.S. If you have not money to send passage fares to your

parents, I have the possibility of making them come here, with the understanding that they will place themselves to where they are assigned; lands of the most fertile, and conditions the best.

With a nervous voice, Pierini told Grace that his agents targeted everyone from barbers to musicians, bricklayers to mechanics—all of whom were looking for a better life, income, or something in between. The agents offered these wide-eyed people free tickets to America, with the promise of work—and land—at the end of their journey across the sea. The Italians were often interested but would say they had no money for the ship's passage. That is when Pierini's company men would smile and say not to worry about it, that they would pay for it. The Italians were expected to pay them back, of course, but easily, over time, as they worked on the farm. Pierini's agents even told prospective workers that the company's wagon would stop at each house at daybreak and hang a large piece of fresh meat on the doorknob. It sounded like heaven to these poor families. At *Il lato esposto al sole*. At *Ed Sunny Sidre*. Sunny Side.

The only thing that the company asked, just as a favor, was that the new recruits not mention this agreement to the authorities at Ellis Island or the Port of New Orleans. The Italians bound for Sunny Side were asked not to mention that the Crittenden Company was paying for their Atlantic passage. The heads of the families were given exact language on what to tell the authorities. These instructions were put on a small piece of paper, written in Italian, that the men studied and learned by heart the whole voyage over. When they reached America, the men tossed these black words into the sea.

Grace wondered why Pierini was telling her this. Pierini sheepishly admitted that while he worked at Sunny Side, he had been acting as a subagent for some of the company's employment agents, earning an extra buck or two off of each new recruit for himself. Pierini took two dollars off each steamship ticket sold. Crittenden then took one extra dollar for himself. It was a nice side job. But a worker at Sunny

Side named Augusto Catalini was jealous of Pierini's powers (and profit) and worked to oust him. So Pierini left and opened up shop on his own as an employment agent in Greenville.

Pierini admitted that he would sometimes see people in his office who had escaped from Sunny Side. When they asked for his help, he would secretly find them work elsewhere. Grace couldn't tell if he did this because he felt guilty or because he wanted revenge on Percy. Pierini then showed Grace a letter from Percy dated March 1907 in which he accused Pierini of helping his escapees find work. Pierini also turned over prepaid ticket stubs, lists of families canvassed, and more letters from Percy. Looking through the letters, Grace knew this was very dangerous for Pierini. "I know that an unfriendly attitude on my part would be an injury to you," wrote Percy, "and I don't want to assume it without cause, but I will."

So this was revenge, thought Grace. They were all in on it. Every last one of them. Everyone but the people working in the cotton fields. Grace thanked Pierini and took the piles of paper to her hotel room, where she read them closely, well into the night. Through Pierini, Grace began to see a new version of Sunny Side. She began to see that lake, cool and inviting, as more of a moat for a prison.

When Grace returned to Sunny Side the next day, something had changed. As she got off the train, none of the tenants would look at her, and whenever she looked over her shoulder, she saw one of the Wrights somewhere in the cotton behind her. To make matters worse, Percy insisted that she leave the plantation at the end of each day. Grace resisted, but he would hear nothing of it, his will resolute behind his sugary smile. Since the boat took two hours each way, that trip alone took a full four hours away from her investigation every day.

At some point over the next few days, Grace was finally able to lose her escort and enter the company store at the part of the island that Percy had first shown her. The words painted on the outside were almost bleached white. A small bell rang over the door as she entered. Grace looked around at the clean counters and sharp concrete floors.

The ceiling was whitewashed. There were fluffy white cotton towels on the back shelves. Hanging from hooks was everything from coffee and tobacco to fabrics and socks. There was even a lit glass case. It did not look like a makeshift courthouse; it looked like a rustic Wanamaker's.

But Grace was shopping for something other than merchandise. Everything good here was behind the counter; everything else was just empty space. Grace had seen farmers come in and ask to look at their books. There was a big wooden riser on the counter that would hold the bound records of each family. They would be allowed to look, if they asked for it, but would almost always leave with a sad look on their faces. And anything she saw people buy wasn't even with bills or coin, it was with "monkey money," little round coins that were stamped "Sunny Side." The plantation even had its own currency.

At the store, a man in straps and shirtsleeves stood behind the counter. He nodded and produced the book for Grace to look at. There was no one else in the room. Or maybe there was. All that mattered was that there, in the fine print of the ledgers, Grace finally read the secret history of Sunny Side. What Grace found was meticulous individual accounting of everything: cotton, machining, ginning, food, and even doctor and priest visits. Percy and Crittenden were charging their tenants for all of those things.

Grace remembered that Percy had told her that they paid tenants an average of $34,000 last year. Subtracting that number from the company profit statements, Grace estimated that the company's profit last year must have been $86,950. But in looking at the books, Grace quickly realized that Percy's quote of $34,000 per family did not include expenses like rent, rentals of mules, ginning expenses, and the transportation, baling, and wrapping of cotton. Grace realized that all of these costs were coming out of the farmer's pocket and going into the company's. The problem was that the farmer's pocket didn't exist, or could never be deep enough. To top it off, the company charged a flat 10 percent interest on everything, including visits to the priest.

Grace finally understood the real horror of Sunny Side. It wasn't physical coercion that had turned these families into slaves. It wasn't chains or whips. It wasn't the voodoo practiced in the dark swamps for luck or love or the loud religion of song that rose from the white churches on Sundays. It was simple economics. It wasn't that Sunny Side farmers couldn't escape chains, it was that they couldn't escape their debts to Crittenden, to Percy, and to their own mortgaged lives. They had sold their souls to the company and were pushing rocks up a mountain only to fall back down again under the crushing weight of that never-ending 10 percent interest that bound them to the island. No matter what they did, most families would never get out of debt. Not only did Sunny Side have its own currency, it also had its own cemetery, located on a green hill with a crooked iron fence. No one was leaving Sunny Side.

But Grace knew that she had to, immediately. As she left the store and walked toward the train, she saw a little girl of about ten years peering at her through the brittle green stalks. The sad girl had yellowing skin, pale lips, and drying eyes. Grace stopped. She could see the girl's bones at the corners of her body, poking out like sticks in a river.

When Grace got back to her room in Greenville, she started to write a letter to the attorney general of the United States of America, Charles Bonaparte.

"Something is radically wrong at Sunnyside," she wrote to Washington.

Before she sent her letter to Bonaparte, Grace sat down with Percy and his wife to discuss her findings. Grace did not want to recommend that Sunny Side be disbanded; she could only imagine what something like that would do to its poor tenants. Instead, she thought that there were simple solutions that would make things better. To start, the workers wanted the free sale of cotton, kinder supervisors, and smaller doctor fees. Grace told Percy that she had heard that farmers who had asked for these changes, especially "those who told that lady," would receive no advances and "could take the road." Percy squirmed. Grace had no more use for airs. Over passed gravy boats and folded napkins, this was now a chess match between two accomplished lawyers. Percy knew that Grace had a report to file. At the same time, Grace knew she was dealing with a powerful man on his own fertile territory.

In her finished report, Grace called the Sunny Side experiment a complete failure. She pointed out that the Italians were tenants in name only, having signed contracts that were written in English, when they could neither read nor write. "Everything is all right," the families were told by the company agents as they made their marks. "Everything is all right."

Grace made it clear that at Sunny Side, hard labor was on one side of the equation, and heavy profit was on the other. With 158 families made up of 900 individuals, the plantation was paying very little yet reaping enormous profits. Though the company made money, it was, as Grace put it, "for the Italian a complete bankruptcy." The company was only making money because they weren't paying their workers; they were keeping them immobilized by debt. According to Grace, the enforcers of this system meant to imprison the immigrants were "men without education whose lives have undoubtedly been spent in driving Negroes."

Grace did add that Percy had promised, at their most recent meeting, to make some real changes. The company had agreed to hire an Italian representative during the picking, ginning, and selling season to better protect the interests of the workers. It was a start, and Grace was glad to include it in her letter. But, overall, it was damning prose. Grace spilled the beans on everything she had: she told of Pierini; of the sad, lonely cabin; the 10 percent; even the girl with the yellow skin. Grace told Bonaparte that she had all of Pierini's paperwork as evidence of a network of agents operating in Italy, the ports, and in Sunny Side itself. She even remarked on the haunting, beautiful Italian women at the camp and how there were "perhaps dangers far more grave . . . which should be investigated." When Grace finally finished the letter, she signed her name in a flowing black script on September 28, 1907. Her last name, Quackenbos, was stopped with a period.

A few days later, Grace came back to her hotel after another day tracking down evidence. She took off her hat and undid her hair. As she sat down to add to her report, she was shocked by what she saw. Her desk was empty. All of her notes, including her interviews with potential witnesses and her invaluable records from Pierini, were gone. Grace moved through the room in a panic. She felt the empty space of the information in the room; it was *gone*. As a lawyer, she understood the grave danger here. Even though she had already sent the letter, this was the evidence itself and thus infinitely more important. The other side of her then became aware that someone had been in her rooms. She was furious with herself. Grace called her assistants. She knew who was behind this. *Percy.* But she also knew she could never prove it. He probably owned the hotel. Grace made some calls to Washington, but it was rapidly sinking in that there was nothing she could do.

A few days later, Thomas Catchings, the retired congressman from Mississippi, returned the stolen files to Grace, having valiantly "recovered" them from an unknown felon. The details were unequivocally vague. Catchings was a notorious associate of Percy. Grace knew the game. Percy seemed to be telling Grace that she could not touch him, no matter what her threats were. He also, very practically, wanted to know what she had, and though it was incriminating, there was no real evidence for what she had been sent to find evidence of: peonage. Now that Percy knew this, he could better plan his counterattack.

Peonage was a tricky thing to prove in this particular case. The Sunny Side contract was impossibly unfair, but it was still frustratingly legal. What Grace needed was proof that the owners were making people stay and work against their will. They already were, in a sense, but not in a way that could be legally seen as criminal. There were no whips and chains as in the turpentine camps. So Grace searched, as she always did, for more clues. For stories.

While Grace did more digging, Percy had gone to Memphis for the largest convention of Mississippi River city officials ever held. Those present heard President Roosevelt belt out a speech about how the in-progress Panama Canal would lead to other ventures like hydro-electric dams and massive irrigation works here in the United States. "The whole future of the nation is directly at stake!" Teddy shouted to the packed hall of more than ten thousand people. The crowd cheered and cheered.

As Percy soaked in this vision of technology and progress, Grace snuck back into Sunny Side to spend another night with a tenant family. But a Wright brother spotted her and ordered her off the property. Grace refused to obey unless Percy himself told her to leave in writing. Before sunrise the next day, a young black man delivered her a note from Percy doing just that. Grace left Sunny Side—for the last time—but sent Percy a note accusing him of "untrustworthiness and ungentlemanly behavior."

In her room, Grace pored over the lists of families living at Sunny Side. The official accounting showed 183 families at Sunny Side. But the priest's lists, which he had slipped her, only showed 158. There were twenty-five families missing. These were the ones Grace was looking for. If she could find them, she might find evidence of peonage.

One by one, Grace began to collect stories of the escapees of Sunny Side. She began compiling a list of names for her report. One group of three paid a boatman to cross the levee at midnight. The small band hid themselves until morning and then crept up to the outskirts of Lake Village, Alabama, in the middle of the night. They wore little more than rags. The dazed men walked into the store. One plunked down ten lumps of monkey money; it was worth fifty cents. The other had a $6.00 small barrel of flour that he sold for $3.50. As they left the store, a man watched them. Crittenden had spies in all the outlying towns. The man contacted Tom Wright, who got on his horse and took off for Lake Village at once. Tom then got on a steam launch, reaching the three men just as they were ready to board a train.

Hearing this story, Grace knew that she was one second away from a federal case. If Tom pulled out a gun or a whip, she would have them. She would have them all. Forcing people to work was slavery. That would hold up.

But Tom Wright had real smart bosses. That, or he wasn't as dumb as Grace had thought. Instead of hurting the fugitives or threatening them, Tom silently took every particle of their poor personal belongings that he could claim under their contracts. The fugitives were allowed to leave, but they were left with nothing but the clothes on their backs.

Grace heard story after story of smuggle attempts, railroad concealments, and late-night swims to escape the green island. The stories were all sadly the same. Then she heard the story of the Muzzi Brenno family. They, like many of their kin, had had enough of Sunny Side and decided to make a run for it in the warm night. But as they tried to make it across the peninsula, they were caught. The Wrights rode high on their horses and ran them down. They had shotguns at their side, but they didn't raise them. The family pleaded for mercy, pointing to their quivering child, sick with fever. The Wrights then took all they had and made them stay in the field all night. Miraculously, the child didn't die and the family made it to Alabama.

The Wrights were obviously smarter than Grace was giving them credit for. She knew they wouldn't screw up Sunny Side. But maybe someone else might. With that thought in mind, Grace began to fish for stories involving Percy or, better yet, the one who stood to lose the most in all this: O. B. Crittenden himself.

Grace found a story of a family who made it all the way to the train. But this story was different. As the family waited on the train, Crittenden himself showed up on horseback, flashing his silver pistol. In every other story, the Wrights would take the escapees' belongings or escort them back by choice. Not this time. In this story, Crittenden got on the train, with his gun, and shoved the people back into the night, back toward the weak light of Sunny Side.

Grace knew that while the Wrights were protecting their paychecks, Crittenden was protecting what he saw as his property. She only wished that Percy had been there, too, but beggars and all that. Grace located the witnesses and prepared the affidavits. On October 25, 1907, Grace sent a wire to Attorney General Bonaparte in Washington, happily informing him that "O. B. Crittenden arrested for peonage." Crittenden, who was well known in the South for his success in the railroad concern, was vilified with the headline MILLIONAIRE HAS SLAVES ON FARM.

Local newspapers began to take notice of Grace's work at Sunny Side. "Who Is She?" asked the *Greenville Times*. The paper called Grace "a lady lawyer who is stirring up the Italian immigrant question from center to circumference."

> She comes with a formidable retinue of employees. . . . She has already closed up one importing joint and has the planters of that vicinity worked up over the peonage question. In other words, she is just raising——, as is usual with a professional woman.

In the wake of Crittenden's arrest, Percy barred Grace from ever visiting Sunny Side again. In addition, he sat down to write a strong letter to President Theodore Roosevelt himself.

Attorney General Bonaparte, who hated any sort of electrical transmission, called for a meeting with Grace. She thought that she was going to get fired. Instead, Bonaparte explained that he wanted her to come to work directly for him, as special assistant to the attorney general of the United States. Bonaparte wanted her to undertake a secret mission to break up the lumber trusts in Florida. She accepted and traveled to New Orleans. Her arrival marked the first time in the history of the U.S. government that a woman served in this capacity under a cabinet member. But she didn't have much time to work.

By November 15, Grace was called back to Washington because the president wanted to hear from her firsthand about the details of her Sunny Side report. She sat down with him in his dark office, and he was much impressed. But the next day, Assistant Attorney General Russell called her in. He read the complaints from the telegram that Percy had sent to President Roosevelt. These were serious charges, Russell said. Grace listened without comment.

"I've kept quiet on this subject heretofore, but I'll do it no longer," Grace said to a reporter outside the attorney general's office. She stopped. "Of course, when you arrest a man on a criminal charge, you would expect his joint owner to fight you, wouldn't you," she asked, her voice getting louder and higher.

Behind closed doors, Bonaparte recommended at a cabinet meeting to cut Grace loose. Roosevelt listened behind his small, round glasses and said no. They should send her to testify in Florida on another case, the president insisted. On November 20, 1907, the attorney general announced that all the charges levied against Grace had been disproved and dismissed.

At his desk in the White House, Teddy Roosevelt read Percy's telegram again and weighed it against the scathing report he had read from Grace about the plantation. In his letter, Percy defended the dream of Sunny Side. He wanted Grace recalled from the South because of her meddling, which was interfering with his workers. Percy also had some strong wishes for the fate of her massive report. "I have no desire whatever to have her report suppressed," Percy wrote to Roosevelt. "I only ask that no publication be made of it and no action taken under it until it has been verified." Roosevelt was impressed by Grace's investigation into the various sins of Sunny Side, but he was also worried about her methods. Still, the president knew that enslavement of a race—of any form—could not be tolerated in the United States. Even in Arkansas.

But then President Roosevelt remembered the time, many years earlier, when he had gone bear hunting in the Delta woods. There, in the deep woods, Teddy had hit it off with a young, enterprising businessman whose name was staring up at him from a letter on his desk. His old friend, LeRoy Percy.

Roosevelt sent another friend, the historian Albert Bushnell Hart, to objectively investigate Sunny Side. After he read Hart's report, Roosevelt wrote back to him:

> I have been very uneasy about Mrs. Quackenbos. She comes in the large class of people who to a genuine desire to eradicate wrong add an unsoundness of judgment which is both hysterical and sentimental. . . . The fact is that on those southern plantations we are faced with a condition of things that is very puzzling. Infamous outrages are perpetrated— outrages that would warrant radical action if they took place in Oyster Bay or Cambridge; but where they actually do occur, the surroundings, the habits of life, the sentiments of the people, are so absolutely different that we are in reality living in a different age, and we simply have to take this into account in endeavoring to enforce laws which can not be enforced save by juries. . . . It is like trying to enforce a prohibition law in New York City.

After her report on Sunny Side was put away on a shelf, Grace did not stay too long in the South. The papers reported on this lady of "prodigious fortune" who used her legal skills toward philanthropy. "Her light has been hid much beneath the bushel," they said.

⚜

A hush fell over the chamber as the woman in black walked into the marbled room to testify before Congress. It was March 31, 1910, and Grace had been absent from Washington—and from America altogether—for over a year. After leaving the South, Grace had embarked on a long trip abroad. The long details of her trip were sketchy, though there was gossip that she had simply had enough after her troubles in the South.

But Grace was not in Washington for idle gossip or talk about a much-needed vacation. She was there, finally, to give her full report on peonage and immigration. In early 1908, Representative Edgar D. Crumpacker of Indiana, a lawyer, motioned for the House Committee on Labor to take up the issue of southern peonage. By March, he wanted Grace's suppressed report released to the committee. By the time hearings were scheduled, it was March 1910. Grace, who had worked on peonage cases for three years, had, for the last year, been traveling through Spain, Portugal, Italy, and Greece.

In her absence, Crittenden had somehow escaped indictment. For the most part, southern newspapers had dismissed the stories of Sunny Side as Grace's own failed attempt at notoriety. Percy himself wrote an article claiming that Grace had been "malicious and garbled" in her treatment of Sunny Side and that she had "no experience." But as the time got closer to her testimony, Representative Clark from Florida again came out swinging against Grace. He called Attorney General Bonaparte a "transplanted bud of alleged French nobility" who employed "a lady bearing the euphonious name of Mrs. Mary Grace Quackenbos, whose field of labor previous" was limited to her own "dear Manhattan Isle."

Assistant Attorney General Russell testified first. He spoke for a half hour. Grace went next. She spoke for two and a half. She talked about her three years as a U.S. attorney, Sunny Side, her travels, and how immigration needed drastic and speedy reform. She told how employment agents hoodwinked young men into forced labor through false pretenses. She showed how "expert masons were sent to a cotton plantation; boys promised work in a licorice factory were sent to a turpentine camp; a tailor to a mine."

Grace was dressed in her customary shadows, which contrasted her armfuls of letters, reports, photographs, and books. During her testimony about Sunny Side, John Sharp Williams of Mississippi, who was a member of the committee, listened carefully. He looked at the photographs with great interest. When it came time for questions, Williams commented that though Sunny Side was surely not an ideal place, it did pay wages and did not have some of the physically cruel practices that some of the other southern sites had. Grace thought a moment and responded by reading a list of camp conditions. Mr. Williams felt vindicated; those were the conditions at Robinsonville, he said, a notoriously bad peonage site. When Grace revealed that she had just read conditions from Sunny Side, most everyone in the room laughed.

Grace explained to Mr. Williams that the Department of Justice was not there to make men laugh but "to compel employers to treat laborers fairly." Their purpose was "not to prevent European labor going to the South, but just the contrary"—to make it work.

After Roosevelt pulled her out of Sunny Side, Grace had not gone overseas just for an extended vacation. She had also gone to uncover the very source of the injustice she had witnessed. She visited every country she could in order to root out these sources of immigration evil. As she listed the ports of call she was received in, some wondered if she had done so under orders. Grace compiled her findings, which she presented to the Senate committee members. Her plan, titled "The Answer to the Immigration Problem," asked for government regulation and registration of immigrants to move them away from the crowded cities and into jobs in less-developed areas: the part of the Sunny Side idea that was good, but with regulation and a moral foundation.

Grace was frank. She said that "Uncle Sam has been negligent of his new wards" and that the "dark days of the slave trade" had arisen again in the form of the "human vampires" who were preying on their very own countrymen.

"It is a matter of so much a head with them," said Grace. "They prey upon the new arrivals as soon as they land." She argued that there should be an immigration employment exchange like they had in Berlin, with a separate department for women. Above all, Grace argued that the immigrants be moved out of the cities they were so magnetically attracted to.

"They don't know that in the rural districts farmers are crying for help," Grace said. "In the meantime tenements multiply, congestion ensues, there is no work for the alien and he either becomes vicious, an undesirable citizen, or ekes out a miserable existence amid the mazes of a city that is full of lures for his unsophisticated rural soul." Dr. Stella, a government advisor on disease, agreed that Grace's plan would also help alleviate the specter of tuberculosis in the tenements.

For those who thought she was merely agreeing with the Sunny Side experiment, Grace shook her head. "The point is that we Americans are exploiting the aliens," she explained. "For while our Federal laws are excellent for keeping them out of the country, we show a noticeable lack of interest in them after they are admitted."

Grace fished around in her folders and held up the card of an employment agent. She read from it: "Any number or nationality of skilled or unskilled laborers furnished. Newly landed foreigners always on hand. New arrivals every week. Kindly call at my office and engage a gang of shortly landed foreigners (Not spoiled from city life)."

Grace ended her testimony with a story that she said was important for the committee to hear. She was in Aquila in late June 1909, in the Abruzzi Mountains of Italy, traveling with Esther Boise van Deman, an American professor of Latin and archaeology with a Ph.D. from the University of Chicago. It was June 30, 1909. They were just an hour away from Palermo, from where Joe Petrosino was killed a few months before.

While waiting at the Hotel d'Italia for a train leaving Aquila, Grace looked across the way and saw a large poster that read AVISO near the door of an Italian barbershop. Grace walked over and looked at the fine type that mentioned a bank at 60 Mulberry Street in New York.

The sign itself was hard to miss. It was three-by-two feet in dimension and had large words with pink and black lettering. On the other side of the shop window was posted a huge billboard advertising the steerage and second-class passage rates of steamers from Naples to New York on the Hamburg-American Line. That sign was eight feet high and colored red, white, and blue. Both signs were in Italian, though Grace could make out words like "bankers" and "jobs." She went inside the barbershop.

Grace and Esther entered the shop and saw the barber sweeping up. The man said he spoke no English and Grace said she spoke no Italian. But Esther spoke both. She told the barber that her friend Grace had a friend in the United States—in Arkansas—who was looking for some imported labor.

"Do many of them go over?" Grace asked.

"For a long while, no; but business is picking up again," the barber said. After a pause where he stared at her, he continued.

"The signora wants to know how it is done—wants to talk with someone who helps laborers to go over." He patted his barrel chest. "I'm the *representante*."

"Are you the *representante* for the steamship company or for the people who go over?"

"Of the steamship company, but I help the people go over. See here," he said, walking toward the back.

The barber stepped to the back of the shop and removed a second eight-foot billboard of the Hamburg-American sailings, just like the red, white, and blue sign out on the street. He showed Grace that completely hidden behind it was one of the edicts issued by the Italian government that warned against trusting employment agencies.

"What kind of a thing is that?" asked Grace.

"Oh, that comes from the government people," the barber said.

The barber then went over to a cabinet and took out a yellow-covered book of about 250 to 300 pages. The entire book contained, page after page, alphabetical lists of all the small towns in the United States, with their respective counties and states, together with six or seven columns of figures placed opposite the names of the towns extending across the entire page. They could not look too closely because they knew he was going to take it away in an instant.

"If people want to get laborers to work for them in the United States," asked Grace, "how would they go about it?"

"They could send over the tickets," the barber said.

"How?"

"Go to the bank. You pay the money, send me the tickets, and I would send over the people."

Grace told a lie, that a "Mr. Frank" wanted contract laborers to work on his cotton plantation and that, in traveling through the mountains, she and Esther had seen what good workers the Italians were.

"But I don't see how you agents send them over," Grace fished.

"A little money for my expenses to find the people." The barber smiled.

"Do you send women?" asked Grace.

"Yes."

"I forgot to ask about children. What about them?"

"Oh yes. One can always use them somehow, and they won't cost much, they're just trifles, we'll throw them in for nothing." He paused. "Very little children," he said.

Piccoli bambini.

"Oh yes," he said, "you can use them for a good many things."

⁂

When Grace was done with her story and the silence gave way to mumbling and paper pushing, she may have looked over to the long table of old men—most of them white-haired and suited—and seen the newly installed senator from Arkansas looking right at her. LeRoy Percy himself had just been elected as a Democrat in 1910. Sunny Side's boss, who had undercut her with the president of the United States and buried her report, was about to serve on the United States Joint Immigration Commission that would decide whether or not to act on her hard-won testimony. They did not act, at least not in the way that Grace had hoped. At the end of the hearings, Grace returned to New York. She would retreat into her life again. She had done enough. She couldn't imagine the life of a crime fighter calling her back.

When Grace got back, one of the first things she did was return the coat she had borrowed three years earlier from Martha Bensley Bruere. As Grace sat down to tea, she looked exhausted. She told Martha that she "had no thrilling adventure to relate . . . her travels were quite conspicuous for their lack of stirring incidents." Grace looked around, remarking that she did miss the "modern accommodations" of home. Still, she had to admit, "it was a very interesting experience and the knowledge I acquired on this trip I could have gathered in no other way.

"You see," Grace explained, "I soon found that it doesn't help the immigrant to jail a few men so long as everybody outside the jail thinking it is good business to keep up the old game. It's like teaching children that the harm in cheating is in getting caught. We have been prosecuting these peonage cases for more than two years, and yet the traffic in immigrants goes right on. Why, one of the worst offenders had himself elected to the Senate and sits now on the congressional Committee on Immigration to investigate his own crimes! I don't believe jails ever solved any real human problems, anyway."

As Grace spoke, she was absently dumping lump after lump of sugar into her tea. She realized her mistake and laughed.

"Oh, do give me another cup," Grace said, smiling.

Grace paused a moment, sensing that Martha wanted to hear more. "If you saw a child that had been neglected or abused so that it had run away from home, wouldn't you try to find out what was wrong with the home or the parents? That's all I did about those immigrants with the whip marks on their backs; followed them into the turpentine camps, from there back to the railroad and steamship companies across the Atlantic, and into their homes. And there I found what was wrong. They were poor, hungry, tax ridden and their Governments didn't care enough about them to protect them against kidnappers."

The immigrants who filed into her office were the growing class of poor inhabitants of the United States. Some numbers had the unemployed hovering at three hundred thousand. Every week, more children came to school in rags. And when the teachers and visitors followed these children into their homes, they found bare, dirty, chilly rooms where the little folk shivered and wailed for food and the mothers looked distracted and gaunt.

"You don't mean they're kidnapped?" Martha asked, shocked.

"Well, it's that, practically," replied Grace. "The whole back country of Italy, Bulgaria, and Greece swarms with agents of the steamship companies who tempt them over with false pretenses of fabulous wealth. Why, one man in southern Greece, nine mule back rides from a railroad station, told me that he had cleared thirty thousand dollars in five years in commission from the steamship companies for luring immigrants to the United States! And right under the nose of the Greek Government!"

Grace sipped her tea, now a little darker and more to her liking.

"For a long time," Grace said, with deliberation, "we have had runaway immigrants pouring in on us and have tried the man's scheme of building a high restrictive fence about our country—and then letting them pull off the palings and creep through! Did it ever occur to any of the legal minds that they might step over to a parent State and say, 'keep your naughty children at home?' And yet we've been doing that very thing."

After Grace left, Martha wondered if her friend was right in insisting that all the world was a neighborhood. Was she right that it was time to take "the bandage off the eyes of international Justice, lay down her sword, get her mind off the thief and the jail, and become a kindly, intelligent mother to the world?" Martha thought that might not be fair. She thought that law school graduates as a whole "were like too many carrots in a row—they crowd and crush one another, and nobody grows very big. But the women who transplant themselves into new fields grow like everything." Martha liked that thought very much.

8

The Giant and the Chair

July 1916

As Grace drove up along the east bank of the Hudson, about thirty miles north of the city, she saw Sing Sing prison rising like a pile of stones by the sea. The prison wasn't tall, not like the buildings she had left behind in New York. There were white structures in the back and a dark tower near the front, all framed by train tracks and wire.

As Grace's car crossed over the bridge and approached the gatehouse, she went through the unnatural routine of gaining entrance to a prison. She flashed a smile beneath her hat at the familiar faces at the door. Grace had reclaimed her role at the People's Law Firm. The woman in black had become, once again, a usual sight in unwelcome places.

Grace walked past the exercise yard, and they took her straight to the Death House, a flat, irregular-shaped building floating like an island within the rest of the compound: a prison within a prison, it was made almost entirely of stone. All of its residents were housed in cells with fairly open bars so that the guards could watch them at all times. There were twenty-four cells in total, with room for three men in each. The cells were never empty, though there were always new faces on the Last Mile, which was what the short hallway was called. At the end of the thin corridor was a green door.

Today, Grace was seeing a client named Gennaro Mazella, who had been sentenced to death for the murder of Antonio Castigliano. Mazella had shot him dead on the street in Brooklyn. He pleaded self-defense, but the jury disagreed. Grace was working to commute his sentence down to life based on new evidence that seemed to back up his claim. She had already gotten him two extensions and was confident of a full reduction. After speaking with Mazella in the visiting area, Grace was stopped in the corridor by Spencer Miller Jr., the young assistant warden at Sing Sing.

"Well, we don't know about Mazella," the warden said, shaking his head. "He did kill the man, you know. But if you're in the saving business, here's a man we all feel confident is innocent and they've convicted him. Take hold of that." The warden began leading Grace down the hall. A recent graduate of Columbia, Miller worked in the deadliest prison in America—yet he was determined to reform it. He knew Grace from her work with the Mutual Welfare League, an organization seeking to abolish the death penalty. Miller once left the prison two days before a double execution to personally scour a stretch of New York tenements for clues to prove their innocence. He was not successful. But Miller kept trying, with each subsequent prisoner who was sentenced to die. That is why he wanted Grace to meet Inmate No. 66335.

As they walked further down the hall, Miller filled Grace in on the particulars of the case. The defendant was a man named Charles Stielow. He and his brother-in-law, Nelson Green, had been convicted of murdering their neighbor Charles Phelps and his housekeeper, Margaret Wolcott, in upstate Orleans County. The crime occurred in March 1915. There were no witnesses, but Stielow had given a full, signed confession.

Miller stopped in the hallway with an outstretched hand. Grace approached the cell on their right. Inside, there was a cot and a shelf. Grace could only see a glint of a mirror. It was being blocked by a gigantic form of a man, standing with his back to her. He was wearing the dark wool suit that was the uniform of every inmate at Sing Sing. His sleeves and pants looked short. His back was massive and strong.

Even from outside the cell, Grace barely came up to the man's chest. So when he turned around, she was surprised to see a shy, chubby face with two, close-set eyes. His mouth was half-disguised by a soft mustache. His hair was thick and curly. Grace looked at him more closely. The skin of this man was whiter than any she had ever seen. Grace introduced herself and spoke with him politely about his case. Charlie Stielow murmured his answers short and to the point. Grace spied some papers and letters on his shelf. She asked very nicely if she might look at some of them. She did so very quickly. All the while, the giant clutched a crusty German Bible. There was one letter in particular that Grace asked if she might borrow. Charlie agreed by nodding. Grace told the man in a stern tone that she could make no promises whatsoever. He nodded once more.

Once out of the corridor, Miller asked Grace what her first impressions were. Grace calmly asked why she had been asked to meet this man. Miller said there were questions about how Stielow's confession was procured. Grace nodded and showed Miller the paper she had taken. It was a handwritten note. Miller recognized it as written by Stielow's eleven-year-old daughter. The letter read:

> *God knows, as well as we do, father, that you are innocent. He knows,*
> *as we do, that you didn't go out of the house that night.*

Miller looked to Grace to see what her impressions were. She looked like she was still listening to the words in the air.

When she got back to New York City, Grace started making inquiries into Stielow's case. She took the train to Albion and checked out the record of Stielow's appeal. She stayed inside for three days over the July Fourth holiday and studied the case materials—all 1,450 pages—carefully reading the tiny, typed pages.

The facts were deceptively simple, yet they formed a story in her mind. Charlie Stielow was a down-and-out laborer looking for work. He met an older man named Phelps who looked at Charlie's massive size and offered him work on his farm in East Shelby at a salary of four hundred dollars a year. Charlie, who had a wife and two children, thought he had won the sweepstakes. Charlie was given a small house, a cow, feed, potatoes, and fuel for his home. Shelby was a bleak plain of pine trees and melting snow, especially in March, but Charlie had only four dollars to his name and his wife had another baby on the way. So Charlie took the job. His mother-in-law, Mary Jane Green and her son, Nelson Irow Green, arrived from Royalton Center to help with the move and the coming baby.

On the night of Sunday, March 21, 1915, at 11 P.M., the Stielows were awakened by the sound of a woman screaming. Charlie ran to the front door, trying to listen. There was only silence. Charlie wanted to go outside, but his mother-in-law stopped him, saying that whatever was behind that door might excite his wife into giving birth too soon. Charlie stood inside the door, chafing at its surface, straining his ears to hear past the wood and into the darkness.

The next morning, at dawn, Charlie woke up, still dressed in his old blue overalls. He covered his head with his favorite black cap, which had a thin front bill. He put on his size 10 boots, their sloping heels just hanging on.

Charlie opened his front door and found Miss Wolcott, Mr. Phelps's housekeeper, dead and cold on his doorstep. She had been shot under the left arm. A late, light snow had fallen the night before, coating her in white. Charlie followed a trail of swaying red spots all the way to the Phelps house, which stood directly across from him on the opposite side of West Shelby Road. Phelps's large two-story house stood out against the withered sky. Charlie ran over and found Mr. Phelps dying just inside his own door with three shots in him. Charlie shouted for Nelson, and they started across the adjoining lots, trying desperately to find a neighbor. They found Mr. Jenkins, Phelps's nephew, who took some bedclothes, wrapped up his straining uncle, and then called the police.

When the police arrived, they found very little evidence, except for the bullets themselves and Jenkins's insistence that a pocketbook with several hundred dollars in it had gone missing from inside. Someone also noticed a single bullet in the back kitchen glass door. There were no weapon and no eyewitnesses except Mr. Phelps, who was in very serious condition. The sheriff quickly questioned Charlie, but only as a formality. No one believed he could be guilty of such terrible violence. He was just the unlucky one who lived on the property. Besides, there were two sets of tracks: one small and barefoot and another harder to make out. The sheriff called for Charles Scobell, of Oneida Castle, who arrived with his big, slobbering bloodhound. The dog snuffled around in the snow. He looked up, then plunked his way along the tree line in a circle toward the henhouse but eventually lost the scent. When Mr. Phelps died hours later, the police put up a $5,000 reward for any information on the crime. Mr. Jenkins asked Charlie to stay on and keep the farm going while they figured out what to do next.

Sometime after, as the snow melted, a private detective named George W. Newton swung into town from Buffalo. He had been hired by the county to solve the case. They already had a suspect by the name of Kirck Tallman, a former worker of Phelps's who had left under unfriendly circumstances. But Newton had a different idea. He began to hound Charlie Stielow instead. Reading the report, Grace couldn't see why. She was surprised, then, to read that on April 20, Nelson Green, Charlie's brother-in-law, confessed to Detective Newton that he had helped Charlie kill Phelps for his secret heap of money.

Grace couldn't understand how the next part happened, but apparently Newton was able to take Charlie Stielow, without a warrant, over to the county jail at Albion. There, Stielow was jailed for two days, after which Newton emerged with a lengthy confession, complete with an X at the end of it. Charlie Stielow had confessed to a story where he and his brother-in-law used a mop stick and a gun to kill and rob Phelps and his housekeeper. Meanwhile, Detective Newton's men had found two .22 caliber guns in Charlie Stielow's barn.

After the confession had been signed, Charlie's mother-in-law came to visit him in jail. She told him that his wife had given birth to a daughter that morning. Charlie was overjoyed. She also told him that Nelson was in jail, too. Charlie was confused and asked her why.

District Attorney Knickerbocker put them both before the grand jury. Nelson Green pleaded guilty to second-degree murder and was given life in Elmira. The court had termed him "mentally deficient." In court, Charlie said he never confessed, but he was still sentenced to die on September 5, 1915. He was taken to Sing Sing—and the Death House—immediately.

Grace read the next part a couple of times. There was some sort of ballistics expert who proved that the bullets were definitely from the nickel-plated, black-handled Young American pistol found in Stielow's barn. Grace didn't know how that could be proved, although she wondered why the defense was not allowed to call a refuting expert.

Grace pushed herself back from the overwhelming words and voices on the pages in front of her and wondered why she was here. Like any criminal matter, there were two sides to the case. The bottom line was that Charlie had seemingly been caught by a combination of bad detective work and backstabbing family politics. There might have been some of the third-degree from this Newton character, but there was definitely evidence to convict. She still couldn't get herself to close everything up. She fished around in the files until she found Charlie's confession: two pages bursting with cramped black type. She touched the paper in her hands. She knew right then that Charlie Stielow was innocent.

Grace wrapped up the Gennaro Mazella case by successfully knocking him down to a life sentence. She knew that they were cheering in the Death House, as the residents always did when one of their own got off the Last Mile. As Grace thought of that small, dense hallway, cheering and loud, she couldn't help thinking of the gigantic Stielow and that small note from his daughter. In July, some newspapers reported that Charlie had already gone to the chair. Grace's breath caught when she heard this, but the papers were wrong. Charlie was still breathing in Sing Sing, though his hours were growing short. She made up her mind. Grace knew that there would be no vacation for her this summer. She was getting used to that.

Grace remembered the Tolla case again and how, in those early years of her career, she had to do everything herself. She was wiser now. She picked up the phone and called David White, Charlie's young attorney, who, though he had made mistakes in the case, had never given up. White wrote Charlie nearly every day and was working hard to get him a new trial. After getting off the phone with Grace, White then contacted the curly-haired Misha Appelbaum, the outspoken leader of the public-morals group the Humanitarian Cult, which met every two weeks in Carnegie Hall. The group was fiercely against capital punishment and now boasted over 100,000 members after just two years of operation. Grace added her own Stuart Kohn, a sharp lawyer who worked with her, as the new head counsel for the appeal. Their enemies called them the "Emotionalists."

Grace was flabbergasted that this case had received almost no press coverage outside upstate New York. Grace knew that she would be busy on the ground, so she made a call to a young writer whose work she liked. Sophie Irene Loeb had been writing for the *New York Evening World* for years, starting with columns about husbands and cooking before running a deep exposé of the lives of New York's tenement children. Sophie wrote about the heaps of choking dirt and refuse that surrounded these boys and girls like a sprawling monster. Sophie despised inhumanity, in all its ugly forms. She changed welfare laws, wrote news articles, and gave lectures. But she wasn't like one of the old temperance reformers with their lace and velvet; she was a young divorcé who wore a short hairstyle with pearls and wrote electric sentences. She immediately agreed to join their crusade.

Someone suggested they contact another Humanitarian Cult member, Inez Milholland Boissevain. She was bona fide famous, beautiful, and rich: her father had made his money in the pneumatic tube business. Her true claim to fame was wearing a flowing gown while riding a white horse named Gray Dawn as she led a sea of suffragists at the inauguration of Woodrow Wilson in 1913. She was a member of the radical National Woman's Party, captain of the hockey team at Vassar, and an outspoken voice for women in America. She got her law degree at the New York University School of Law in 1912 after being rejected by Yale, Harvard, and Cambridge because of her sex. She also famously said that it took only ten minutes a day to complete her housework. Inez worked for a time at Osborne, Lamb, and Garvan, where she had to investigate some of the crueler conditions at Sing Sing. At the time, Inez wanted to see what it felt like to be an inmate, so she had herself handcuffed to one. With their defense team now formed, Grace took off for northwestern New York. She knew that her role in this case was not that of a lawyer. She needed to be the detective.

Grace arrived in Buffalo and took a room at the Iroquois, a stylish hotel done up in the French renaissance style. As soon as she was settled in, Grace set out to investigate what was left of the crime scene. Orleans County in July was full of apple trees, now out of their full bloom but still green and bright. About three miles south of Medina, the largest town in the county, stood the town of Shelby. When Grace finally got there, she counted about a dozen small houses, a grocery store, a saloon, and a church, all placed around four corners, where the two main roads crossed. Grace continued on to a mile-length stretch of road to the town of West Shelby. The houses there, white and flaking, were set at long distances from each other, separated by farmland. There were trees and fields and broken fences.

In a town this small, Grace knew that people tended to know each other's business. So even if the murderer knew everyone in town or was a complete stranger, someone must have seen something. In the following days, Grace followed up on rumors all over Shelby and greater Orleans County. In Newton's Corners, where Phelps had hired Stielow, people in coveralls with dogs gave her strange looks. Most people liked Charlie Stielow, but they disliked outsiders even more. Grace learned that Phelps was said to be a rich but miserly man, in possession of a secret fortune somewhere close around his person. He hired tramp labor for nothing. Grace looked into a few of his previous employees, but didn't find anything. She did hear a few people tell of a rag picker named Erwin King who had been seen around the Phelps house earlier on the day of the murder. And there seemed to be evidence—a strange third place setting at the table that morning—that suggested Phelps had a houseguest that night. There was also an unknown man at the funeral who had acted strangely aloof. These were the ghosts that Grace was chasing.

Back at the Iroquois, Grace checked in on the telephone with Kohn and Loeb. Parts of the story were starting to spill into the papers, which they all agreed was good. But they had to try something else if they wanted a reprieve for Charlie. The clock was ticking. Luckily, Grace had a new theory on where to start.

Detective George Newton was the head of Byrne's Detective Agency and took any job presented to him. The famous Pinkerton agency did, too, but they had a higher standard of work, at least according to their advertisements. But Byrne's rates were cheaper. And Newton got results, though clients knew better than to ask how. While Grace was picking around Shelby looking for clues, Newton was in New York City tailing some man who was supposedly cheating on his fiancée. It was a "hotel job," as they said in the detective game. To tell the truth, Newton hadn't even seen the man; he just took the job and was biding time until his client, some old rich lady, called again. Her daughter was the fiancée. Poor gal.

Newton finally got the call that afternoon. Mrs. Wintergreen, the mother, asked if Newton might give his report to her lawyer in the city, a man named Mr. Welch, who had an office over at 80 Maiden Lane. Newton agreed; he put on a tie and headed over. He knew how paranoid these rich society types were about their secrets. They needed everything to be official.

Newton sat down with Mr. Welch—a typical lawyer—and made up a bunch of stuff about the man cheating on the fiancée. He made it sound good, but not too sensational. Just enough to shock Mrs. Wintergreen when she heard the report. Newton said he needed more time and resources to know for sure, which of course meant more money. Welch was sympathetic; he knew the game and was just here to placate his client, who had money to burn. As they were finishing up, Welch asked Newton about the Stielow case he had been reading about in the papers. Newton's name had been printed as the star detective who got the giant murderer to confess.

"Well, you see, that was part of my method," replied Newton, proudly leaning back in his chair. "I wanted to get him all excited and worked up, letting him think we had the real murderers. I told him a whole lot of things about this and that, made a lot of motions, got him excited, had my two men there with me and at the psychological moment, I rushed at him, grabbed him, shook him and threw him against the wall and said: 'Charlie, who murdered old man Phelps?'"

Welch soaked in the words. He then asked Newton if he had hit Charlie.

"Well," paused Newton. "Not very hard. Charlie said 'I don't know.' I rushed at him again, grabbed him by the throat and said 'You _ _ _, who killed Phelps?' 'I don't know, I don't know' he said. I grabbed him again and said 'Come along with me.'"

Newton continued. "We brought him over to the hotel and held him there all night . . . I finally told him that if he would tell me that Nelson shot Phelps, I would let him go to his wife. We got Nelson, who used Stielow's confession against Nelson and worked the two of them against one another. Nelson said that he held old man Phelps while Charlie shot him."

"My God" said Welch, clearly impressed. "That was a clever piece of work. Your rushing at the man like you did at the psychological moment practically scared the confession out of him. How do you account for this?"

Newton smiled. "That was the master mind over the weaker victim."

Welch smiled himself at that last line. As he did, he stood still for a moment. Welch called to the adjoining room, and a stenographer came out with a transcript from a Dictaphone. Newton's shoulders fell into a slump. The whole conversation had been recorded.

"My name is Stuart Kohn," said Welch.

Newton locked eyes with the man speaking in front of him. Newton knew that Stuart Kohn was part of Stielow's defense team. But they had never met. A moment passed. Until now, Newton realized. "Mrs. Wintergreen" was probably Grace Humiston herself, he thought. Newton slumped in his chair, defeated, as the rest fell into place.

Once the group went over Newton's confession, Grace told Sophie to write the piece she had been preparing for. On July 18, readers of the *New York Evening World* read the full story of Charlie Stielow and his struggle for justice. In her article titled "Man Facing Death," Sophie assured her loyal readers that "[t]he most vivid imagination of Sherlock Holmes could not evolve more dramatic elements than those which surround the case of Charles Frederick Stielow." She went on to relate the entire story of the Dictaphone sting that had been thought up by Grace. Sophie repeated some of the leads they had made in the investigation into Charlie's innocence. She also made the point that even the officials at Sing Sing thought Stielow was innocent and deserved to be free. And, after her article, countless readers agreed.

On the Friday before the execution, Sophie was supposed to make the final plea for clemency to Governor Whitman. But earlier that week, her own health failed her. Sophie's doctor diagnosed her with nervous exhaustion and told her that it would be suicide for her to go to Albany. The doctor said that she should obliterate the Stielow matter entirely from her mind or face protracted illness and possible death, an impossible request for Sophie Loeb. By Tuesday night, she had a new project in mind.

Meanwhile, Inez Milholland was going from Albany to Albion, drumming up support for Charlie's release in the form of a petition to the governor. The only sleep she was getting lately was on trains. When Inez finally arrived at her home near Westchester, she too collapsed into bed. Sophie Loeb phoned her just before dawn. Even confined to bed, Sophie was serving as the group's de facto organizer. Sophie excitedly told Inez about her newest idea: she wanted to hold a public rally in Medina to garner more signatures for Charlie before their last trip to see the governor. Inez, though exhausted herself, agreed immediately. She hopped on a train that day and convinced Misha Appelbaum and Stuart Kohn to help. Inez then went to Medina to secure the theater and start advertising. She sent out riders on horseback onto the roads and trails stuffed with handbills announcing the event. Sophie called Grace, who was still tracking down the story of a mysterious rag picker. Grace agreed that the event was a good idea and set off in a car.

On July 27, six hundred people came to the Delmar Theater in Medina to hear about Charlie Stielow. They came in wagons, buggies, and on foot from all points within a radius of ten miles. Grace, who had been on the trail of some leads in Shelby, arrived during the day. Sophie got reports at her bedside.

When the lights dimmed and the clapping stopped, Misha Appelbaum walked to the microphone. "For the sake of the spirit of 1776," he shouted, "we must save this great, dumb giant in the shadow of death!" Dr. Frederick Parsons was next. He was an alienist who worked out of Sing Sing to evaluate, when necessary, the mental state of prisoners during their appeals. Parsons had examined Stielow at length and wanted to share his conclusions.

"He is little more than a clod of earth," Parsons said of Stielow.

Parsons was followed by Kohn, who, without any variance of tone or emotion, gave a step-by-step description of how Charlie would die in the electric chair. He told them all how Charlie would be strapped in, the skullcap placed on his head, and the switches flipped to unleash searing volts of lightning through his body. The crackling current, blue and wide, would stop his heart cold after two or three pulls.

The room was silent when Grace then walked up the wooden planks of the stage, dressed in her customary black. She told the audience a few facts about the case and how she hoped that they would be convincing to the governor. But when Grace realized that she was speaking to the people, and not the governor, she took a breath, and started telling a different story. Grace told that dark theater how she had visited the Stielow family home that afternoon. When Grace walked in, their mother dried her hands on her apron as Grace was immediately swarmed by the Stielow children. In the theater, Grace then held up the letter she borrowed from Charlie, written by Ethel, his eleven-year-old daughter. Grace read the words in a trembling voice. When she got to the end, she explained how Ethel signed it with fifty kisses and the message "May these be a blessing to your heart." With that, Grace gestured to her left. There, in a private box, was the Stielow family, all of them except their father, who was far away, locked in a cell. Grace motioned for Ethel to come up to the stage. The little girl stared out at the crowd. She looked out at all the faces behind heavy glasses. She said, in a very small voice, "I know Papa is innocent," and her words became water. Grace helped her off the stage to applause.

Inez then alighted on the stage as if on a breeze. "My friends, you are your brother's keeper," she sang out. She said that the only man she had brought with her on the trip from New York City was the most powerful man she knew—her Lord and Savior, Jesus Christ. The crowd thundered their approval. Everyone knew who she was. She was married now, to a Dutchman named Eugen, but Inez still stood for suffrage, "avid for life and impatient for a world fit to live in." Inez loudly accused Governor Whitman of treating this case, with his endless indecision, as a stepping stone to some greater political office. He was a notoriously deadly government servant and had even sent NYPD lieutenant Charles Becker to the chair for killing a small-fry casino owner in front of the Hotel Metropole. "Have mercy on us, dear Jesus," Becker had cried, as the black helmet covered his face. When the current flowed and Becker pushed against the groaning leather straps, his lips pulled across his teeth as the crucifix he held in his hand dropped to the cement floor.

"Society is the better," Inez shouted, "the kinder, for the distillation of the milk of human kindness. The worst that can happen is that a murderer should receive life imprisonment instead of death." When she finished, her chin high, the deafening cheers seemed to press against the wooden floors and walls.

As Sophie sat by the phone that night in nervous anticipation, the team finished gathering over five hundred signatures. Inez was the first to call and tell her how well it went. The Stielow family retired to the nearby Hart Hotel. They had never been to such a place before and ate a meal there as a family. Or the closest to one they could be. They wore plain blue summer clothes. Roy, the youngest boy, who didn't understand where his papa was, grinned behind his shiny spoon. It broke his mother's heart.

The plan was that the Stielows would travel with Kohn and Applebaum to Albany to make one last plea to the governor. After that, they would go on to Sing Sing and take Charlie home. Alive or not. When a newspaperman asked Ethel if she was looking forward to the trip, she said, "We'll be awfully glad to see Papa." The Stielows' trip was completely paid for by a collection taken up by the other fifteen residents of the Death House at Sing Sing. The warden couldn't remember a stranger, or more telling, invitation.

But Grace was not going to Albany. She was going back to work. The rally was a nice gesture, perhaps even necessary for the press, but it was not going to stop Charlie Stielow from going to the electric chair. Grace knew that. They needed to work for some luck. The next day, Grace got a call from Mrs. Voorhees, a woman who lived on a farm near the Phelps place. She told Grace that five days after the murders, a hobo had come to see her. Grace had been looking for a ragman for weeks. Mrs. Voorhees said that this man had said something very puzzling.

In Albany the next afternoon, Charlie's legal team, fresh from the rally the night before, emerged from their long meeting with Governor Whitman with grim looks and long faces. In the governor's office, their evidence had consisted of affidavits, forensics that the bullets contained marks that proved them not to have been fired from a pistol found in the barn, and the words of three physicians—including Dr. Bernard Glueck, one of the leading alienists in the world—that Charlie Stielow did not commit the crime.

Whitman said his decision was final.

Appelbaum called Sophie and told her that the governor had said no. Sophie was devastated. Kohn had shown him the Dictaphone records, but the governor said it didn't change the actual facts of the case itself, especially given the evidence from the bullets. Loeb called Inez and begged her to go lobby Whitman herself. Inez took the train to Albany, but was told the same thing. Afterward, Inez called Sing Sing to tell the prison officials that Charlie Stielow was not going to be pardoned. After a silence on the line, the prison operator said that they could still get a stay, but only from a justice of the state supreme court. At the Albany train station with the rain pouring down, Inez called Sophie immediately, but the line was busy. Knowing that Sophie was probably working the case, Inez knew it could be busy all night. Just then, Inez saw that her train had arrived. She knew that if she got on the train, she wouldn't be able to talk to Sophie for several precious hours. But Inez would be closer to home, where she might need to be for this new plan—if it even was one—to work at all. So Inez got on the train, a prayer on her lips.

At Sing Sing that night, Charlie's last meal was potatoes and chicken, followed by a piece of ice-cold strawberry shortcake. Stielow was then moved to the Last Dance, the final cell on the Last Mile, as his last earthly possessions were cleaned out of his cell and divided among the rest of the residents. John Hulbert, the bald executioner (who was mostly just an electrician), got very nervous as he checked switches, wires, and volts.

While in Albany, Grace stayed at the Ten Eyck, going over her new evidence from Mrs. Voorhees. Her story was that her family had taken in a hobo one night as a boarder and fed him some supper. This man had strangely brought up the Stielow murders a full day before the papers reported on it. She was sure of it. Mrs. Voorhees also remembered that the man had strange dark spots on his clothes. She said that his name was O'Connell. He was quiet but smiled a lot, Mrs. Voorhees said. At one point, he cracked some kind of odd joke about the last old man who had served him dinner. Mrs. Voorhees didn't very much feel like laughing.

Grace looked around for tramp haunts under bridges and near fire pits. But she couldn't find O'Connell. She heard a rumor that he had supposedly shot his own favored buckskin yellow horse with a .22 the morning after the murders. She kept looking on the road but could find no sign of him. Then, she realized that she had not found him because he might not be free. Not too long after that, Grace located him in an Auburn prison. O'Connell had been convicted for a murderous assault, having shot at a man named Lewis Brown. O'Connell was known in the trade as a "gun man."

Clarence O'Connell came from Medina. His family were what the locals called swamp angels. His father had been an unlucky gambler of poor character. Last year, O'Connell's mother left her boyfriend for his best friend—Erwin King. The three remained friends, all three of them, and lived a gypsylike life around the fuzzy Pennsylvania border with Clarence and his own small family for the better part of last year. They traded horses and committed crimes.

Clarence smiled when he said that he had no idea where Erwin King was. They had a falling out, he said. Had she come all this way for nothing?

Grace had to find King right now.

⁂

It was very late on Friday night, July 28. Justice Charles L. Guy of the New York Supreme Court was in the well-appointed library of his Convent Avenue home, selecting a book before bed. The phone rang. He answered it.

"This is Sophie Irene Loeb speaking," said the voice on the phone.

"Oh, yes," the judge answered. He paused, checking the clock on his mantel. "I assume that you would not call me up at this hour unless something urgent was at hand?"

Sophie didn't stand on ceremony. She had a history with this particular judge.

"Judge Guy, you can save a human life!" Her voice wriggled a little, so she took a moment to bolster it.

"Judge," Sophie said again, more firmly, "do you remember saying, not long ago, that I had the mind of a man and the heart of a woman, and that where an issue involving both heart and mind were concerned you would take my opinion against that of most men? Did you mean that?"

"I remember perfectly saying that," the judge said. "And I should not have said it unless I meant it."

He paused again.

"What can I do?"

"There is a man in Sing Sing," Sophie explained, "condemned to die at a quarter to six o'clock tomorrow morning—this morning, for it is after midnight now—of whose guilt there is the gravest doubt. I know that no jury cognizant of all the facts in the case would ever have found him guilty! I am familiar with every bit of the evidence produced at the trial, and I have evidence that neither judges, jurymen, nor district attorneys have seen—parts of it I secured myself."

Sophie told the short version of the story, especially of how Stielow had been before the courts nine times and been sentenced or resentenced to death in six of them. Three times notices went out to the necessary legal witnesses for his execution, and twice the executioner had made the trip to the chamber. He was there now. Sophie explained that new evidence was available only today, so Stielow's only hope would be a stay of execution by a justice of the New York Supreme Court.

Judge Guy listened. Sophie could almost hear him thinking through the line.

"My dear Miss Loeb," the judge finally said. "It is impossible for me to act unless I have sworn testimony before me. I must see his new evidence before I can sign a stay."

Sophie was ready for this.

"The new evidence is on its way," she said.

At that moment, Inez and her husband were en route from Westchester County with the documents that the governor had, on that same day, twice declined to act on. After Inez had told Sophie about finding a Supreme Court justice, Sophie immediately thought of Judge Guy, whom she knew and thought highly of. Sophie told Inez to get on the train for Manhattan. Sophie then called Stuart Kohn, who got in his car in Stony Brook and headed to the city. They would be there in two hours, carrying the Dictaphone transcripts that had failed to move Whitman.

"You must see Mrs. Boissevain and Mr. Kohn," said Sophie. "They, with Mrs. Grace Humiston, have been working night and day to secure this new evidence. Mrs. Humiston is developing important clues at the sight of the murder right now."

Another pause. Sophie swooped in.

"I should come to your house, Judge, only I am confined to my bed with neuritis and am so weak that my nurse is holding the telephone to my ear while I am talking to you.

"Promise me that you will take up the case tonight," Sophie asked. "They will both be at your house by half-past two o'clock."

Justice Guy didn't hesitate any longer. "I shall hold court at any hour they may arrive."

At three thirty that morning, Kohn finally drove up to the home of Judge Guy in Manhattan. It was a white-knuckle drive in the dark. Kohn was surprised to see two police motorcars already at the curb. Apparently, there had been reports of a suspicious man lurking around the judge's home sometime past midnight. The cops produced the man from the shadows: it was Misha Appelbaum, who had been waiting for Kohn to arrive. He said the judge had gone to bed but would get up and hold court in his library when they were ready.

Inez arrived soon after, and they realized the brief they had prepared was not completely ready. So, at the suggestion of the policeman, the motorcars put off at full speed for the all-night Western Union telegraph office on 125th Street. As they spilled in, they saw only one typewriter on the premises. As Kohn finished up his last revisions with a pen, Inez dictated the final lines of the brief to Eugen, who plucked out the letters on the keys.

When they returned back to Convent Avenue, Justice Guy was waiting in his library. It was a quarter past four in the morning. Charlie Stielow was scheduled to die at quarter to six. Inez showed him the affidavits and evidence. The Justice read them thoughtfully, with no sense of anger. When he was done, he agreed that this new evidence must be considered and issued a stay of execution until eleven o'clock that night.

Justice Guy picked up the phone and asked for Sing Sing. Once the connection to the prison was established, Guy was informed that both Assistant Warden Miller and Warden Osborne had left in protest of Charlie's pending execution, leaving Principal Keeper Dorner in charge. Justice Guy told him that the execution was to be put on hold. But Dorner replied that, unless the order for the stay bearing the justice's signature was physically put into his hands, he must proceed with the execution as planned. Those were the rules.

Stielow was scheduled to die in a little over an hour and it was twenty-seven miles to Sing Sing.

Kohn, who was normally the quiet, matter-of-fact one, sprung to action. He had a fast motor and was positive he could make it. So, at twenty-two minutes to five o'clock, Kohn started off with the signed order for the stay in his pocket. The policeman called Central and told them not to interfere with a speeding car headed for Sing Sing.

Kohn had devoted his life to the absolute nature of the law. But tonight, as he barreled up the road in the dark, pushing his mechanical car past its limits, he was consciously doing the opposite in favor of what he perceived as the greater good. As he passed through Yonkers, a cop who had missed the order jumped out in back of him and shot at the back of his tires. Kohn kept going.

There was a hint of dark blue in the sky above Sing Sing by now. It was five o'clock in the morning when the thirteen witnesses were summoned to the Death House.

On the other side of a partition, the executioner was tinkering with the apparatus attached to the squat black chair. Stielow had already said good-bye to his wife and two little children earlier that night. The children were asleep as Laura Stielow waited on the veranda of the warden's house, watching the sun rise over the blocky prison buildings, coming up behind the Westchester hills.

Dorner alone knew that a stay might be coming, but he didn't tell anyone because it was still such a long shot. He had no idea if that had really been Judge Guy. Still, Dorner stood at the outer door of the prison, glancing at his watch and praying for time. Dorner knew Charlie Stielow and did not want to officiate his killing.

As the sky tipped to yellow, the honking of a horn was heard on the road. At twenty-three minutes past five, Kohn's car turned the corner and flew toward Dorner, his hand outstretched from the automobile's window. Dorner ran alongside the car and snatched the letter. As he disappeared inside, Kohn's car finally reached a halt, and he followed Dorner inside, running.

At home, Sophie Loeb was trying to stare at the clock and the telephone at the same time. When the phone rang, as she knew it finally would, she answered it. It was Kohn. He had gotten to Sing Sing with only fifteen minutes to spare. Charlie was saved.

That afternoon, Inez and Mr. Kohn finished up the full paperwork and submitted it to Justice Guy. He issued an order returnable in Rochester on the twenty-third of the next month to show cause why a new trial should not be granted to Charles Stielow. Justice Guy ordered a stay until after the hearing and determination of the motion. As both attorneys got some much-needed sleep, Sophie Loeb was visited by Mrs. Stielow and her children, who wanted to give their thanks in person. As they surrounded her bed with smiles and small hands, Sophie was overwhelmed by their bright-eyed gratitude. But she knew that Charlie was not wholly out of the woods yet. They had to find new evidence that would finally reunite him with his family, once and for all, outside of prison walls.

In a small room in the Little Valley sheriff's office, Grace Humiston had her eyes finally fixed on Erwin King, the man whom she had been chasing around upstate New York for the better part of the summer. At two separate times over the past few months, she thought she had been fairly close to being shot in her pursuit of him. In the end, Grace had finally just gotten lucky. The sheriff found King working odd jobs at a hotel. They snatched him up right away and called Grace. The crowded room included Sheriff Nichols and his wife; the justice of the peace, Pratt; the surrogate, Larkin; and Martha Hughes, a stenographer. It was August 10, just over ten days since Charlie Stielow had come a quarter turn of the clock away from being killed.

Grace sat down across from King. He was tall (over six feet) and dirty, but his clean-shaven face was self-assured. Grace nodded to Larkin. She wanted him to ask the questions so that there would be no question of impropriety. She had ridden with King in the car all the way from Buffalo just to get a read on him. King seemed surprised that she actually had some power here.

"Do you know what the statement you are making is?" Larkin asked.

"Yes," King replied.

"Do you know what it might mean?"

"I do not know whether it will be the electric chair or life sentence."

Larkin paused. "Knowing that this might mean the electric chair for you, will you still make this statement?"

"Yes, sir. I have got to a stage where I do not care."

"Would you just as soon make this attempt if you knew that it meant the electric chair?"

"Yes; I feel that I ought to."

"Is it the truth?"

"Yes, sir."

"Has any one threatened you if you did not?"

"No, sir."

"Have you had anything to drink to-day?"

"Not a drop."

"Are you ready to make a statement in regard to the Phelps murder at West Shelby?"

"Yes, sir."

"Now go ahead and tell us what you know of this murder."

"I got up to Medina on a Sunday around toward 4 o'clock, and went into Kelly's Hotel and got to drinking," King said. "I was drinking beer and something else in this hotel, on the back sitting room, as the bar was closed. No one was there but the bartender. I was there two hours, or perhaps longer. I do not know just what time it was when I left, but it was dark and the lights were on. I met O'Connell on the corner of Main and Centre Streets and he said that he wanted me to take a ride with him, and I said all right."

"Where was his rig?" asked Larkin.

"It was over in Rundell's alley," King replied. "He had a light spring buggy. I got in with him and we started up Centre Street, going toward Shelby Basin. We just got out of town and he presented a quart of whiskey and we drank quite a little. When we got near to Shelby, he said 'I want to do a job and want you to help me, I know where this is a lot of money. I will get the money and split with you.' And I was fool enough to go with him. I said to O'Connell: 'Do you think that we can get this without much trouble?'"

King continued. "When we got pretty near to Shelby, he stopped in a hollow of the road and hitched the horse, but he drove on the grass for quite a ways before he stopped and hitched the horse. When I went to get out of the rig I almost fell out because I was so drunk. When we started up toward the house I said 'Why this is Old Man Phelps!'"

King said that he could see from the window the old man sitting in the middle room. He could not see anyone else. So he circled back around to the kitchen door and went in from the back way. From inside the door, he picked up an old broom. He pulled it outside and hacked off the end with an old axe that stood there. King and O'Connell then went up to the back door and rapped on it with their fists. Their breath hung in the icy night air.

"Yes?" They heard the old man get up, his footsteps making their way to the door.

Phelps opened the door, and the men walked right in.

"You both get out of here!" Phelps yelled.

O'Connell hit Phelps with the stick. But Phelps had a hold of the doorknob, and he reeled around and fell toward the stove. He collapsed in a heap on the ground.

O'Connell started to look for the money when a woman in her nightdress fled by, leaving through the door they came in. The door swung shut, but not tightly. O'Connell shot once through the door.

"Did you hear her holler?" asked Larkin.

"I thought I heard a noise, but I did not look."

"What did O'Connell do next?"

"He turned around and shot Phelps three times, I think," said King. "All the shots hit him."

"Did he groan?" asked Larkin. They needed to prove Phelps was still alive when O'Connell shot him.

"Yes," replied King. "He made a little noise and moved his leg a little. I do not know what O'Connell did with the gun, but he went into the next room and came out with the money. I do not remember of seeing any purse, but he came out in the kitchen with the money. I thought that I heard a noise outside, so I said: 'Let us get out of here.' He handed me $100 and I put it in my pants pocket. It was all in bills and he had quite a wad in his hand, it was all paper money, and I did not see any silver. When we came out I said to him: 'You go your way and I will go mine.' He took his rig and drove away. I went up the road quite a way, pretty near to Reynold's hotel: then I cut across to another road and went to Alabama Centre and then to Alabama Station."

He continued. "Just as I got in front of the Dry House I met a farmer driving, and I asked him where he was going. He said he was going to Akron, and I asked him if I could get there quicker by riding with him than waiting for a train, and he said yes. I do not know who he was. He had one horse and a buggy."

"Where did you go?" asked Larkin.

"I rode from the east side of the railroad back to Akron, to the American Hotel. The farmer tied his horse under a shed there, and I asked him if he would not go and have a cigar; but he said no, he was in a hurry to get back home, and he went up the street. I went into the hotel."

"How long did you stay in Akron?"

"I stayed there all day, drinking a little."

"Where did you stay?"

"I stayed in Parker's livery stable," King said.

Grace pulled up to King, and she read him the letter from Ethel Stielow claiming her father was innocent. The one with the drawn signature of "fifty kisses." When Grace was finished, she stared at King. He was weeping softly.

"I'm the one that killed Phelps and Mrs. Wolcott—not Charles Stielow," King said. He then—at Grace's insistence—repeated it to the sheriff and then to the judge.

"King," she said, "just raise your right hand."

They had a full confession. They were all celebrating inside because nowhere in that story—nowhere—was Charlie Stielow's name. Once everyone was notified, the feeling was equal parts exhaustion and elation. Even King himself seemed relieved. When asked why he had confessed, King said he wanted "to do a manly thing." He was then taken back to the jail. After King's confession was finalized in shorthand after midnight, the authorities mobilized. District Attorney Knickerbocker sent his car over to convey King to the jail at Albion.

The next day, Grace found out that King had retracted his entire confession.

"This is a malicious, absurd, evil lie!" Grace shouted. "King couldn't make a declaration of that kind of his own free will!" She was fuming in her own way. "It's amusing, really," she said, "to think that those who are so determined to get Stielow into the chair must stoop to charges of this sort." Grace immediately got on the phone with Knickerbocker. Grace asked to see a copy of the retraction.

"I wasn't in the room when King made his statement," Knickerbocker replied. "I haven't seen a copy myself." Grace was stunned. How could the district attorney not know if there was a copy? Was King being held as a legal prisoner? She asked if there had been a warrant sworn out against King on the murder charge. On the other end of the line, Knickerbocker hesitated.

"Wait a moment," he said. Two minutes passed before a strange voice came on the line.

"Hello?"

"Why, I was talking to Mr. Knickerbocker," Grace said.

"He has gone out," the voice said. The line clicked dead.

That afternoon, Erwin King, who had done a good job of disappearing after the murders, took to the newspapers to make his case as visible as he could.

"That Little Valley story was a lie," said King. "I wish I had never seen that gang at Little Valley. I would be all right now. This lady, Mrs. Humiston, I did not know who she was; never saw her before.

"I was not introduced to the lady," King said, almost proud of himself. "We got out of the city and they talked about this trial of Stielow. They wanted to know what I thought of it. I told them they had the guilty man, and she told me she thought she was going to get some information from me. I told her I did not see how."

King then said that Grace had offered him a bribe. "If you will confess that you did this crime you will never be locked up long, I have it fixed with the governor," is what King said Grace allegedly told him. "It will be down in black and white. There is $4600 in Albion and I will see that you get $3000 of it."

King admitted that sounded good. So he said he lied and told Grace that he and O'Connell did the deed. But now he felt that was wrong.

"I told her we done it and I told her the wrong story," he said.

"You now say this is entirely untrue," asked the reporter.

"Yes, sir," said King.

As Grace made a direct appeal to Governor Whitman, the case—and her defense team—was all a scramble. Kohn and the others were convinced that King's turnaround was purely political. Kohn and Sophie began working again on an appeal for Charlie. Inez had left for a speaking tour but was checking in regularly over the telephone.

Grace knew that the only way to fix this was to talk to King again, who was still in jail. She knew she could reverse his course, but her every request was denied. Grace had no court order so the sheriff couldn't let her speak to him. But a thought occurred to Sheriff Bartlett. He went over to King's cell and asked him if he wanted to see anyone.

"I wouldn't deny myself to anyone," King said.

Bartlett brought in the visitor. She was dressed entirely in black.

"I've expected you these three weeks," King said, unsurprised. Grace had to admit that King looked better and didn't smell of booze. They held the interview in Sheriff Bartlett's bedroom because the lawyers feared his cell might be wired with a Dictograph machine.

This time, Grace had no time, nor tolerance, for pleasantries. She sat down right in front of King and asked the questions herself.

"King, do you still say I gave you money to make the confession? You're an honest man, King. You can't look me in the eye and say I gave you money."

"I can, too," King said, looking away from her. "I'd never be here today if I hadn't met you and been offered money to confess."

"King, that's a lie," said Grace. "You know I never offered you money. Before this case is settled you'll admit it. Look me in the eyes and tell me you were given money by me."

King refused both requests.

A month later, Charles Stielow was denied a new trial and was given an unprecedented seventh version of his original death sentence, to be carried out on December 11, 1916. They were running out of hope. Meanwhile, Inez was still in California on a speaking tour. She was riling up a packed suffrage rally in Los Angeles when she keeled over from exhaustion. Consigned to the same rest that doctors had prescribed to Sophie Loeb, Inez called her old friend from her bed to check on the case. When Sophie told her that Stielow was still on the Last Mile and that the governor was debating a commutation, Inez was furious. She talked to her father and made him promise to stay in contact with the Stielow team and render them any assistance they needed. "You will see to it, won't you," she finally asked Sophie, "that every effort is made to cheat the electric chair of this innocent man?" Sophie agreed, catching something different in her voice. Inez died on November 25, 1916.

Sophie Loeb wrote a eulogy in the *Evening World* titled "The Example of Inez Milholland." Loeb wrote of her "dear, dear friend" by telling readers that you could always find her not in the usual spots for women, but in asylums, Sing Sing, and political marches. "How easy it might have been for so lovely a creature as she to sit idly by," Sophie wrote. "But no. She could not enjoy the world while it suffered . . . she went forth to fight and used every asset to gain something for others, even unto the very end." Inez, according to Sophie, was

An example for the idle rich girl who is poor indeed, whose time hangs heavy because it is full of nothingness. An example for the pretty girl who believes that all life means is to smile and dress. An example of the woman of brains who hides them under her marcel wave because she has become a parasite. An example for the woman who thinks that she can gain love when she acquires a man's bank account. An example for all womanhood.

Four days after Inez's death, Governor Whitman agreed to chair a public hearing on the Stielow case. Grace argued vigorously that law enforcement had completely mishandled the case from the start, resulting in a fabricated confession from Stielow. She again referred to her own confession from King, which was made in the presence of several witnesses. Grace also pointed out a clue that she had noticed all the way back when she first met Charlie Stielow. Whitman listened.

A few days later, the governor came out to address reporters. He had made his decision.

"I realize that a governor," Whitman said, "who interferes with a judgment of the courts of this state, without good and sufficient cause, is himself committing a lawless act." He continued, even as hearts sank all around him. "I believe that Stielow is guilty," Whitman said. "And I believe that King's confession is a lie." In their heads, the reporters were already making plans for the dreaded final trip to Sing Sing. Whitman said that even though he believed all of those things, the principal facts were not about his opinion. Whitman said he knew, after all his trial experience, that "no jury in this country would have convicted Stielow of murder in the first degree with the King confession before it." The reporters almost stopped writing. "I commute the sentence of the court to imprisonment for life," said Governor Whitman.

Soon after, Whitman conducted his own secret interview with King. When King swore up and down that he was innocent, the governor slapped down on his desk a pack of letters that King had sent from jail. They had never reached their destinations. These messy letters had been written to all manner of friends and accomplices. A November 15, 1916, letter from King to Joe Kinnie read:

> *Friend Joe Kinnie I hear that you Been squealing on me. Know you know that if you tell on me it would Bee the way that they would send me to the Chare. You know what I said to you at parkers Livery. Know one knows But you and you Can save me from the Chare.*

As a result of his conversation with King, Whitman appointed George H. Bond to conduct a special investigation into the original murders. King eventually confessed (again) that he and O'Connell were the murderers. Newton, too, was found to have promised Stielow a special role in law enforcement if he signed his confession. The most persuasive piece of evidence though was a report that concluded that although Charlie had a working command of about 150 words, his signed confession used 369. Grace had known this all along. When she first met Charlie, she listened to his words carefully and realized how few of them there were. Stielow and Green received full pardons from Governor Whitman on May 8, 1918.

The Stielow case was so popular in the press that Hollywood filmmaker Lois Weber tackled the story in her 1916 movie *The Celebrated Stielow Case*, which she rushed to finish in order to sway public opinion on the case. In the film, an uneducated farmhand faces execution for a murder many believed he did not commit. After finishing the film, Weber submitted it to the National Board of Censorship. They asked that all references to Stielow be eliminated in favor of the more generic "John Doe." Weber agreed, and the film appeared in theaters less than a week after Stielow's death sentence was commuted. The film was considered the most influential work on the death penalty of its time in terms of its ability to start conversation and generate opinion and argument.

Grace had gone back to New York City after Charlie's sentence was first commuted to life. She agreed to consult on the governor's report, but she was not worried about the outcome. She had more pressing concerns in the city.

A girl had gone missing.

9

The Manhunter of Harlem

June 1917

Grace Humiston stood in the street on an early summer morning and looked up at the Metropolitan Motorcycles shop. Grace didn't know if Ruth Cruger was alive or dead, but she had a feeling that this place held the key to answering that question. She just didn't know how. Grace was still wearing black, even in the summer. Certain lines had come to her face these days, but that's not what she was thinking about. Her eyes were dancing around a new kind of mystery. She remembered the words she had said upon taking the case. That long-delayed rest and vacation would have to be postponed yet again.

Grace craned her neck and took in the tall glass windows that ran almost ten feet high across the front of the store. They were framed in dark wood. The white lettering read MOTOR CYCLES STORING on the left and AUTO SUPPLIES on the right. There were tin signs for Mobil Oil that hung still in the early heat. A single globe lamp hung off a pole in front of the entrance. A huge billboard for graham crackers—as big and long as the shop itself—rose off the roof and into the bluish sky. On the sign, a boy was crunching happily away, frozen in time.

Cocchi's shop was only a story tall. The building to the right was double that. People there had already begun peeking out of windows to see what new commotion the Italian's shop had brought to Harlem. A man in white pajamas with his hair combed over and a mustache watched from under his own heavy window, hunkered down on his elbows. His wife joined him, a mug of something in her hand. They half watched and half chattered. The inside of Cocchi's shop was dim behind the smoked glass.

Since Grace had joined the Cruger case, it had stalled to a slow, frustrating stasis. The police were confident that Ruth had simply eloped. Most agreed that, given the scrutiny that Ruth's character was receiving in the press, she was probably just too embarrassed to come home and announce her happiness to the world. Cocchi, though probably a dodgy character, was no killer. He had only left town because he feared an Italian witch hunt with his name at the end of it. The papers, having reported on every single cockamamy clue, had now focused their attention elsewhere. The massive headlines about the war in Europe had edged out everything else onto the next page.

So there Grace was at the store, walking by without trying to look too obvious. Since the store had been broken into several weeks ago, Mrs. Cocchi had refused all interior searches, as was her right. Grace's eyes darted under her black hat to note the details of the world around her. The store was open but looked empty. There were two signs in the window that said MECHANIC'S HELPER WANTED and SELLING OUT. Cocchi's absence had clearly caused business to plummet. On the outside, to the left of the front door of Cocchi's shop, was a narrow stairwell that sank into the ground and served as a separate entrance to the basement. Grace walked near these stairs as unobtrusively as possible to get a better look. The area in front of the basement had a dirt floor and was older, a different color even, than the ledge under the windows. Here was an elevation of about four feet, behind which was the coal vault under the sidewalk.

Grace knew, like it or not, that all of the evidence they had—all of it—was circumstantial. The police had searched the cellar at least twice with multiple people and found nothing but absence. The rest was gossip and headlines. Why was Cocchi missing? Because he had taken the girl? Because he had been spirited away by the same fiends who had taken poor Ruth? Or because he was afraid of becoming a scapegoat? Was there any kind of clue in the paperwork here that would tell them where Ruth had gone? Or who had taken her to a cab? These questions couldn't be answered yet. But they needed to be asked.

Grace paused, considering the possibilities. Perhaps Ruth and Cocchi were the happy couple in this after all? That was a possibility, whether Henry Cruger cared to admit it or not. Grace did not, at least not yet. That version of the truth seemed remote given the facts of the case. When she was hired in March, the first thing Grace did was to lock herself in her office for a straight week to study every scrap of paper related to the case. The second thing she did was hire Julius J. Kron.

Kron, her comrade in arms from the old peonage days, was now also in the city, working as a private detective with the Martin Donnelly Detective Agency. When Grace contacted him, Kron was wrapping up a case in Detroit. He immediately boarded an eighteen-hour midnight train straight to New York City. The next night, Grace and Kron had dinner at the luxurious Hotel Manhattan on Madison and Forty-second. Kron wore his customary checked dark wool; Grace, her usual black. They picked up menus that claimed "Food will decide the war," just as they tried to decide between city staples of clam cocktail Manhattan, clear mock turtle soup, or rice pudding. There was also deep-dish apple pie with cream, served on flat plates.

There, among the white tablecloths, high-backed chairs, and palms, the two partners, now older, talked business, just like the old days. She called him Kronnie. He called her Mrs. Humiston, without any hesitation. Grace told Kron everything she had so far. He was the only one she did that with. "I want you to meet Mr. Cruger, the girl's father," Grace said, between sips of tea. "He is a mental and physical wreck. If this isn't solved soon, he'll be in a sanitarium."

When they left the hotel at eight, Grace gave Kron the bulk of the files she had on the Cruger case. There were hundreds of typewritten pages. Kron took the papers home and studied them all night long, making big blue pencil marks over promising leads. In the morning, he blinked his eyes, took an icy shower, and ate breakfast. Before leaving, Kron kissed his wife Estelle and three young daughters good-bye. Kron stared at his oldest for a few more moments.

The air was warm outside for late April. Kron's apartment was in the west eighties, so he decided to walk to Forty-second Street through Central Park. He wanted to get the facts straight in his mind before he reached Grace's office. Ruth Cruger had left her fashionable apartment house at 180 Claremont Avenue on February 13 to pick up her newly sharpened ice skates at Cocchi's store on 542 West 127th Street. She was never seen again. What Kron couldn't figure out was how a girl of eighteen could disappear in broad daylight in such a crowded section of the city. Three days later, Cocchi—who had been cleared of any wrongdoing by police investigators—also disappeared. Walking along, Kron watched kids already playing in the fountain as their parents laughed outside the immobile stone rim. They were holding on for dear life, screaming as their clothes got soaked.

When Kron arrived at Grace's office, he found her already talking to Henry Cruger. When Grace introduced Kron, with no small amount of the usual hyperbole, Henry's eyes pleaded at him from under his bushy eyebrows.

"Mr. Kron," he said. "Won't you find my little daughter? Someone is keeping her—she would never stay away—she would never have gone away."

"We hope to, Mr. Cruger," Kron replied, through his thick Hungarian accent. He continued with a lie meant to make the man—the father—feel better. "Just remember that of all the thousands of girls who disappear every year, over ninety-eight percent are located." Kron managed a persuasive smile.

"Yes," Henry cried, "but where?"

Kron had no immediate answer.

Henry again insisted that his Ruth had no love affairs, was quite fond of her family, and would not have stayed away without any communication. Henry repeated his fears that Ruth had been kidnapped by a passing motorist or met with an accident and was in a hospital unable to identify herself. Or it was possible that, since it had been a bitterly cold day, she had stopped in some doorway to warm herself and had come to harm there? Cellars, vacant lots, and flats in the section were searched. When no further clue had been revealed after forty-eight hours, Commissioner Woods, at Henry's insistence, sent out a general alarm. Since then, there had been countless dead-end rumors and vague tips, and the fear that there was still something waiting for them in all that melting ice.

Once Henry left, Grace and Kron mapped out a plan. Grace would investigate Ruth Cruger while Kron would try to learn more about Cocchi.

"Kronnie," she said, "you are the only man I can trust to dig up the real facts. There is something crooked behind the whole thing." Kron had sensed that, too. There had to be something that everyone else had missed.

Grace's part of the investigation required leaving the office because this was not a legal case. Not yet. They had to be discreet. So Grace put her black hat on and searched vacant lots and old buildings by herself. She spoke with Ruth's classmates at Wadleigh High School and friends of hers from church. She also talked to Seymour Many and some of the Columbia boys whom the police had already questioned. But Grace had heard enough to support her initial feelings about Ruth Cruger's character. Ruth had been going out occasionally (and secretly) with some college students, but she was not, as the police were saying, a "wayward girl." Grace was unsure about much of this case. But she was getting very sure of that.

That is how Grace found herself at Cocchi's shop, staring at nothing she felt was probably something. Grace walked casually because she knew no one would look twice at her if she behaved normally. Her black hat shielded her face and allowed her to blend in. Satisfied with her investigation of the store, she moved down the street. A few doors down from the shop, she met a garage man and asked about Cocchi.

"There's something phony about that guy," the mechanic said. "Cocchi kept his shop closed for three days after that girl disappeared." He thought about it a minute. "Mind you, now, I'm not saying a word, but he put a sign up 'Closed for Repairs' and he kept the door locked."

The man also said that Cocchi had hired a twelve-year-old neighborhood boy named Herbert Roemmele to work for him before and after school hours. Grace asked if this boy had been working with Cocchi when Ruth Cruger went missing. The man thought a minute and said that was the day the boy was fired. Grace found the boy easily; he lived only a block or so away. Grace didn't have any children of her own, but her sister did, so she knew how to talk to them. When Grace got to the door of the tenement, she stared up the beetling cliff of dirty windows. After finding the apartment, Grace talked to the boy's mother, who agreed to let the lady lawyer have a brief interview with her son.

In the room with Herbert, Grace smiled and asked him if he could draw. When the boy nodded yes, Grace asked if he might draw the inside of the motorcycle store for her. Kind of like a map, she said. Herbert dipped his head and got to work drawing a sketch of Mr. Cocchi's shop for her, though in his sketch it was disappointingly bare. Herbert drew six lockers on one end, which he said policeman used for their raincoats and lamps. Herbert got more talkative as he drew. He told Grace how on one particular day the giant sidecars were all standing on end and placed to cover up the rear of the store. "Like boats," Herbert said. That day was in February.

On that day, Herbert told Grace, everything was normal. Herbert went to the store after school as usual. He remembered that Mr. Cocchi told him he was too busy to be bothered. But that wasn't out of the ordinary. Herbert remembered playing with Mr. Cocchi's little son Athos out on the street, but Mr. Cocchi came out and said they were making too much noise.

Herbert said that Mr. Cocchi was smoking a lot of cigarettes and seemed upset. He told Grace that it was probably because of Mrs. Cocchi. They were always fighting. When Herbert went back to the store after school the next day, several policemen stopped him and sent him to Brooklyn for some nails, which they said were needed by Mr. Cocchi. Herbert heard hammering. "When I came back after school," said Herbert, "the shop was locked up. He was busy in the cellar."

The next day, Herbert again showed up to work.

"You clear out," Mr. Cocchi told Herbert. "I don't need you anymore."

On the third morning, Herbert saw Mr. Cocchi's name in the newspaper. He went down to the store and shouted to Mr. Cocchi, but he could not get in. The door was still locked.

After raising a ruckus for a few more minutes, Mr. Cocchi came up the outside steps from the coal bin, snatched the paper from the boy's hands, and ran back into the cellar. In an instant, Cocchi was up again and ordered the boy to buy two more newspapers. When Herbert returned, Mr. Cocchi grabbed them again and hurried back into the cellar.

"What do you suppose he wanted with three newspapers?" Grace asked.

"Oh, I think he was building the morning fire," Herbert said.

Grace thought that it was beginning to look more and more like Cocchi was the man she wanted to talk to the most. She headed back to her office to look over the evidence again to see what they had missed. Grace remembered her training from Dean Ashley at NYU: look at the facts of the case and then work in the spaces between them.

When Grace arrived at her office, it was mobbed by newspaper reporters. She thought they might be looking for another statement from her on the Cruger case. They were, but not for the reason she thought.

There was news.

✤

The reporter wiped his brow under the hot Italian sun. The afternoons were even quieter up here, in Bologna. As the reporter walked up the path to the low building, he started to wonder if this wasn't just another wild-goose chase. Milt Snyder was a reporter, so he thought in terms of stories and their worth, but he also knew when they just plain fizzled out. At the same time, as the longtime globe-trotting correspondent for the *Sun*, Milt had done some of the work on the Petrosino story, so he knew never to discount the impossible. So once Milt's editor caught word of the news, Milt was rapidly dispatched from Rome to verify its truth. The *Sun's* motto was "If you see it in the *Sun*, it's so."

As he got closer, Milt shielded his eyes from the sun and saw a man sitting in the June sun amid the colorful bones of a broken bicycle. Milt pushed back his hat.

Are you Alfredo Cocchi? Milt said in perfect Italian.

Yes, the man said, surprised. Milt's eyes focused. There, indeed, was Alfredo Cocchi, on his knees, tinkering with a drive chain.

When Milt Snyder said his name, Cocchi seemed surprised. Not by the fact that someone had found him or that the person had an American accent, but by the fact that someone was looking for him in the first place. Cocchi told Milt that he had been in Bologna this whole time, living with his father and his brother Arturo at 7 Via Poleso, working in the family bicycle-repair shop. When Cocchi spoke, Snyder looked at the man. It was strange to see the dark face that had been inked all over the papers now grinning and come to life.

"I am well known here," Cocchi told Snyder, wiping off his hands and offering his hand. In Bologna, he had not made the slightest attempt to hide his identity.

Cocchi swore that he knew nothing about Ruth Cruger's disappearance. He had actually heard that she had been kidnapped and was living somewhere in Europe. Cocchi's claim called to mind quaint, crooked streets and rambles around dark, silent cathedrals. Whom was she with? And why? Cocchi waved his hands as if the question were a noonday fly. He was astonished that he was even being asked these things. He had no knowledge of them. He seemed genuinely hurt.

But Milt was a true reporter. He mentioned to Cocchi that, because of the many unanswered questions about the case, the United States might try to extradite him back to New York for trial. Cocchi seemed to be offended by this. He explained to the reporter that he had abandoned a good business and returned to Italy after ten years because his wife was crazy, not for any other reason. Cocchi didn't understand why this was so hard to understand. The timing with the missing girl was merely coincidental. His wife had become unbearable, Cocchi said. She was excessively jealous and nosy. He referred to her only as Maria Magrini, her maiden name.

Snyder turned the conversation back to Ruth Cruger. Cocchi explained again, as he had all those months ago to the police, that he had met the girl only once in his life, when she had come to get her skates sharpened.

"She was a pleasant faced girl," Cocchi admitted. "But there was nothing extraordinary about her."

10

The Pale Man

With the news of Cocchi's appearance in Italy in early June, a significant amount of legal and political machinery began turning its gears to get Cocchi extradited back to the United States so that he could be questioned about Ruth. But since this was Italy—in the shadow of the First World War and the Petrosino murder—officials on both sides were not cooperating. Given the tense political atmosphere, insiders knew that there was little chance of an extradition. Even though Cocchi had been found, the Italian government refused to even arrest him.

"I have heard from him once," Maria Cocchi admitted, back in New York. "He told me he was living with his father and brother in Bologna. He said nothing about that girl. I shall be glad if they bring him back. It is like him to run away and leave me.

"He did it before, while we were betrothed, and left me in Italy," Maria explained. "Then he sent for me to follow him and we were married. I hear also from my sister who is visited by Alfredo every week. He tells my sister many lies. He told her he sold his machine shop for much money and left me $5000. He did not sell the shop." This seemed believable. There were rumors going around that Maria Cocchi was already trying to sell the motorcycle store.

The news of Cocchi's appearance affected Mrs. Cruger quite differently. "I am overjoyed to learn that this man has been found," she said. "And now I hope, since the police permitted him to slip through their fingers, they will see that he is brought back here. I have always maintained that Cocchi knows what became of poor little Ruth. The police may congratulate themselves on the finding of Cocchi, but it seems to me they were very lax." Stifling back tears, she urged reporters to talk to Mrs. Humiston.

"Circumstances had come to light," Grace said, "which made it appear extremely likely that Cocchi knew all about the girl's disappearance." Grace revealed that her investigations into the records at the American consul in Italy showed that when Cocchi arrived, he had good clothes and plenty of money. This was "striking, because it has been established pretty well that he had only $15 and was dressed in his working clothes when he dropped out of sight." Grace said that "if he could be induced to tell where he had obtained money after he went into hiding, the mystery would be near a solution." Her reasoning was sound. Grace was working the case, not getting caught up in the personalities involved.

"It isn't going to be an easy matter to extradite Cocchi," District Attorney Swann told the press. "All we have against him at present is an abandonment charge preferred against him by his wife. That is not an extraditable offence." But it might, he added, generate "leads which will enable us to connect him up materially with the disappearance of Miss Cruger."

Grace thought about going to Italy herself to look for Cocchi. She would have already been on a boat, she knew, in her younger days, but she felt fairly certain that Ruth herself was not there. There was also the small matter of the war. The Atlantic had already become uncertain terrain, masking the terrifying U-boats that slowly wound their way beneath the waters. Grace knew that if they didn't find Ruth, then any case they had against Cocchi would fall apart completely. If that happened, Cocchi could live in Italy, free in the sunshine, for the rest of his life. Finding Cocchi didn't solve the mystery.

A few days after Cocchi was found in Italy, Grace was in her office thinking about what to do next when she looked up to see Commissioner Woods himself at her door, hat in hand. She didn't skip a beat.

"Alfredo Cocchi was the man we wanted," Grace said, matter-of-factly. Some believed her, though a great many seemed to believe Cocchi's explanation of things in the paper.

"Come now, Mrs. Humiston," Woods said. "You have nothing on Cocchi and you know it. Would you expect a Grand Jury to indict him with only your evidence against him?"

Of course, Grace knew that the commissioner was right. In truth, there was still no physical evidence to connect Cocchi to anything. And the reports from Italy were threadbare at best—just that Cocchi had been found, living in plain sight, and the Italians refused to arrest him without a formal charge. All that meant even less when Woods phoned Grace the next morning.

"Well, we've found Ruth Cruger," he said.

Grace stared into space, holding the black receiver in her hand. She was utterly shocked. She had been working for nearly a month under the secret premise that Ruth was long dead. She hadn't told the family that, of course, not in so many words. They were still hopeful, but Grace had to be more practical. Could Ruth truly be alive? She felt surprised and happy at the same time.

"We found her, all right," Woods said. "She's alive and well in Mount Vernon, living with some man. She even admits who she is."

Hearing Grace's silence, Woods filled it with his own authority.

"Why don't you and Mr. Cruger go up there to see her yourself this afternoon? I'll send an officer with you."

As they drove up to Mount Vernon together, Grace noticed how overjoyed Henry Cruger was. She had not met this version of him before, only perhaps imagined him as an inverse of the sad Henry she had seen every day. She couldn't help feeling sheepish about demanding Cocchi's arrest and for denying that Ruth had eloped. But she was quite happy to be wrong. The answer was always the simplest one, not a great conspiracy. Once they reached the rooming house at the address Woods had given them, Henry jumped out of the car and ran up the stairs to the apartment.

As Grace and the police officer walked the steps, they could hear the landlady talking with Henry.

"She's gone," the lady said. "She went to a hotel this morning."

The woman gave them the number of Ruth's new location. Grace wondered if she was running from her father or had just needed a new place. As Henry started down the stairs back to the car, Grace turned to the landlady and asked a question. Henry stopped to listen.

"Are you sure the girl is Ruth Cruger?"

"Positive," the landlady replied.

"Did she admit it?"

"She didn't exactly admit it. But I asked her, and she laughed."

Henry didn't say anything as he walked slowly to the car and stepped in. At the hotel, they found her almost immediately. Grace could see a slight resemblance, but it was only very faint around the eyes and mouth. It was not her. As they drove home in silence, Grace watched as the green trees of the mainland gave way to an island of boxes and blocks, almost toylike, though the closer they got, it became all too sharp and familiar.

Later that afternoon, Grace walked in the office and slowly sat in her chair. Her secretary told her that Kron had phoned.

"It must be something important," she said. "He said for you to call him as soon as you got in."

Grace sat down and called her detective. They connected easily.

"Mrs. Humiston," Kron said. "I've got something on Cocchi."

An hour later, Kron sat across from Grace at their customary hotel meeting place. Kron told her that he had uncovered new information that might be relevant. For one, Cocchi was no stranger to girls. Kron found that girls would often visit the motorcycle store and drink wine with Cocchi late into the night while he would sing Italian songs. "A Lothario," Kron told Grace. "No pretty girl could pass by that store without him noticing and saying something in an attempt to get her to come inside." There were also rumors that his shop had been a meeting place for all sorts of gamblers, racketeers, and loafers. But there was more.

"A former landlord reported that Cocchi," Kron said, almost whispering, "under the name of Lou Marinaro, used to sneak girls into his repair shop for trysts with customers." Kron discovered more assaults, but no one pressed charges because they feared a public scandal for their daughters.

Kron looked over his shoulder and dropped his voice even lower. He told Grace about someone he talked to who used to live on Cocchi's street. Her name was Madame Mureal and she was a French actress who lived at 111 Manhattan Avenue with her sixteen-year-old daughter, Philippa. Their house was across the street from Cocchi's motorcycle shop.

When Philippa's bicycle broke one summer, her mother sent her to get it fixed by Cocchi. He was always smiling and seemed like a kind man, sometimes waving at them from across the dusty street. When Philippa came back, her bike not only fixed but wiped clean, the girl opened her hand to show her mother the rose that Cocchi had given her. On another occasion, he had given her a red box of candy. Philippa's mother became worried and took to watching her daughter through the windows.

One day, Philippa came home more excited than usual. She told her mother that Cocchi had offered to take her riding in the sidecar of his shiny motorcycle. She asked her mother's permission.

"I refused," Madame Mureal said. "How thankful I am that I did."

Another time, Philippa went over to see if Cocchi could attach a small motor to her bicycle. Cocchi wiped his hands on his rag, looked at her bike, and said he'd do it cheap. Just for her.

"Oh, really?" said Madame Mureal, when her daughter told her.

"Yes," said Philippa. "Because he told me he likes me."

As Madame Mureal watched from the window, she saw Cocchi and her daughter go into his store. She said, "I saw Cocchi and Phil come out of the shop and go down the basement steps from the sidewalk. I thought at first that maybe the motors were kept down there, and he had taken her down there to show them to her. But suddenly I had a sort of presentment of harm, and I ran breathlessly down the six flights of stairs to the street and over to the shop. When I reached the head of the basement steps I heard Phil screaming *Mother! Mother!* I started down the stairs, calling her name, and it was not until I called with all my might that Cocchi released her and she came flying out, sobbing and shaking with terror. The sleeve of her dress had been ripped loose from the shoulder and on her arm and neck I could see the spots already turning blue from the grip of the man's fingers.

"I want all mothers to know," Madame Mureal went on to say, "how easily these things can happen. There was that man, right across the street from us, and yet he dared to commit this deed in broad daylight within a few yards of Phil's home. I wanted to go at once to the police and am sorry now that I didn't, but for Philippa's sake I moved away instead. Phil did not even then understand her danger. 'He tried to kiss me, mother' she told me and 'I became frightened.' "

She continued. "We had been following the Cruger case rather closely because Philippa had been slightly acquainted with Ruth, but it was not until I picked up a paper on Sunday and saw this Cocchi's picture that the connection dawned upon me. In fact, I had forgotten the name of the motorcycle man on Manhattan Street, until his face stared at me from the paper. I was so unnerved by the discovery that I fairly shook. I recalled that man's face on the day Philippa had rushed to me from his grasp, his leering eyes, that bestial look."

As Madame Mureal noted, "There were other girls in the neighborhood who visited that shop. Phil used to tell me what a 'nice man' Cocchi was to all the girls. As soon as I found that this Cocchi was the same man who had lured my daughter into his shop I reported the whole matter to Commissioner Woods."

As Grace took this all in, Kron looked around before dropping his voice to a hush. Kron told Grace that he had strong evidence linking Cocchi with a secret Sicilian organization, though he was not sure how deep it ran. He suspected Black Hand involvement. Kron also found out that, in 1915, Cocchi had been the roommate of a doctor who had committed suicide after being questioned by police in connection with the death of a young girl. The doctor was supposedly part of an abortion ring.

Grace had a damning point of her own to add. When first questioned about the Ruth Cruger disappearance, Cocchi had several deep scratches on his arms and face. This had never shown up in any of the early testimony or news pieces except on an evidence card that Grace had seen. They knew this was possibly very telling. Of course, given what they were finding out about Cocchi's wife, the marks could just as easily have been made by her. But there was enough to focus their search now. Henry Cruger had never trusted Alfredo Cocchi. Now, neither did Grace.

Kron pulled out the newspaper clipping that included a few photographs of Alfredo Cocchi. He was handsome. In one, his chin was at a slight angle as he regarded the camera, almost defying it. In another, the thickness of the print and of his eyebrows made his eyes look like dark stains. In another photo, he wore a hood, with the slightest of smiles. They were seeing someone new now. Something worse. And he had been under their faces the whole time.

"This man," Grace said, "should have been behind bars years ago."

"We'll make up for that," said Kron.

As they sat there at the table, these crimes they had spoken of seemed to sift through the air between all the happy, hungry people around them. They—Grace and Kron—had their own secret now. But they needed evidence to catch him. They needed to get into that mysterious cellar. Grace thought for a moment and then asked Kron a very bizarre question.

She asked him if he knew how to fix a motorcycle.

That night, Kron took out some ragged clothes and puzzled over a borrowed motorcycle repair manual. He stayed up late, with the aid of coffee and light, trying to figure out how to fix an all-chain drive.

The next morning, Kron knocked on the door at Cocchi's store. When Maria Cocchi answered, Kron told her that he was here for the job. She looked him over and then asked what experience he had.

"Several years," replied Kron quickly, looking her directly in the eyes.

"Then get to work," Mrs. Cocchi said. "Clean out that clogged gasoline on the red one first."

Kron paused for a second. He had never monkeyed with a motorcycle before. He had a car of his own and could tinker it up all right, but he'd have to experiment with the cycle. And he hated these clothes. But she was standing right there, watching him.

"What are you standin' there?" she said. Kron heard her emphasis on "there" and looked down at his feet. He was standing on an iron grating that had hot air blowing up from the cellar. It was late spring, so there should be no need for heat, Kron thought. He wondered if there was equipment down there.

"Why I'm looking for a place to hitch my coat," said Kron, stalling.

Mrs. Cocchi pointed with her thumb to a nail on the wall. As he hung up his coat, Kron asked, "Is there any other helper here, ma'am, if you don't mind me askin'?"

"I do mind you askin'," Maria answered, mimicking him. "Don't ask so many damn questions!"

For a week, Julius J. Kron, the Hungarian detective who could not be bribed, fumbled and bluffed his way through motorcycle repairs as Maria Cocchi watched over him like a hawk. Kron would commit the bikes' maladies to heart, learn how to fix them at night by reading the manuals, and try to put this knowledge into effect the next day. He had surprising success. The more daunting exercise was dealing with Mrs. Cocchi.

All the while, Kron reported back to Grace everything he was learning about the shop. They would meet at her office or in hotels, and he would pass on the information. The one-story building itself was largely taken over by motorcycles, most of their repairs now far overdue. There was a workshop in the cellar, but it was only accessible through the outside stairs in the front. Mrs. Cocchi never let him go near there, Kron told Grace. Whenever he needed tools, Mrs. Cocchi would bring them up herself. Kron didn't think she trusted him, or anyone, for that matter.

Grace had also hired a young female detective named Marie Vanello to gain Mrs. Cocchi's confidence. Grace had her rent a room from Mrs. Cocchi, who was obviously in dire need of cash. Kron would see Marie sometimes, in passing, but would not acknowledge her. Grace's plan looked very promising. Her people had already closed in around Mrs. Cocchi, who suspected nothing.

On the fifth day of Kron's new job as a mechanic, a customer brought in a motorcycle that needed three of the front wheel spokes replaced. All Kron needed to do was to solder it—but the equipment was in the basement. Without pause, Kron began to put on his hat and coat. Mrs. Cocchi stopped him.

"Where you going now?" she asked.

"The smithy. To get these spokes soldered."

"You don't need to go to no smithy," Mrs. Cocchi said. "I'll take you down-stairs and you can use the heater there."

Kron put his hat and coat back on the tack. He made sure to control his breathing and his eyes. Mrs. Cocchi wiped her hands, and he followed her outside the shop. At the front sidewalk there were four steps that led down to the cellar. As Mrs. Cocchi remained standing on top to watch the store, Kron jumped down. Mrs. Cocchi kept an eye on Kron as he went inside.

When Kron entered the basement, he tried to take it all in as quickly as possible. There was no lavish furnished space or medieval dungeon; there was only a workbench, a massive tool chest, some rags in a corner, and the slick smell of motor oil. There were two windows facing the front small alley. Kron scanned the wooden boards on the floor for new damage or shiny bright nails. But even the dust was uniform. Kron knew that the police had already searched this room twice. It certainly looked like it.

"Don't you see the heater there in front of you?" Mrs. Cocchi shouted from the stairs. There was a pause. Kron looked around again for a footprint or a scuff—anything. He started searching the back wall when he realized he had taken too long. "Never mind, come on up," Mrs. Cocchi said, quickly. "Take the spokes to the smithy." At that moment, Mrs. Cocchi's high-pitched voice convinced Kron of two things. One, there must be some kind of tiny clue in that basement, and, two, that the jig was up.

Kron grabbed the spokes and scrambled up the stairs. He could hear a customer in the shop upstairs. Maybe she just didn't want him in the cellar unattended. Maybe there was nothing down there after all. The tools were valuable, but not as valuable as what he was looking for. There was no secret cell or hiding place. Or at least he had not seen one. It was just an ordinary cellar. Maybe Mrs. Cocchi hadn't noticed the length of his absence. But when he came up the stairs, he saw her eyes locked on him. He instantly knew that his time down there had been too obvious.

"I know you now!" she shouted. "You're another one of those detectives that chased poor Al away—you're no mechanic! You're hounding after him still even after—." She broke down, crying. "Get out! Get out!"

As Kron was pushed out into the street, he now understood what Grace had been telling him this whole time. There had to be some clue in the cellar. The plan had worked beautifully until he got in that basement and blown his cover. He had failed her. Kron slouched and sighed and walked away from the store, back toward square one.

That week, a half-Indian prisoner in the Tombs banged his cup against the bars and said he had something to tell the police. His name was Stephen Smith and he said that Cocchi had hired him a few months ago to haul away a huge pile of dirt he had dug out of his cellar. Smith, who had been in jail since April, said that Cocchi also asked him a very strange question.

"Don't you want to go to Mexico?" Cocchi had said, according to Smith. "Dozen of pretty American girls have been taken down there." Grace was interested in the lead, until Smith tried to commit suicide and refused to speak anymore.

This was hardly the first time someone had brought up white slavery with regard to Ruth Cruger. But now Grace was beginning to think it might be more than just a rumor. In fact, she'd been following a thread of this on her own. She called Kron into her office. He was still disappointed over his performance at the store, but Grace didn't have time for spilled milk. She wanted to get him back in the game. Grace told Kron she had another lead for him, a person of interest who might have actually seen Ruth Cruger.

"She says that she was lured last winter by the leader of a gang of South American white slavers," Grace said. "She says she may have been in Cocchi's cellar. I want you to talk with her."

Grace sensed Kron's hesitation. Not only had his pride been wounded by being exposed by Mrs. Cocchi, but, Grace knew, he hated white slavery cases. Half the time they weren't real, Kron always said; when they were, they were impossible to prosecute.

"Listen to her story before you jump to any conclusion," Grace pleaded.

The detective still wavered. Kron looked like he wanted to jump on a boat to Italy and just shoot Cocchi for putting them through this.

"Don't be hard-boiled, Kronnie. Have a little patience with her. She has been through some horrible experiences."

Kron finally agreed. Grace called the witness and arranged for her to come into the office later that day. When she did, Kron sat her facing the light. He studied her. She was brunette and pretty.

"I don't know just where to begin," said Consuelo La Rue, who was dark in complexion and had a Spanish accent prowling on the edges of her words. Kron remembered that Cocchi once lived in the Spanish section. There might be something here after all. Kron studied her more carefully. She had rouge on her lips. He could tell she was one of the new generation of girls who shopped and traveled without an escort and was of the age and disposition to attend dances on the roof of the Astor Hotel, which lasted through the evening and well into the next morning.

"Well, begin at the beginning," Kron said. "Where did you meet the man who lured you to Cocchi's cellar?"

"At my dressmaker's, on West Fifty-eighth Street."

La Rue proceeded to tell the story of how she had met a handsome man of Spanish nobility. His full name was the Count de Clemens, but she called him "the count." Kron noted that she told the story with some hesitation but no embarrassment. And there were certainly plenty of counts in the city these days.

The count was perfectly charming and invited her to tea at the Plaza. They had several dates before he finally invited her to his apartment on West Fifty-eighth Street between Fifth and Sixth Avenues. "I went to meet his uncle," La Rue said. "He was a most aristocratic-looking gentleman with white hair."

"What happened next?" asked Kron. Now he was getting interested. The uncle game was well known among detectives. It was a common graft where a man posing as the uncle of the initial suitor would sweep in to request money, kidnap the girl, or worse.

"We had a glass of wine," La Rue said. Afterward, the count called his chauffeur and offered to drive her home. She agreed, but then things took a terrible turn.

"The wine must have been drugged," she said. "I woke up in that dreadful cellar."

Kron looked right into her eyes. He noticed a distinct lack of horror in La Rue's voice. But he remembered the Mureal girl and listened with an open mind.

"I managed to escape by giving the man who acted as guard all the jewels I was wearing at the time." She sat motionless before Kron.

"Will you please describe the cellar," Kron requested.

Her hands clasped together. "I can't tell you anymore. Those white slavers, señor—they will kill me."

Kron glanced across the office to see if Grace was with a client. He saw a black sliver of her through the door, seated and alone. Kron excused himself and passed into her office.

"Well, Kronnie, what did I tell you?" Grace asked. "She wouldn't tell me her address, but I knew you would get it out of her, and find out who this count was."

"She is either mentally unbalanced or a drug addict," Kron said.

"That may be so," Grace agreed. "But I believe that girl has some information we want, and I mean to find out. Try to get her address."

Kron took down the address and sent La Rue home. The next time they met, at a restaurant, Kron asked her to more fully describe the secret room where she had been held.

"It was beautifully furnished in rich Oriental style," said La Rue, speaking with an obvious effort. "Divans and little cot beds, deep-piled carpets, softly shaded lamps. There were two very beautiful girls there. I promised to go back for them. . . ." She paused. "But I didn't and for that I deserve to be punished."

Kron studied her. "I'll tell you what we'll do," he said. Kron told her that they would take the subway uptown. But they could not talk or act like they knew each other. She nodded.

"We'll get off the train at 125th near Cocchi's," Kron said. "I want you to walk ahead of me. When you are opposite the place you believe to be Cocchi's cellar, drop your handkerchief."

"Will you do that?"

She nodded yes.

When they got into the square, steel train, Kron grabbed one of the fat, looped tan handles above. As the train clacked forward, Kron absently read the ads for folding Brownie cameras and refreshing Coca-Cola. La Rue sat on the longitudinal seating as they rattled across the bridge. The trains, though new, had already carved their own necessary space for internal theater. People thought about people and destinations, never the train or ride itself. Many riders thought of the Mineola millionaire August Belmont's alleged private car, clad in mahogany and silk mulberry drapes, hidden somewhere on the IRT. People wondered if it existed, or if it was a part of their own train, in secret down the rail. Kron thought of La Rue's sensational story. It sounded like something out of *Arabian Nights*.

When they got off at West 125th, Kron held back, giving La Rue time for a head start just in case anyone was watching. But not too far. The sidewalks were busy, making it difficult to stay together. As Kron made the turn onto the street, he saw La Rue walking briskly toward Cocchi's shop. Her walk reflected her stories. There were a few people gathered outside of it, as was the norm these days given all the news in the papers. Kron looked around. He had to make sure he didn't run into Mrs. Cocchi, so he dipped his hat and let the shadows pull him. He looked ahead for La Rue.

When she reached Cocchi's shop, La Rue kept walking. Without a glance or a moment's hesitation, she kept going. Kron picked up his pace. Not taking his eyes off her, he grabbed the arms of Tom Fay, one of his men who was stationed near Cocchi's place as a watcher. Kron ordered him to follow La Rue all night, no matter what happened next. He pointed her out with his finger. Fay nodded. Kron then sprinted and overtook La Rue, pulling her into a doorway.

"Why didn't you drop the handkerchief?" Kron asked.

"Because someone was watching me," she whispered. "I know my cellar was where all those people were standing."

Kron knew this was a lie. He had been in that cellar, and there were no pillows or silk for miles. There could be no grand adjoining chambers, either. Next door lived an old Irish lady named Mrs. Donnelly, a churchwoman, and on the other side was a very respectable family with many children.

"You are all unstrung," Kron said. "Come over to this candy shop," he said, motioning to the establishment on the corner. "Have a malted milk. That will do you good."

"Oh, I couldn't let you do that," La Rue said, pulling away. "They would kill me." She looked around in a frightened manner. "I think I had better go now." She turned to leave.

Kron thought fast. "While you are drinking it," Kron added. "I will go into one of the telephone booths and report." Kron could tell that she had been racking her mind for a getaway. She agreed.

Kron showed her into the corner candy store. There were rows of Goo-Goos, Heath Bars, Turtles, and white Life Savers. A young woman with untidy blond hair and a grimy apron waited on them. When she came back with their order, she delicately planted two glasses of malted milk on the marble-topped table. La Rue gave a shudder. This place was clearly not one of her usual haunts. La Rue looked from the drink to Kron. To save her further embarrassment, Kron excused himself and went toward a telephone booth.

After Kron had given a telephone number, he glanced toward the spot where he had left La Rue. She was already gone. As soon as the connection was put through, Kron described the results of his up-town journey to Grace.

"She is another irresponsible person," Kron said, furiously. "One of those border-line psychopathic cases." Kron hung up.

That evening, Kron's man called to tell him that he was successful in tailing La Rue after she had left the candy shop. She was living in a shabby tenement house on West Fifty-eighth Street. Tom reported that she had lived there several months and was regarded as something of a mystery by her less eccentric neighbors. Kron was surprised. He wondered why a woman of her apparent breeding—and he was convinced of that—was living in a slum. What was she hiding? Kron checked his watch. It was never too late for detective work.

Kron rang the janitor's bell at La Rue's building. The door was answered by a shaggy-haired giant of a man. He had blond hair and light-colored eyes. Posing as a credit investigator, Kron asked him questions about La Rue but received only silence. Kron handed the man a good-size greenback and explained whom he was looking for.

"She is of medium height, slender, a Spanish type, and dresses very well," Kron said. "She has rung up bills at the largest stores and has given as her references the names of prominent Spanish counts and barons. Now, that money is yours if you know her."

Kron could tell that the janitor had eyes for La Rue.

"Miss La Rue knows a great many barons and counts," the janitor said. Kron heard a distinctive Slovakian accent in his words. "They used to come very often right here to this house," continued the janitor, "driving up in their rich limousines. Without doubt she is the lady you seek. If she used another name—that is her affair." Kron handed the janitor the money and suggested there was more, but only if he had more to say.

The janitor obliged. He said that many fancy-looking men, most of them exotic in nature, had visited La Rue. Many of the other residents were convinced that she was a princess in disguise. More than once the sound of violent quarreling was heard. Or something like it. La Rue had few women friends, but once or twice young girls had been her guests for short periods. The large janitor didn't recall that she had been recently missing. Kron walked away from the tenement house and made a call to Grace from the corner. He had no more desire to talk to Consuelo La Rue. Her life was an act, and she was a distraction. They needed to get into Cocchi's basement.

The next day, Kron went to see Deputy Police Commissioner Guy Scull about getting into the cellar. Scull was a step below Woods, but he still had power in the department. A Harvard man, Scull had been a Rough Rider with Roosevelt, a treasure hunter in the Caribbean, and followed Buffalo Jones deep into Africa. When Scull was married in 1914, he told Woods he would be back to work that same day. "If you are," said Woods, "I'll fire you."

"I'm sorry, but I don't see what I can do for you, Mr. Kron," Scull said. "The building was searched through by this Department and nothing at all was discovered. I am perfectly willing to do anything I can to help you out, but the only thing I can suggest is that you get some corroborative evidence, and apply to the Magistrate of Washington Heights for a search warrant. If you want men to aid you in the search, you may call on the Captain of the Fourth Branch and tell him you talked this over with me."

Kron went back to Grace. Together, they got to Magistrate Green's office just after noon. He was about to go out for lunch. Green invited them in and listened, his stomach rumbling, as they told him about the cellar, the boy Herbert, and everything else.

"The police have been all through there," Green explained, sighing. "I'm afraid I can't give you one unless you have new evidence."

But that was the whole problem. Grace was positive in her mind that there was something there that might provide a clue to where Ruth was, but she was also mindful that there was always a chance that they wouldn't find anything. They could be sued by Mrs. Cocchi for several hundred thousand dollars in damages. They would be made fools.

"Talk about the cup of Tantalus," Kron sighed.

"I wish I could do something," Green said. "But the only suggestion I can make—and it isn't an official one—is that you ask Captain Alonzo Cooper of the Fourth Branch Detective and see if you can bluff an entrance."

When they visited Cooper, the next desk in line of the men who were in power, Grace implored the captain. "I've simply got to go over each inch myself in order to satisfy myself that I am overlooking nothing," she said, somewhat uncharacteristically. "Just give me two men to help me search the place." They were desperate. Cooper surprised them with his answer.

"I'll go with you myself."

For the first time in days, Grace felt like she might be able to get her investigator into that basement. Mrs. Cocchi wouldn't dare try any of her tantrums on the captain. He was a tall, majestic chap, six foot five, exceedingly handsome with a military bearing.

Maria Cocchi met them on the street. Her eyes focused on Kron.

"You back again. You won't get in here." Then she turned to Grace.

"You, Mrs. Humiston?" she asked.

"Yes," Grace replied.

"You snooping around long time."

Grace and Kron dropped back as Cooper doffed his hat, opened his arms a bit, and smiled as he talked nicely to Mrs. Cocchi. After their conversation, he returned, shaking his head.

"It is useless," Cooper said. "She has evidently seen a lawyer and knows her rights."

They all stood in silence, looking at the building.

"What is the place next door?" Kron asked, pointing to the left.

"That's an old gin-mill," Cooper said. "The place beneath was a gambling dive; it used to be raided every week or so. If you want to scout around there, I'll give you a couple of men."

Grace thought his voice sounded almost too kind. But the history of the building was interesting and possibly a lead. Cooper replaced his hat and told Kron to hang around. He promised to send Detective McGee to help him. As Cooper left, Grace walked down the street. Things had changed. Kron had had his cover blown and other leads had turned up cold. Grace saw the busy candy store on the corner near Cocchi's store, the one where Kron took La Rue.

Grace thought about Kron's comparing this all to the cup of Tantalus. He was always a surprise. In mythology, Tantalus was invited to Zeus's table, where he overindulged and stole the food of the gods, sharing it with mortal people. In an attempt to make amends, Tantalus killed his own son, chopped him up in a pot, and served him to the gods as a sacrifice. The gods were most displeased. As punishment, Tantalus had to stand in a pool of water in the underworld beneath a tree filled with luscious, dangling fruit. Every time Tantalus reached up for a bite, or scooped a hand below to slake his thirst, the fruit or water eluded him. It was a myth, or more like a lesson, about needs versus wants. The cup of Tantalus was an actual drinking vessel that embodied the same lesson. If overfilled, the cup would cause the liquid to disappear completely from the cup. Grace was as frustrated by the clues she was getting in this case as she would be drinking from such a container. Everything led back to that store—every story, every clue, and every imagined footprint—and Grace was frustrated that she couldn't get in to search it herself. The overflow of clues notwithstanding, the trail had run dry.

But the cup wasn't really magic. It was invented by the ancients as a practical joke—or perhaps as a way of keeping their servants from stealing their wine. There was a hidden space inside the base where the liquid was held. The cup cheated. Grace knew someone was cheating here, too.

They needed to do the same.

11

A Door to the Underworld

Julius Kron and Detective McGee, who told Kron to call him Frank, searched and dug through the old building next to Metropolitan Motorcycles for a week, but all they found was garbage and dirt. Everything stuck to everything else, and the dust clouded the air. When Kron and McGee would come back out onto the street, it looked as if the building itself was swaying in the heat. Nothing seemed completely certain here.

As they came up empty-handed, day after day, Kron chomped his cigars, and McGee's massive body was drenched in sweat. The neighborhood hawks would poke their heads out of their windows and jeer at the unlikely pair. Many of them were friends of the Cocchis.

"Don't mind them, Kron," McGee said, tucking his tie into his shirt. "We'll have the laugh on them all yet." But that laugh seemed a long way off.

Meanwhile, Grace had opened up a temporary headquarters in the back of the candy store on the corner. She knew they had to be as close as possible to Cocchi's store in case an opening presented itself. Grace told Kron to hire some local day laborers to be at the ready in the candy store. They sat there with picks and shovels leaned against the wall, eating Squirrel Nut Zippers and popping Necco wafers.

Mrs. Cocchi was still barring any entry to the motorcycle shop so they drank Jersey Creme sodas, biding their time.

After a week of digging, Kron stood with McGee outside Cocchi's place, both of them sore and weary. Kron was at least glad he could wear his wool pants again. As he looked down, he noticed the lid of a coal chute, large and heavy. He followed its invisible trail under the sidewalk and stopped.

"Frank," Kron said, stooping down to lift the lid.

McGee saw the same invisible trajectory in his mind. This chute emptied into the vault under Cocchi's sidewalk to deliver the coal. Right next to the cellar. McGee helped Kron open the iron circle to see a dark entranceway. Kron lit a match and saw some coal lining a tunnel of darkness. As guessed, it looked as if it ran down under the sidewalk at a slow angle. He ran his fingers through the coal. It was mixed with dirt. Kron lit another match and saw flecks of something in the black, flaky substance. Chloride? Lime? Kron started to move his hand in when the shadow of Mrs. Cocchi appeared over him.

"Steady there, Mrs. Cocchi," said Frank in a soft voice.

"This is a public highway," Kron shouted, scrambling to his short, full height. He had finally had enough. "I am at perfect liberty to go down there—and I'm going. Frank, arrest her if she makes any more monkey-shines. Right now give me a lift down this chute."

Mrs. Cocchi narrowed her eyes but retired to the door of her shop. She knew that Kron was right—he was technically on public property. She watched them from the doorway.

Kron shifted himself down the narrow chute as McGee stood up top. Inside, Kron saw more of the white specks on the walls, though just little flecks here and there. The floor was lost in what looked like several feet of newly dug earth. Kron tried to clear the floor with his feet, then more hurriedly with his hands and arms. He turned black as night. As Kron lit his last match, he felt something hard under the floor. As the match sputtered out, Kron's eyes widened.

"What have you found down there?" asked McGee.

Kron was covered with black coal, and he was worn and hollow-eyed, but his smudged face wore a look of satisfaction. "What we've been looking for," he said. Kron instructed McGee to get everyone down here at once. And to bring a searchlight. McGee left, leaving the lid open, letting in a beam of hot sun.

A few moments later, the lid clanged closed and Kron was again shut in darkness.

He heard a laugh and realized that Mrs. Cocchi had sneaked over and replaced the lid on the street. It was dark and quiet and there was a door beneath his feet, and he had no idea where it went. He listened to the scampering of something and hoped that Frank would come back soon.

※

"Hey, are you there, Kron? What the devil happened?" It was McGee, pulling open the lid. Some time had passed, though McGee had only gone up the street to the candy store.

"Mrs. Cocchi," Kron replied, disgusted. "Get the men down here as fast as you can before I pass out."

Grace walked up to the opening and looked down, amazed. There was a door set in the bottom of the dirt. It was battered and almost destroyed, but it was a door. They brushed off the dirt and coal and lifted it up before setting it into a corner. It was not on any hinges. But it did cover an oblong hole, a vault, six feet by six feet, which someone had broken into the cement floor. The flash lamps glinted at its rounded corners.

"Bully for you, Kronnie," Grace said.

After her detective was hoisted out, Grace told everyone to hold tight and wait at the candy store. She then went to the borough president, then the Bureau of Sidewalks and Vaults to apply for the right to tunnel under the sidewalk through the coal vault. She knew there would be a legal question over this eventually, and she wasn't going to take any chances. Grace also asked around to see who the plumber was who had installed the pipes in the cellar.

"He's dead," said Mrs. Cocchi.

But Grace didn't believe it; she still suspected that Mrs. Cocchi always knew more than she was saying. After searching through building permits and talking to construction company officials, Grace indeed found the plumber. He gave Grace a diagram of the building, but it didn't have what she was looking for—a way into that damned cellar. Grace had to think.

When Grace returned, she walked past the candy store and made a quick, prearranged sign with her hands. The two laborers, Peter McAntee and John Spittle, saw her through the window. They grabbed their tools.

As they turned the corner, they walked directly down to the motorcycle shop in a group. For the first time, there was no subterfuge. They were going in under Grace's direction. Mrs. Cocchi appeared with her baby in her arms and shouted, "Where are you going?" Just as her men approached the coal chute with their tools, Grace reached into her dress and waved the permit she had just obtained from the borough president in Mrs. Cocchi's face. People from the neighborhood began to gather and point. Grace gave the order, and the flash lamps lit an area almost too narrow for a child.

Mrs. Cocchi returned to her chair in front of the store. Defeated, she sank into it. But then she started smiling. She began bouncing her baby on her knee.

"They won't find anything," Mrs. Cocchi said, to anyone who would listen.

"They're crazy."

Grace and her men found nothing that first day except for more of the white substance that looked a bit like plaster. It had finally been identified as quicklime, which Kron had suspected all along. Later in the day, a sudden downpour of rain forced all the onlookers to head for cover inside Cocchi's shop. There they stood, in the cool store, looking at the silent, single-eyed motorcycles. Grace gave the order for the men to come up out of the watery vault before it flooded. Grace politely asked Mrs. Cocchi if her men might use the inside door to the coal cellar by the front stairwell. Maria politely refused.

As the rain blew down, the men had to be drawn out by rope, dripping wet, through the filthy outdoor chute. All of the people on the street felt worn out and cold. This grand display of digging was, like everything else thus far, an endeavor that led to nothing but more empty space. There was no evidence to be seen. Grace, wet, grimly vowed that digging "would be resumed to-morrow."

The next morning, the police department put a hold on Grace's promise until they could figure out if her permit was actually legal. By late afternoon, the assistant corporation counsel agreed that the borough could authorize such an action—the opening of the vault underneath the sidewalk—but only if there was no permit for its presence in the first place. The underground of New York was still relatively uncharted. Just as the city built up, some saw the world beneath as an untapped resource for train tunnels and living space. Some forward thinkers dreamed of pneumatic tubes swooshing passengers out to Coney Island. A permit for the vault was searched for, but none was found. So at five o'clock, the police obtained a digging permit from the commissioner of public works to allow Grace and her men to keep digging.

The next day, June 13, the skies had cleared, and it was hot again, though the rains had helped loosen the earth a little bit. As Kron, McGee, and his laborers dug, one of their flashlights caught something shiny. They fished out a tin sign, just like the ones hanging outside the motorcycle shop. It looked brand new. Then they hit an oil can. Then another sign. Kron pulled out a huge empty gasoline tin. These artifacts came out of the pit and were carefully placed to the side.

The next thing they found was a newspaper. They handed it up to Grace. It was an Italian paper dated July 15, 1916, almost one year earlier. At the bottom of the hole were hard, dark stones. They tried the pickaxes, but they just sparked against the rocks. They tried to lift the stones out, but they were too heavy. So they got a block and tackle from the toolbox and hooked it up. The men threaded the rope through the pulleys and worked them out, back and forth. Eventually, the stones came up and out and into the air. The men piled them into the corner. They looked into the blackness and saw something small. It was white.

The thing looked like a flower. Once it was free, they passed it up to Grace. She shook it loose as clumps of dirt fell to the ground. It was small and light. She turned it over in her hands lightly and recognized it as an embroidered corset cover, once beautiful, now crumpled and dirty. It had not been long in the ground. Their stomachs were in their mouths.

Someone shouted. They had found something else. Kron lifted the small object out and stared, speechless. He brought it up to Grace, slowly. It was a small piece of rounded, discolored bone. Grace turned it in her hand like a jewel. No one could see her face under the black hat. She handed it over to Kron. He placed it in his pocket.

As a crowd gathered to peer down the chute, Grace looked at her watch. The vault was almost completely cleared, as far as they could tell. She headed for the car. Where are you going, they asked.

A wedding, said Grace. They stared at her in disbelief. But Grace didn't care. She was already late.

Before she left, Kron spoke with her in private. "There's no guesswork there," he said. "Cocchi didn't bury a ten-gallon tin of gasoline under that load of coal for any other reason than to fill up the space."

"That hole was intended for a grave," Kron said.

There was just one problem: no one was in it.

"Station three or four guards outside the place before you leave," Grace ordered. "Give them instructions to note everyone who calls at the place and to follow anyone who leaves with any suspicious-looking bundle." Grace gave another quick look around. "So long, Kron," she said.

Some of the men couldn't understand how the lead detective on a case this big could leave for a wedding, but Kron understood. That was Mrs. Humiston.

The men kept digging until they heard the shovel hit something hard and loud. The worker tapped it.

"A box, probably," McAntee said, wiping his forehead. "Might take about half an hour to get it out." He paused. "But it's 5 o'clock now and my quitting time."

They seemed so close now to what everyone was thinking, but no one was talking about. This wasn't a secret chamber. It wasn't an elaborate hiding place. It was a hole in the ground. It was something they didn't want to say.

"No," said Kron. "It will take a good four hours to get that box out—if there is one—at the rate we've been digging to-day. Better call it a day's work, and we'll go at it again in the morning."

When they emerged into that late afternoon light, McGee went last, padlocking the chute. By this time, real crowds had gathered in the streets about the shop, and the police had thrown a cordon of lights around the cellar entrance. Someone made an announcement to the crowd, which had grown with each passing hour. The crowd groaned and murmured, some among them even offering to pay for the workers' overtime. There were plenty of reporters. But Kron was adamant. He was not authorized to pay for any overtime.

"I'm bossing the job," he kept saying.

"What are you going to do now?" McGee asked. "We're on the right track, I'm telling you."

"We could go ahead and dig," Kron said. "But I'm hungry and awfully tired."

Kron wasn't lying. But he wasn't completely telling the truth, either.

Kron was indeed hungry, and certainly tired, but he was by no means off the clock. So after leaving his partners and workers, Kron worked his night hours. That was the only time he could get any real work done by himself. McGee was all right, for a cop, but Kron had some things that he had to do for Grace first. So Kron took the bone over to Doctor Alling of Columbia University.

"Those are butcher's bones," the doctor said. "Nothing human about them. But they are very fresh. Apparently somebody is trying to play a trick on you."

Reached at the wedding, Grace didn't seem surprised. "We expect to go on with the excavation in the Cocchi cellar to-morrow. That cellar has been under suspicion for some time, and it should have been dug up a long time ago." Privately, Grace was wondering if they might be able to legally tunnel all the way into the actual cellar through the sidewalk vault.

"Naw, the whole place would fall down," said the plumber she called up. "You'd have to get a mason or buy the place," he joked. When Grace talked to Kron on the phone for the last time that night, she said, "Meet me outside Cocchi's cellar to-morrow. To-morrow will write the finish to the Cruger mystery."

But Kron still had one more task to accomplish. He had put it off long enough. He took the corset cover, which was just a scrap of a thing, and took it over to the Crugers' apartment. It weighed more heavily in his pocket than it should have. Mrs. Cruger was too ill to look at it for more than a moment. Mr. Cruger stared at it for a very long time. He said he was sure that the apparel had not belonged to his daughter. Going home, Kron wondered. They had labored long in the earth and found things that meant nothing. Kron felt as if someone was mocking them.

The next day, Kron was still tracking down leads as Grace used their newly unearthed discoveries to convince Swann to open an immediate investigation of Alfredo Cocchi by the grand jury. Grace was still intent at getting to the actual cellar. After reading of the so-called horrors found in the vault yesterday, a substantial crowd had already gathered outside the motorcycle shop. There were men in suits and white straw hats. There were children, too—pushed up to the front, their fathers' hands pressed flat against their chests.

From down the street, Kron, McGee, and their two workers headed toward Cocchi's store. Grace was nowhere to be found—she was presumably at court—but had left instructions with Kron to try to negotiate an entrance that didn't involve the coal chute. Kron held up a hand and walked to the front door. He needed to get the cellar keys from Mrs. Cocchi. After he knocked, he saw her on the other side, separated by the dark glass. With a grand jury opening an investigation and all the things they had found, Kron thought she might be willing to finally bury the hatchet. She was, but not in the way he hoped.

Mrs. Cocchi opened the door with a hammer in her hand.

"Get out of here, or I'll throw this hammer at you!" she shouted, her eyes flashing.

Kron stopped in his tracks. She raised the black mallet high above her head.

"I don't care if the whole Police Department and a regiment of soldiers came here! No more digging in my cellar!" She pushed forward and Kron ran back to the sidewalk.

"She told me to get out," Kron told McGee. "She won't give up the keys."

McGee looked at Mrs. Cocchi from the street and thought he might as well give it a try. He walked up, and she actually let him inside the store. Kron watched closely through the glass. They could see McGee show Mrs. Cocchi his badge, shiny and solid. Mrs. Cocchi looked flushed and waved her hands. McGee trudged out, defeated. Apparently, there would be no digging today. They weren't going to fight her in the streets. Kron had to tell Grace. A grand jury investigation didn't mean they had a warrant for anything.

That afternoon, Aaron Marcus, who was Mrs. Cocchi's attorney, issued a statement that said any further excavations would be refused because the crowd that had gathered frightened away prospective customers.

"Mrs. Cocchi's attitude is not an unfriendly one," said Marcus. "She has helped the authorities with the investigation in the past."

By five o'clock, Grace had arrived on the scene with good news. The Commissioner of Public Works had granted her a full digging permit, including the cellar. Grace's men resumed their work in the dirt. The so-called "box" was just another sign. But before they could get any further, Grace was summoned back to court for obstructing the sidewalk with the big pile of dirt that her men had been unearthing. Grace knew that Mrs. Cocchi's lawyer was behind the complaint.

He was good. Grace hired wagons, on her own dime, to cart away the soil. But then the court summoned her again, saying that the dirt had belonged to the landlord and couldn't be removed without her say-so. Grace was ordered to return it. For the rest of the week, Grace went back and forth between the bench and Cocchi's shop. The workers waited in the candy shop. Nothing was getting done. By Friday, at the end of another long week, the court ordered her to stop digging altogether by the end of Saturday.

City officials were not being helpful. Deputy Police Commissioner Scull said of Ruth and Cocchi that "there was no connection between their disappearances." "There was no such thing as abduction," Scull said to reporters. He had never seen it happen before.

"No one has ever disappeared in such a manner in New York," agreed Captain Cooper.

That night, Grace went back to her office. It was now the middle of June and almost three months' hard work had gone for nothing. They had expended all this time and work tunneling toward a small basement that the police had already searched at least twice. Even Kron had found nothing in his brief time down there. They had found some things under the sidewalk, but nothing even remotely conclusive. Were they grasping at straws? At nothingness? Cocchi himself was halfway around the world. That night, Henry Cruger visited Grace, as he did every night, anxious for the day's report. They sat around her office, now quiet, not knowing what to do or say. They had less than a day before the digging permit expired.

A thought occurred to Grace that if a building inspector could look over the basement, he might find something they overlooked that could translate to a real, honest-to-goodness warrant. Henry Cruger piped up that he knew an inspector named Paddy Solan who worked in the Erie Railroad offices. Solan was summoned to the office and agreed to help. He had an Irish accent and wore a suit that seemed strapped to the shoulders of his short, thin frame. As they worked up a plan, Grace went to make a few more calls.

The next morning, on Saturday, Solan, disguised as a laborer (at Grace's suggestion), followed Kron and McGee to the cellar. Grace was late, as usual, but Kron knew they had only so much time left before their permit expired. He looked at his watch. The streets were clear so they started without her. They looked at the door, which was locked, and the stairs, which were now impassable because of all the dirt and debris. They would have to go through the coal chute.

Solan, because he was short, went down through the sidewalk first and into the vault. He was surprised by all the dirt that had been dug up. When he got to the basement door leading to the cellar, he shouted up to the street and asked McGee if he could go in. McGee stuck his head in and told him to hold on; there was something going on outside.

Up on the street, Kron stared at the front of the motorcycle store. Something was different. He had been looking at that store for so many weeks now that even the slightest difference was glaring. Then Kron saw it—Mrs. Cocchi had taken away the SELLING OUT sign. Kron asked around the crowd. Someone said she had sold it to an auctioneer. One of the diggers groaned. A new owner could make things infinitely worse for them, especially if it meant the property would have to go through a lengthy auction procedure first. Some wondered if it wasn't a ploy to get out from under the permit that was expiring today. Or perhaps Mrs. Cocchi knew what was coming and wanted to make herself scarce. Normally, she would be watching over them like a hawk. Kron looked around. She was nowhere.

But Kron, who had spent some time around very smart people the past years, saw a brilliant plan at work. By selling her store, Maria Cocchi could now make the case that Grace's digging had ruined her sole means of income. She would then have a good case when she sued Grace—and perhaps Kron—for trashing her store. This might be Maria Cocchi's last-ditch attempt at cashing out before she had nothing—destroying her enemies in the process. Kron guessed that this would probably put a halt on their permit until the property changed hands. They would be stuck yet again.

Grace finally arrived, customarily late, and Kron rose to tell her the bad news. She saw the men sitting in the dirt and dust. Grace pointed for them to get down there.

Into her basement.

While they had been digging under the sidewalk, Grace had contacted Edward Lind and Charles Greenbaum, the real estate auctioneers in charge of selling the Cocchi store. For weeks, Grace had been using her secretly planted aide, Marie Vanello, to try to urge Mrs. Cocchi to put her house on the market. When she finally did, Grace immediately began the paperwork to buy it. The plan came together flawlessly, and the property was sold on June 16 to Mrs. Grace Humiston, Esq. Mrs. Cocchi had no idea. Kron smiled. At least he was right about this being a brilliant plan.

Grace couldn't make it down the narrow coal chute, so she watched as her men, with flashlights, were lowered into the vault. Entrance through the chute would be difficult and require a bit of elbow grease, but they had most of the day. So instead of staying and being useless, Grace went to her downtown office to check the morning mail. She knew that this whole process would take a good long while, and she had other work to do.

As soon as Grace walked into her office, her phone was ringing. Grace picked it up. It was Kron.

"Mrs. Humiston," her old friend said. "Hurry back here."

Grace drove as fast as she could. When she got close to the store, she stopped because of the sea of people who had come out of nowhere. It looked like a parade was going on. She stopped, got out of her car, and ran the rest of the way to the store. There had to be over a thousand people here, draped over one another, looking at something in the center of it all.

When Grace finally arrived at the store, there were reporters and people everywhere. There was a kind of ladder set up over the broken stairs. Grace, under her black hat, pushed her way into the cellar and disappeared from view.

Minutes later, when Ruth Cruger came out of that cellar, into that beautiful June afternoon, she was carried in the air by the men who had spent so long looking for her. Her body was held in a thin cardboard box, closed tight with a belt. A single dark glove lay crumpled on top of the interim coffin. As she was raised up, the men in the street took off their hats.

Their sons, watching their fathers, all did the same.

⚜

Earlier, after Grace had left for her office, the men descended into the silent cellar. Kron scrambled down first into the darkness. A single electric bulb looped down off the uneven ceiling of the basement. It sparked hot white. The brightness lit the scar on his face.

Kron ducked his head so that it missed the edge of the stone ceiling. He palmed his hat and snapped on his unlit cigar. He surveyed the entire room, looking into its webby corners.

Hello? he asked.

The room smelled of damp cement, oil, and wood. There was no furniture. The compactness of the room seemed to freeze everything. McGee and Solan followed Kron in. McGee barely fit. Solan, in overalls, was darting around. He looked at everything with purpose.

As the men moved around and kicked at the floor, it felt like an underground church.

They looked up to see a chute that reached all the way to the first floor. There should have been a flue, but it wasn't there.

There were pipes and a tin sign and some saws, but otherwise the room was empty except for a huge workbench against the wall. There was a large bag in the corner of the room that looked like quicklime. Kron stepped in slow circles on the planked flooring. They walked into the corner, where exposed brick lay against the bottom half of the wall. These New York basements were forgotten places, with everything stretching up. The down of things was always left behind. The cop started taking off his coat, then his drenched vest.

Solan examined the massive workbench. He motioned, and everyone helped him move it. They pushed it to the side and stared downward. The floorboards were gone. Instead, in the cement floor, they saw a door, set into the ground like a gate.

Kron pulled back the door and stared into a black space. He couldn't see or sense the bottom. Kron jumped straight down.

It was almost impossible to breathe. He kept going.

Several feet down he saw her.

When they lifted her out, they did so in silence and as delicately as they could. She was tied up. Her legs had been pushed up parallel to her chest, where they were tied around her body. Kron immediately cut the ropes. On her left hand he saw a ring with the initials W.H.S. Kron left to make two calls.

She had a bruise on her forehead.

After Grace came down into the basement to see the girl she had never met, she went back outside, her head in her hands. People took her picture. Henry Cruger had just arrived with Reverend Pattison and came up alongside Grace. He looked in her eyes. One of the diggers walked out of the store and held out his hand to Grace. Inside was a small wristwatch. Grace gave it to Henry. He glanced at it once, turned it over, and read the inscription on the back. He then gave it back to Grace. He whispered something to Pattison, who nodded. Then Henry turned away silently. His shoulders were drooping. As he disappeared against the grain of the crowd, he seemed barely able to walk. He had eyes, but it seemed he could no longer see.

When the late evening editions hit the street, the newspapers reported on the tragic end of the mystery. *The Brooklyn Daily Eagle* on June 17 ran the story that was being repeated across the country.

RUTH CRUGER'S BODY FOUND IN COCCHI CELLAR

The body of Ruth Cruger was found yesterday afternoon buried under a wooden flooring at the extreme rear end of the cellar, where Cocchi's work bench stood. A score of police detectives had raked the cellar over a dozen times without finding it. The discovery was made by J.J. Kron, a private detective employed by Grace Humiston.

A big wooden chest containing tools was found to be fastened to what appeared to be the dirt flooring. The dirt, however, covered a wooden flooring; to this the chest had been fastened. When the boards were pried up, Kron and Detective Frank McGee of the Fourth Branch detective bureau, who was left on the case after the other detective had been sent to other work, saw a pit three feet wide and about six feet deep. Kron jumped in before taking a good look, and then discovered that he had landed upon a body, very much decomposed.

The body was that of a girl. It was bent nearly double and the arms and legs were folded over the torso and tightly bound with rope. The skull had been crushed, as if by a hammer blow, and a towel was twisted around the neck.

The coroner removed the body, pressed several dozen witnesses into duty, and held an inquest at the nearest police station that lasted into the night. Further identification of the body was confirmed when her hat was found in the grave and pointed out by her mother at their Harlem apartment. They found a policeman's uniform as well, though it seemed old. They found Ruth's ice skates, stained dark with blood. An indictment charging Alfred Cocchi with murder was returned by the hastily summoned grand jury. Testifying were Lagarenne, McGee, Helen Cruger, Peter McAntee, and Dr. L. L. Danforth, the Cruger family physician.

Maria Cocchi was detained as a material witness. Before being taken into custody, she was allowed to go back to her home on Manhattan Street to get clothes and see her two children, who were left in the care of neighbors.

"I am amazed to learn of the discovery of the body of the missing girl in the cellar of my husband's shop," Mrs. Cocchi said. "If he killed her, he was not alone in the crime. He is too much of a coward to do anything like that by himself. I hope they bring him back here and if he is guilty I want to see him punished." The police then took Mrs. Cocchi's young daughter, who was ill, and placed her in a city facility. When Maria finally broke down, it was because of that fact: "My children's father is a murderer," she said. That night, a cable was sent from Police Commissioner Woods to Italy.

It contained two words:

HOLD COCCHI.

12

A Second Guess

They should have found that body," Mayor Mitchel said, almost to himself. He turned to face the crowd in front of him. "It is regrettable that the police did not find the body at the time they made their first search," he said, more loudly. "When a police officer searches premises and there is something that is to be found there and ought to be found and they fail to find it, there is no excuse. They should have found it," the mayor repeated. The newspapers were reporting that this was just the tip of the iceberg.

"Mrs. Humiston, they say, had some tip," a reporter said. "Why wasn't it possible for the police to get that same tip?" "I don't know," replied the mayor. "It may have been possible. Perhaps the officers assigned to the case did not do their work well enough." Someone else brought up Grace's latest claim in the papers that she knew of at least twenty-two other girls who were missing in the city. It had come out in the paper that Captain Dan Costigan had also searched the shop with his men—but nothing.

"I do not know what girls have disappeared," the mayor admitted. "If their cases have been reported to the Police Department they will be on record there."

"Do you think it calls for a shakeup in the detective department?"

"I don't express an opinion as to whether it calls for that or not,"

Mitchel said. "That is one of the things which diligent inquiry on the part of the Police Commissioner, which is now under way, will develop."

From his own perch at Command, Arthur Woods knew that he had to choose his next actions carefully. Like Mayor Mitchel, Woods could only look on as the press denounced the men under his command. People were calling for Woods to be fired. Grace had been right this whole time, thought Woods. Cocchi had taken the girl. Woods shook his head.

Woods called in Inspector Joseph Faurot. He was the detective who had sent the handsome Hans Schmidt, a priest, to the chair in 1906 for killing his pregnant housekeeper and cutting her up into slippery pieces. Woods ordered Faurot, who had been mastering the new science of fingerprinting, to do an in-depth, very public investigation of any police wrongdoing in the Cruger case.

"Spare no one," Woods growled.

The sad body of Ruth Cruger had been found, but there was still a chance to make some kind of amends. Woods knew that justice for Ruth Cruger would not happen without a great deal of work and luck. For one, they needed physical evidence that Cocchi had killed her, though no one was doubting that anymore. No one knew if Cocchi had even been arrested yet. Woods feared that he might have already fled Bologna. The possibility existed that Cocchi had even gone off to war, in which case they would probably never see him again. Cocchi could be lying in a pile of flowers somewhere in France, with dirt in his ears and mouth. Woods also got in touch with the district attorney, Edward Swann, to see if the case had any connection to the traffic in white slaves. They had the body, but there was much they didn't know.

Swann kicked the grand jury into action, which he selectively populated with several Italian delegates to avoid community backlash. Swann had been appointed by special election the previous year. He was a Tammany man, tied to the political machine named after the three-story brick building on East Fourteenth Street where Democrats had smoked victory cigars on election night since 1830. But Swann was new to the politics of the city and was also eager to prove himself. He had helped Henry Cruger earlier in his investigation, and now he was eager to do more.

※

Early the next day, people walking on the sidewalk of West Eightieth Street looked up quickly when they heard something shatter in the sky. Those who were fast enough thought they saw a pretty young woman jump through a third-floor window and fall into the vacant lot yawning between the buildings.

A beat cop on the street spun around and ran toward the space that had swallowed her. When he turned the corner, he saw a small body, in a dress, lying still on the hard ground. She started to move. She was alive. He took three shrill pulls on his whistle for help. Gray bone was protruding from her crumpled left leg.

"He's up there," she gasped, turning her head. She pointed up to the building, to the sky.

"The men," she said, seeing the cop's confused look. "One grabbed me by the throat and said 'I guess you'll not tell anymore.'"

The cop tried to quiet her as the ambulance arrived. As they pulled her onboard, the woman pulled on his hand.

"Please," she asked, "tell Mrs. Humiston." The girl was in a great deal of pain. "Two men had tried to murder me because I gave Grace Humiston information."

The woman said her name was Consuelo La Rue.

"If you only knew what I've had to go through," she said, on the way to the hospital. "They told me they'd kill me, for what I'd done."

Grace was summoned at once. When she finally arrived at the Polyclinic Hospital and was ushered into the emergency ward, her face was deadly serious. When she tried to see La Rue, Grace was told that the police were limiting her visitors. La Rue was apparently unable to tell a coherent story, and the doctors were worried about her state of mind. As Grace stood in the hall, Inspector Faurot appeared to speak to the press. He said that he was going to charge La Rue with attempted suicide, even though he admitted there was a mark on her throat as if she had been choked. Faurot also said that he had made another important discovery but thought it best to withhold it until he found substantiation. Grace was furious that the police would not permit her to even talk with La Rue and that they already seemed to be dismissing the girl's claims. Grace doubted that Faurot had even spoken with La Rue in person.

As La Rue laid in her hospital bed, Captain Cooper stood outside the door, talking with the guards. Grace walked by and stopped.

"I have absolutely nothing to say," Grace said.

"No one asked you to say anything," he replied. Only days ago these two people were helping each other. Now they were at odds. Grace knew why. The entire city was blaming the police for failing to find, and perhaps even save, Ruth Cruger. And the police, at least some of them, were blaming Grace for making them look bad.

As the press converged on the hospital, clogging up its thin halls, the assistant district attorney, Alexander Rorke, who had questioned La Rue at the hospital, said that the young lady had maintained a mysterious reserve. The police could not confirm if La Rue had any relationship to Ruth Cruger. A reporter at the hospital finally spotted Grace hanging around the back and asked her if it was true, if La Rue had given her the information needed to find Ruth Cruger.

"To answer that now would do more harm than good," Grace responded, after a moment's pause. "I feared for Miss La Rue's life. She telephoned me that her life had been threatened and I had a private detective searching for her."

That afternoon, the police reported that an examination of La Rue's apartments on the second floor of 215 West Eightieth Street revealed a broken mirror and an overturned chair, but no other signs of a struggle. Neither was there any trace of either of her mysterious visitors. There was also a calling card with a name that was found in

her room. The name was prefixed with "Count." In the hospital, La
Rue told police that when she had been kidnapped, months earlier,
two white slavers were with her, accompanied by the men. She said
that she was led to a grave and made to view the body of a girl they
said was Ruth Cruger. La Rue said that she was warned the same
thing would happen to her if she tried to escape.

La Rue was too badly injured to be questioned any further. So
Captain Cooper pulled up a chair and watched over her bedside.
Sometime later, one of his men came in and whispered in his ear
that Grace wanted to talk to him in the hall. He left La Rue's bedside
and walked into the hall. He regarded Grace, alone.

"I thank you for ordering me out," she said, referring to the earlier
incident.

"I don't understand your remark," said Cooper.

"I shall see Commissioner Woods in the morning," replied Grace.

"All right, then, I have nothing more to say to you," said Cooper.

Grace got on the phone and complained directly to Woods that
she had been ordered from the room by a captain, but Cooper denied it. Governor Whitman, who was in the city for the day and staying at the Hotel St. Regis, showed keen interest in the development
of any part of the Cruger case, including the La Rue matter, which
he intimated might eventually come before his desk. He didn't say
anything about Grace Humiston, whom he remembered quite well.

Later that night, Rorke revealed that another attempt had been
made on La Rue's life while she was recovering in the hospital. A
strange man had been seen in the hallway near her door before cops
chased him away. A rock had been thrown from the roof of an adjoining building. The attached note was in Spanish and warned that
she would be killed if she talked. The papers also reported that a
man with a gun had been detained wandering her hallway in the
hospital. The police proceeded to limit La Rue's visitors in order to
protect her against injury or intimidation. Two policemen remained
on guard at all times. The police refused to comment further, saying

only that her story strongly corroborated rumors that powerful forces were seeking to shield Cocchi, who, the day before, had been indicted in absentia for the Cruger murder. There was a rumor that Cocchi had supposedly threatened vengeance on anyone connected with his prosecution. Papers reported that Cocchi was a member of the dreaded Camorra and that its agents had made it possible for him to escape to Italy. Some of the papers were now reporting that Ruth's body had been found folded in two, with her ankles at her face. To New Yorkers with long memories, it sounded eerily like the murder of Benedetto Madonia by the Morello gang in 1903. Madonia was found stuffed in a barrel, unmercifully contorted in the same ugly way.

Grace had heard enough. "This girl is a victim of white slavery," she told the press. "She offered to help me in the Cruger case and insisted all along that I should dig up the cellar, not because she had actual knowledge of the case, but because of her knowledge of the methods of white slavers. I am satisfied that the gang that made the La Rue girl suffer tried to kill her last night. They knew she was in touch with me, and they were afraid that she would expose them after the Cruger case had been cleared up."

Grace looked at the reporters. "Not a word to-day," Grace begged them, ominously. "The publication of the La Rue girl's story means that two more girls may be killed."

The next day, a meeting occurred at the DA's office between Grace, District Attorney Dooling, and Captain Costigan to discuss La Rue. Grace conferred with Kron over dinner that night. Could that girl really have been right the whole time? Kron wondered if Grace had been following up with La Rue after he had dismissed her story. Faurot's men were digging up cellars all over the city based on La Rue's testimony. For all the girls who had gone missing in different places across the city, they had apparently never checked the basements.

"Rorke believes as I do," Grace said, "that the girl's story is true. To-morrow morning he is going to take up the matter with the Police Department. This is our great opportunity to wipe out one of the biggest gangs of these ghouls. They are going to give me a score of detectives to work on the case," Grace exclaimed. "We are going to clean out the whole rotten crowd."

Kron sat with his drink and shook his head. At his core, he was, first and foremost, a detective. And he remained skeptical of La Rue. He felt he was being led by the nose.

"That's great," replied Kron. He was glad that Grace was going to work with the police. But he still had his doubts. "I'm never keen on being mixed up with white-slave cases," Kron said. "You haven't only the trouble of getting your man, but you have the 'victims' to win over. If they won't testify, or if, as is so often the case, their testimony is declared worthless, all your labors have been for nothing."

Meanwhile, the papers had begun to recognize Grace for her solution of the Cruger case. "Mrs. Grace Humiston continues to make things hum," one reporter wrote. Henry Cruger made good on his word and gave Grace a check for one thousand dollars for finding his daughter. "I refused to accept the check and he refused to take it back," said Grace. "If he continues to refuse I shall use the money as a foundation for a fund to establish a home for girls in the country, as a memorial to Ruth Cruger."

On June 20, *The Evening World*, which had been liberal in its coverage of the Charlie Stielow case, ran the names of all the girls in the city who had gone missing since January 1 of that year. They printed eight hundred names in that edition. The list—with names like Rachael Phillips, Becky Levy, and Mary McBride—started on the front page and continued for three subsequent pages of small black type. The newspaper also urged that a fund be started to build a public monument to the fallen Ruth Cruger. The idea was first proposed by Benoni Tabijian, a news dealer who lived in the Crugers' neighborhood. "I suggest a monument over the grave," he said. He thought it should read "Ruth Cruger, died to save her honor."

As the police tried to make headway into the attempt on Consuelo La Rue's life, the mayor, on the advice of Woods, appointed a commissioner of accounts, Leonard M. Wallstein, to investigate why the police department failed to find Ruth Cruger. On June 21, Mayor Mitchel also announced that he would keep Woods on as police commissioner. "I believe the city as a whole has felt that the work of the police department was and is steadily improving," the mayor said. New Yorkers read it in disbelief.

Leonard Wallstein was the perfect man for the job of ferreting out police irregularities. For one, he was unusual in that he was not a Tammany Hall Democrat. In 1915, Wallstein investigated the city coroner system and found that most of the coroners—who were appointed, not elected—weren't even doctors, but included plumbers, musicians, and even a milkman. Wallstein found that at least half of recently filed death certificates were incomplete or wrong, making them useless to investigators. Suicides, abortions, and many murders were simply labeled "death," if they were even labeled at all. Wallstein watched coroners sip from their flasks in open court as their records amounted to nothing, sabotaging hard-fought prosecutions. Wallstein gutted the coroner's office, making many enemies in the process. Wallstein had a high, pulled-back hairline. His quick eyes pierced at his frightened subjects from behind near-invisible glasses. For the Cruger investigation, the mayor had given him the full power of a justice of the state supreme court to summon witnesses and compel testimony. Wallstein was dangerous because he was beholden to no one but the truth. The phrase he hated most was "passing the buck." He would not stand for it.

The first thing Wallstein did was to visit Cocchi's shop. He walked out the whole miserable place, now stamped down by feet and mostly empty. He worked his way to the rear room and into the basement, delicately putting his toes into corners. His silver cuff links shone in the darkness. There had been new discoveries at the shop since Ruth's body had been recovered. A list, written in Cocchi's handwriting, had been found in a desk; it was filled with the names of girls. They were ostensibly customers, but their presence on a separate list made investigators wonder if this wasn't a secret ledger of some kind. The first name, Elsie Goldberg, had already admitted to being attacked by

Cocchi. Another new discovery made the police look even worse: all along the heat register, which ran from the floor to the cellar, were small spots of human blood. Wallstein could still see them.

Wallstein then went with Inspector Faurot to the Fourth Branch detective house to interview Captain Cooper. When Wallstein left, he took a number of books and reports with him.

"I shall begin the investigation immediately," Wallstein told the press. "The hearings will be open to the public and will begin tomorrow on June 21, Friday morning, in the Municipal Building in Room 1200. All who have been guilty of misconduct, malfeasance, or negligence may be discovered and punished." He promised there would be no stepping on toes of the other investigations, especially Swann's fledgling grand jury.

The night before Wallstein's remarks, Henry Cruger wrote a letter to Mayor Mitchel. He put it in his pocket and carried it himself to the mayor's home at 258 Riverside Drive. Then Henry went home, took out an envelope, and sent his letter to the *New York Herald*. They ran it the next day, on June 20, 1917.

"The work of the department has been marked by great stupidity, if not inspired by ulterior motives," Henry wrote. "They refused to send out a general alarm until the lapse of twenty-four hours and they said Cocchi was a reputable business man." Instead of trying to find his daughter, Henry said that the police only wanted to find "some flaw in her character." Instead, "[t]he much boasted efficiency of the Police Department was proved to be a hollow mockery by the persistent work of a woman," wrote Henry. Henry called for Woods to be removed from office. He also had no faith in Wallstein's inquiry. "Any investigation," wrote Henry, "by the present Commissioner would not be worth the paper the report was written on."

A couple of days later, Henry was in his apartment, now draped in black, when he received a personal letter from the mayor of New York City. Mayor Mitchel apologized to the accountant who had lost his dear daughter. "We will leave no stone unturned to determine why the work of the police was not more effective and to make as certain as possible that such things do not occur in the future." The mayor tried to absorb the blame of his men. "I want to assure that my inquiries," he wrote, "into the matter convince me that the Police Department held no theory which in any way reflected upon the character of your daughter and that no statement containing such a reflection ever issued from the Office of the Commissioner. You have been misled in this regard. In fact, I am told that their investigation revealed nothing in any way discreditable to your daughter. For the failure of the police to discover the body and to prevent the escape of the murderer there is no excuse. Culpability will be established shortly, and whether it consist of mere stupidity and incompetence, or of worse, it will be punished." The mayor also defended Woods. "Through a period of unprecedented stress and public excitement," Mitchel wrote, "a well-disciplined, well-organized, loyal and foresighted Police Department has insured and maintained public security, tranquility and order." He signed it "Very truly yours."

Henry Cruger's emptiness could not be filled by even emptier political speak, no matter how well intended it might be. During the search for his daughter, Henry Cruger had disobeyed almost every request of the New York Police Department. He had no regrets about that. He was even glad when the letter from Mayor Mitchel later ran in the paper for all to see. Henry couldn't help imagining what the outcome would have been had the police actually believed him in the first place. Now, as he looked across his apartment, its chairs empty, he felt as if he were in that basement.

Henry had started writing his letter to the mayor, as floating thoughts and words, as he followed his daughter's body to her grave. Ruth Cruger was quietly buried in Kensico Cemetery in Valhalla, New York, in Westchester County on June 18. The papers reported that her body was encased in a casket sealed with steel and lead. The only attendees were the Crugers and Mrs. Grace Humiston. As Henry led his crying, bundled family back to the car, his letter stitched itself together in his mind.

The night before Ruth was taken to her rest, the papers reported that ghouls had stolen some of her personal effects. Thieves had taken a gold stickpin and five shell hairpins from the little bundle of trinkets that had been placed in a shallow metal tray next to her body in the morgue.

13

The Pointed Finger

There were so many people elbowed into room 1200 that workers had to fetch benches and camping chairs just to accommodate them. The crowd consisted of uniformed policemen, detectives, and maybe six or eight women, some of them still in their teens. Squirming around tables in the back were members of the press, with their overcoats, notebooks, and pencils. They had all come to the very new, forty-story Muncipal Building at One Centre Street to find out how far the police had slipped up in not finding Ruth Cruger. People walking in saw a gilded figure spark on the top of the building. The statue depicted a woman holding a shield and a five-point crown meant to symbolize the five boroughs of New York finally come together as one. It was called *Civic Fame*.

The rumors that were passing across the chairs only served to charge the air even further. A few hours before the hearing, Captain Cooper and Detective Lagarenne had been relieved of duty by Commissioner Woods and put on official suspension. Also suspended was Frank McGee, who had been alongside Kron as they dug through the street and into the black cellar. Lagarenne and McGee were the primary detectives of record on the case, and Cooper was their immediate supervisor. They were all expected to testify.

When Wallstein walked in, he stopped all the hushing with a

glare. He began by asking any members of the police department who were present to rise. Eight men stood up in their dark blue, heavy uniforms. Everyone stared at them. Wallstein instructed them to leave until they were called to the witness stand. Some of them exited more slowly than others.

The first witness called was the acting chief of detectives, Captain Alonzo Cooper, who gave his age as forty-five. He had been in charge of Fourth Branch since August 1, 1914. Cooper knew that he was fighting for his career, if not more than that. Wallstein himself did all the questioning.

"I asked you to make a search of your branch for all papers in connection with the Cruger case," Wallstein asked. "Have you found any others?" Wallstein looked everyone in the eye when they answered him, even if they mostly did not. Cooper nodded and handed up a bunch of papers he said were found in Cocchi's private desk drawer. Wallstein looked through them quickly. One of the items was an Italian passport.

"When did you get this?" asked Wallstein.

"Shortly after Alfredo Cocchi went away," Cooper answered. "February 16 or 17, I think."

"Who gave it to you?"

"Sergeant McGee."

"Where was it found?"

"In the home of Cocchi and his wife."

Wallstein turned it over in his hands. "Has it been out of your possession since then?" he asked.

"Yes," answered Cooper. "I think some of the detectives had it at times."

Cooper then passed up a small brown book that was about four or five square inches. Wallstein asked Cooper to identify this item and where it was marked for the clerk.

"It's the Record Book of the Fourth Branch and the entry of Feb[ruary] 14, 1917," said Cooper.

Wallstein read the entry aloud. It was a short announcement that

Ruth Cruger, eighteen years old, was missing from her home on Claremont Avenue. She had last been seen at 2 P.M. on February 13. Lieutenant William Brown was listed as the officer who took the initial complaint.

"How many cases of missing persons have been reported to your branch in the last year?" Wallstein then asked Cooper, switching gears.

"I can't answer that, but I can find out by telephoning to the department."

"In the last year, what detectives have been assigned to such missing persons?"

"Detectives Lagarenne and McGee."

Commissioner Wallstein then produced a deep yellow card from the sheaf of papers. Cooper identified it as a D.B.B. card, which contained a memorandum of the time of the initial report and a description of Ruth Cruger. Cooper looked at it and proclaimed that the message had been sent at 10:15 on February 14.

Wallstein continued. "Is it a rule of the Police Department to delay for twenty-four hours the sending out of a general alarm?"

"I can't say it's customary, but it frequently occurs," answered Cooper.

Wallstein then asked why, under the category of "Publicity," the word "Yes" had been crossed out in favor of "No."

"Is it the custom of the bureau to be guided by the person making the complaint as to whether there is to be publicity or not?"

"Yes, it is. The officer receiving the complaint has no discretion. There are no specific orders on it."

Wallstein adjourned the proceedings for lunch.

In the afternoon, Wallstein called up Victor Blady, a friend of Cocchi's who was always seen around the shop and was known by the nickname Jersey. Blady said that he was in the shop between nine and nine thirty on the night the Cruger girl disappeared. This contradicted what a young errand boy said, who saw Blady between six thirty and seven. A report that one of the uniforms found during the cellar excavation fit the six-foot-five Victor Blady perfectly was neither confirmed nor denied. Blady's story was that he was there because of keen interest in the motor sled that Cocchi invented, built, and drove on Broadway last winter. Blady testified that there were other men in Cocchi's shop when Ruth went there at noon and left her skates. Wallstein wanted to know what they were doing. If it was digging, it could prove that the whole thing was a premeditated act. Blady said he didn't see anything out of the ordinary. Blady's final comment was that he thought "the crime may have been committed by a woman, moved by jealousy, who, since the murder, has been shielded by the police department." Blady's testimony was dismissed as that of a personal friend.

The next day, Maria Cocchi arrived to give her testimony, and the room welled with anticipation. As Wallstein started his questioning, Mrs. Cocchi fainted, causing the room to gasp. She recovered—steadied herself—and returned to her chair. She nodded to her interpreter. Wallstein kept his questions very focused on the police activities in the case. He was not interested in idle gossip. Neither was she. She silently stuck out her hand and produced a white card. Wallstein took it and turned it over. It read:

Take care of Alfredo Cocchi. He's O.K.
BILLY EYNON

When Wallstein read the tiny card out loud, the crowd nodded and the reporters wrote. Everyone knew that Billy Eynon was an active motorcycle cop. Wallstein was very familiar with these types of cards, though he wished that he were not. The holder of the card could show it to any motorcycle squad member who had pulled him over for speeding and walk away without a ticket. According to his wife, Cocchi had gotten it from Eynon for working on his bike. Cocchi apparently liked to speed. But it wasn't the card itself that cast a shadow over the proceedings, it was the phrase at the end: "Take care of Alfredo Cocchi."

"There were always policemen around his place of business," Maria said. "I have entered his shops many a time and found him talking mysteriously with policemen. I never heard what they were saying. They did not talk when I was around." Maria paused for a moment before continuing. "Always," Maria said, "he worked hard to get money so he could go back to Italy and live like a prince. He was good to his children, but stingy with me. He could not keep away from women." The rumor circulated that her son and daughter had been taken away from her and placed with the Children's Society.

Maria also mentioned Edward Fish, the private detective who was also a friend of Cocchi, but apparently Wallstein's men could not find him. According to Maria, Fish had once been a policeman.

As the testimony wore on, the story that was slowly being patched together was that Cocchi and the motorcycle police seemed to have been involved in some kind of grafting operation. The scam would work, more or less, when motorcycle cops would hand out their summons to citizens for minor traffic infractions. Later, through an emissary, these cops would approach the citizen and say that their ticket could be fixed if they went to see someone such as Cocchi, who would then offer to fix the ticket for a price. Once the exorbitant price was paid (in cash outright or by buying a profoundly marked-up item from the store, such as a monkey wrench), the profits were split between the fixer and the cop who originally issued the ticket. The summons itself, written in pencil, would be erased and used again. Cocchi's connection to Eynon, his tight relationship as repairman to the motorcycle squad (he had spare cop uniforms in the store lockers), and other drifting rumors seemed to be solidifying the overall picture of Cocchi's police ties.

One of the last things Wallstein did that day was to motion to one of his men, who then brought a small folded cloth to his desk. When Wallstein unwrapped it, the crowd took in the sight of a long, sharpened table knife with a metal handle. It had been found in the rear of the basement where the body was discovered. The knife was identified as Cocchi's. He kept it in his desk drawer on the street floor of his shop. Wallstein momentarily held it aloft, suspended in midair, all eyes upon it. The tip was invisibly sharp.

The policemen who testified all asked to sign a waiver of immunity from prosecution. When they got to the stand, the general police defense was that they had no idea what they were dealing with in Cocchi. They had no experience with such a rare and obscure type of crime. They claimed that there was nothing in their experience to help them in arriving at a correct conclusion. There was no motive, they argued, until the autopsy of the body revealed that the young woman was slain by an assassin of a kind rarely found in this country—a "ripper." They admitted to being completely unprepared for this kind of monster. Wallstein knew from the coroner doctor's report that Ruth had been cut through on the left side of her body in a mysterious way. The cut had severed some of her intestine, but it was more of a surgical wound than the stabbing kind.

Missing from the hearings was Grace Humiston, who would not make her evidence public. "That evidence has," she said, "in part, been turned over to Commissioner Woods by me. I shall give the remainder to the authorities as soon as I consider it wise to do so." But just as Grace seemed to be willing to retreat into the background, another detective stepped forward to trash the police work on the Cruger case. William J. Burns was still the most popular detective in America. His detective agencies bore his name with a shield and eagle, and he boasted offices in "the principal cities of the world." He was also a successful author of several dime-store versions of his most famous cases. He was still being referred to as the American Sherlock Holmes.

Burns blustered accusations against the district attorney, claiming negligence and inefficiency equal only to the police department itself. Burns declared that District Attorney Swann's staff refused to listen to his own (correct, he said) theory of the murder, which sounded, to the reporters, much like the theory put forward months earlier by Grace Humiston. Burns claimed that the DA's office told him months ago to back off, presumably to stall his correct conclusion. When reached for comment, Swann shook his head. "I had nothing to do with having him removed," Swann said. "These statements are false. It is not true that I was urged to dig up the cellar by Burns."

"I was retained by the Cruger family when the girl vanished," Burns revealed. "We traced Cocchi to West New York and had evidence which we believed connected him indubitably with the disappearance of Miss Cruger. One thing we firmly established was that Ruth Cruger never left Cocchi's shop. We even asked for a permit to search it, which was denied. He told us to lay off. Soon afterward we were put off the case."

Burns detective James Downing said they had found a neighbor, a Miss Goldberg, who went to hire a motorcycle from Cocchi. She went to a small back office to sign a receipt. Once there, Cocchi became greatly excited. His eyes gleamed, and he grasped her around the waist. She screamed and struggled, but he held her fast. With a quick upward movement of her hand, she struck him under the chin and then twisted his nose and face. She then got away. When reporters finally asked Henry Cruger about Burns's role in the case, Henry said that he fired him within a week because he failed to do anything other than cash his checks.

As the testimony was winding down for the day, more whispering could be heard among the crowd, causing Wallstein to look toward the back row disapprovingly. Information was spotty, but it seemed that a series of cables from the United Press station in Rome said that Alfredo Cocchi had finally been arrested in Bologna and was being held on the charge of murder. Earlier that month, Maria Cocchi had written a letter to her brother in Italy, asking that he deliver it to her husband.

"Tell Al," she wrote, "that when he went away I was penniless. I struggled along the best I knew how until I sold the shop. Then I was beginning to be happy. Then they found the girl's body and since then I have been a prisoner and my babies have been taken from me.

"Get from Al all he knows about the murder," his wife wrote. "Tell him to send me everything, particularly the names of anyone who was in it with him. Ask him who aided him in escaping, who gave him the money to go back to Italy, and for the new clothes he wore. Please tell him to give me everything he knows so as to clear his conscience and also the names of his babies and their mother. If Al does this they will let me return to my babies."

After Maria wrote the letter, Judge Wadhams in the Court of General Sessions issued an order transferring her from the Harlem prison she was in to an institution where her one-year-old baby girl, Georgette, had been cared for since Maria's arrest. The baby was ill, and Mrs. Cocchi, who was very worried over the child's condition, was approaching a state of nervous collapse.

Back in the hearing, the rumor was confirmed. The Italians had arrested Cocchi.

⁂

At the end of the long stone corridor, cell 68 felt very far away from the rest of the world, and not just because it was in Bologna. Monks had lived here once, in this tower of darkness, but coming down the hall now were Italian detectives. When they reached the cell, they looked through the bars. The prisoner was huddled in the corner, seemingly asleep. He was still, just like the bars set in the powdery stone. When the guard let them in, the prisoner's legs suddenly began to scramble. He struggled and kicked as the men pushed him up against the rough, cold wall. There was shouting and moving as the men pushed their faces in front of him, spitting fast questions. Fists and arms moved in the darkness. When they were done, they let him sink to the floor. The men would return many times that very same night, often only minutes apart, to repeat their interrogations.

At daybreak, Alfredo Cocchi, Prisoner 15,372, weakly asked for a physician. His eyes were red, and he was shaking. The physician examined him and said he was fine. A guard gave Cocchi some bread. He ate it quickly.

When Cocchi first arrived at the prison of San Giovanni at Monte, they scratched his name in ink across one of the pages of its thick books. They first put him in cell number 5, up in the tower itself. Cocchi had a cellmate there who asked questions during the hot days and nights. But Cocchi wouldn't speak. After the other prisoner disappeared, Cocchi was moved to a solitary cell somewhere belowground. A church stood at the foot of the tower. Inside the church was a colorful painting of Saint Cecilia, her head looking up as she listened to invisible music. Somewhere on the altar was a relic, a white knucklebone belonging to Cecilia herself, who, once married, asked her husband to respect her holy virginity. When Cecilia was later martyred, she survived for three days after being struck three times in the neck by a sword.

In his dungeon cell, Cocchi knew he was beneath all of these things. One day, hours after the detectives left, someone else made their way to talk to Cocchi. His steps were slower and heavier. Judge Zucconi, the assigned magistrate for Cocchi's case, nodded at the guard to open the cell so that he and his law clerk could enter.

The judge was determined that this trial go according to the Italian way. Cocchi, sitting down in the corner, tried to compose himself as a gentleman. He ran his hand over his dry hair and straightened up. Cocchi's eyes looked as if they had been hollowed out. The judge asked Cocchi about his life in America.

"My machine shop gave me a satisfactory position," Cocchi said, slowly. "I earned sometimes $100 a week." Cocchi spoke very matter-of-factly. The clerk transcribed his words.

The judge then asked what happened on the day in question in New York. Cocchi said that his wife and he had quarreled, but that was it. "I had never seen Ruth Cruger before she came to my shop to have her skates sharpened," he said.

On the second day the judge came in, Cocchi looked even more pitiful. Cocchi reiterated that all he did was sharpen this poor girl's skates. He mumbled something about some Italians in the store when she was there, but, when pressed, he didn't repeat it. Cocchi was always looking elsewhere. No one had gotten a really good look at him yet.

"I had never seen Ruth Cruger before she came to my shop to have her skates sharpened," Cocchi said again during Zucconi's next visit, or maybe even the one after that. Cocchi looked away at the wall or at something else. He was shaking again. The dungeon cell was cold.

Judge Zucconi started to push from his chair to leave. Maybe another day passed. Interrogations, long ones, took time. There was no clock in the room. Zucconi kept visiting Cocchi but never got any further. "From the very beginning Ruth did all in her power to attract my attention," Cocchi finally said. "I felt something strange when her dark penetrating eyes were fixed on mine."

The judge sat still. Cocchi had said "Ruth."

"I was still more disconcerted when she came again February 13th to get her skates," said Cocchi, now trembling even more. "An overpowering attraction for the young woman seized me. What happened afterwards seems like a dream." Cocchi looked at the wall. "My memory at this point fails me utterly." He kept speaking, but the shaking cut off his words. Almost like it was laughter.

"It must be true I attacked and killed her," Cocchi said. He looked at the judge, almost as if he wanted confirmation. "But God help me I didn't mean to." Cocchi said she must have fallen and hit "some vital spot." Cocchi said it must have been an accident.

Cocchi started to tremble and shake even more, to the point that sweat began pouring from his brow. The guard was summoned, and they at first thought Cocchi was having an epileptic fit. No one in the prison had ever seen anything like it. They called for the doctor.

On June 25, 1917, the same day in New York City, Helen Cruger, Ruth's sister, arrived in Wallstein's interrogation room. She wore a black-and-white checked suit, a brown straw toque hat trimmed with brown leaves and flowers, and low-cut black shoes. People stood up when she walked in. Wallstein asked that she not be photographed, in accordance with her wishes. The press photographers, who had been scrambling for any new photo to print, put down their hollow cameras and watched her with their eyes.

Helen sat down and told Wallstein that she had tried to meet with Chief Inspector Faurot three days after Ruth disappeared. When

Wallstein asked why, Helen said that she had information to share about her sister's disappearance. Helen had strongly suspected Cocchi after their brief but strange encounter at his store. But she couldn't get in to see Faurot. She even had a letter of introduction that her father had helped secure. Wallstein looked at the letter—which was perfectly customary—dated February 16, 1917, and addressed to Faurot. Since Helen was told that Faurot was out, she talked to Lieutenant William Funston instead.

"I told the whole story from the beginning," said Helen, who spoke in a low-pitched, agreeable voice. The people in chairs could see the resemblance to her sister. "I tried to point out that this was not one of the ninety-nine cases that the police said girls always were found in," she said, holding on to her tone. "I told him that was the line they were working on and I argued the point with him," Helen said. "I told him all the reasons why they should not regard this as one of the ninety-nine cases." Helen told the lieutenant that Cocchi had ready answers to her questions and that they sounded almost rehearsed. She also said that all the policemen she had talked to—and she paused because this was important—had called him "Al."

People looked at each other and understood. Wallstein's inquiry wasn't just meant to understand how the police had failed. His questioning was meant to determine, just as an early rumor had suggested, if the police had possibly been involved in the very crime itself.

14

⚜

The Man Who Laughs

The Italian doctor took Cocchi out of the cell and gave him a glass of clean water. When Cocchi returned, he was much calmed. As Cocchi's words stopped and started in his mouth, he still shook slightly. He continued with his story.

"When I returned home I was like a person in a trance. I remember speaking of this peculiar mental condition as though I was ill." Cocchi paused. "I had been constantly quarrelling with my wife. This day, the 13th, when I ate my mid-day meal at home, I drank five glasses of California wine to make me forget my trouble." He paused to drink more water.

"In a nervous condition I went to my shop about 1:20 o'clock, when there immediately entered the girl who before noon had left her skates for sharpening. She was very beautiful and I lost my head. When she went to the rear of the shop to get her skates without seeing me, I barred the street door with a block of wood. Then I started to embrace the girl, but she was very strong and threw me backward. I tried again and succeeded, despite her resistance.

"I picked her up and dropped her into the repair room," said Cocchi, matter-of-factly. He stopped for a moment. "She fell about twelve feet below, striking a motor cycle sidecar on her side, but she was not hurt. All the while she was screaming 'Police! Police!'" He stopped again. "When I joined her in the lower room, my head was gone. I tried again to embrace and kiss her, but again did not succeed; she was so strong. I said 'Please don't say anything, I have two children,' but she would not listen." He seemed to be seeing it play out before him. Cocchi looked away again. He said the next part slowly, while still shaking. "Finally, exasperated by her resistance, I grabbed in my left hand a stick of heavy wood a yard long and struck her twice or thrice across the back of the neck, holding her with my right hand. She groaned and sank down.

"I swear before God and man that I did no carnal violence to the girl," Cocchi said earnestly. "If she had pardoned my first offensive act and listened to my prayers to tell nobody I would have let her go without touching a hair of her head. This is my first offense, but it is of such a nature that I cannot believe it to be true. The greatest punishment is to think what suffering and agony my wife and children are undergoing, as notwithstanding our misunderstandings, we love each other most tenderly."

Judge Zucconi listened as his clerk wrote furiously. The story had obviously changed, but his ears had missed something. The judge pressed Cocchi for specific details about Ruth's death. After admitting hitting her with a block of wood, Cocchi had ended his story there. Cocchi collected himself, then continued.

"After I had seized her and tried to throw her down I got scared," Cocchi said. "I remembered my wife."

The judge pressed him, but that is all Alfredo Cocchi would say.

The judge ordered the clerk to show Cocchi his confession. The clerk scrambled to complete it, then handed it over. It was dated June 25, 1917. Cocchi signed it.

When they were done, Cocchi seemed relieved. "I feel myself acquitted morally, but I am ready to undergo the legal penalty of my country," he said. Cocchi had two requests. He wanted to see his father so that he might relate a message to his wife in America. He also wanted to see the newspapers of the day. The judge refused both. Once he and his clerk left, Cocchi stood up and walked to the far end of his cell. Readying himself, Cocchi took a breath. He ran as fast as he possibly could and launched himself, headfirst, into the opposing stone wall.

⁂

In America, news of Cocchi's confession was met with towering black headlines. People wanted him deported directly to the chair at Sing Sing with no stops between. As soon as Cocchi's confession was made public, Maria Cocchi announced that she had more to say. This time, she was questioned by the assistant DA, John T. Dooling. She had not been arrested following the discovery of Ruth's body, but she had been detained. She was not sure what the difference was. Her eyes were dark and heavy from not sleeping. Her husband, for he was still that word to her, had been found halfway around the world. The first time she tried to testify, she was too agitated. She fainted and had to rest. Maria was still being held with her one-year-old daughter and it was taking its toll. She was going to "tell everything."

For four hours, Maria talked in a loud, rapid pitch. She was in a greatly excited state. She told of her husband's many love affairs, both perceived and real, and his flirtations with the girls on the street. When Dooling pushed her on her husband's whereabouts on the day Ruth Cruger disappeared, Maria remembered that Edward Fish had begged her to let him stay in the bicycle shop alone after Alfredo had fled to Italy. Maria told him no. Maria also told Dooling that within forty-eight hours after her husband's disappearance someone had forcibly entered the motorcycle shop at night. She thought it was Henry's Cruger's private detectives, but now she wasn't so sure.

In Italy, Cocchi was recovering from his head injury in his cell. His jailers took away any towels, suspenders, bedsheets, and utensils left in the room. They threatened him with a straitjacket. His guard detail was increased. There were also rumors that certain factions of Cocchi's family were going to try to help him escape. There had been only one escape in the fifty-year history of the prison. Just three years ago, a lone prisoner succeeded in twisting free the iron bars in his window. The prisoner got to the roof and leaped to the nearby church tower, where he concealed himself in the confine until he could slip away into the Italian night.

Because of Cocchi's suicide attempt, the judge had ordered Professor Augusto Murri, Italy's famous nerve specialist, to gauge the prisoner's fragile mental state. Murri subjected Cocchi to an extensive examination. "The prisoner is now physically in a bad condition and mentally weak," Murri concluded. But his conclusions were clear: "Although he has spoken of suicide, he hasn't the courage to commit it," said Murri.

As Cocchi lay in his cell, dazed and slowed, taking turns mumbling to himself and singing out loud, his friends and family in Italy started a fund to halt his extradition. Cocchi had earlier confessed to a friend that he was terrified of the American electric chair and all the souls it had sucked dry. Some wondered if his fear of the chair might have been the cause of his detailed confession in the first place. If found guilty in Italy, he would face a long imprisonment, but he would remain alive.

In the wake of Cocchi's confession, the Bologna police began a thorough investigation of his mysterious life. When Cocchi left Italy ten years before, he was in love with Maria Magrini, a servant to the Cocchi family in Bologna. Alfredo promised Maria that he would marry her if she followed him to America. Cocchi left, and she eventually did follow, with a female friend in tow. Alfredo and Maria were married soon after, on October 3, 1907. Days later, Maria Cocchi accused her new husband of cheating on her. Cocchi wrote a long letter to his family confessing to numerous vague misdeeds, but he promised to mend his ways. "She's so jealous," he wrote of his new bride.

There was also some uncertainty as to how Cocchi had even made it back across the Atlantic. Cocchi said that he sailed on the French ship *Manchester*, under the name Louis Lerdi. No one asked for his passport. Other evidence put him on the *Giuseppe Verdi* from Jersey

City using someone else's passport, though the picture was of Cocchi, taken at a New York photographer's office a week after Ruth disappeared. Cocchi supposedly made efforts to escape from the ship at several ports but finally succeeded at Naples. All of these different stories claimed to be true.

Last November, Cocchi had written his family to say that he was thinking of returning home to join the colors of the Italian army. Shortly after Ruth vanished, a letter arrived at the Italian Cocchis from Maria. She said that Alfredo had eloped with a girl who was eighteen years old and had taken all of her money, all fifteen dollars of it. She worried about Athos, who was "almost dead from privation and fright."

In his private office, Judge Zucconi seemed disturbed. He was keenly aware of contradictions in Cocchi's confession. What Cocchi had described in his cell was an instantaneous crime of passion. What they had found in New York was the work of something else. Which man did they have in that cell? The picture they were learning of Cocchi in Italy was that of "an unbalanced adventurer with anarchistic tendencies." A close investigation of letters revealed that Cocchi was suffering from "a horrible type of degeneracy manifested by attacks on children." Zucconi couldn't trust him, so he couldn't underestimate him.

When Cocchi first returned to Italy undetected, Francesco Baroncin, husband of Emma Magrini, Maria's older sister, was worried that Cocchi had harmed his family. Baroncin persuaded Cocchi to go out to dinner one evening. Baroncin ordered the wine. "He did not tell me exactly how it was committed," Baroncin told police, "but his meanderings indicated he had killed the girl." Though there were "certain details that even a man of that sort is ashamed to tell," admitted Cocchi's brother-in-law. Cocchi's father and brother insisted that Cocchi had told them nothing. Baroncin also told the police that Cocchi's father had once traveled to New York to visit his son, but had left—sometime between 1913 and 1915—because of some sort of attempted violence. Baroncin said that Alfredo Cocchi was a "degenerate by heredity."

Cocchi's defense lawyer was Signor Venturini, who was the best defense lawyer in Bologna—twenty-five years earlier. He was now seventy-five, creaky, and angular, but he still knew the law like few else in the city. Even though Venturini was Cocchi's defense lawyer, he had not yet been allowed to see his client. Venturini went to court and made an official complaint against the secret manner of the investigation thus far and asked why he was not allowed to see Cocchi. Venturini also argued strongly against his client's extradition. When the court seemed to snicker at him, Venturini referred to articles in the Italian penal code that he said not only did not admit the possibility of Cocchi's extradition but prevented the Italian government from trying the prisoner for a crime committed abroad. "This cannot go on" he said. "The law exists, and cannot be violated. It is a matter of honor with me, to see that the prisoner gets a fair trial, as I have undertaken in my old age to defend all poor Italians whom I can serve." He shook his finger and his eyes blazed. Venturini would not be underestimated, either.

Venturini's great worry was the length of time that would pass before his client's trial. The Italian government still had to determine if Cocchi was an American citizen or an Italian subject. The trial could slog on for months as records were pulled and men argued. "I am guilty, and I want to pay the penalty," Cocchi repeated from his cell. "Why spend your money on a lawyer? I won't see him," he said defiantly. It was not clear who was paying for his defense. "I would rather know the worst at once than live in this uncertainty," Cocchi said. He allegedly told his father, several days before his arrest, that he was going to plead insanity.

On June 26, a woman slipped into Bologna very quietly. She was taken to Judge Zucconi's rooms to be questioned. When the interview was concluded, the person returned home to America. The secret witness was reported to be an American woman who came to

Italy for the sole purpose of giving testimony concerning the motive for the crime and the circumstances behind it. The name and address of the woman were not made public. The press speculated it might have been a Miss Cruger, though they offered no proof.

⁂

When Wallstein reconvened his hearings on June 26, it was for Captain Cooper to testify for the second time. This time, Wallstein had questions about Detective Lagarenne. Cooper said that Lagarenne's report was recorded on a large blue card that indicated he had searched the premises. The card also mentioned Lagarenne's interrogation of Rubien, the taxi driver who claimed to have seen Ruth Cruger. The card summarized Rubien's statement that a man had called him to bring his taxi to a jewelry store at 127th and Manhattan. There, the man beckoned to a girl, got in with her, and Rubien took them to the subway station at 127th and Lenox. Lagarenne stated on the report that he believed this girl to be Ruth Cruger.

"Did you ask him how he came to that conclusion?" Wallstein asked.

"Yes, and he said it was on account of her appearance, her clothing," replied Cooper.

"Did you accept this as conclusively as Lagarenne did?"

"No, they have to show me."

"Were you ever able to locate the man reported as accompanying this girl in the taxicab?"

"No, sir."

Wallstein wanted to talk about the motorcycle squad next. A group of them were at a restaurant near Cocchi's when they learned that he had disappeared. As soon as they heard, they jumped on their bikes to Fourth Branch to tell the captain. Wallstein specifically questioned John L. Ochsenhirt and James Haggerty, both motorcycle cops who knew Cocchi. Ochsenhirt admitted that he was in the store earlier on the day that Ruth disappeared. He was also the man who reported that a girl and a young man had been seen in a taxicab in the neighborhood on the same night. The entire motorcycle squad was ordered to report the last two years of their paperwork. Twelve of their number had already been suspended due to the graft inquiry.

Dooling, fresh off his own interrogation of Maria Cocchi, was the next to stomp up to Wallstein's table. He was chomping at the bit to talk. He knew that he was not here to be pointed at and accused. He was here to share what he knew.

"Three facts," Dooling said, "proved that there were accomplices. First, the toolbox in the shop weighed seven hundred pounds and could not be lifted by one man. Second, the removal of the hot air flue and its replacement after the girl had been dropped through the improvised trap, required at least two persons. Third, more than one person helped carry away from the premises the earth that was taken from the tunnel grave." The flue Dooling was referring to was the heating passageway from the first floor of the store to the cellar, which they were surmising Cocchi used to transport the body for burial. The coroner, Dr. Otto Schultze was next. He did not fear Wallstein. He testified that the smears on the tin around the hole in the floor were indeed drops of human blood.

In Italy, Cocchi seemed to be finally exhibiting a proud kind of remorse. "I am racked with grief," he said. "I cannot bear the remorse. I would like to go to the front and be killed in the first line." Police had found that Cocchi had tried to enlist in the Italian army the year before, only to be rejected. The word "deformity" was typed into his application file. In Italy, Cocchi underwent corrective surgery to fix it, but the procedure left him unable to lift heavy weights.

Cocchi even talked about the search of his cellar by Lagarenne and McGee. "The reputation I had with the police was so good," he said, "that these detectives told me they made this inspection merely to be able to say that they had done it." Cocchi then admitted that when the detectives searched his basement, Ruth's body wasn't even covered in the ground. Cocchi also elaborated on some of his name changing and trickery in getting back to Italy, though it didn't add up. "Gueiseppe Gesundheit" was quoted in an Indiana paper explaining that Cocchi's name was "pronounced the easiest possible way, just ordinary 'cock-eye.'" But in Bologna, Cocchi seemed immune to real scrutiny, humorous or otherwise. Cocchi even told Milt Snyder that while in Bologna, he had begun an affair with a young girl.

"I did it just as a joke," Cocchi said.

In Bologna, detectives had found a letter that Cocchi wrote to his brother Joseph dated November 27, 1916. After telling his brother that his business was doing very well in America, Cocchi asked, "How are things going on in Italy? Would you advise me to come back? It would be a godsend for me to have some relative here to look after my business. My son is too young to realize what a dirty mother he has. Maria does not care about the shop and we have always been quarrelling. She is having me shadowed by private detectives because she says I am after other women. I . . . cannot get on with Maria. I cannot even go to my house, and during the last week have been having my meals out.

"She is an unfortunate wretch," wrote Cocchi. "All our quarrels are due to the fact that she listens to the gossip of people who are Germans. She says we are a family of murderers and that I had to escape from Italy, where I would have been in prison. Had we been in Italy, I do not know what I would have done to her. If I had peace at home I would be the happiest man in New York. . . . All my work during ten years will go to the devil and my children will have nothing left, but at least the scenes of jealousy will end."

This was the first time Cocchi had written to his family in ten years.

In New York, Wallstein continued focusing his magnifying glass on the police. In Italy, Cocchi had confessed, but he had a sharp lawyer and there was no physical evidence connecting Cocchi to the murder. He admitted to hitting Ruth with a block of wood, but no one had found it, leaving unanswered questions. As Cocchi smiled and told his endless stories, Judge Zucconi couldn't tell if he was just stupid, desperate, or playing at some dark, larger game.

Cocchi ended his letter to his family with a list of his customers, who included, in his words, the "best people of New York." "All the policemen who have motorcycles come to me for repairs," bragged Cocchi. But his last lines took on a chilling countenance:

"A day of reckoning will come through to all my enemies in this country," Cocchi said. The judge wondered exactly what that meant.

15

The Sliding Number

On June 28, Leonard Wallstein finally called for the testimony of Lieutenant Brown, who had taken the first phone call at Fourth Branch on the day Ruth disappeared. Wallstein wanted to know why Brown had not officially reported her missing until the next day. Brown claimed that he honestly didn't remember what happened. Given the volume of calls, this was certainly understandable, so Wallstein let him take the casebook into an adjoining room to refresh himself with its contents and perhaps spark his memory.

When Brown returned, he handed over the book, and it was once again placed into evidence. The small book was then slid across the table to Wallstein, who opened it up to the date in question. Wallstein dipped his nose and read the page through his thin glasses. He stopped and looked closer. His eyes flashed on Brown.

"Were you alone while you were looking up these complaints?" Wallstein asked.

"Yes," said Brown.

"Did you see that this '4' had been changed to a '5'?"

Brown hesitated.

"Yes," Brown said.

Wallstein looked even angrier. Someone had changed the 4 to a 5 in the Cruger entry and thus, February 14 had become February 15. And thus Lieutenant Brown couldn't be accused of delaying the investigation.

"Did you make that change?" Wallstein asked sharply.

"No," Brown answered.

"Is that your handwriting?"

A pause. "It is," Brown said.

Wallstein stared at him. "I strongly suspect that you made that change yourself," he said, "and if I can prove it, I shall see that you are punished." He waved his hand. "You can come back at 2:30," he said. Brown protested that he had been under observation while examining the casebook. Wallstein wouldn't even look at him.

After a short recess, Wallstein returned. His face was red. "I find after examination," he said, his words coming with difficulty, "that no one was watching Lieutenant Brown during his absence from this room when he was working on the complaint book. While I strongly suspect that he did tamper with the book, I do not wish to make the charge at the moment." Wallstein knew Brown had done it, but there was no way to prove it.

"I answer telephone inquiries," said Brown. "I make $2,250 a year and you accuse me of having altered the records?"

"No, I don't accuse you," said Wallstein. "But I strongly suspect you."

When the hearings ended that day, new stories began to surface about the case. According to the *Sun*, Cocchi's father, while visiting New York a few years before, attempted to attack Maria Cocchi. The scandal was hushed up, and the father was forced to return to Italy. Mrs. Cocchi reported it to a policeman, but nothing was ever done. Maria had told the district attorney that she took the policeman's badge number and still had it written in her prayer book.

News had also come that Cocchi had hid himself for six days at the Society for Italian Immigrants before leaving New York in February. Cocchi said that he was housed at a loading house along with a hundred other Italians waiting departure. After staying in port for an extra two days, the ship finally cleared on Washington's birthday.

The loading house was under the direction of a priest named Father Gaspar Moretto.

The reporters and detectives descended on the Saint Raphael Society House at 8 and 10 Charlton Street that same night. When he opened his door, Father Moretto, who was young, short, and heavyset, was much surprised to see a pack of reporters. Moretto admitted that he knew Cocchi. He had gone to his shop about four or five years earlier to have a motorcycle repaired.

"No detectives came near me," Moretto said, "but Miss Cruger's sister came here with a very nice young man, a Catholic, and asked me if I knew anything about Cocchi. I am sorry, I told them, but I don't know anything about them."

"Have you seen him since February 13th?" one of the reporters asked. There was a long pause. Father Moretto replied in broken English.

"When a man comes to a priest and talks, the priest can say nothing about it," he said.

"We are not speaking of the confessional," said the reporter. "We asked if you had seen Cocchi since February 13th." The priest became even more disturbed. He half turned away, wrung his hands, started to speak, hesitated, and finally turned to them.

"If the Judge asked me in court—" He left the sentence unfinished. The question was repeated. Father Moretto then turned, without replying, and entered the house.

A few moments later, he appeared once more on the doorstep and said firmly, "I have not seen Cocchi now."

"You mean that you have not seen him since February 13th?"

"That is what I mean," said Father Moretto, shaking his head vehemently. "I have not seen him." Then, after a pause, he went on:

"If you watch the papers, in a few days, you will see that Cocchi has gone insane—but I am not a doctor." He then went back inside, closed his door, and refused to come out again.

At Maria Cocchi's next interrogation by Swann, her lawyer told the district attorney how some prison officials at the Harlem jail tried to force her silence about any police friendships with her husband. One of the guards told Maria, according to her attorney, "that if she continued to involve policemen in the Cruger case, she would be killed as soon as she left the prison."

On June 29, Detective Lagarenne finally appeared before Wallstein. There were many questions as to how he was in Cocchi's shop the day after Ruth disappeared and did not suspect—or thoroughly search—the very ground he had been walking on. Many of the people in the audience already knew his name; in May 1914, he had been commended for obtaining the arrest and conviction of the great criminal Gregario Giordano, which Wallstein noted in the record. Lagarenne was a hero, which is why he became a detective.

"You suspected Cocchi?" asked Wallstein.

"No," answered Lagarenne.

"Why did you never have him under surveillance?"

"I can't recall."

"Did you talk to the neighbors about his character?"

"No."

"You weren't interested in that until he disappeared?" asked Wallstein, with a hint of contempt.

"No."

"Did you believe Cocchi when you talked with him?"

"I did," answered Lagarenne.

"You thought she was a voluntary runaway, didn't you?" asked Wallstein.

"That was my opinion."

"Well," said Wallstein. "Your opinion was wrong and absolutely immaterial."

Wallstein paused, staring the man down. He was clearly not going to give him anything.

"You did not lift that workbench up?" asked Wallstein.

"No."

"Why didn't you ask Cocchi to remove the workbench?"

"I don't know."

Wallstein then asked if Lagarenne had once been placed on trial for failing to prevent a burglary on his patrol post. Lagarenne admitted that he had.

"Well," said Wallstein, angrily. "You are excused, and you don't have to come back."

That very night, Wallstein sent a letter to Commissioner Woods urging that Lagarenne be brought up on charges of gross negligence. In writing up the charge, Woods noted that Lagarenne "failed and neglected to keep Cocchi under surveillance and didn't open up easily accessible and locked areas, including drawers and closets."

The next day, Detective McGee followed his partner on the stand, though telling a somewhat different story. McGee answered every question with a full answer and admitted that he could have done a better search of the cellar. This enormous, sweating man who had helped dig out the cellar with Kron even started to weep. "In sight of God and man," McGee said, "I did the best I could on that search. I did everything I could." Wallstein looked at him from across the table. He had seen McGee's dossier. He had once shot at a fleeing burglar who was running down Broadway. McGee ordered him to halt, but the thief kept on going. McGee stood still and shot him through the neck, then walked slowly up to the wounded criminal with his gun drawn. He found a shaking, bleeding boy.

"Your testimony gives me the impression you are honest," Wallstein said. That night, he sent Woods a similar request to bring McGee up on charges, but in a more forgiving tone. Wallstein was feeling pressure and wasn't any closer to the truth. He began extending the hours of his hearings and started to call more and more witnesses. He called Reverend Pattison, who testified that he had baptized Ruth last Easter and that she was a wonderful girl.

Reverend Pattison revealed that when Ruth first went missing, Henry Cruger asked him to accompany the police as his proxy on a mission to chase down a clue. The police were going to visit a midwife's house somewhere in the Fifties after a tip said that Ruth was there. Reverend Pattison rode there with two detectives. As they approached the house, the slimmer of the pair winked to the reverend that the entire building was given over "to treating girls." "It was too bad to see a girl like Ruth Cruger in a place like this," said the other detective. When they found the girl, in the back of the building, the detectives said she was very good-looking. But she wasn't Ruth Cruger. The reverend told Wallstein that if he wanted "any proof of the good character of Ruth Cruger he could have it from the lips of 600 people, the congregation of the Washington Heights Baptist Church."

Captain Cooper, the former head of Fourth Branch, was called up again. He seemed to have taken the hint from Lagarenne when Wallstein asked him about the day Ruth was reported missing.

"I can't recall," he answered. "I don't remember."

Cooper told Wallstein that he sent two motorcycle men that night to Cocchi's. The cops said they knew Cocchi, so they offered to go fetch him. When he heard this, Wallstein exploded, as much as he could.

"Captain Cooper," Wallstein demanded, "I want answers. It is inconceivable that a man of your experience and age should remember so little of a very important part of this investigation. I don't think you want to help me." Cooper left, his mouth still shut.

When Edward Fish finally walked in to testify, the crowds made it difficult to see. His name had been part of this investigation from very early on, but no one had been able to find him until now. Mrs. Cocchi had accused Fish, a former cop and friend of her husband's, of breaking into her house while she was in prison. Fish guffawed and told Wallstein that he had been in Bloomington, Illinois, the whole time. He was short of cash and had to write home for railroad fare to come home to New York. That's why he had been so long in appearing. Once that was out of the way, Fish denied ever seeing Ruth Cruger and denied being a go-between between Cocchi and the cops in the alleged ticket scam. Fish was accompanied by his lawyer.

But, yes, Fish admitted. He was a friend of Cocchi's.

Swann, meanwhile, had been in touch with the State Department about a possible extradition. The people in Washington recited a very sobering statistic handed down from Frank Polk, the same man who had been shot in the cheek all those years ago in the attempt on Mayor Mitchel's life. He still had the scar. Polk related to Swann that "of twelve Italians tried in Italy for crimes committed in the Unites States, during the past four years, not one has been convicted."

While Swann's office still held out hope that they would be able to put a living, breathing Alfredo Cocchi on trial on American soil, Commissioner Woods quietly tried to work his own angle. Judge Zucconi had turned down any official police envoy, so Woods sent a man named Joseph Grigg to report on Cocchi and any other evidence the Italian police were finding. But Grigg was not a cop; he was a reporter for the *Sun*. Woods deputized him in secret and gave him his orders. Having done work in London, Italy, and France, Grigg was perfect for the job, and Woods hoped that Grigg could keep an eye on the case for him.

Once Grigg arrived in Italy, he was threatened almost immediately. He was soon named in papers as Woods's personal detective. Within days, Grigg received Black Hand letters that told him he would share the fate of Petrosino if he didn't abandon the case forever. Woods considered pulling him back but did not.

By early July, Wallstein was thinking about calling Inspector Faurot, Captain Costigan, and even Deputy Commissioner Scull himself to testify. Readers who were following the hearings in the papers were anxiously awaiting upcoming witnesses as if they were hitters coming in to face Bob Shawkey. For though grand jury records were confidential, quoted testimony from the Wallstein hearings was reprinted almost daily on the front page of the *Sun*. Readers were especially waiting for July 6, when Grace was scheduled to at last tell the whole story of her successful search for Ruth Cruger's body. To prepare, Wallstein planned to work through the weekend.

Just before the July Fourth holiday, Wallstein called Henry Ankenmann, one of Cocchi's errand boys, who had worked at the shop until August. Ankenmann gave Wallstein the names of a number of

motorcycle cops whom he had seen rub elbows with Fish. Ankenmann also said that he did not think that the source of Cocchi's
supposed clout was anything other than friendships with the local
motorcycle policemen who worked in his neighborhood. After all,
wouldn't it make sense that the Harlem motorcycle shop owner knew
all of the Harlem motorcycle cops?

Ankenmann did admit that he helped Cocchi dig under the sidewalk pavement outside the shop. Cocchi had told him it was part of
some plan to bring motorcycles into the cellar more easily. Cocchi
said it was because he needed more dirt to fill in the floor of a path
under the sidewalk. Ankenmann also remembered how Cocchi once
boasted that he did not need a motorcycle license because he knew
the police so well.

When Independence Day came, New York City was ablaze with
red-and-blue streamers and portraits of the new symbol of America,
a fictional character called Uncle Sam, who had white hair and stern,
glittering eyes. On July Fourth, Governor Whitman ordered Wallstein's investigation finished. Without any warning, Whitman asked
that all evidence and paperwork be delivered to District Attorney Swann
for the transition to a grand jury investigation. Summons were served
that same day on several officials at police headquarters and at Fourth
Branch. As the feared envelopes slid across desks, into mailboxes, and
into shaking hands, policemen looked up in anger and disbelief.
Whitman assured everyone that shuttering Wallstein's inquiry would
be only temporary and that it would resume sometime in the future.

Wallstein gathered every square inch of paperwork he had and
sent it down the line to District Attorney Swann, the Tammany Hall
man. Wallstein, who was the chairman of the same Humanitarian Cult
that had helped Charlie Stielow years before, worried what might
happen to his case now. Mayor Mitchel was equally furious. "We were
attempting, and I think succeeding in our attempt, to make a complete investigation of police methods," he said.

As Wallstein was leaving the city to take a delayed vacation, he commented on the astonishing ease with which his investigation had been shut down. He told a reporter that he had been asked "to fade out of the case . . . and that he was now in the act of fading." "I have stopped dead in my tracks," Wallstein said. New Yorkers understood his tone. Many felt the same way. They felt like pieces on a game-board dwarfed by large, invisible players.

"The issue in this case," said Wallstein, "was boneheadedness vs. criminality. Boneheadedness was proved. Criminality has yet to be proved." This meant that for all of the finger-pointing and outright tampering of evidence, there was a good chance that no one would be punished. As Wallstein left the stage, Assistant District Attorney John Dooling and Alfred J. Talley picked up the grand jury investigation, which would be presided over by Judge McIntyre. Instead of working on their golf game over the holiday, as they had planned, the staff was recalled to look over legal transcripts. They laid out their papers on tables in places emptied of their usual workers. They read and searched for answers.

In Italy, Judge Zucconi was equally frustrated by the presence of outsiders in his business. He had read about Joseph Grigg, the man sent by Woods to keep an eye on things in Italy. Zucconi called him in; he wanted to explain a few things about the Italian judicial system. American newspapers were starved for news from Bologna. The transcripts had already been unofficially leaked; rumor and news were becoming the same thing.

"I understand how great is the interest in America," Zucconi said, "to find out if possible, through the Cocchi case, whether any connivance existed between the American police and the series of so-called elopements of girls under age that have occurred frequently, without, as a rule, the men culprits being discovered.

"The law is equal for all," Zucconi explained. "As long as the investigation lasts, no one can be allowed to interfere with it, directly, or indirectly. I hope America will not take offense if, while we are not allowing even the accused's lawyer to see the papers in the case or interrogate the prisoner, we also forbid the representative of the American police having any such privilege."

The Americans had questions for Cocchi, but they were not allowed to participate in any process—even discovery—of Cocchi's trial. Zucconi, and Italian law, had frozen them out. Zucconi then added that they could submit their questions through the magistrate, though this would take much longer than they were usually accustomed to.

"What must be put clearly before the American public and its authorities," the judge said, "is that so long as the investigation lasts absolutely no one can have official information regarding the developments in the case, nor be allowed to communicate directly or indirectly with the prisoner. This prohibition extends even to the members of his family. His old father, whom I understand is heartbroken for what is occurring, cannot visit him, and his wife, if she were here, would not be allowed to see him.

"I can foresee that it will last several months," Zucconi said, confirming the Americans' fears. "In fact, while awaiting with keen interest the American newspapers containing the descriptions of how the body was found, we cannot conduct the examinations on such unofficial reports, but must receive the official, legal evidence from the American authorities. This means a long delay." The judge had closed the door, for the most part, on any American involvement. Cocchi would be tried as a son of Italy.

※

On July 10, Zucconi once again made his way into Cocchi's small cell. This was his eighth visit in more or less as many days. He was carrying something in his hand. Zucconi had tried to eliminate distractions because he still had work to do. Though Zucconi had refused to share information with officials in New York, they had certainly shared it with him. Cocchi had been able to smuggle out a note to a relative that read, "Get them to leave me alone and not try to make me talk. I am suffering too much. I am ready to serve my sentence in prison, but wish to do so in Italy, my beloved country. I do not wish to die in a foreign land in the dreadful electric chair."

Zucconi had just gotten the official physician's report from New York City. He and his clerk were let into Cocchi's cell again. The judge began reading some of the grisly details.

Compound fracture of skull.

Wound on left side of abdomen severing descending colon.

Left ureter & small intestine.

On the report, Dr. Benjamin Schwartz, the coroner's physician, ended his summary with a single word:

Homicidal.

Cocchi looked trapped and anxious. Zucconi told him that, according to the report, Ruth's watch had stopped at 2:10 P.M.

The silence that followed in the cell felt like a stop as well.

"I was in terror," Cocchi said, quietly. The judge stared.

"I hit her with my fist and cried: 'You promise to keep quiet!' She clawed at me with her hands and screamed again. Then I struck her and she fell, still fighting, to her knees."

The judge nodded as the clerk began to write.

"She got up," continued Cocchi, almost oblivious to their presence. "I jammed my fist against her mouth. I tore her clothes. She was so strong and resisted so much I could not rip her dress from her. She screamed.

"I was scared. I struck her again and threw her to the floor. Her head struck the floor. She was dazed, but not unconscious. I grabbed a wrench and hit her. Dazed as she was, she kept fighting. I feared every minute that someone would rush in. I dragged her to the hole in the floor (a heat register) and threw her into the basement."

The cell was quiet. Cocchi continued, his eyes on fire.

"Her head struck the concrete and she was still. I jumped down after her. She still tried to struggle. I grabbed a round stick of wood in my right hand and struck her over the head. She moaned and rose to her knees. Three times I struck her. She moaned again and sank to the floor."

He continued. "The blood was coming. I put on a pair of rubber gloves to keep the blood from my hands. I dragged her to the coal hole with a rope around her body. She was still warm."

He added, "It was not difficult."

The judge stared at him. He knew Cocchi was not finished.

"Then I attacked her," said Cocchi.

There was more silence in the stone cell.

"Afterwards, I dragged her to the coal hole and pushed her in head first and doubled her body up. I covered her with a box. I left things that way until after the police came the next day. The body was in the coal hole covered with a box, but they didn't see it.

"They didn't see it," Cocchi repeated.

Alfredo Cocchi's final thousand-word sworn confession revealed that Ruth Cruger's body was barely hidden only a few inches from where the detectives were standing when they first came to investigate. Policemen questioned the ease by which Ruth and Cocchi could have passed down the air flue, hinting that Cocchi might have removed part of it ahead of time to make the opening bigger. They also noticed that nowhere in Cocchi's confession was there anything about digging the hole, making detectives wonder if he had done it beforehand.

As he left the prison cell for the last time, the judge was satisfied that there was enough for a trial. He looked at Cocchi and finally saw the monster he always knew was there.

⚕

Swann felt that everyone in New York—every man, woman, and child who could read a story in a paper or hear it on a stoop or windowsill— wanted Cocchi to burn in the black chair at Sing Sing. Even in the absence of proof, they wanted blood. But Swann knew the reality of the moment. The Petrosino case seemed to show how little the Italian police cared about working with the Americans. To make matters worse, the war was dividing nations. At least Swann could take solace in the fact that Alfredo Cocchi was no longer surrounded by thin bicycles but by solid iron bars.

Edward Swann had inherited the Wallstein case, but he had been working on it himself for months. He appointed James W. Osborne to take full charge of the investigation of the police. "I will go wherever the trail leads," said the special prosecutor. As the investigation pressed on, it became clear that the phrase "go see Cocchi" was commonplace advice given to people who wanted to "fix" their tickets. For a small fee, a ticket could disappear as easily as a swipe of the eraser. Cocchi and the police, it seemed, had first developed a relationship over their machines that had grown to include other mutual activities.

Stories began to surface that Cocchi had run a betting book on the horse races right out of his garage. The results of the New York, southern, and Canadian tracks were received by telephone at Cocchi's. One witness told Swann of a cop who placed a 20-to-1, five-dollar bet with Cocchi and was now owed a hundred dollars. Swann told him to tell the officer not to hold his breath. Another witness said that, although Cocchi kept the book, he was not the principal person. "He had a man of means as his backer," the witness said. A manager of prizefighters was rumored to have bankrolled the operation. Some thought it could be the Camorra itself. Swann was now asking jurors to sit an extra hour each day.

Grace was one of the first to testify as part of the new grand jury proceedings. After her testimony, Osborne declared that it was "one of the most interesting and remarkable stories I ever heard." The jurors then went to see the motorcycle store. They walked around in silence, especially in the cellar.

Grace knew that if Cocchi were to return, he would die in the electric chair. That was against all of her beliefs, but she still said that "every effort must be directed toward bringing him back to this country." She knew that the benefits would be too great. "One case of this sort," Grace said, "fully proved will expose much and root out a big gang in this city. I suppose I'll get my head punched for saying that, but I believe that Cocchi knows more about these cases of young girls than any man in this city."

Cocchi kept issuing a flat denial of any collusion with the police.

"Not only was there no connivance between myself and the police," said Cocchi, "but it was dread of the police which caused the crime."

Grace disagreed. "Cocchi didn't escape just to save himself," she said. "I believe it was suggested to him to get away."

Only parts of Grace's grand jury investigation made it to the papers. The final, tell-all testimony of Grace Humiston that had been so eagerly awaited in the Wallstein hearings had been distilled to only a few vague lines. The full story of how Grace had solved the case of the missing skater had not yet been told. So, after some persuasion, Grace agreed to do something that, unlike the other endeavors in her life, she was almost completely unsure of.

An interview.

16

Mrs. Sherlock Holmes

On the tenth floor of the building at Madison Avenue and Forty-second Street, Grace nervously arranged the roses on her desk. The half circle of reporters around her desk seemed to inch forward. Grace's black eyes fell against her dress of purple silk. She had decided to soften her dark wardrobe as of late, if only in the form of a lacy white shirt.

Before she answered even five questions, the telephone rang. "Yes, this is Grace—that you, mother? *Tut, tut,* I am not overworking myself. No, really, I'm not. Oh, mother, do you mind tucking away my gray dress; it's on the chair nearest the dresser, and will you see that the plants are watered?" Grace hung up and smiled to the reporters when the phone rang again.

"Oh, no," she said, to some perceived congratulations. "Don't talk about me, my dear, but little Ruth." As Grace chatted away, the reporters in the room took notes as they studied her for clues. One noted that Grace had a merry laugh. Another wrote that she reminded him of the late Joe Petrosino. "William J. Burns looks like a detective," wrote a reporter, "but Mrs. Grace Humiston does not at all look like an investigator. You may see her type presiding over civic or mothers club meetings." Another wrote that it was like dropping in at Baker Street and having Holmes throw the pipe, the violin, and the hypodermic out of the window and begin to discuss how many strawberries make a shortcake.

Some of the reporters had done a little digging into the woman in black before their visit. Her family had roots in old New York. Her father was Adoniram Judson Winterton, an influential member of the Baptist Church. Grace grew up in the city and graduated from Hunter College in 1888. She taught for a time at the Collegiate School at West End Avenue and Seventy-seventh Street. After her first marriage to Henry F. Quackenbos, a doctor, ended, she took an evening class at the NYU law school. Five years ago, she married again, this time to a former co-worker of hers at the Legal Aid Society. He was a Yale lawyer named Howard Humiston; they were married in Peru and lived togather with his mother. Rumor said that on their steamship honeymoon to London, the boat came down with typhoid fever. Grace saved the day by single-handedly instituting strict quarantine procedures, thus getting them safely back to England. The story surprised no one.

There was talk that Grace first studied law only to understand the management of the large property of her family. Grace said that upon the death of her brother some years earlier, she became trustee of the family estate. But her becoming a lawyer was about more than that. One month after her firm was opened, there were 120 cases on her docket. She had the respect of lawyers and judges. She was called the "People's friend." She was a protector of the poor who also loved the Ladies' Mile, the Midtown shopping paradise that included Bergdorf Goodman, Best & Co., and Tiffany, all anchored on the street by the Flatiron Building.

Once Grace got off the phone, the reporters readied their pencils for her actual words. Almost on cue, she spied Kron lurking in the outer office. She motioned him in. She was determined not to go down alone.

"Kron is a remarkable man," Grace said. "A splendid investigator. When I was investigating the peonage cases, I had to do some work among the Hungarians. So I went to a Hungarian newspaper and asked for a capable man who could talk Hungarian. I got Kron. He had not been working long on the peonage cases when he was offered a bribe of $500. He came right to me and told me about it. We set a trap for the would-be bribers and marked money was paid in the old Astor House. We caught them and sent them away. I knew I could depend on Kron."

Grace had succeeded in embarrassing her old friend. Reporters then asked Kron about the working habits of his employer on the Cruger case. "How many hours did Mrs. Humiston work?" someone asked.

Kron shrugged. "Sometimes eighteen and twenty-one hours. She ate her meals in the office here. She is absolutely tireless."

Grace shook her head. "I may have done that occasionally, but as a rule I put in only fifteen or sixteen."

"How did you solve the Ruth Cruger case?" another reporter asked, cutting right to the question they were here for.

"Because," she said.

The room became quiet again.

"I started out with the conviction that Ruth Cruger was a good girl," Grace continued, her head nodding. "I knew that one of her training and character never would figure in an elopement or anything of that kind. Working on this conviction of mine, I knew that the police theory of 'waywardness' was all bosh and that Mr. Cruger's repeatedly expressed belief that his daughter was being forcibly detained was correct—or at least partially so."

As the reporters took her words down, they observed details about her. Her eyes were puffy, for one. She wore no earrings but had a thick white locket around her neck. She wore a large blue stone on her left ring finger. Her desk was very messy.

"Ruth was a good girl," Grace said again, sitting below her painting of the Madonna.

Grace put up her glasses and very professionally went over the rough timeline of the case: "We eliminated every clue that led outside New York City. I searched morgues, cemeteries, and hospitals. I became convinced the girl had been murdered and Cocchi could solve the mystery. We investigated the cellar and found the police search of the place had been superficial. We subjected the man's record to the closest sort of scrutiny. For more than five weeks we clung to our investigation without having a single clue to work on. We were simply convinced that sooner or later we would find the body, and, although there were times when the task grew heavy our little band managed to keep cheerful. We went after Cocchi just because that was the common sense thing to go after we had established his horrible reputation."

Grace moved up in her chair. There were papers piled off to the side with names scratched in ink on their spines. "I've noticed that some folks are saying that I found the body because I followed my intuition. Every time a women does make a discovery somebody pipes, 'Intuition!' Let me say that, in this instance it was just plain everyday common sense on the part of Kron and myself, backed by a determination to keep going until the case had cleared up."

She added, "There never was a time when we felt like giving up. We knew that Ruth was a model girl, that she had disappeared, that she had been murdered, and we intended to prove to others—yes, the police among them—that we had the correct view. There was only one unpleasant feature in connection with the search and that was the vile slanders about Ruth that kept cropping up again and again. It may be interesting some time to ascertain just where they all came from."

Grace took in a breath. "That day we started to dig I knew that our search was ended. Hole after hole was made and although nothing came to light, we were convinced that every time a shovel went into the earth, it might disclose what we sought. What happened . . . you know."

Reporters could sense that the topic should be altered. A reporter asked her about the new nickname that the papers had been using for her: Mrs. Sherlock Holmes.

"No, I never read Sherlock Holmes," responded Grace, laughing.

"In fact, I am not a believer in deduction. Common sense and persistence will always solve a mystery. You never need theatricals, nor Dr. Watsons, if you stick to a case."

Another asked her views on the women's vote. Grace thought of her friend Inez. When they worked on the Stielow case together, Grace had dreams of bringing Inez on as a full legal partner when it was all over. She never had the chance.

"I am not a suffragette," Grace said. "But I certainly am not an anti-. If giving the vote to women could abolish white slavery or the other nefarious practices, if it could make better the lot of womankind then by all means let us vote. As a matter of fact, I'm much too busy to ally myself with any organization for or against suffrage."

Lastly, someone asked if she preferred life as a detective to life at home.

"As between a professional career and home?" Grace asked, surprised, her eyes lighting up. "Assuredly, I prefer home—possibly that sounds old-fashioned. Well, to me there's nothing like my home." She smiled, and everyone laughed, if only in release. Their questions, even light ones, could not mask the deep occasion of this story's end. There was silence again. But Grace found more fire. Though Ruth had been found, Grace vowed to get to the root of the problem rather than endlessly toil in its wake.

"Vice conditions here in the city are astounding," Grace said. "The 'good people' of New York are as much asleep to the nastiness of their city as the nation appears to be to the seriousness of our war. The records of the police department show hundreds of girls disappear every year. There must be many whose vanishing is not reported to the authorities because of the notoriety."

She continued. "There are little, harmless looking shops scattered all around some of the high school and public schools," Grace said, her voice rising. "Loungers of the most depraved type infest these places and watch the girls going to and from school. When a girl is insulted in one of these places, she usually broods over the horror of it. Never could she tell her parents, for she feels she is partly to blame. Little by little her seducers batter down her moral stamina and soon another girl is 'missing.' "

Grace observed, "New York does not yet realize how systematic the danger is for the girls who live in it. The public readily says, when a girl disappears it was as much her fault as the man's.

"I know better," Grace said.

The woman in black had a plan. "What I think is needed is a bureau, supported by voluntary contributions that would prevent girls from getting into the hands of these beasts, rescue them if they were already snared, and then cure them of their moral ailment. Why, had I the power, I would cause to be inserted in the laws of every state an act that would make the tempting of a girl a serious offense, punishable by an adequate penalty, I would call such practice 'criminal persuasion' and I think that if the white slaver knew he violated the law at the beginning of his 'trade' there would be fewer girls in the underworld."

She added, "I would have agents throughout the city, but the headquarters of the organization would be out of town—on a farm, best of all. Once the girls were rescued I would send them out to the farm, where their environment would be entirely different. Secluded there even from their own kind with light work to do, placed where nobody except the attendants—all women—would know of their past, the girl would start life anew. If funds are provided, I think the best plan would be not to have the bureau part of the police department but, of course, to work in full sympathetic co-operation with it. If this bureau is made powerful enough it can do something the police and public sentiment have as yet failed to do—wipe out immorality in this city."

The reporters were struggling to keep up.

"In one year," Grace said, "828 persons disappeared from the streets. In three of the five boroughs there were 244 murders. These conditions indicate either that New York is the most criminal city in the world or the police force is inefficient." Grace said that in her three-month investigation, she found twenty-two cellars where girls were made victims of men. But she couldn't do what was needed. Even her hunt of Ruth Cruger was incredibly difficult, she admitted, far more so than it should have been. She paused and dropped her voice a bit.

"I found myself blocked by some mysterious person at every step," Grace said.

She sighed. "I have been utterly tired out by my work on poor Ruth," Grace admitted. "Let the public show that it wants something of that sort, however, and I am willing to drop everything and begin the work."

"Why couldn't the police have found the same thing?" someone asked.

"I don't know," was Grace's reply. "I don't know why they didn't. Something told me to keep on digging and I just couldn't stop, although they told me that I was foolish. I was told that there might be a civil suit. I was not to be dissuaded by that.

"You put two and two together," Grace said, simply. "That is, you do if you are a woman. If you are a man you don't, or you get the addition wrong. 'She ran away with the dago;' 'they quarreled with her at home;' 'girls won't stand for strict parents' were some of the theories put forward by members of the city's police and detectives. And all the time the child's body lay buried beneath Cocchi's cellar, and someone helped Cocchi to escape."

When a reporter asked, "Do you still believe capital punishment ought to be abolished?" the reporter wrote that Mrs. Humiston declined to answer. "It hurt her," the reporter wrote.

The long article published in the *New York Sun* after the interview built Grace up like one of the new Gotham skyscrapers. The accompanying photograph featured the smiling face of the woman, clad in black, who had found Ruth Cruger. Mrs. Humiston was now the mystery confronting readers. Who was this woman who solved the crime that had so baffled the police? And how did she accomplish it? "She never gives up on anything," the reporter said. "She shuts her teeth and goes on and on, no matter what happens. Trying to stop her is like flashing a red flag in a bull's face."

"She would have made a detective," the article observed. "Indeed she is a detective."

But she wasn't in it for fame, it seemed. "It may well be," reported the *Sun*, "that she does not care a rap for her own gain or her own reputation in all this. You feel that when you are talking to her that she is above self." After all, "she is a born and bred New Yorker," the reporter said.

This was not the same Grace Humiston with ebony hair who darted about the South in disguises and rode mules over Italian mountaintops. Grace now had more wrinkles and, after the Cruger case, clearly needed some rest. But that was all just appearance. At forty-eight years old, her words—and what was behind them—commanded more authority than ever. The reporters in that room now understood why. The nation could hear it, too. After the articles came out, Grace's mailbox was soon flooded with requests by desperate parents begging her to look for their lost daughters. The *New York American*, a staunch supporter of Grace, even hired a "missing-girl editor" to keep up with the topic. Grace was even reported as having signed an exclusive contract with the Hearst family of newspapers to only speak to them.

A laudatory tribute to Grace appeared in the *New-York Tribune* in the form of a poem, "Lines to Mrs. Humiston," written by Alice Duer Miller. "Lines to Mrs. Humiston" was certainly complimentary, but it had a wickedly sarcastic tone of warning to it:

> *Oh, Mrs. Humiston, oh, Mrs. Grace*
> *Humiston, can it be you have not heard*
> *The last, the master-word?*
> *You haven't without doubt,*
> *Or else you'd not be out*
> *Milling about*
> *Doing man's work, when home is woman's place.*
> *A woman's duty is to praise and please,*
> *To make men feel proud, competent and strong.*
> *Never to hint by word or deed or glance*

That not all men have qualities like these:

That's very, very wrong.

Besides, it kills romance.

Oh, strange it seems to me,

You do not see

That deeds like yours imply a criticism,

And criticism vexes,

And makes antagonism

Between the sexes.

I know, of course, what you will say,

The thoughtless, weak excuse that you will make—

You wished to help young girls. A great mistake!

For in the end,

My friend,

You'll find the only way.

The gentle, charming, yielding best of ways

Is to stay home and praise

All men,

And all they do,

However strange;

And to condemn

Women, and all things new—

Ay, any change.

❧

New York faced a hot summer: many days reached ninety-six degrees, and by midsummer 142 people had already died from the heat. A man living in the Pennsylvania countryside claimed he had found the body of Satan himself, petrified near a riverbank. Cocchi was in jail, and Ruth was being mourned, but the trail of evidence connecting Cocchi to her murder was similarly hazy. Authorities had Cocchi's confession but very little else. The La Rue story was being pressed by Inspector Faurot and his band of diggers. Meanwhile, William J.

Flynn, chief of the Secret Service, had identified a new suspect in the case named Jose A. Del Campo. This man had been inquiring about La Rue's condition and had recently given her a large sum of money. When questioned about La Rue, Del Campo would only say that "she comes from one of the best families in Argentina." With the aid of the police, Flynn was investigating a larger South American white slavery ring that stretched all the way to Buenos Aires. The police were now convinced that "Cocchi and his associates systematically plotted the ruin of young school girls . . . planning to ship them to Latin-American countries after they had been disgraced."

In the grand jury hearings, the heat was making the long days feel even longer. When Assistant District Attorney Talley began his questioning of witnesses at the end of July, it was with the same old questions: Where were you on February 14? What did you see or hear? In late July, the person answering those questions had his legs dangled beneath him under the chair. Arturo, Alfredo Cocchi's young son, called Athos by his father, told Talley that he was in his father's shop after three o'clock on the afternoon of February 13 and that he heard his father and one or two other men talking in the cellar. This was the day of Ruth's death and was several hours before her disappearance was reported by her family.

Athos was sure of the date because it was the day after Lincoln's birthday. He knew the time because it occurred when he came home from school, when he would usually go down to the shop to play. The current police theory was that Ruth was killed at two in the afternoon. Her watch had stopped at two thirty.

"Papa was not in the shop when I got there," Athos said. "But through the hole in the floor where the heat comes up, I heard him and other men talking in the cellar. I started to go down stairs, but Papa met me and made me go back. The back room of the shop was locked."

Talley let the boy off the stand. He had heard enough. He thought of him playing in that basement, alone and unaware.

As the grand jury hearings proceeded, Grace was in court for some other matter. She had just filed an injunction against the Universal Film Manufacturing Company for their newsreel "Woman Lawyer Solves Ruth Cruger Mystery," which included views of Grace on the day Ruth's body was found. The newsreel was part of the Universal Animated Weekly series that ran before most feature films. When Grace saw it, she was furious. The particular portion of the film that Grace objected to was a still photograph, used alongside ordered story cards, that told the news of Ruth's body being found.

Judge Ordway ruled that Universal Animated Weekly was not entitled to the protection afforded a newspaper, which could use any outdoor photo without permission. Instead, the court ruled that the exhibition of moving pictures was a business, pure and simple, originated and conducted for profit. The judge ordered the newsreel pulled pending the trial of the action, in which Grace asked for $100,000 in damages for the unauthorized use of her picture.

Ordway concluded that Grace had the right to object to the unauthorized use of her picture because she was not "the commander of an army, a visiting Ambassador, or even a public official, but a private citizen entitled to be protected in her right of privacy." Grace appreciated the irony. Grace could sue because she was a private citizen, although her newfound celebrity was pushing those limits. Her image and name were now in the paper almost every day. A wire story noted that "the newspapers are full of her: lawyers, philanthropists and policemen are making reputations out of her." Grace was eventually awarded $2,500 in damages.

Just as Grace's star was rising, so too was the name of her right-hand man. Frederic J. Haskin, a reporter who wrote a syndicated information column, asked Kron—"the one man who has probably put more time and thought on the missing girl problem than any other person"—for an exclusive. According to Haskin, Kron had been "barely mentioned" in the accounts of the case, even though his "originality of method and variety of adventures make him a fair candidate for Sunday newspaper publicity." Kron defied easy categorization: he wasn't an Arbuckle or even a Watson. He was more than just a side-kick.

The story that ran on Kron had none of the lavish illustration that Grace's did, but its portrayal of the detective as a "five feet four, Hungarian, and modest" man who led an "intensely practical life" helped fill in the missing pieces of the mysterious investigator. "When Mr. Kron sets out to solve a crime," the story said, "he not only goes back to the very beginning of the incident but to the very birth of the criminal." He traced Ruth Cruger's history from the day she was born. Mr. Kron wasted no time on theories concerning a false sweetheart. He knew that he "was on the track of a criminal mind of the worst order."

Kron said that the case began to crack for him when he found two men who told him that on two successive midnights in February they had seen Cocchi lope out of his cellar, his clothes black with dirt. Kron knew right then where he had to look. He had seen this type of monster before. A few years ago, the chief of police in Buda-pest called Kron back home to help solve a horrific murder. Kron sailed over the Atlantic to a small kitchen of a farmhouse, where a woman had been found with her throat slashed. Her thirteen-year-old daughter was missing. By the time Kron arrived, the girl's father had gone mad. Kron's search of the house revealed something shiny lodged in the crevice of the stoop of the door. It was a single American dime. Kron also found a handkerchief in the kitchen stove. It was covered with blood. The make of the bandana was American.

Kron found an American working as a barkeeper in a village not thirty miles away. When Kron stepped into the bar that night and saw the man, nervous and looking over his shoulder, he knew instantly that he would have his confession. Gaining his confidence, Kron heard the American confess that he had been a former employee on the farm and had been infatuated with the daughter. He had known her since she was a baby.

When the American tried to carry the girl away, the mother screamed. So he killed her. When the girl resisted, he killed the girl.

The American buried her small body in the big Hungarian woods. Kron stepped away and phoned his friend, the chief. Together, they excavated the girl's body that night. Kron didn't tell the reporter what happened—or what they did—to the American.

When Kron returned home from Budapest, he was contacted to help with a similar case in New Jersey. The police had captured a German American, whom they believed murdered a little girl in a lonely stretch of trees, but, try as they might, they could not construct a strong case. Kron assumed the personality of a man of the underworld who was very rich but something of a fool. Kron befriended the suspect and began throwing his money around. They lived, ate, and dined in the same places. Kron soon knew the whole life of this man, all except the murder, which he scrupulously avoided as a topic of conversation. Kron had a longer game in mind. He hired an Italian to stand by a certain tree in the stretch of woods where the girl's body had been found. Kron told the German that the Italian man had been saying things about him. The German seemed nervous, so Kron offered to take care of it for him. They crept up on the Italian. Kron took out his revolver and shot the Italian dead. They fled the woods.

The next day, Kron showed the German copies of the newspaper that said an Italian had been murdered in the woods. The German, moved by Kron's help, finally confessed to the murder of the girl. He didn't know that there was a Dictaphone in the next room. When the police stepped in, the German realized his betrayal.

Kron had used blank cartridges, a dummy newspaper, and patience to send this killer to the New Jersey electric chair.

"There are born criminals and those who are made so," Kron told the reporter. "The born criminal is the man who carefully plans his crime; the made criminal is one who commits it in a moment of passion." Kron never had sympathy for the former, but he could sometimes feel it for the latter.

After the Cruger case was solved, Donnelly made Kron manager of the detective agency. He was proud of his man, but he also recognized an opportunity when he saw it. Their ads in the New York City directory were updated to reflect the change:

> **DETECTIVES solved Ruth Cruger mystery; reasonable rates. J.J. KRON, Manager, Donnelly's Detective Agency, III Broadway, Phone 7476-Rector.**

Across town, Grace was also contemplating a change. After the publicity that followed the Cruger case, police and city officials were tripping over themselves trying to hire her. District Attorney Swann offered Grace a full-time job as an investigator of white slavery. Grace had made Swann look like a fool, but he recognized her new political power. Observers wondered if he wanted her closer to draw on her skill, to save face, or to keep an eye on her.

In addition to receiving job offers, Grace had people wanting to work for her. One day, a very tall, very pale woman with short hair appeared on Grace's doorstep. She was dressed in full khaki uniform with a thin belt and a flat helmet. She introduced herself as Miss Christie Harrington and straightaway volunteered her services as Grace's personal bodyguard. She was part of an initiative started by Commissioner Woods called the New York Women's Home Defense League, a group of civilians whose job it was to patrol the parks and guard the children against white slavery perils. She wore high leather boots.

Around the same time, Grace officially announced that she was giving up her law practice. She was going to devote herself, full-time, to stamping out white slavery and ending the missing-girl problem once and for all. Society women of influence and wealth lined to back her, including Mrs. Felix Adler, who had suggested she look into the Ruth Cruger case in the first place.

"I have seen so much and hope to be able to accomplish so much on behalf of girls who are constantly meeting the same risk that cost Ruth Cruger her life," Grace said. "So I shall give up my law practice and devote every energy I possess to this fight against white-slavers."

*

"I know of other victims," remarked Grace, "and I only wish I could afford a house in the country where I could protect them. If some wealthy person would only pay the rent I would do the rest. . . . I know of twenty-two cellars where young girls have been brought by men and made their victims. . . . I would like to get hold of the Police Department list of girls who have disappeared. Ninety per cent of them, I feel certain, are under the control of men."

And thus the Grace Humiston League, whose goal was to raise one million dollars in order to endow a national organization for the protection of womanhood, was conceived. One of New York's best citizens, who remained anonymous, said he would personally contribute fifty thousand dollars. Grace said she looked forward to serving under a board of trustees to grow an enterprise that would eventually spread to every major city in the United States. Grace applied as an incorporator for the Morality League of America, along with Cathy de Nemethy, Izola Forrester, Helen de Nemethy, and Hannah E. Frank.

In late July, Grace finally accepted an offer of employment from Woods to be a police special investigator. She was even allowed to carry a gun. But she didn't care about any of those things; she wanted something far more formidable. She wanted subpoena power. Per U.S. Code, section 2321, Grace wanted the ability to require witnesses to appear in court and produce evidence under threat of prosecution. She needed this authority because, she said, "with seven hundred cases under investigation, the time expended in such efforts is a handicapping factor." She asked Governor Whitman for this power in person. On July 21, he declined. She felt as if he would always decline her. When people asked her why she picked the cop job over Swann's, Grace swore that it was not political. "I assure every one that politics has no more to do with my actions than it has with the tides," she said. Her position with the police came with great fanfare in the press. It also came without salary.

A few days later, Inspector Faurot announced to the newspapers that they had finally found the cellar that Consuelo La Rue had been imprisoned in. Faurot came out to talk to reporters. They all held their breath for more news of the white slave ring that had encircled their city. Faurot marched to the front and held up a small black book. The newspapermen stood on their tiptoes. There had long been rumors that members of the Black Hand carried a manual called *The Code and Ritual* that contained all the secret rites and names of their order. These small books were supposedly housed in special, dummied-up gauntlets along with small bottles of arsenic and ground glass. The Black Hand was so difficult to stop because there was seemingly no unified rhyme or reason to the secret organization. Having one of these books would be an incredible victory for law enforcement.

Faurot raised the book even higher. He had a smile on his face. Maybe the case had been broken after all. Faurot explained that his investigators, who had been working to substantiate La Rue's claims, had found this black volume in her possession. They felt it solved the mystery once and for all.

Except it wasn't a secret handbook of crime. Faurot was holding up a novel. Consuelo La Rue's story of being kidnapped by white slavers had been stolen from a book.

The Insidious Dr. Fu Manchu, by Sax Rohmer, was published in 1913 and was the first in a series of thrilling novels about the villainous Fu Manchu, aka the Yellow Peril from the East. Tales of murder, white slavery, and remarkable escapes from death were the hallmark of Rohmer, and this volume was no exception. In the book, Karamaneh, the heroine, is a girl of great beauty whose description corresponds strikingly with that of La Rue. The young woman is taken captive and held in a luxurious apartment, where she is threatened by seeing the grave of another victim. The villain, the mysterious Chinese criminal lord, has the power of life and death over his captive women. Ads for the book in the papers claimed that "these are no ordinary detective stories." Faurot said that La Rue had given the book to friends, recommending it highly. The book was eventually mailed to a friend in Havana but returned to New York as undeliverable, which is how Faurot found it. In the book, several people are made to commit suicide by jumping out of windows. There are blindfolds, veiled cellars, and men who hold the complete will of their charges in their hands. Faurot noted at least twenty other passages that coincided with exact specifics in La Rue's story. The briefing was ended with Faurot noting that La Rue's real name was Mrs. H. T. Clary and that she had family in California, including an eleven-year-old son named Harry. When the *Sun* reported the end of this strange story, they said "And so it goes. Copies of 'The Insidious Dr. Fu Manchu' and of THE SUN for the last days of June may still be had while they last."

At the time, one of the most popular films was *Poor Little Rich Girl*, starring America's sweetheart, Mary Pickford. In the film, the maid gives Mary an extra dose of sleeping medicine so that she can go out. Mary experiences a surreal, imaginary world inspired by her real-life friends. The world includes places such as the Tell-Tale Forest and the Garden of Lonely Children. People wondered whether La Rue's story happened the same way, like a kind of self-hypnosis. Where did this story come from? Was it drugs, delusion, or just a wild, public lie? Two shadowy men would later be indicted for blackmail in the La Rue case, but for the most part New York readers felt as if they were coming out of a haze.

Reporters tried to reach Grace for comment, but she was out of the city. She was in Annapolis.

On another big case.

17

The Marked Neck

The first thing that Grace noticed about the house in front of her was that it had only recently been painted white. The color was still bright and thick on the wooden planks. Someone had been paid to do it too, from the looks of it, which also told her something about the husband. He was too busy to do it himself, possibly, or just didn't go in for that type of thing. That, or his line of work didn't lend itself to physical labor. Grace already knew that she was right on that guess. The husband was in naval intelligence.

The house stood almost perpendicular to the sidewalk, separated only by a narrow front porch. As Grace walked through the front door, she found herself in a small, square room with a couch, a library table, and a Graphophone. There was a chimney and mantel lined against the other wall. Looking straight ahead, Grace saw an open door. When she passed through its frame, she gasped to find herself in the bedroom. The room was a mess. There was a white dresser with its drawers open. Clothes were scattered on a dark rug that was decorated with golden, interlocking shapes. The brass bed in the middle of the room was bowed and looked to have a feather mattress. In the corner, Grace saw a wooly toy lamb placed near a book about babies. The mattress on the bed was soaked in blood.

Grace walked through the dining room and saw the mahogany

sideboard, then the bathroom, filled with the usual appointments of a young couple. As she was about to leave, Grace stepped out onto the rear porch and looked out the back. Past the tall weeds at the far end of the short yard, she could see shapes moving through the five-foot-tall plank wooden fence. She had been told there was a Negro community there, just on the other side.

A day earlier, Grace had been in New York, when a call came in from the *Washington Times.* Grace assumed it was for yet another quote about Ruth, but it was not. The editor told Grace that there had been a murder in the naval city of Annapolis. They wanted to hire her to solve it. As trial preparations were beginning in Italy for Cocchi, Grace was staying out of it. She had already called for Cocchi's extradition, but there was really nothing more she could do for poor Ruth Cruger. So she agreed to listen.

The facts of this new case were both sad and mysterious. The Brandons were a young, newly married couple living in an Annapolis row house. On August 8, 1917, Val, the husband, came home from work to find his wife, Lottie May, murdered in their bed. There was barely any physical evidence, and everyone had an alibi, including her husband, who worked for the navy. Grace took a moment to think on the phone, negotiated some, and then got on a train to Washington.

When Grace arrived, the first thing she did was to interview Valentine Brandon, the young husband. He was a stenographer with the navy, in the Experimental Division. When they met and clasped hands, the thin man stood tall with his head angled downward. He told Grace that he had married Lottie May a year ago. She had come from a family of nine. He told her of their home life. Val was clearly heartbroken.

"After I bury my wife in Washington, I shall return to Annapolis," he told Grace. "I will sell my household effects and leave here for all time."

Grace then took a machine to Annapolis and the Brandon home. Grace entered the house without speaking and walked through its rooms in silence. When Grace got back to Washington, she passed the Capitol and remembered her time in those halls, walking across that flat marble, arguing about immigration. She kept going. In front of the iron fence of the White House were a line of gray ladies in tight black boots. They wore sashes and had flags colored purple, white, and gold. They held large signs that read "Mr. President What Will You Do for Woman Suffrage?" and "Mr. President, You Say Liberty Is the Fundamental Demand of the Human Spirit." Some of the other signs referred to President Wilson as "Kaiser Wilson." Grace saw them and thought of Inez. "Just a year ago they were married," reported Alissa Franc, of the *Washington Times*, "and in a few weeks a tiny stranger should have entered their doors." At the time of her death, Lottie May Brandon was seven months pregnant.

On August 11, three days after the crime, Grace had her first exclusive column on the front page of the *Washington Times*: "Lottie Brandon's murderer was undoubtedly someone Lottie Brandon had known," Grace wrote. She also didn't believe that the murderer was from the nearby Negro community, as the police were hinting at in the papers. Lottie's diamond engagement ring had remained on her thin finger. "A Negro would almost certainly have committed a theft while in the house," Grace said, matter-of-factly. She also believed that the horrible act was premeditated. "Very few crimes start all in a moment," wrote Grace. "The genesis and ramifications of this tragedy may date back several years." Grace called out in print for evidence and leads, promising that "this murder mystery is going to be solved."

Grace had also interviewed the Brandons' neighbor, Mrs. King, who was certain that there had been another man in Lottie's life. Mrs. King told Grace that Lottie had confided in her about a man she had been engaged to for three years before she met Val. The man was tall and dark, but Lottie would never say his name. Not out loud. "That other fellow thought a lot of her," Mrs. King whispered. Lottie, according to Mrs. King, had to break it off because of her parents' objections to his religion. Lottie kept a photograph of him somewhere in the house, Mrs. King said. She also told Grace that Val was always jealous of his wife. He would not let her dance "because he could not bear to see another man's arm around her waist."

Since coming to Washington, Grace had been working for twenty-four hours straight. She was trying to absorb the particulars of the case before all the fiends ran and hid in the dark. Grace noticed that the house itself had many blind spots, leading her to believe that Lottie had been in the kitchen when the murderer approached her from behind. Grace guessed that the assailant entered while Lottie was washing dishes, partially choked her, dragged her into the other room, threw her onto the bed, and afterward hit her on the forehead. Grace also noticed something on the photographs of the body. There were small, crescent-shaped marks on Lottie's neck. Grace thought these might be fingerprint marks, possibly of a woman assailant.

On the same day of Grace's first article, Lottie May Brandon was laid to rest in her hometown of Baltimore. Her husband accompanied her body on the train. In her article two days later, Grace recommended that Lottie's body be exhumed so that a more scientific, methodical study could be done of the marks on her neck. Grace knew this was a bombshell request, but there was so little physical evidence at the site—none, really—and the eyewitnesses were faulty at best, so she felt as if she had no other choice. "Let us work from the beginning and in a scientific manner," Grace wrote in her column. "We cannot have fallen premises from which to work."

As Grace continued her investigation, the Annapolis, Washington, and Baltimore police were busy picking up threads from all sorts of directions. Everyone had a theory. Church sermons titled "A Mysterious Murder or Who Killed Lottie Brandon?" were delivered to bursting congregations. The police, under the direction of Marshal Carter, thought they had identified a primary suspect. On the day Lottie was killed, "two colored girls" saw a man wearing a pink shirt escape the Brandon home, but they were deathly afraid to come forward. The girls consulted their mother, then a minister, before going to the authorities. The man they saw was a worker at the ice plant of Parlett and Parlett, they said. When Lottie died, the police found a half block of ice melting on the Brandon front steps.

When Val Brandon left his wife that fateful morning, he gave her a one-dollar bill that he left on the buffet. That afternoon, the suspect was seen at Martin's Bar, watching people play pool and drinking beer, where he changed a dollar bill for drinks. The suspect claimed he had won it playing craps. An inveterate drinker and gambler, "Scoop" (his nickname) lived with a woman just around the back of the Brandon home. The police tracked him down and arrested him. His face was badly scratched. They brought him into the sheriff's office. They locked the door and slowly circled the suspect, who sat chained to a chair. His name was John Snowden, age thirty-four. He was "unusually black," according to the papers.

At the sheriff's, Snowden's chair was up right close to the table. Marshal Carter and his men presented all of this evidence to his face. One of the men then hit Snowden in the head. Carter took out his gun. It hovered at Snowden's temple. Carter threatened to shoot him. A bottle of whiskey was brought in. Carter ordered Snowden to drink it all. The pistol was still there. Snowden choked down the brown liquid. Carter then told the prisoner to take his clothes off. The men pulled the chair back. Marshal Carter asked him if he had killed Mrs. Brandon.

"No sir, no sir," said Snowden.

Carter nodded and his men pulled back John Snowden's arms and tipped the chair back farther. Carter turned the gun around in his hand and brought it down hard, crushing John Snowden's balls down to nothing. Snowden's eyes went blank and he vomited. Then he screamed.

He did not confess.

Carter and his men knew that all of their evidence, no matter how many papers it sold, was circumstantial. So the various offices and factions finally listened to Grace, and on a rainy night, they set aside the withered garland and dug up the casket of Lottie May Brandon.

Val was kept away from the gravesite, but they let him walk outside Emergency Hospital, where they conducted their exam. He walked around and around.

During this second autopsy, the fingernail marks on her neck were found to be inconclusive. But the chief doctor, Dr. Walton Hopkins, looked under Lottie's own fingernails and found what he proclaimed was black skin. Dr. Hopkins also said that someone had assaulted her. When they finished, the men took her back to the Sardo funeral home, then back to Glenwood cemetery. When they placed Lottie May back in the earth, they replaced the flowers as carefully as possible. Val did not stay to attend this second ceremony. One was enough.

Ella Rush Murray was married to the pastor whose advice the two girl witnesses had sought. A local columnist, she had read Grace's reports and was profoundly affected by them, especially by the exhumation of Lottie's body. Murray wrote in the *Washington Times*:

> Only a woman knows just how precious to her is her own body. Only a woman knows that to a woman the chief horror of a violent death is the fact that autopsies are involved; that all the care a woman has exercised to keep her body sacred and inviolate is forgotten, and the alien hands of everyone investigating the case are privileged to examine.

> And today when they lay her away for this second and last time; when Mrs. Lottie Brandon as a tangible thing passes out for all time from this murder investigation, may it not be possible that the mental image of Lottie Brandon as he last saw her, smiling up into his face, kissing him good-by, with the light in her eyes telling of the great hope that she was cherishing—may it not be that that image will so persist that Val Brandon will never rest.

Grace had been right again. Her suspicion to reexamine Lottie's body had resulted in new evidence, though in a slightly different direction. Grace wasn't sure about that. There were other new theories now, including Lottie's having sudden-onset eclampsia, which had killed her cold in her bed. But that skin under her nails, and this man who lived outside the backyard, were questions that couldn't be dismissed. One of Lottie's shoes was in the living room, not the bedroom. And her underclothes had been taken off. These were only pieces of a still-incomplete puzzle, but Grace had helped find them. The Baltimore police, who had still failed to get a confession out of Snowden, weren't as pleased. Detective Dougherty of the Baltimore police said that Grace was only an "amateur detective" who was in D.C. representing the New York Police Department. She was a carpetbagger.

"I am a lawyer, and investigator," responded Grace. "And as such am trying to solve the mystery of the murder of Mrs. Brandon. As to the 'amateur detective,' it seems to me that Dougherty and some of his associates of the Baltimore police have played this part to perfection."

She added, "They failed to rope off the premises where the murdered woman was found—didn't interview Mrs. King, and so forth."

The next day, Grace was with Detective Dougherty and his men as they were going to question the wife of John Snowden. As the police car rolled to the curb, Grace began to step in.

"You cannot get into this machine, madam," said Dougherty. Grace didn't understand. There was plenty of room on the seat.

"Why not?" she said. "I am a member of the New York Police Department." She flashed her shiny new badge.

"I don't care whom you represent, madam, you cannot go in this machine," Dougherty said firmly. "I know that you are a newspaper reporter and that you are writing articles for a newspaper about this case under your own name." He shut the door.

"You're not giving that Negro a fair show," said Grace, quickly. "I'll get a lawyer for him."

"That's your privilege," Dougherty said. "You can do what you please. If you wish, you may follow me in another machine."

"I won't follow you!" Grace said.

"Well, I shan't be sorry if you don't," he replied.

William J. Burns, Lady Jean Doyle, and
Sir Arthur Conan Doyle (*Courtesy of Library
of Congress*)

Grace Quackenbos (*Author's collection*)

Illustration of Grace at the
People's Law Firm (New York
Times, *June 11, 1905*)

Antoinette Tolla (Actual Detective, *March 23, 1938*)

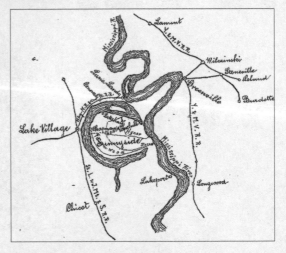

Grace's map of Sunny Side (*from* Report on Sunnyside Plantation, *Arkansas*)

Workers at Sunny Side
(*Courtesy of National Archives*)

Grace Humiston (Geneva Daily Times,
June 26, 1917)

Charles Stielow (from Report by
the Special Deputy Attorney, 1917)

Inez Milholland (Publicity photo)

Sophie Irene Loeb (Publicity photo)

PRETTY GIRL SKATER STRANGELY MISSING

Ruth Cruger, 17, Left Home Tuesday on Errand and Disappeared.

POLICE SEARCH IS IN VAIN

A Graduate of Wadleigh High School, Her Family Say She Had No Attachment.

Newspaper headline (New York Times, *February 16, 1917*)

Ruth Cruger (Actual Detective, *May 4, 1938*)

The Cocchi family (Actual Detective, *May 4, 1938*)

Police Commissioner Arthur Woods
(Author's collection)

Henry D. Cruger (New York Evening World, *June 25, 1917*)

Grace Humiston (*Author's collection*)

Julius J. Kron (*U.S. passport application, 1923*)

Ruth Cruger (Actual Detective, *May 4, 1938*)

Basement of the motorcycle shop (Actual Detective, *May 4, 1938*)

Crowd outside the store *(Author's collection)*

(Actual Detective, *May 4, 1938*)

The trial in Bologna (Chicago Daily Tribune, *December 19, 1920*)

John Snowden (Afro-American, *March
7, 1919*)

Mrs. Grace Humiston (*Author's collection*)

Skating at Van Cortlandt Park, New York City by Walter Appleton Clark (Harper's Weekly, *March 1897*)

For more images and artifacts, please visit MrsSherlockHolmes.tumblr.com.

Grace knew that Dougherty and his men had given Snowden the third degree in Baltimore. She knew they had done terrible things to him. But she also knew that the man had scratches on his cheeks and that Lottie's fingernails had skin under them. There was also the matter of the ice on the doorstep. Grace couldn't deny that. But she still felt as if he was being railroaded.

The whole town was shaken by the case. Alissa Franc summed up the shock: "We have learned that a woman can be murdered in a little row of houses with friendly neighbors surrounding her on every side, watching her movements, as such neighbors do.

"And we pause to think," she said.

John Snowden was charged and remanded over for trial. Grace quietly visited him once before she left. She remembered all the other prisoners she had talked to over the years, all staring at her from locked rooms. She left for New York City. The evidence had run its course and she was hailed in the papers for having solved the case of Lottie May Brandon.

18

Her Last Bow

Glasses clinked together as people looked toward the podium in the Café Boulevard on Second Avenue. The ballroom was filled with women in dresses, the "Vere de Veres of the East Side," all with an eye toward the empty podium in front. The occasion that night, on November 15, 1917, was the annual banquet of the Women Lawyers Association. The keynote speaker was none other than Mrs. Grace Humiston herself, fresh off her latest victory in Baltimore. The specialty of that night's festivities was further heightened by the recent vote to allow suffrage in New York. Celebrating that moment with rousing speeches were Katherine Devereux Blake and New York Supreme Court Justice Charles L. Guy, among others. They, of course, saved Grace for last. When she finally arrived, the women at the tables pointed with their gloved hands. They greeted her with warm, thankful applause as she was introduced as the hero of the Ruth Cruger case. Dressed in black, Grace seemed to take in the light of the room itself as the clapping grew before finally settling down.

The year had been long for the woman in black. There in that room, layered with white tablecloths and champagne glasses, it was the perfect time for Grace to tell her oft-repeated story of starting out as a nighttime lawyer and of her work founding the People's Law Firm. She talked about the muggy southern turpentine camps and of

Sunny Side, and of the innocent men and women she had worked to set free. When Grace talked, it was always more about the cases than it was about herself. When she spoke of the Cruger case, it seemed like a shadow was crossing her face.

For the association to invite her to speak was a great honor. This was her year, after all. Not only had she solved the Cruger case, but she had been given her own independent bureau within the New York City Police Department for the sole purpose of finding missing girls. She had spawned a deep investigation into police corruption and the madman Cocchi was about to be tried in Italy. Grace talked about the importance of her work with the police department—as the first consulting woman detective in New York—and the ongoing work she was doing in that role. She had just begun writing a series of syndicated newspaper articles about white slavery, wayward girls, and immigration that included case details and advice for parents. Grace was being asked to consult on cases all over the country. In this room of lady lawyers, she was not only one of them, she was the best of them. The applause was strong.

It was a wonderful speech, the ladies agreed, as they smiled at each other over their own clapping hands. Grace motioned to them all. She was not done talking. Not yet.

Grace mentioned Camp Upton, the brand-new army training camp on Long Island near Yaphank. It had been built as the primary staging ground for New York's brave draftees for the Seventy-seventh Army Division before they left for France and Germany. The camp had just opened in September and was still a busy hive of soldiers, workers, and personnel. Many in the crowd had a brother, friend, lover, or husband who had gone, or feared going, to Camp Upton. They all knew what the camp really was—a jumping point to the trenches of the war.

"At Camp Upton," Grace said, to the quieted room of lady lawyers before her, "there are six hundred girls who are about to become mothers—who have no husbands.

"It has been reported to me," Grace continued, over the sudden silence of the crowd, "that seven of these little mothers are dead. I have proved the facts of this in the case of two of them and am going down tomorrow to get the facts in regard to the others."

The large room with the white tablecloths and crystal glasses became quiet. But there was a familiar anger underneath it all. In a corner of the room, a reporter wrote furiously, checking with others to make sure he had heard that number correctly.

Six hundred girls.

The next day, the commanding general of Camp Upton was in his office, a wooden house on a small hill in the center of the camp's skinny parade ground. General J. Franklin Bell stood at his window and watched his camp at full life. Because the camp had very low buildings, you could see the house from almost anywhere you stood. Carved out of the marshlands in a remarkable space of four hell-bent months, Upton was built upon sixteen thousand acres of cleared Long Island brush five miles around. Its goal was to house and train 44,000 men, give or take, all under Bell's iron command.

Once the camp finally opened on September 5, 1917, New Yorkers made up the first 30 percent of its tenants, who took five days to get there by the Long Island Railroad. When six hundred men left Carlton Avenue in Brooklyn on the same day, there was semi-rioting. Five women fainted right there on the street. There were girls kissing every man who was leaving. This first wave was of single men; the army didn't want sons or fathers. Not until later. Once they arrived at Upton, the boys were given sixteen weeks of intensive instruction in theoretical and practical warfare. Like the song, it was "Goodbye Broadway, Hello France."

Bell was a two-star general. His white hair was parted down the middle with the sides clipped up high. His wool, button-down army uniform framed his serious face. He wore a tank watch and round glasses. The camp police stood watch in a tower across from his office, looking down at the cars and men. Bell knew the reporters were on the way. And perhaps others. Perhaps even *her*.

In front of him, on a desk that held troop assignments and maps of France, was a copy of the *Washington Post*, which contained the story of Grace's allegations. Bell sat down at his desk and wrote an official response. There was music playing in the background. With Bell, there was always music in the background. Bell took pride in practical instruction, but his other goal was to create soldiers who could not only fight but also sing. He purchased musical instruments and mass quantities of copies of popular songs to create what he termed the greatest chorus in the world. At Camp Upton, Long Island, "A singing man is a fighting man," General Bell said.

"It is not possible that even one girl could have died at Camp Upton much less seven," Bell wrote. "Since references in the morning papers to Mrs. Humiston's address were called to my attention early this morning, I have been diligently investigating every possible source of accurate knowledge or information. These efforts were begun nearly ten hours ago, and thus far I have been unable to locate any one who has heard of anything furnishing the slightest foundation for Mrs. Humiston's allegations."

"I cannot conceive of any such condition existing here," wrote Bell, "and I don't believe it does exist. I don't see how such conditions could exist without my hearing of them, and I have heard of no such conditions."

"I have been expecting a call from her all day," the general said. "It is now 6 P.M., but I have not heard of Mrs. Humiston being at Camp Upton. I shall continue this investigation, and if I ever succeed in finding any foundation whatever for Mrs. Humiston's allegation I shall frankly disclose what I learned to the press." Bell signed the letter sharply and had it sent off to the *New York Times*. He looked back out onto his camp, now darker and slower, and wondered if Grace Humiston was already here without his knowing it, hiding somewhere in the shadows in her black hat.

Behind the scenes, Camp Upton began taking immediate precautionary measures. All the outlying saloons were closed and higher security measures were imposed, including the frisking of all visitors, even women. In addition, federal deputies patrolled not only the camp but also the locality around it. Bell reiterated the grand standing order that "No women are permitted to be in company barracks after retreat in the late afternoon. And at no time are they permitted to go about the camp unescorted."

After Bell's statement ran in the newspaper, another reporter asked him if there would be any special precautions this Sunday, which was always visitor's day at Upton. Bell finally flashed some anger.

"Look here," he glowered, with an old whisper of a Kentucky cadence. "If you think Mrs. Humiston, or any others person, can think of any measures we are not already using I shall be glad to put them into effect." But Grace Humiston couldn't be reached or found anywhere. To the public, Upton was full of wholly American, New York boys. The *Brooklyn Daily Eagle* ran accounts of their individual exploits like they were one-reel comedies. Newly arrived Private James F. O'Brien calmly halted an important second lieutenant on the company street and borrowed a match. Charlie Holmes said, "It makes me sick to hear that mess call. I have to wash about a million pots and pans in the kitchen every day." John A. Beyer said he would "give a whole lot of money for twenty minutes in Brooklyn." Major Morris, who commanded "the Negro troops, caught a bootlegger in camp today, and confiscated three quart bottles of gin." While a score of the men watched, he poured the liquor on the ground in front of his tent. One of the sentries, with a grin from ear to ear, saluted and said, "Please sir, I would like to sleep with ma nose on that spot tonight, if you don't mind."

When soldiers first arrived via the Long Island Railroad, passing through miles of evergreens and cleared-away brush, they were shown to their barracks and bunks. There, they were greeted by a gift: their own personal Bible, generously donated by the Scripture Gift Mission of Philadelphia. Each Bible contained a special foreword written just for the soldiers of Camp Upton. It read:

The Bible is the word of life. I beg that you will read it and find this out for yourselves. You will not only find it full of real men and women, but also of things you have wondered about and been troubled about all your life, as men have been always, and the more you read the more it will become plain to you what things are worth while and what are not.

It was signed "WOODROW WILSON." New recruits, for they weren't even soldiers yet, came from all the boroughs to read those black words.

While at Upton, these men would train in "going over the top," the practice of climbing out of an actual trench with a fixed bayonet attacking a prone dummy. "Bell's Boys," they called them. When they showed up, clean and shaved, under a big sky that men who had never left Brooklyn before could only stare at, Bell addressed them all, down to the very last man. Irving Berlin was somewhere down in that crowd. There were rumors that Henry L. Stimson himself, Grace's old boss and the former secretary of war, was coming to Upton as a lieutenant colonel.

"You have entered into this war wisely." The general's voice boomed across a field of men. "I have had experience in three wars. And I would be ashamed to look my fellow citizens in the face if I died before I took an honorable part in this war.

"It doesn't matter so much when a man dies as how he dies," Bell said. "When he dies as a craven spirit he dies forever, but when he dies like a hero he lives forever." Bell then invited all those in the audience who had sons or relatives in the service to meet him up on the stage. As people filed up the wooden riser and crowded forward, he shook their hands, sometimes two at a time.

"The world was on fire," these fighting men were told.

*

The sun was nearly set, and it was already past seven thirty. The man and the woman walked in ragged step toward the two-story wooden building. There were three white columns on the top with the letters A, M, and C on them, all topped by American flags, whipping in the wind. There was a patio up front, and they could smell food inside. The man was nervously eyeing the front door.

The bell on the door jingled as the couple walked in the door of Acker, Merrall, and Condit's, the combination diner, hotel, and department store that served the whole of Camp Upton. To their right, they could see a lunch counter, just like the ones in the city. Ahead of them was a more sophisticated, sit-down restaurant. They saw a waiter in dress clothes serve a few men in uniform. To the left was what looked like a department store, full of everything from cigars to cans of tomato soup. It felt as if they were smack-dab in the middle of Thirty-fourth Street, not out here in the middle of Long Island.

The man saw a small desk located by a stairwell, signifying the part of the building that was the hotel.

"Can we get a room here?" the man asked the clerk.

"Yes, for man and wife," the clerk replied.

The girl had curls and looked down shyly. She was young. The man with her was considerably older, around forty. He took the book from the clerk and wrote down a name. The clerk said that their stay could not exceed forty-eight hours. The couple had no luggage. They started up the stairs to the room that had been assigned to them on the second floor. A few moments later, the man called down to the clerk and asked him to send a bellboy, to which the clerk replied that the place was a camp, not a hotel.

On the second floor, the man looked up and down the hallway, nervously, before finally shutting the door. The man stepped into the room and looked out the window to see Camp Upton, buzzing with activity in the Long Island twilight. Men ran, flag squads curled, and birds could be heard in the underbrush of the dusk. As the light outside finally gave out, he turned back to the room. The girl was sitting on the bed.

❧

The longer Grace was missing, the more the newspapers demanded to see the evidence behind her claim. Officials in the War Department said that her charges were absurd. They asked the Committee of Morals, headed by Raymond B. Fosdick, to begin a formal investigation.

"There are a few unfortunate girls near every camp, and we can't help that under the circumstances," Fosdick said. "Mrs. Humiston's story is damnable because it gives the impression that our boys in uniforms are wild animals, when, in fact, they are behaving themselves in splendid fashion."

There were rumors buzzing across Long Island that Grace was seen at Patchogue, sixteen miles away from Upton, and that her detective, Kron, was at Center Moriches, eight miles away. But neither called on General Bell. If they did go to the camp, they did not make known their true identities.

After a long week of taking hits in the papers, Grace's voice finally surfaced in a surprise, defiant response in the *New York Times*.

"I have been informed of the death of two girls down there," Grace said, in no uncertain terms. "By people who saw them assaulted. One of these little girls was found in the bushes near the camp, the other some distance away. Do you think that I would be foolish enough to say what I did if I didn't have the facts to back it up with?" It was hard not to trust the woman in black. But she refused to present her evidence or eyewitnesses.

"I am going down to Camp Upton shortly," Grace said. "To get facts about the other five deaths. I don't intend to advertise the day on which I shall visit the camp. I don't investigate that way. When I am ready to do so, I'll bring the proofs forward to the proper authorities."

Fosdick responded again, short and direct, in the very next edition of the paper.

"The American armies are clean," he said.

"Let Secretary of War Baker ask me to investigate the conditions about our camps," Grace responded. "Let him guarantee me a free hand in the investigation, giving me time, money, and a pass to all the camps and I will show him that what I said was true. But there must be no attempt at whitewashing the matter if I prove my statements."

Grace was still adamant about her evidence. "I will not divulge a fact until I am ready," she said.

A day later, Grace planned a trip to Washington, D.C. "I will take enough facts and proofs with me," she said, "to convince Secretary Baker that I ought to conduct an investigation for the Government. If my offers to investigate are declined, I'll bring prosecutions upon my own authority. If I am not backed up, I'll give the facts I have to the public, and let them judge what conditions are.

"I have the facts in black and white," said Grace. "I have the names of the girls who are dying at Camp Upton. I have witnesses to verify what I say. But I shall disclose nothing to any one, save, the secretary of war, if he will listen sympathetically. The information which I have received has been given to me in confidence. As a lawyer I cannot violate that confidence unless it is for some good purpose. I shall not try to refute what my critics say. I think the facts which I can produce will be sufficient to refute them."

A few days later, an aide walked into Bell's office and informed him that their internal investigation had uncovered something he needed to see. About ten weeks ago, there had indeed been a rumor that the dead bodies of two girls had been found near the edge of the camp. Bell listened quietly. The aide reported that the story was investigated at the time and a number of correspondents for New York papers—who also heard it—endeavored to run it down to a fine point of certainty. But so far, no one had been able to find any foundation for the rumor or to ascertain how it originated. The only fact the army could determine was that the rumor had its birth before any of the drafted men had even arrived at camp.

There was always gossip. On any given weekend, New Yorkers read stories of Upton soldiers taking Long Island brides in nearby Patchogue. And though enlisted men were not allowed to have wives or girlfriends stay at camp, the officers had more leeway. Major O. K. Meyers's wife was pregnant when she came to camp and gave birth to the first official child born there. News reporters used a little poetic license and named the baby "Uptonia."

But there were, like the story of the two girls, darker rumors, too. Though soldiers had not reported until September, the workers who were actually building the camp had been there since July. There were rumors of suicides, sunrise shootings, and attempts at poisoning wells. Upton officials insisted that there were no violent murders, though there were plenty of drunk workmen causing trouble in the neighboring towns. The men were "raw recruits: mentally and physically."

From the beginning, the army insisted that Camp Upton would not be located near any places where vice might thrive. At the same time, J. M. Power, a U.S. marshal, made a round of the surrounding towns, where it was rumored that houses of ill repute were preparing to establish business just as soon as the camp reached full swing. Traffickers in dope were said to be ready to devote all their time and energy to a new customer in uniform. After all, most of these men were from places like Brooklyn and Hell's Kitchen. They were not all bank tellers and tailors. There were many brass knucklers, bootleggers, and gunfighters in their lot. They were regular fellers. The infamous Gas House Gang even had an Upton chapter within the camp itself.

That is what gave General Bell pause: the origin of this particular rumor's blooming just before the soldiers arrived. The workers were a shady lot, and not just because they weren't military. Greater Long Island was so worried about these Camp Upton builders that a local judge, Joseph Morschauser, and a sheriff, Amza W. Biggs, met to hold a public forum on morals at Upton before the soldiers even arrived. The justice said he thought that these conditions of vice existed; the sheriff said that he knew positively they existed.

"That is no Sunday school crowd out there," he added. "If that isn't the worst bunch of crooks that ever landed in one spot I'm no judge of human nature. They even take the tires off of your car while gasoline is being put into it." The outlying counties threatened jail and physical punishment. "Give a few of these fellows the limit," he said. "We've got a little room left in our jail." Local officials' only consolation was that Upton's military police was largely made up of former members of New York's finest. They would have to count on the police keeping the crooks in line.

⚜

Back at the hotel, after the Camp Upton room door closed on the young couple, a knock came. There were two men, one who identified himself as a Secret Service agent. They entered and saw the young girl look up at them. She was writing down a list of the items in the room. The man she was with stood near the bed, staring at them in disbelief. The agent asked if they were married.

The couple was arrested and separated. The men led the girl through the narrow spaces between the wooden buildings to the military police. The girl with the curls listened as she was arraigned. She did not say anything.

The officers did the same to the man, though they took him to a different room. When they asked how he knew the girl, the man said he'd been introduced to her at a party by another woman.

A woman dressed in black.

19

Army of One

"What is your name?" the Secret Service agent asked the man they had taken from the hotel.

"James C. Adkins," he replied.

"When were you employed at Camp Upton?"

"Some time about the middle of August, as a carpenter."

"What had you heard?"

"I had heard there was two girls found dead."

"Where did you say they were found dead?"

"It was when I was working on the ice plant that I heard it. They didn't say where they were found dead, only they said on the edge of camp."

"Whom did you hear that from?"

"Some of the carpenters that I was working with."

"Had they seen these two girls?"

"No: they didn't say that they had seen them. They asked me if I had heard about the girls being found here. I said I did not hear about it."

"And you told this to Mrs. Humiston?"

"And I told this to Mrs. Humiston that I had heard this from them, and she asked me what was said, and I told her what the boy had told me. I have his name: his name is Constable, as well as I remember."

"About when was it that carpenter told you this?"

"As well as I remember it was about four or five days before he was laid off, or before he quit, rather."

"You told Mrs. Humiston what you had heard from them about these two girls being found dead in the vicinity of the camp?"

"I told you I was working in the camp on the ice plant and one Sunday I did see some girls lying down on the ground and some soldiers sitting by them talking."

"Where was that?"

"On the furtherside of the ice plant, where the trains come in."

"What time of day was that?"

"About 2 o'clock in the afternoon."

"That was the first day you saw Mrs. Humiston?"

"Yes, sir."

"Then you saw her again?"

"I think it was two days later."

"What did you say to her?"

"I told her I had been trying to find out about the crimes being done."

"Where did you see her again?"

"Wednesday evening at the dance, at Terrace Garden."

"What did Mrs. Humiston say then?"

"She said she had heard about the girls and who had taken their bodies away when she was going to investigate."

"Did she say who took their bodies away?"

"No, she didn't say that. I had met the civilians and I told her I had heard of men coming out here and registering at this hotel as brother and sister and also as man and wife."

"When was the next time after that you were there?"

"I think yesterday at noon."

"What did she say?"

"I think she said something about the boys going out and registering as brother and sisters and also as husband and wife."

"What was the sense?"

"What I understood was that any one could come down here and register and stay overnight and go back the next morning to the city, and I think from that they come out here under the pretense of seeing friends. And I told her what I had heard. When I told her that she said something about my coming out."

"And when you told her you would come out what did she say?"

"She said she had a girl she could trust."

"To do what?"

"To come out to camp and ___."

"Did Mrs. Humiston ask you if you would be willing to come out here at the camp and investigate what would happen if you called at the hotel for a room with a young woman and registered as man and wife?"

"Not in those words. She said that she would like to know the true conditions of this camp and as a citizen I was willing."

"Was she to pay your expenses?"

"No, sir, I pay my own expenses. I done this as a citizen of the country to find out if the things here was true. That is what I want to know."

"Let us resume with the question of providing the girl. Now, then, when you told her you would come out, what was it she said?"

"She said that she would get the girl. I didn't know who the girl was to be only this afternoon. I met her at the Penn station."

"At what time?"

"About 4 o'clock."

"When you met them at the station what did Mrs. Humiston say?"

"She told me to find out about the conditions at the camp. First she introduced the girl."

"What name did she give her?"

"The name she gave was Miss Francis."

"Then did you make your plans with the girl on the way out here?"

"We was to come out and register and catch the next train out to the city."

"What time did you go to the hotel?"

"It was a little after 8 o'clock when we went to the hotel. A little after 8 o'clock. We didn't get there in time to register and catch the train back to the city."

"As soon as you did that did you start for the station?"

"We saw there was two single beds, and then we came out and I tried to get a taxicab back to the station. I couldn't get a taxicab so I tried to get back to Patchogue."

"I am trying to get out how you earned your $5. What would you have established by what you did?"

"What I intended to do was to leave the young lady in the room to-night, and I told her I'd stay out and if I saw we registered as man and wife."

"You'd stay out in the morning and go back to town? You wouldn't tarnish her reputation?"

"No, sir, I'd no intention of doing that."

"How would you do that and go back by the next train?"

"I would not have stayed if I could have got this train."

"No, you said you planned to stay in the room for the night."

"That was after we missed the train. We made the plan when we missed the train."

"What did you tell the hotel people when you came in?"

"I just registered as Mr. Pendleton from Kansas City."

"And did you tell the clerk the occasion of your being there?"

"Not a word that."

After Adkins answered their questions, the agents also questioned Miss Francis. She looked down at her shoes and refused to answer any questions. Except that her first name was Adeline and that she lived with Mrs. Humiston. After Adkins and Miss Francis were examined, they were sent back to the hotel, where they were required to register under their own names and were assigned to separate rooms, the young girl being placed in the charge of the matron of the hotel.

The next morning, Adkins left on the first train. Miss Francis followed on the ten o'clock. General Bell told reporters that Grace had not given him any of the names of the supposed "dead girls" or of any eyewitnesses who saw them. Bell said she was "peddling gossip."

That day, a search was made of the barracks. A letter was found addressed from Adkins, who had been a carpenter during the camp's construction, to Sergeant Penland, who was currently in the Army Cooks and Bakers School. Penland, at one time, had been Adkins's bunkmate.

Dear Friend:

Will now try to write you a few lines to ask a favor of you as well as to tell you what to do in order to get tickets to the dance free. I am helping Mrs. Humiston by doing (keep this to yourself) some detective work in regards to girls under 17 years of age being enticed from their homes to white slavery and I have told her about the way girls done near the ice plunt when we were working on same one Sunday and also about two girls being found dead near the camp while I was working there, and now she wants as many of your sergeants 1st class as she can get to do so to come over to her office and tell her what you know about the conditions of the camp and how the girls stay over night there.

Come over Wednesday and bring all the men you can get to come with you and I will show you all a good time. Hoping to see you all on Wednesday evening and with best wishes to all the boys I am

Your Friend,
Jas. C. Adkins
435 East 15th St.

The letter was dated November 20, five days after Grace's speech before the Women Lawyers Association.

On November 26, Grace received a telegram from Secretary of

War Baker. "You are quoted in morning papers as making serious charges against United States soldiers," he wrote. "It is requested that you come to Washington immediately."

"I made no serious charges against United States soldiers," Grace replied. "But at a dinner of women lawyers, I mentioned certain conditions which have been reported personally and by letter to my office. Mr. Fosdick's telegram is not expressive of the sentiment of my address." Grace offered to work for six months—for free—to help the Department of War get to the truth. She even hoped that she and Major Bell would become good friends. "It takes two to make a right, you know" she said.

William H. Zinsser, the chairman of the Subcommittee on Civilian Co-operation in Combating Social Diseases, had his own views on Grace's behavior regarding Camp Upton. "She has not been willing to cooperate with any of the bodies that have been working to see whether anything has been done or to report any 'hearsay evidence' that has come to her," he said. "She rather chooses to adopt a sensational method of flaunting a hysterical charge, outlining a condition which does not exist, and perhaps in one interview doing more to spoil the work of months than anything which has yet come before the public, at least in this locality."

The next day at Grace's office, two military men walked in. They were not potential clients. They sat down with Grace and Miss Francis to take their official statements. Grace admitted to the whole plan of sending the couple to Upton. The only reason Grace's plan had failed was because of a dance she gave a few days previous where one of the attendees—Sergeant Penland—saw Miss Francis for the first time. On the night of Adkins and Francis's secret visit to Upton, Penland recognized her as she passed him by in camp. He then tipped off the military police and Secret Service, who hightailed it to the hotel room.

The press, who had begged Grace for evidence during this long ordeal, were not kind to her now. The *New-York Tribune* editorialized that "Mrs. Humiston may, in her way be doing what she considers good work, but is it necessary that twenty-five or thirty thousand members of a United States army unit, or any other organization, should have their character shaded in this manner?" The *Brooklyn Daily Eagle* called it "a disgraceful experiment":

> Charges of wholesale immorality at Camp Upton or any other camp are not to be sustained by casual experiments designed to trap hotel clerks, they are to be sustained only by the production of evidence. No such evidence has been presented by Mrs. Humiston. All that has been so far received from her is a proposal that if the Government pay her expenses she will go after the "evidence." The Government does not need to waste a penny on her. An indignant public opinion has sufficiently discounted her charges. . . . To the man who lent himself to this disgraceful experiment nothing need be said. . . . As to the girl . . . she should be removed by law, if need be, from all contact with the woman who employed her on this disgusting errand.

"I hesitate to say anything which would seem to dignify the activities and statements of Mrs. Humiston," declared Secretary of War Baker. "What she has so far done seems to have begun in irresponsible slander upon the army and ended in a futile and disgusting trick."

> Soldiers are not saints. . . . Reformers, too, are only human, and frequently a misguided zeal o'ertops judgment. Mrs. Humiston's motivations may have been admirable. Her performance has been deplorable, and its effects vicious beyond description. A scandalous accusation has been lodged, not against individual soldiers or cantonments, but against soldiers in general, facts to sustain which have not yet been produced by this woman. The charge has been spread far and wide, and wearers of the uniform have been discredited, regardless of their personal character. Yet the most discreditable thing in the whole affair has been done and admitted

by Mrs. Humiston itself. Any servant of this country should be free from the attack of sensation mongers.

Government officials and reporters were calling her claim of six hundred girls "the greatest exaggeration" and added that she was simply "seeing things that ain't."

Grace had apologized for her methods but was sticking to her story that she had evidence of vice at Camp Upton. She told the papers that she had three cases with facts that were "absolutely straight" and would vindicate her. She said that she had evidence of two infantry soldiers who had attacked two fourteen-year-old girls and held them in a Bronx rooming house for ten days. Grace kept repeating that the army had actually instructed her to investigate Upton in the first place as part of a secret operation. Fosdick disagreed: "The army has not been directed to cooperate with her in her investigation." He was quoted in the Upton newsletter, the *Trench and Camp*, that she had not "one scintilla of evidence."

Grace finally had a meeting with Major Gardner of the inspector general's office on Governor's Island, which lasted three hours. According to Grace, she furnished him with full affidavits and witness reports about the three cases, including the Bronx kidnapping. But the commander of the regiment refused to place the men Grace named under arrest. Grace's response was biting: "If more of our Generals were like General Pershing and would order men shot who attack women, we would have fewer problems on our hands."

As December approached, the shining reputation of Grace Humiston as a peerless detective was no more. The criticism against her seemed never-ending: "Her vague and preposterously incredible charges of immorality at Camp Upton," wrote *Brooklyn Life*, "show to what depths of depravity and mendacity a morbid imagination coupled with an inflated ego induced by a little notoriety can cause a woman to descend. Her achievement in the Cruger case has evidently turned Mrs. Humiston's head completely, but imagine a woman posing as a public informer of morals inducing a young girl to ruin her own reputation in order to supply some shadow of evidence to sustain the would-be reformer's extravagant charges. It would be well for this lady barrister to change her mind or have it thoroughly fumigated."

More ridicule came from "The Rookie's Diary" in the *Brooklyn Daily Eagle*, a column allegedly written by an Upton army private. "The men in my squad were discussing her refuted charges and her nasty attempt to manufacture evidence after mess this evening," he wrote. "I have been reading the papers and I never did take the woman or her charges seriously."

"Corporal" was another soldier who was quoted, further down the column. "If I had my way I would see that the proper punishment was imposed upon that woman. The Major General disposed of her in short order and to make the job more complete Washington disowned her. But being discredited does not have any effect upon her. The men I know personally in the National Army do not feel that justice will be done them until the woman who threw the mud is forced to remove the smirch."

On December 19, the Cosmopolitan Club on East Fortieth Street held an event to honor Sara C. Douglass, one of the first women police officers in New York City. The event also featured Miss Miner, who was head of the Committee on Protective Work for Girls at Camp Upton. There were smiling, flowered ladies everywhere. Miss Miner delivered a patriotic speech, and as she was stepping down from the dais, she was asked about Mrs. Humiston and the Upton disaster. Miss Miner said she was glad to be reminded, since she had meant to bring it up.

"Absolutely false her stories are," Miss Miner said, with emphasis. "The conditions about the camps are wonderful. We know, because we have had expert investigators there. Here is one of them." She drew Marian Goldmark up to the stage, who spent October investigating conditions at Camp Upton.

"Of course, we don't mean that nothing unfortunate ever happens there," said Goldmark. "There are silly girls and bad women attracted by uniforms, and there are bad soldiers of course. But the conditions are wonderfully clean, as clean as they could possibly be, and there is no truth in Mrs. Humiston's stories."

As Goldmark spoke, a man stepped in through the back door of the room, framed in its shadow. When Goldmark saw him, she stopped speaking. After a moment, she smiled and said that police commissioners were busy persons and must not be kept waiting. She gestured to the back door and introduced Commissioner Woods.

Woods took the stage with a smile. In truth, he was on his political last legs. "I am on the eve of a period of my life when I will not be so busy," he told the crowd with a smile. They all knew that the next mayor would want his own police commissioner. But instead of being nostalgic, Woods plunged into his subject, which was about the necessary human touch of police work.

"Poverty," Woods said, "is one great cause of girls leaving home, ignorance of parents is another, and drunkenness on the part of the father." He told of one girl who ran away because "she was so large for her age that she was ashamed to go to school, and her father beat her to make her go.

"That is the kind of work I like the police to do," said Woods, his grave face lighting up. "I admit I disagree with my friends who want to spend their efforts teaching Sing Sing men to knit, and so on." He paused for effect. "I'd rather prevent boys from landing in Sing Sing!" The crowd laughed and cheered.

When Woods was done, Captain Williams spoke next. He told stories of missing girls found by the police.

"Too bad we got to lose Commissioner Woods," Williams said, shaking his head. "I've been in the department twenty-one years and I haven't seen any like him. Surely the new administration can't afford to fall behind the pace he has set."

Sara Douglass then took the stage in all her glory. She told of the girls she had scolded and sent home when she found them on the streets with strange soldiers. "I'm just crazy about uniforms," some of the girls would confess to her. Sometimes, she had to rescue youthful soldiers from women. Everyone laughed at her stories. She announced with pride that the mayor's committee was trying to add ten police-women to the role. Everyone clapped at the historic announcement. The very next day, as police power for women was being expanded throughout the city, Commissioner Woods revoked the police commission he had given to Grace Humiston. Woods also took away the authority given to her chief detective, Julius Kron.

"Mrs. Humiston has done a great deal of good work," Woods admitted. "But I have not felt that I could take any responsibility for the Federal investigations which she has been carrying on." Woods announced that all of the New York City detectives working under Grace would be reassigned. The police records in her office would be removed. Woods revealed that an internal investigation, conducted by Inspector "Honest Dan" Costigan, had been completed ten days ago. The report concluded that Grace had done fine work "so long as she confined her activities to New York." According to the report, Grace's caseload was repeating, even overlapping, the work already being done by other detectives. It recommended that Grace be replaced by Lieutenant Grant Williams, who would now head the Missing Persons Bureau.

Woods refused to go into detail, saying only that this action "demonstrated the wisdom of having the work done by regular policeman acting under officers at Headquarters." Woods would not comment if the Upton controversy had contributed to the move. He said that the police department couldn't concern itself with that kind of thing. Woods did say that he had sent Grace a letter asking for her resignation earlier in the month and had offered to talk to her in person. But she was unreachable.

After Woods's announcement, the committee appointed by the mayor to help Grace in white slavery cases met at the Bar Association and demanded that Grace finally give up the evidence for the charges she had made about Upton. The stormy session ended in failure. The next day, its members all resigned, and the committee disbanded. The announcement that Commissioner Woods had deprived Grace of her shield was also followed by news that the Ruth Cruger Emergency Fund and the Grace Humiston League, founded by a number of prominent society women, had parted company with Grace early in October.

On December 30, Grace was still not in her office. Izola Forrester answered the phone and told reporters that Grace was ill at a hotel in Washington and that she would make a statement later. When reporters called on Grace at home (just to see if the Washington story was a ruse), they found only a woman named Mrs. Frankel, who was living with Grace at 307 West 100th Street. She had nothing to say. Privately, her friends complained that Grace was being persecuted because of her claims about Camp Upton. Grace was still telling her friends that she had acted with full authority from the secretary of war. The *Washington Post* said that the Department of War "had been cooperating with the women lawyer in an investigation of moral conditions at various army camps." The source for the story of the two murdered girls was never found, though it was confirmed that Camp Upton was populated with 142 former New York City policemen, many of whom had been there since the camp was constructed.

When the holidays came and went that year, most people had forgotten about Ruth Cruger, though she sometimes came unbidden to the thoughts of mothers and fathers as they watched their own happy children. Ruth was, of course, never far from the Cruger apartment in Harlem, once again covered with the snow that carried so many cold memories. On New Year's Eve, on the last day of 1917, Grace Humiston wrote a final telegram to Commissioner Woods. She accused him of playing politics and challenged his right to remove her without a hearing.

Thank you for your expressions of praise made yesterday to Miss Forrester concerning my work for girls, and your statement that it is beyond criticism. I am informed, however, that you suggest my resignation because you deem my recent criticism of conditions surrounding military camps either inadvised or unfounded.

As I have written you, investigations now proceeding with army officers will, when completed, establish the fact and remedy conditions which may require change I cannot believe that you or any one else will prejudge accuracy of statement.

Differing opinions may properly exist as to whether public statement of truth is inadvisable, but I submit that in any event no criticism that has arisen because of these statements has been in the least directed against you or your department, and now that the matter has dropped out of public attention I earnestly urge that it should not again be brought to public issue by you at this last moment of your administration.

Grace then told the newspapers that she was planning on resigning anyway because of the incoming mayor, but it rang a little hollow.

20

The Assassin Strikes

As 1918 began, Grace decided to keep her practice open at her main office on the third floor of 50 East Forty-second Street. There were clients, though not as many as six months ago. Whether the lower volume of clients was a result of the war, Grace's tarnished reputation, or something else, Grace didn't know. But people still came in looking for help, especially when they were desperate.

So it was no surprise one afternoon when a man, around seventeen years old, walked into her third-floor office. He slipped off his coat and hat and hung them on the post outside the door. The secretary was busy, so Julius Kron stepped up to greet him and take down his information. There was always room for a new client.

"I've come to see Mrs. Humiston," the young man announced.

"She's not in," said Kron. "Why did you want to see her?"

"I'm going to kill her," the boy said.

Kron looked at his face. He could instantly tell that the kid was serious.

"Well, if I can't kill her," the boy said slowly, "then might as well kill you!"

The boy picked up a chair and circled Kron with a cold look in his eyes. There were two young men from the Morality League and four other clients in the office. They ran out the door immediately. Josephine

Geisinger, the operator for the office, entered the room and gave the boy a disarming smile. He put down the chair.

"Be calm," she said. "What's the matter?"

"I'm going to kill Mrs. Humiston," he said. "But I'll kill you first." The boy lunged forward with the chair, throwing it at Kron. The detective dove behind a desk as Geisinger sped into the secretary's office, locking it behind her. As the young man banged on the door, she and four other young women took shelter under the desks. Josephine pulled the phone with her under a desk and demanded to be connected to the West Thirtieth Street police station.

By this time, Samuel Bustwick, another private detective who was in the back of the office, ran in and squared himself up against the assassin. The boy eyed him before he pulled an eight-inch blade out of his shirtsleeve. Behind a desk, Kron palmed a small object from an inner pocket. Bustwick pointed at the boy's knife. "You better put that up," he said. The boy grabbed a chair with his other hand and chased after Bustwick, striking a glancing blow on his head. Bustwick staggered back. At the same time, Kron stuck his head out the window and blew the police whistle he had retrieved from his person.

Private detective John Goudart, who worked at another firm on the third floor, was in the hallway when he heard the whistle. He saw the hat and coat outside the door and ran in. On the street, a traffic policeman named McCarthy looked up and saw Kron pulling on the whistle. Taking a moment to count the floors and windows, McCarthy took off for the front entrance.

When McCarthy entered the room, the boy was advancing on the detectives. The knife was on the floor, and he had pulled an eight-inch cast iron stove lifter out of his hip pocket. He raised it to pound down on Kron's head. The boy turned around, and policeman McCarthy floored him with his right fist.

The assassin was charged with felonious assault. His name was George Toomey, seventeen, of Tompkinsville on Staten Island. He was sent to Bellevue for observation. Grace returned a half hour later to a very messy office. When she saw Toomey down at the police station, she recognized him. He had visited her office a few days before.

"He said I was talking about him behind his back," Grace said.

Grace admitted that since her police badge had been taken from her, she had received many threatening letters, and she intimated that she wouldn't feel safe until she got it back again.

The police made a statement saying that they had received an anonymous telephone message that a murderer was going to call on Mrs. Humiston at six P.M. The police sent a detective to her office to check it out. The detective had arrived at six, waited until seven, and then left. There was no one there. Grace declared that she knew nothing of the message or of this detective.

In the press, Grace was now being portrayed as faded in both appearance and power. "She isn't even pretty," one paper reported. "Almost middle-aged—wears her hair parted in the middle, and she doesn't frivol." Her office was still "besieged by countless parents" even though "a fashion display had the power to lure her quite as easily" as a real crime. This type of pigeonholed thinking toward middle-aged women was widespread. Newspapers ran advertisements for Lydia E. Pinkham's Vegetable Compound, "especially adapted to help women" through the critical time "between the years of 45 and 55 . . . often beset with annoying symptoms such as nervousness, irritability, melancholia, heat flashes which produce headache and dizziness, and a sense of suffocation." That was how some people saw her.

A year after Ruth's disappearance and murder, the motorcycle squad had been completely revamped and the Fourth Branch had been reorganized. William Eynon, Willard A. Helms, Thomas Kerrigan, and John Ochsenhirt, all motorcycle men attached to traffic squad C, were found by the courts to be in violation of rule 39, which covered the issuance and returns of tickets.

On February 22, Detective Lagarenne was finally convicted, after an eight-day trial, of dereliction of duty in the Cruger case. The jury concluded that Lagarenne had failed to adequately search the cellar and had not given Cocchi the focus he deserved. It didn't help his case that Lagarenne not only called Cocchi "Al" but also told Henry Cruger that Cocchi was a respectable man in the neighborhood. The conclusion was that Cocchi was a man who serviced police bikes and was a favorite with cops. The jury deliberated for four hours before handing their decision to Justice Goff.

During the trial, attorney Frank Aranow, representing Lagarenne, made the point that "the finding of Ruth Cruger's body in the cellar of Cocchi's bicycle repair shop was entirely due to Lagarenne and his brother officer, Frank McGee, and no one else. Mrs. Grace Humiston, who took all the credit for the finding of the girl's body, was not there at the time it was discovered, nor had anything to do with the unearthing of it."

Frank McGee's trial was next. Following special prosecutor James Osborne's lead, Lagarenne even testified against his longtime partner by identifying his signature on some reports. The court found gross negligence not in the way the case was investigated by McGee but in the way Ruth's disappearance was initially reported. After the first call from Henry came in, the lieutenant on the desk, William Brown, failed to accurately record the call, leaving a fourteen-hour gap between Henry's desperate call and the assigning of the case to Lagarenne and McGee. Unlike his former partner, Frank McGee was acquitted, but not without incident. During summation, McGee's attorney, Aranow, had strong words for Prosecutor Osborne.

"Would that I had the power in my hand to indict officials for neglect of duty," said Aranow, "I would have indicted Mr. Osborne for neglect of duty because he said things to this man (he pointed to McGee) in front of the Grand Jury which he knows is a lie. I don't make any mistake in that." At the end of the long table in front of the jury, Osborne rose to his feet.

"Do you mean to say that I lied?" Osborne shouted. He rushed across the room and tried to land a right hook at Aranow, but it weakly sailed past him through thin air. Osborne slowly fell on his own elbow. As the judge banged his gavel and officials jumped in to separate the two, one of the bailiffs snickered, calling Osborne's punch "a Mary Ann upper cut." When order was restored, Osborne approached the bench, his head bowed in shame.

"Your Honor, I humbly apologize to you. It is the first time in a practice of thirty-five years that I have allowed my temper to get the best of me in court."

The last person to be tried was the biggest fish, Captain Cooper, the former head of the Fourth Branch detectives. On August 3, 1917, Cooper had been indicted by the grand jury. Judge McIntyre fixed bail at one thousand dollars. When the trial phase began, only one juror was selected when Justice Goff declared, at the request of Osborne, that he was sure there wasn't enough evidence to convict Cooper. The judge dismissed the indictment against him.

On April 18, 1918, John Lagarenne, the only one to be convicted, went before Justice Goff for sentencing. Lagarenne was offered the choice between a $250 fine and 250 days in jail. John Lagarenne paid the money and was released. When the final bill for the investigation came out of the comptroller's office, the district attorney had spent $7,302.01 for "Special Expenses in Connection with the Murder of Ruth Cruger."

That same month, in a different courtroom in Baltimore, John Snowden was found guilty of murdering Lottie May Brandon. The jury deliberated for thirty-five minutes. Snowden, who had never once confessed, nearly collapsed in court at the verdict. The judge waited a week to sentence him in hopes that the volatile atmosphere of marchers and crowds would settle down. Neither the *Times* nor the *Post* ran the story on the first page in an attempt to defuse a violent reaction. On February 13, 1918, Snowden was sentenced by Judge Duncan to hang. The governor would fix the date.

By October, the case finally reached the court of appeals. It is there that the world finally heard Val Brandon's full story. On that fateful day, Val took the ferry from the experimental navy station, walked through the front door of his home, and whistled. There was no response, so he walked through and went into the bedroom. He saw his wife on the bed. Already seven months pregnant, she was lying on her side. He called her name, but there was no answer. He began to worry if she was sick or had fainted, so he walked up to her and touched her shoulder. She still didn't say anything. All of the shades were drawn. He left the room, then the house, and went to the neighbor's house.

From there, Val went down to the bakery, where they tried to telephone for a doctor, without luck. Val then ran into a Mr. O'Neill, who went to go get a doctor. O'Neill told Val to go back to his house and wait. By the time Val arrived at his home, the doctor had just arrived.

"Did you see your wife after that?" the prosecutor asked.

"Not until late that evening. I got in there, and the doctor went in to the middle room and shut the door and left me in the front room with some of the neighbors; I didn't know really what happened until late that night when several detectives came around and took me with them and I identified the body of my wife."

"You didn't lift her up to see whether she was fainting or she was dead?"

"No, sir."

"That is all you did, laid your hand on her shoulder?"

"Yes, sir."

"That was as far as you went?"

After receiving no answer, the prosecutor resumed his questioning. "On Tuesday night after you retired, it has been testified you had intercourse with your wife. What did you do after that intercourse? What was done, what did your wife do?"

"She got up right away and went out in the other room," Val said, his eyes downward.

"What did she do?"

"Well, she didn't tell me what she was doing, but I know what she was doing."

On February 22, Governor Harrington said that he would meet with any last-minute petitioners at eleven o'clock in his office. All other appeals had failed; only a single man's mercy remained. Somewhere between two hundred and four hundred people showed up, many with signs and song. All of the jurors who convicted Snowden, save one, were present, having signed a petition for his release. Sixty leading white businessmen signed the same document and stood out in front with the crowd. A band played gospel music outside.

Ella Rush Murray was there too, as well as the mother of the two girls who were the key witnesses, Edith Creditt and Mary Perkins, who had since moved from the area altogether, having become scared for their safety. Murray had changed her mind about Snowden and now wanted him freed. Grace was there as well, though not as a reporter or as an ad hoc detective. She wanted Snowden—the man she had helped convict—to be freed.

Snowden's sentence weighed heavily on Grace because she knew she had helped put him there mostly through circumstantial evidence. So she had returned to Baltimore to do the thing she did best—set the dead free. She had been working on the case since she last left Washington. But Grace had something more than argument; she had new evidence about the Brandon marriage. Grace had knowledge of a "mysterious friend" and an alleged confession by Val Brandon that was overheard as he was dreaming.

Governor Harrington listened to Grace. But he still believed that the case was simple at heart. "I was inclined to think it was robbery," he said, "and for that purpose the woman's stockings were taken off, believing that she kept her money in her stocking and that coming into contact with the white woman's flesh aroused the beast within him and he committed the greater crimes, murder and rape. He has had a fair trial," the governor said. "It is not up to me to try this case. I will not interfere."

On February 27, the night before the scheduled execution, two companies of infantry with fixed bayonets, ordered up by the governor, appeared at the jail to patrol any unruly crowds. The city was under martial law. Snowden had only been to school for six months of his life. Earlier that day, the sheriff passed out white tickets of admission to anyone who wanted to witness the hanging of John Snowden at daylight. Inside his cell, Snowden was still proclaiming his innocence, meekly and quietly.

Grace was still trying a full range of legal tactics, but the governor was unswayed.

"I am firmly convinced of Snowden's guilt," he said, "and you can appeal to me until Doomsday for 'clemency' and you will not get it. I wish that my lips were unsealed and I could tell you all I know, and they will be unsealed if necessary."

Grace then allegedly tried to induce Ida Burch—one of the witnesses who claimed to have seen Snowden leave the Brandon home—to change her testimony. The district attorney told Grace that she would be arrested if she continued to badger his witness. Murray rushed to Grace's defense and said that the DA's bullying was just "one of many endeavors made by certain interests to discredit a woman who was appointed assistant to Attorney General Charles Bonaparte by President Roosevelt." That old title still carried weight in Washington. Murray also revealed that she was "strongly warned by three highly prominent men, all connected with the case, not to bring Humiston back to Annapolis." Time was running out, but Grace had, as always, one more card to play.

Inside the jail, as John Snowden looked straight at the camera in front of him, he could hear hammering somewhere in the background. The sound of iron and wood was strangely comforting. Snowden was wearing his brand-new blue suit, black tie, and black shoes. The suit fit nicely across his broad shoulders. Another man walked in, and Snowden could feel the muscles in his legs fly away into air.

"Marshal Carter," Snowden said to the man. "I want to say before I go, that I forgive you for the way you treated me in that sweatbox in Baltimore." A man then took his photograph. Snowden did not smile. The words attributed to him appeared in a newspaper.

Outside, a band played. John Snowden could hear lots of footsteps as he walked out to cheers and song. He walked up the stairs.

Many people in the crowd said that it was a good thing that John

Snowden was a client of Mrs. Grace Humiston. She had met with him just last night, and they all knew she was working on some last-minute plan.

When the hood was placed over John Snowden's head and he dropped through the trapdoor to his death, his body swinging in the chilly Annapolis air, over one hundred people stood outside the jail singing "God Will Take Care of You." His body, in the best suit it had ever worn, was taken down and given to his sister. A three-hour funeral followed.

A few hours before he was led to the gallows for the murder of Lottie May Brandon, Snowden had said a few words:

In a few hours from now, I shall step out of time into eternity to pay the penalty of a crime I am not guilty of. God knows that I am telling the truth, and after I have been hanged, I am asking the authorities to please continue to search for the murderer. Though I have suffered, if it would have proved to the world that I was innocent, I would have willingly gone through that awful degree again. . . . I could not leave this world with a lie in my mouth.

A few days after the execution, the sheriff's office received a printed letter from Washington, D.C. It read:

I am sorry you killed Snowden today. He is not the guilty man. I am the man. I could not stand to see another man live with my heart so I put Lottie May out of my way. I hope his sins fall on my head. He is not the man. God will bring things right some day.

The letter was unsigned.

21

The Invisible Places

Bologna was a medieval town once dominated by tall stone towers, piled up into the cloudy sky. But over the years, most of these towers had fallen, having been destroyed by invaders, or having been built too high and hopeful to begin with. Of the few left, the most famous were the two—the leaning Garisenda and the taller Asinelli—that could be seen from anywhere in the city. The Asinelli had been used by medieval philosophers to study the rotation of the earth. During the Second World War, it was a post for rescue efforts. The Garisenda ominously leaned toward the ground. Dante referred to the tower in the "Inferno": "like the Garisenda looks / from beneath the leaning side, when a cloud drifts / over it, so that it seems to fall."

The towers could be seen from the square of the beautifully ornate Barochi palace, where Cocchi's trial was to be held. The outdoor piazza was always filled with a moving, murmuring crowd, who were now discussing every detail of the family history of Cocchi and commenting on the identities of the ten jurors. Venturini, Cocchi's lawyer, argued that his client had never lost his Italian citizenship. This had been ratified, some thought, by the fact that Cocchi was a reservist in the Italian army. Even though Italy did have an extradition treaty with the United States, she did not give up her citizens lightly. Especially in times of war. So Cocchi was stuck in his dungeon cell, with his father and brother forced to provide food from outside for him, as was the custom. As all parties prepared for his trial, the mayor of Bologna sent a formal letter to the New York City government to express his deep regret and shame over Cocchi's horrific acts.

On June 23, 1919, Alfredo Cocchi, son of Giocondo, born at Malalbergo on June 24, 1881, appeared before the Italian court of assizes at Bologna, accused of attempted rape, murder, and giving misleading information while entering the kingdom under a series of false names.

Inside, the court of assizes was dark and wooden, very much like a church. The high ceilings had dark panels with small lights. Yellow murals on the walls served as background to white marble statues of men in robes. The floor was stone, and a high chandelier watched over the room like an ironwork cloud.

Now, two years after Cocchi's confession, Judge Zucconi was gone. Chief Justice Signor Bagnoli now sat in a wide, wooden chair on one end of the room. Chairs lined the sides. On a riser stood a few more rows of stiff-backed chairs and the dreaded cage, where the accused would stand. A balcony set out on the opposite wall. The center of the long room was ready to be filled—as it was every day—with somehow different versions of the same story.

After the room filled and it was time for Cocchi to testify, they let him step into the middle of the court. He looked nervous. Despite all the buzzing in the square, it was not expected to be a long trial. The Americans needed a trial, and the city needed to just put Cocchi away in that cell for good. These proceedings were a foregone conclusion. Cocchi had already confessed to the crimes so no one was expecting any surprises. It would just be a matter of how much his lawyer could pare down his sentence.

Free of cells or shackles, Cocchi started walking down one end of the space in front of the bench. Some wondered if he might make a swift run for the doors. Instead, Cocchi began to talk, gesturing with his hands, pointing through people and at things that weren't there, to show where things in his bicycle shop were placed thousands of miles away and several years before. Cocchi noisily moved desks and pointed to clerks to act as stand-ins for pieces of furniture and people. He started to tell the true story of that day in his shop.

"I was talking to the signorina," Cocchi said, pointing to the clerk in front of him. Cocchi told how Ruth Cruger had come into his store to have her ice skates sharpened. Cocchi was, to all present, a glittering fool, talking and waving at ghosts.

Cocchi turned swiftly. He motioned to the lawyer on the other side of the room. "Then my wife struck her on the back of the head with one of my tools." The gallery of people froze.

"It was not I who struck the fatal blow," said Cocchi, "it was my wife. I hid the body to protect my wife."

As the courtroom rose as one, the enormity of Cocchi's words reached the judge. Not only had Cocchi just retracted his confession, but he had just claimed, in front of the entire court, that his wife, Maria, was the real murderer of Ruth Cruger.

Judge Bagnoli roared for order. He instructed the prisoner to finish his story.

"Not I, but my wife, in an excess of furious jealousy, killed Miss Cruger," Cocchi said, his hand on his chest. "I had accused myself in order to save the mother of my children Athos and Georgette, but as I knew from the documents of the lawsuit that she is very adverse to me, I thought it would be better to tell the truth. And as an action was brought against her in America for this murder, I wish to know how she could escape the condemnation."

The prosecutor asked what happened next.

"I took the body," said Cocchi, "and tried to conceal it in the cellar but the door was not large enough." The prosecutor asked, pointedly, how he made her fit. Cocchi paused. "I sawed the body in two," he said.

As the room again erupted into loud shouting and finger-pointing, the judge kept his eye on Cocchi, who had the same steady stare that he always did. As order was called, the prosecutor shouted, "Was she already dead?"

"Yes," said Cocchi. "Yes."

When the room quieted down, Cocchi produced a new laundry list of witnesses that he wished the prosecution to investigate. A number of them were known to prosecutors, but a number of them were not.

The next day as court began, Signor Venturini, now seventy-seven years old, stood before the judge. His client, Cocchi, stood on the prisoner's platform, quiet and remote. He was on full view for anyone who dared risk eye contact with him. Everyone in the room was still thinking of yesterday. Prosecutor Mancuso said that Cocchi's display had ruined any sort of sympathetic angle. "He gained nothing by his dramatic presentation," Mancuso told the press. "Of course, it is certainly his plan to have his trial postponed again and again so that he will be entitled to receive his friends and his meals in prison instead of suffering solitary confinement. Cocchi knows that he is a doomed man. That is why he is playing for delay."

Venturini approached the bench with a letter. He explained to the judge that he had received this some time ago and had thought it the work of a crank. But recently, he had been in contact with the writer, who confirmed that every word was true. Venturini thought it might be important to share with the court now, especially in the wake of yesterday. The judge wondered how much of a surprise that was to Venturini.

The judge took the letter in his hands. It had a postmark from New York. He looked at it, and his expression changed. He handed the letter back and asked Venturini to read it. The old man held it up, adjusting it to his eyes.

Room 850 Municipal Building
New York City
August 18, 1917

EXCELLENCY:—*However much I may desire the extradition of Alfred Cocchi, and the meting out to the monster of the extreme penalty for his crime in the country of its committal, I think it would be a great and grievous mistake to deliver him to the American authorities for the present. . . .*

I, for one, do not believe that Cocchi's confession is the truth—at least not the whole truth. There is not one iota of proof how, when, where, why, or by whom, the Cruger girl was slain. There is no certainty as to whether her body was buried in the cellar before or after Cocchi's flight. It is almost a moral certainty that <u>Cocchi's shop was one of the stations of the White Slave System:</u> *that the Cruger girl had fallen into the hands of the slavers while at school; and that her death resulted from attempted abortion. I take no stock in the findings of an autopsy or post-mortem on a decayed body over four months in the grave and especially if the autopsy be performed by an employee of the prosecutor, and there is proof that the prosecutor is a shielder and shelterer of White Slavers.*

I lost a fine girl, 21 years of age, and, like the Cruger girl, a student, but at Hunter College, not at Wadleigh High School. I live in 115th Street, about forty feet across the street from the Wadleigh. My girl died at her home on the 1st day of October, 1916. The unaccountable suddenness of her death, and the attitude of certain people in the locality, led me to make an investigation which resulted in the discovery of a complete branch or district of the White Slave System, headed by a manager named Lawrence, whom, I am credibly informed, is the financial backer of a chain of dives and saloons, and a particular personal friend of Edward Swann, District Attorney of New York County. The various quarters of this system are located two blocks from the Wadleigh School. My girl fell a victim to the fiends, and died as the result of abortion, after suffering about a year of unimaginable agony of body and mind. I got all the evidence, with over a score of witnesses, to present the case to the Grand Jury; but Swann refused to prosecute—refused to do anything in the matter. On December 1st I appealed to the Governor, and was promised that my case would be considered, but although I have renewed this application twice since then, nothing has been done—and nothing will be done.

Now, Ruth Cruger passed these slave dives twice a day, going to and from school. Is it likely or credible that she had sufficient self-control to escape the allurements of the slavers? The ways of these fiends are too insinuating and seductive for an unsophisticated school-girl to resist them. There is the dance-hall, the suave exquisitely dressed dude, the sympathetic soda-water and ice-cream dispenser, the handy capsule of chloral hydrate in the soda-water— and the sleep! Even an automobile was not lacking as part of the apparatus of this slave gang for whisking the victims about the city—the very mobile so often seen in Cocchi's shop. The Cocchi-Cruger case is, of course, no concern of mine; but if my surmise is correct, that both girls were victim of the same gang, it is of prime importance to me that Cocchi be preserved alive in Italy until he is exhaustively examined by the Italian authorities regarding the matters here disclosed, and until my case gets an open hearing in New York.

There has been a regular campaign of noisy hysterics worked up by a lot of shady self-promoters in regard to the Cruger murder, and Swann was not slow to take advantage of the confession and switch the murder matter, with the adroitness of a juggler, into a police "graft" inquiry.

Your Excellency's most obedient servant,

J. J. LYNCH

P.S.—Further and fuller details will be forthcoming if desired.

On July 24, 1919, the president of the Italian assizes issued an order to suspend Cocchi's trial while they explored these shocking new claims.

"It seems now opportune, or better necessary," the judge said, "after the new crimination of the said Cocchi, and to improve the actual debate—that the acts of the American judicial authority concerning the said Magrini be examined thoroughly." The court needed to find out if Maria Cocchi could be implicated, if the letter about white slavery was legitimate, and if there were other records in America that would be necessary to continue the trial. Cocchi was now providing Italian authorities with dozens of names of people he said should be questioned in New York. Across an ocean, Swann said that Cocchi's requests—or tactics—were "absolutely ridiculous and preposterous." "This is merely a belated attempt to shift the blame," he said.

What had begun two days before as an exercise in formality had spiraled into pandemonium. In the end, Cocchi was taken back to his familiar cell, under no formal sentence and free of any fear of extradition. There was no date set for his trial to resume. With no eyewitnesses or real physical evidence tying him to the crime, Cocchi, though still behind iron bars, was feeling free.

✤

In New York, Julius J. Kron was running his own private detective agency out of a twelve-story building known as the Vincent on 302 Broadway. The store had previously been a gun shop, and you could still smell the powder, especially in the spring. Kron now had his own office, his own secretary, and several detectives who worked for him, including a woman. His letterhead had his name twice, first as Julius James Kron in the top center, and then in the right header above "The Principal." He also listed himself as "Former Special Agent, U.S. Department of Justice and as the Chief Detective of the Morality League of America." As the Morality League, the old team of Grace and Kron still ferreted out kidnappers all throughout the city. They rescued Gladys Benson of Yonkers and Muriel Flynn of Mount Vernon at 125th Street and Seventh Avenue. After the fifteen-year-old girls were taken to the Children's Society, they told a story that led to the arrest of two men, Harry Wurzberger and Irving Breslau. Grace and Kron were finally catching not only the victims but also the perpetrators of these acts, whether they were actual kidnappers or just smooth-talking scum. They rescued Evelyn Rose, twenty, from August Wuttereich, twenty-two, an assistant engineer at an ice plant on Atlantic Avenue. The names and places of their conquests continued to appear in the papers.

Not every case was a headline. Kron did plenty of investigative work, which New York City had an abundant supply of. Some nights it was shadowing. Sometimes it was records work or tracing. Sometimes it was just messy. Ralph E. Woods was a civil engineer who came to Kron's office with a blank stare. His wife had taken a new job and was getting home later and later at night. Kron went to work and, within a week, led a raiding party on an apartment at 38 Barrow in Greenwich Village, where Don Luis R. Alfaro, the young nephew of the Panamanian minister to the United States, resided. When they barged in the door, they found Alfaro in a white bathrobe. There was a red dress lying on a table, along with a pair of silk stockings. Ralph, the angry husband, found his wife, Mrs. Edla G. Woods, twenty-six, of Astoria, hiding in the dark closet. Ralph immediately demanded a divorce—and custody of their son, John, two. These cases repeated like days of the week.

Grace had survived the threat on her life, but after the Brandon case had finished, Grace had gone from the most celebrated woman in New York City to something of a pariah. But she was still trying to save the girls of her city. After a few failed starts, Grace opened the Manhattanville Be Kind Club in June. The purpose of the club was to be a place where women could listen to lectures, engage in sporting clubs, and be safe from the perilous streets. The club also had a "nursery home," where mothers could leave their children when they were at work.

That summer, the club opened its doors with a lecture given by Grace. A welcome dance followed, which carried an admission charge of five cents to defray the rent and lighting costs. Grace knew that there were many dance halls in the area known as places of vice; she thought that her club would provide a place she could control and oversee. This was a new endeavor for Grace—and she was a bit over her head, as always—but she knew that here, on the ground, is where the front lines in her war really were. As the music played and the young people danced, a gruff man flanked with two policeman walked in her door.

The man, Captain Gargan, of the police department, asked for Grace and informed her that he was going to shut her dance down. He claimed that there were "vicious loafers" on the street corners around the lights of the Be Kind Club. He said that some of them were dancing with the girls, some of whom were no more than thirteen years old. Even worse, Gargan found out that Grace had no license to operate a dance hall. Grace was shocked. She had talked to the appropriate bureau at City Hall, and they told her she didn't need one.

Gargan loudly ordered that the dancing be stopped. Girls and their partners stared at him from the floor. Gargan said that until a license could be procured, everyone had to leave. Dancegoers said that Gargan was very insulting to Mrs. Humiston and acted in a way not fitting a policeman. Grace was so upset that she tendered her resignation as sergeant of the police reserves—the last official link she had left to the police—right then and there. Captain Gargan gladly accepted it.

The charges against Grace for operating a dance hall without a license were dismissed in the First District Court. The court said that she was not running the hall for profit so there was no charge to pursue. Grace told the court that she would apply for a license right away even though she was still convinced she didn't need one. She told a reporter from the *New York Times* that Ruth's body had been found in Captain Gargan's precinct. Most people knew what she meant, though some actually said it. "Apparently the police never forget or forgive," wrote Richard Spillane in *Commerce and Finance*. "No Camorra or Mafia is more vindictive. They will 'get' Mrs. Humiston yet," Spillane wrote. "That is, unless there is enough decency at Police Headquarters to stop it."

Grace was also working on opening a similar club on Long Island called the Castle, but the local Beechhurst community voted against it. She had a series of properties financed by her sister Jessie and hoped to rekindle the Be Kind Club as the Grace Club, but securing a permanent location—always a problem in New York—remained an issue. Grace went to suppers and book clubs and still gave talks. And she was still practicing law when people came to see her. She wrote essays for newspapers. But she was, in the public eye, much diminished. But Grace never stopped. Located at 7 Manhattan Street, the original Be Kind Club, before Gargan shut it down, was just around the corner from the old motorcycle shop where Ruth Cruger had died. By trying to help the girls in that same neighborhood, Grace was perhaps still working that sad old case, long after Ruth had gone.

22

The Witnesses' Revenge

Three years to the day that Ruth Cruger disappeared, the Honorable Joseph F. Mulqueen in the Court of General Sessions in New York heard the last testimony in the case against Alfredo Cocchi for the crime of murder in the first degree. It had been three long years. And no matter how much anyone involved barked to the press or the government, they all knew that Cocchi wasn't coming back to New York. They were surprised they thought he ever would. The only good news was that the trial was finally going to resume in Bologna. Or so they were told. For three years, Cocchi had been sitting in jail—but free of sentence or threat of extradition. And with this new trial, he had the possibility of actually going free.

So much had changed in New York, as it always did. Woods was long gone; he was now a full colonel in the army. Edward Swann was hanging on as the district attorney, but the Tammany bosses were trying to push him out. Swann had tried, numerous times, to get either his assistant, Talley, or Maria Cocchi to go to Italy as his proxy. Swann thought that if he had an ironclad witness, this nonsense would finally end. But although officials in Italy assured Maria of her safety, the U.S. government could not. No matter what officials promised, Maria Cocchi was terrified that, after her husband's story, she would be detained in Bologna for murder. Swann knew that part of his job was to explore Maria Cocchi's role in the events of that murderous day so long ago.

Swann looked at the request from Italy for the depositions of witnesses named by Cocchi.

Swann didn't know what Cocchi's plan was—and he wanted no part of it—but he also knew that providing the depositions might be the only way to assist the case. He began trying to find all of the named witnesses and schedule them into the Court of General Sessions to give their testimony. He tried to locate and organize all the documents of the case, but they had been spread across many different departments. With all the overturn in personnel, some of it was missing altogether. Swann found what he could and sent it all off to Italy. It would never return to America. And then, when he was done, Swann set about answering the new questions from Italy. He was going to do his job, even if no one else cared. Even the papers would become jaded, wondering if "perhaps our grandfathers will be able to tell us something about that ancient crime."

Swann hung his hat on humanity. The new forensic sciences of his profession were certainly persuasive, but Swann believed in good old-fashioned testimony. "The very essential of justice," Swann said, "is the veracity of the witnesses. Without it the true facts cannot be ascertained, and there can be no such thing as an even handed administration of justice." Swann knew that it was now up to the very people involved in the case to put Cocchi away for good—or tell the truth at last.

Swann first interviewed Edward Fish, who had been the subject of much scrutiny three years ago. He was now a salesman for the Goodyear Tire Company. At the time Cocchi owned his cycle shop, Fish stored his motorcycle there. Fish said Cocchi and his wife fought frequently, but only in Italian, which he didn't understand. Fish's fiancée of ten years, Elizabeth Mitchell, repeated the same thing, and told stories of them all riding together on motorcycles in the free air of the country. Elizabeth was friendly with Maria but admitted that Maria never confided in her about any domestic troubles. She stopped and thought for a moment.

"The only subject of our conversation I recall was about her baby," Elizabeth said. "She seemed to me to be very much interested in her children." Helen Beck, another new witness on the list, said the same thing. She and her husband, John, had lived in the same house as the Cocchis on 75 Manhattan Street.

"Did you help secure an abortion for Maria?" Swann asked, referring to Cocchi's claim that she had.

"It is untrue," Helen said. "I never secured a physician on any occasion for Mrs. Cocchi." Helen said that the first time she had spoken to Mr. Cocchi was when Mrs. Cocchi returned from the hospital after giving birth to Georgette. Helen visited her and the baby at home to help and got to know them and the boy, Athos. Mrs. Cocchi never made any complaint.

"So far as I was able to observe," Helen said, "Mrs. Cocchi was a faithful and devoted wife and a good mother. She was an exceptionally good housekeeper and always kept her home in a clean condition, and was always interested in the care of her children."

Since the first trial, Swann's investigators had found a record that Cocchi and his wife had consulted with someone at the court of domestic relations on September 24, 1915. The probation officer they saw was named Rose McQuade. Though her memory was fuzzy, McQuade's notes revealed that the couple had been fighting. On McQuade's advice, the Cocchis agreed to return home and live together. In her notes, McQuade wrote that "no formal complaint was made by the wife against the husband."

"I am unable to say whether or not she is the same woman," McQuade said, "because of the lapse of time, and the fact that I have interviewed many thousands of women in similar cases since that time."

Swann was confident that he had enough testimony to refute Cocchi's claims about neighbors and secret abortions. But there were a few people left to talk to. When Cocchi's trial had been suspended three years ago, one of the reasons was the enigmatic letter from J. J. Lynch, whose letter to the Italian court during Cocchi's original trial ground the proceedings to a halt. Swann found him easily.

"I am an accountant by occupation," said the fifty-eight-year old Lynch, with an Irish accent. "I am employed by the City of New York and have been so employed for the past 20 years." Swann showed Lynch the letter that he had sent to the Italian courts three years ago. Lynch admitted it was his handwriting.

"I had a young daughter," Lynch said, quietly, "who died." He went on to explain that he thought her death had been caused by the same criminal agencies that killed Ruth Cruger.

"From my personal investigations," Lynch said, "I was of the opinion that the said Alfredo Cocchi was in some way connected with the persons responsible for my daughter's death. I thought that if he were brought back to America, the prosecution against him would be helpful to me in bringing to justice those responsible for the death of my daughter." He wiped his eyes. He admitted that he had no facts to connect them.

Swann made him say it again, though he took no pleasure in it.

"I am personally in possession of no facts and no information in any way directly or indirectly connected to the disappearance of the death of Ruth Cruger by the said Alfredo Cocchi; I never knew Ruth Cruger in her lifetime. My daughter never knew, to my personal knowledge, Ruth Cruger in her lifetime. I never knew Alfredo Cocchi."

The Reverend Gaspar Moretto testified on February 9. In his forties, he was still a young, strong, and good-looking man. He had a soft smile with some gray at his temples. Cocchi named the priest as the man who harbored him as he waited in New York before escaping to Italy. When questioned by the police and Helen Cruger during that time, Father Moretto had only intimated at things, avoiding them directly. He was more forthcoming now.

"I am a naturalized American citizen," he said with gusto. He explained how he was ordained in Italy but came to the United States in

1903. He was still attached to the Saint Raphael Society, an Italian mission. Reverend Moretto visited Ellis Island every day, he said, to help the Italians with their spiritual needs as they arrived under the shadow of a giant, expressionless woman who had been hammered from copper.

The reverend knew Cocchi through Ernesto Bregagnolo, a member of the society who had a motorcycle. "In the fall of 1914," Moretto said, "I remember one occasion when Mrs. Cocchi called at the Mission." She asked Moretto to talk to her husband because he was being unfaithful to her with other women. "This, however, I never did," said Moretto. "I had not seen her husband before this occasion except the early summer of 1914. The next time I saw Alfredo Cocchi was in the early evening of the 15th of February, 1917." Moretto had been on Ellis Island, leaving on the late afternoon ferry for home at four forty as the sun rolled west. The reverend had arrived back at the mission around 5 o'clock.

"When I arrived there," Moretto said, "Alfredo Cocchi was waiting for me. I was informed by one of the sisters attached to the mission that he had been waiting for two hours. He spoke to me and requested me to hear his confession. I then heard his confession according to the rites of the Roman Catholic Church. Under the rules of the Roman Catholic Church and under my vows as a priest, I cannot disclose any part of the confession," said Reverend Moretto. Swann stared at him.

"I never saw Alfredo Cocchi after this day," Moretto said. Then he stopped as if he had remembered something.

"I am informed," Moretto said, "that Alfredo Cocchi was married on the 3rd day of October, 1907, at Ellis Island, and that I was the officiating clergyman. This is undoubtedly true, but I have no distinct recollection of the marriage. I do recollect that when Mrs. Cocchi saw me at her husband's shop in 1914, she recognized me as the priest who had solemnized her marriage at Ellis Island."

The next witness was a young blond woman who turned heads when she walked in. Her name was Mary Probst. She had also been named by Cocchi as a possible witness, and when she spoke, it was all business. "I am employed as a packer in the candy factory of D. Auerbach at 640 Eleventh Avenue," she said. Mary Probst told the story of how she lived with her parents in the same house as the Cocchis and helped out with paperwork and cleaning. "I frequently made out statements and bills for Alfredo Cocchi," she said, "because he could not read and write English." Her father was the janitor of the building. It was on 301 West Eighty-third Street.

"One day while I was dusting the house and helping my father," Mary said, "Mr. Cocchi met me in the hallway." She paused and looked at the judge, who nodded. "He opened his trousers and exposed his private parts. Mrs. Cocchi immediately followed him out of the apartment after this occurred and called me back into her home. I told her what occurred, and she told me not to tell my mother or anyone else. I promised that I would not."

Mary then recalled how, several weeks later, she went to the motorcycle shop with a friend to get two bicycles to go for a ride. Cocchi was always happy to loan them bicycles. When Mary returned on her own, Cocchi put his arms around her and embraced her. Mrs. Cocchi entered the store and got very angry with me. "She told me to leave the store," Mary said, "and not to come there again." The court asked Mary her age. "I am nineteen years of age," she said. At the time of the events she was relating, she had been fourteen.

Several more girls whom Cocchi named as witnesses were also summoned. Francesca Triolo was twenty years old, dark haired, and very quiet. "He never made any improper advances to me," she said. Florence Leonetter was seventeen and worked at a tea store. She said that Cocchi would sometimes give her and her brother rides in his motorcycle sidecar. She paused. "I frequently saw Cocchi in front of his shop; he always used to smile at girls when they passed by."

Agnes Powers was older, married, and had two children. Her husband was an inspector at the *New York Globe*. Powers told Swann that in late 1916 she visited Cocchi's shop to have a baby carriage repaired. She liked his work, so she went back six or so times after. The last time she went, on a Sunday, she had to leave the carriage for an hour or so.

"I returned at two o'clock," she said, "and he took the carriage to the back part of the store, and he asked me to come in the back and sit down. I sat by the baby-carriage, and my baby started to cry. I bent over the baby and Cocchi came over behind me and embraced me and acted in a disorderly manner. He asked me to kiss him and he tried to kiss me. I had 35 cents in my hand which I was offering to him, when he took my hand and tried to place it on his private parts; he also placed his hand on my breast; at the same time he attempted to kiss me. I kept pulling back. I succeeded, however, in tearing myself away and making an outcry. When I released myself from him he said to me: 'You don't owe me anything.' "

Mrs. Powers ran out of the store with her baby and the carriage. When her husband got home from work, she told him everything. He went over to Cocchi's in haste. Cocchi said it was all a misunderstanding. It was his helper, not him who had done this outrage. Her husband returned with a policeman, but the store was closed. So she let it go. When she was shown her testimony, Mrs. Powers signed below the line that read: "The acts related above by me were not done by any helper, but were done by the defendant, Alfredo Cocchi."

Swann also summoned a number of men whom Cocchi said would speak to the quarrelsome nature of his wife. Joseph Caggiano would sometimes help with the billing at the shop. One day, Maria Cocchi took him aside and told him that her husband was running around with other girls. Caggiano remembered one time when the couple was arguing, Cocchi told his wife to be quiet. Maria then tried to grab at one of the tools lying around the shop. Caggiano couldn't remember if she actually swung it at him, but he did remember one time when she threatened it.

"This is what I have to put up with," Maria Cocchi had told him. It was sometime late in 1913 or early 1914. Frank Bauer was another machinist who similarly worked on and off for Cocchi. "I personally never saw him act improperly towards any women who came into his shop," he said.

One of the last names on the list had been a difficult man to find. Victor Blady still lived in Jersey and was a chauffeur now, though he was not presently employed.

"I remember reading about the disappearance of Ruth Cruger," said Blady. "Sometime around Lincoln's birthday. . . . I have no recollection of having seen him either on the 14th or 15th of February, 1917." Blady knew Herbert Roemmele, Cocchi's helper, too. Blady's next words were chosen very carefully, and almost rehearsed:

"I have no distinct recollection of having taken Herbert F. Roemmele, Alfredo Cocchi, and the latter's own Athos in an automobile driven by me, from Cocchi's shop to Manhattan Street," Blady said. "I will say, however, that I have on several occasions driven Alfredo Cocchi and his son and Herbert F. Roemmele from Cocchi's shop to 75 Manhattan Street, but I cannot say that I did so on the afternoon of February 13th." Blady had been suspected of being the mysterious driver. Blady claimed to know of no difficulties within the Cocchi marriage, though he did remember one time when Mrs. Cocchi told him that her husband had a girlfriend. Blady said he didn't want to get involved.

Leah Brinckmann, German, was married with five kids. For the past nineteen years, she had also been the janitor of the house adjoining Cocchi's motorcycle shop. "I never talked with him except to bid him the time of day," she said of Cocchi. "I know his wife; I frequently saw her in front of the premises. She used to sit outside of her husband's store with the children, and I often talked with her."

Brinckmann told a story how Maria Cocchi had accused one of her daughters of spying on her at the park, presumably on the orders of her husband. Maria Cocchi asked Brinckmann, and she refuted it, but when the daughter in question came home later, she was crying. She was eight or nine. She said that Mrs. Cocchi had slapped her. "I did not speak to Mrs. Cocchi after that day," Brinckmann said. "I believe this occurred in July, 1916." She paused a moment. "Mrs. Cocchi always appeared to me to be a hard-working woman," she added. "Neat and clean, and took good care of her children." Leah's daughter remembered nothing of the incident.

John Lagarenne came as the next-to-last witness. He was wearing his police uniform. The man who stunned the room with his terse, one-word answers three years ago finally seemed ready to help. "I am now," he said, "and since the 16th of October, 1905, a member of the Municipal Police Force of the City of New York with the rank of Sergeant." He didn't mention his conviction at the end of the Cruger inquiry or his time away. He still lived in Brooklyn and made a point to say that he had been assisting the DA in locating the witnesses on Cocchi's list. The only person he couldn't find was a Miss Wells, though he searched the post office and rode up to Middletown, sixty-eight miles away, where she had lived in 1916.

The next witness was very well-known to Swann, though he had not seen her in some time. Maria Cocchi walked in and sat down.

"I reside at 37 Old Broadway in the borough of Manhattan," she said. "I am the wife of Alfredo Cocchi, now waiting his trial for the murder of Ruth Cruger in the County of New York. I have been shown the documents where he said it was me. I, his wife, in fit of jealous fury. I desire to say that this statements are false.

"My husband states that he accused himself in order to preserve a mother to his children," she said. Calmly, Maria Cocchi proceeded to refute her husband's claims against her. Swann asked her about her husband's claim that she had attacked him with a hammer.

Mary Probst, as her own testimony had said, lived in the same house as the Cocchis with her parents. Her job in the Cocchi household was "to clean up and take care of the home and fix their bed each day." The arrangement seemed to be working very well until one day, Mrs. Cocchi claimed, she received an unsigned letter. It read: " 'Mary Probst, instead of taking good care of your home, is taking good care of your husband.' " Maria added that the writer said they "had seen Mary Probst go into my husband's apartment after 10 o'clock at night, also at 6 o'clock in the morning." Maria said she destroyed the letter in a fit of rage.

Days later, Maria was getting the mail when she noticed a letter in the Probst box with her husband's handwriting on it. Maria slipped the letter out, opened it, and read the letter. There was a five-dollar bill inside. This letter read that he wanted to meet her that evening at Seventy-second Street and Riverside Drive. Maria said that she brought the letter and showed it to Cocchi.

"What happened?" asked Swann.

"I quarreled with my husband and he struck me," Maria replied.

"It was Christmas morning, 1914, when I found Mary Probst in bed with my husband," Maria said. "I chased her out of my room and she was in the hallway asking for her clothes." Edward Fish, who was her husband's friend, was there at the time. "He saw her in the hallway naked," Maria said.

Maria composed herself. "All of our quarrels were caused by his improper conduct towards me and my child by his intimate relations with other women. My husband frequently remains away from my bed and home on various occasions sometimes one and two nights each week. I was not dominated by jealousy," she said, matter-of-factly.

"What about the doctor?" asked Swann, referring once again to Cocchi's insistence that Maria had sought an abortion.

"Mrs. Beck never secured a physician for me on any occasion when I was either pregnant or ill," Maria said. "She never secured a midwife. I never attempted to abort or cause to be aborted while I was with child."

As the witnesses left, Swann knew that he would probably never see them again. That thought stayed with him as he himself left the building. That, and a nagging thought that he could not dismiss. How had they missed this? How had they all missed it?

Swann packed up the testimony and ordered it to be sent to Italy. He also wondered, considering how damning this all was, if they weren't still playing right into Alfredo Cocchi's hands. It was almost as if Cocchi was prosecuting himself, either to seal his fate in Italy, free of the chair, or to protect someone else. Swann had another piece of new information that he contemplated sending along as well but was uncertain what effect it might have.

In Bologna, the trial of Alfredo Cocchi resumed on October 24, 1920, and lasted four more days. The new testimony had been offered for the record. Though neither state nor federal prosecutors had been able to extradite Cocchi, Swann had finally been allowed to send Owen Bohan, as assistant, to testify to the new information gathered in New York. So, on the last day of the trial, the judge allowed it. Owen didn't say much. He testified that Cocchi's wife had been exonerated by the police upon further testimony and was an upstanding member of society. At the end of his statement, Owen also said that Cocchi's eldest daughter, Georgette, was dead.

The room stopped as everyone turned to look at the prisoner's face. Cocchi stood alone in the dark prisoner's cage. He wore a dark suit and was almost completely covered in shadow. His face was nearly white. Someone took a photograph of him.

Cocchi had previously testified that he made his original confession of guilt to protect his beloved wife and children. His second confession was, according to Cocchi, to save his children from his insane wife. Judge Bagnoli scowled. The American, Swann, had affected this trial after all. Owen explained that after a long illness, Georgette Cocchi, Alfredo's daughter, had died on December 6, 1918, of pneumonia. She was only two years old, having been born right before Ruth Cruger's murder. Owen added, almost mercilessly, that Athos was doing well at school.

Cocchi collapsed in his cage in the courtroom.

When it was time for the verdict, the judge looked at Cocchi and spoke in Italian. The American reporters and photographers who couldn't understand the language only knew what happened when Alfredo Cocchi collapsed. Their translators handed them sheets of paper with misspellings. Cocchi was convicted of the attempted rape and murder of Ruth Cruger in New York. In their statement, the judges said that they thought his fury was caused by Ruth's spurning. They concluded that he killed her to avoid having a witness and getting in trouble. They also convicted him for traveling under a false name. Cocchi's claim that his wife had done it was ignored utterly.

The Italian criminal code, the Zanardelli Code as it was known, provided strict sentencing guidelines, though the punishment decreased if the crimes were committed abroad. The code demanded 25–30 years for murder. For rape, it suggested one to six years. There were some other reductions and mitigations that had to be quibbled and negotiated over. Signor Venturini was able to take a few years off because of some discrepancies in the language. In the end, Alfredo Cocchi was sentenced to 27 years, 2 months, and 26 days for the murder of Ruth Cruger. Venturini maintained his optimism; he hoped that a future king would pardon his client outright. When Cocchi was taken back to his cell, he went on a hunger strike. For that, he was sentenced to ten years of solitary confinement. He was then allowed in the common prison population, to disappear among the killers and thieves.

In the end, it was determined that there was no vast web of white slavers tailor-made for the newspapers, only deep, unknowable evil, now consigned to a cage.

23

Her Dark Shepherd

In 1919, Grace and Kron were still working together as the New Justice Detective Bureau. Grace had also put together a magazine called *New Justice*. Its purpose was "to call women citizens to their civic responsibility for young girls in every untoward condition of life." They charged $1.50 a year for a subscription. In November, the New York Supreme Court, on appeal, ruled on Grace's suit against *Universal Animated Weekly*. The court decided that the newsreel she had been featured in was different from a photoplay, another popular genre of the day in which real events were acted out by professional actors in magazines or on film.

A photoplay is inherently a work of fiction. A news reel contains no fiction but shows only actual photographs of current events of public interest. The news reel is taken on the spot, at the very moment of the occurrence depicted, and is an actual photograph of the event itself. The photoplay, as the result of fiction, retains its interest, irrespective of the length of time which has elapsed since its first production, whereas, a news reel, to be of any value in large cities must be published almost simultaneously with the occurrence of the events which it portrays. This news service, as far as it goes, is a truthful, accurate purveyor of news, quite as strictly so as a newspaper. While a newspaper account conveys the news almost entirely by words, the news service conveys the same by photographs with incidental verbal explanation.

If a newsreel was more like a newspaper, then it could print publicly taken photographs without permission. Newspapers were allowed this power because they functioned as the truth of the world. The initial judgment was thus reversed, and Grace was ordered to pay back the damages. The images that were being contested showed Grace walking out of the motorcycle store, smiling and bowing.

Now in her fifties, Grace Humiston was still taking cases, speaking at club luncheons, and writing the odd article here and there, but she was not nearly as popular as she had been. She was having money problems, too. Real estate deals and overspending on staff had thinned her resources. The Grace Club was now operating at 147 East 21st Street in Gramercy Park, where businesswomen and girls could rent comfortably furnished rooms for eight to twelve dollars a week. The building itself had thirteen bathrooms. But running such a facility had frequent unforeseen costs, and the club, Grace's great idea, had to close. In late March, Grace petitioned the New York State Court to be paid for having represented Stielow all those years ago. She was seeking compensation for all the old business she had never had the time—or the need—to request before.

Grace never stopped reading the papers. In the summer of 1926, she saw a case that gave her pause. George Bittle was a taxicab driver condemned to the electric chair for the murder of Rufus Eller, a Buffalo jeweler. A man named Frank Minnick had hired Bittle's cab. He was already dead for the crime. Grace quietly checked into the case. She then took a ride to visit Bittle in prison. The old excitement seized her again. She would set this man free. When she arrived, she told the man behind bars that she had new evidence that might help his case. But George Bittle knew who Grace Humiston was. He refused her help and sent her packing.

Grace disappeared into the shadows after that. Though she mostly stayed out of the crime limelight of the dailies, Grace was still out-spoken about the city she loved. She railed against the city's night court system, where judges had the power to imprison anyone who walked through the courtroom doors. She worked with the Morality League and the Girls' Vocational Club, which had just two rules: Never mention your past, and Never stay out all night. She continued to express her strong thoughts on the police who had embraced and then abandoned her. The same went for the federal lawmen. When Hoover said that the nation should conserve food, Grace fired back that they should instead conserve girlhood. When a columnist asked her if smoking lowered the morals of a woman, Grace said no, and that any woman had a right to do so, though privacy would be ideal. "I do not like to set any standards for women," Grace said, "for I think there should be a single standard in everything for men and women. But then, on the other hand, a 'womanly woman' is somehow more universally convincing and more admired by the best of both men and women."

Grace was still getting mail from mothers whose daughters had gone missing. "How can girls disappear from the face of the earth in these days of civilization, Mrs. Humiston?" wrote one anguished mother. Grace quickly realized that she could not answer every letter. So she began a series of columns, titled "Our Missing Girls," hoping to tell the rest of the nation what she had learned. As always, Grace fell back on stories—on cases—to get her ideas across. She wrote of a "well dressed confident Western mother" who walked into Grace's office seeking help for her lost daughter. "You are the average American mother," Grace said, "the woman who doesn't know a tenth of what is going on around you in this very world you and your girls live in." That is why she wrote.

"Every day of the 365 in the year," Grace wrote, "two hundred and seventy-seven girls shut the doors of their parents' homes in the United States and turn their back on the places where for years their lives have been molded. Two girls a day from Chicago. Two every three days from Detroit and Cleveland. One a day from St. Louis, Boston,

Philadelphia, Washington, Pittsburgh, Kansas City and scores of other larger cities in the country. They leave no word. It is the last time. Whether the door which shuts be the white-painted wood one of the country farmhouse or the iron-grilled gate of the city apartment. For one of every three of these girls will never return. In many cases these girls are of striking personality, initiative, and business ability."

Some of the papers printed photos of artifacts from Grace's personal collection, including letters from girls begging for help along with actual missing person reports. One was for Esther L. from Akron, Ohio, a stenographer who was last seen at the Strand Motion Picture House in New York. She wore a dress from the May Company and had a graduation ring. She was sixteen years old. Some wanted Grace to find Dorothy Arnold next. The wealthy heiress disappeared on December 12, 1910, when she left a Brentano's bookstore on Fifth Avenue. Grace said she would search out all possible clues.

Grace warned of the lure of the photography studios, where phrases—"Wonderful! Such poise! Such command! Who is the girl!"— could weaken a young girl's resolve. She spoke of nightclubs and bungalows and "blackout parties." Her "Rules for Avoiding Trouble" included "Don't go out to dinner with your boss" and "Be a little cruel to yourself—remember that the movies are only reel life, not real life."

Grace had files upon files of information on girls gone missing from five-and-ten stores, coin-in-the-slot restaurants, and the waiting rooms of large department stores. Sometimes, she got letters from the girls themselves, too terrified to come home. "Has anybody been looking for me in the last twenty years, do you know?" one girl asked. "Not a day passes," said Grace, "but someone is seeking someone else. The search for the missing girls is an endless search."

On holidays and odd Sundays, Grace would leave her apartment at the Vanderbilt at Thirty-fourth and Park and step over to the Osborne, on Fifty-seventh and Seventh, right across from Carnegie Hall. She would ride up the open shaft elevator to her sister Jessie's new apartment. She went alone. Her nieces and nephews would stare and consider their Auntie Grace, a black figure framed against the high, corniced ceiling. Jessie, who always smiled and laughed, would welcome her in and talk about her plans to organize a trip to Connecticut to see the family sites or to travel by car across the country. Grace was a lawyer and detective; Jessie, a church lady whose husband, Harry, had a seat on the New York Stock Exchange and blood ties to the founders of the Baptist Church in America.

Sometime after Christmas, during one of these family visits, Jessie pulled Grace into a room and sat her down. This was a reversal of roles. Jessie had always been the helper, investing in real estate with Grace and cosigning loans for Grace's many-titled ventures. But Grace could tell immediately that something was wrong. This wasn't about money. Grace listened quietly to what her sister had to say. What Grace heard from Jessie that day were the kind of whispers she had heard during her entire career. This was a subject matter she had to approach very delicately. But Grace's sister needed her help. That was all that mattered.

In addition to being a mother and wife, Jessie Day was an influential member of the Madison Avenue Baptist Church. She and Grace's father had been active as a Baptist, and their sister Nelly had even married a pastor. The impressive church at East Thirty-first Street and Madison Avenue was cornered by four towers of dark brown wood and steep, fluid steps. The leader of the Madison congregation was the Reverend Dr. George Caleb Moor, who had come by way of Brooklyn, where he was pastor of the Baptist Temple there. He was a rising star in the clergy: a passionate, handsome family man with a wife and child. He was a very hard worker; he once had to stop during a sermon because he was on the verge of a nervous breakdown after part of his church had been destroyed by fire.

Moor did not shy away from the secular world in his work. As he delivered a sermon titled "Is the Kaiser the Anti-Christ?" two men in the front row ducked their heads and made a hasty exit. As they disappeared, Moor remarked that he hoped they would at least come back for his lecture on Russia and the czar. It was the first in a series of six sermons titled "Thrones and Dominions vs. the Throne of God." But Moor was not all political brimstone. He also delivered a series of lectures titled "The World's Great Rivers." Moor was, by all accounts, a wonderful church leader.

On the night of February 19, 1922, a meeting of the membership was called by the trustees of the church. Held in Sanders Hall, the church auditorium, the meeting was closed to outsiders and press. Once everyone arrived and was seated, the doors were locked shut. A reporter for the *Times* stood outside, prepared to wait it out. Sometime later, a small group of elderly women emerged, flustered and fanning their necks. As more time passed, the reporter watched younger women leave in shocked states, their handkerchiefs to their mouths. "This is a disgrace," one of them said. "We will not stay in there while she reads that statement, but we intend to go back and cast our votes when she's through."

When the doors were finally opened at twelve thirty in the morning, the *Times* reporter was told that during the meeting, Jessie Day had produced the diary of a young female parishioner. With Grace seated beside her, Jessie stood up straight and started reading it aloud. Some of the older members of the church left immediately. As Jessie progressed further in the diary, more women also found themselves unable to remain. Many withdrew, some so shocked by the narrative that they became hysterical. What Jessie was reading was disturbing because it implicated a church member in having an affair with this young girl. The man being accused was Reverend Moor, who was seated directly across from Jessie and her sister.

Once Jessie was finished, she quietly sat down. After heated discussion, the church voted to retain Moor. They then voted to expel Jessie Day with a vote of 64 to 43. A longtime deacon, W. S. Foster, who supported Jessie during the meeting, was also charged by Moor himself with "acts unbecoming a Christian and a church member." Foster was also expelled 72 to 17. Moor's wife had remained in the meeting the entire time. At its close, she said she was "tired, but very happy." Moor was scheduled to preach later that day; the title of his next sermon was listed in the newspaper as "Feeling Gray."

Jessie and Grace were stunned. They had actual physical proof—a diary!—that Moor was behaving indiscreetly, but they still knew that accusing him would be a gamble. Jessie had now been stripped of her church membership, one of the most important forms of identity a New York society woman could claim. But they were not going to give up. Another longtime church member, Dr. Hall, also called for Moor's expulsion, so another meeting was held, with Jessie and Grace there to support his cause.

As Grace sat there with her sister, she watched as Moor and his people again came into the room. Grace saw someone in the back pushing a wheelchair. She felt Jessie's hand press upon her arm in a very hard way. Grace looked closer as the man was wheeled in. Her shoulders fell. It was their brother, Adoniram Judson Winterton Jr.

There was shouting in the room. Grace stared at this white-haired man who looked like her father. She looked at this man, her brother, whom she once told a whole room of reporters was already dead.

Once things quieted down, Adoniram was given the chance to speak. He rose and denounced his sisters, saying that they were unfit to take communion and that he himself had been forced to withdraw from the church by the abuse of his family. When he sat down, his words still hung in the air.

Grace explained to the room, in a quiet voice, that Adoniram had been in a sanitarium and was very sick. She said that Moor "dug him up and brought him there" only "to embarrass her." Grace asked that all of the remarks, including hers, be struck from the record. When they finally got around to Hall's case, the church board offered him immunity if he retracted the charges against Moor. Hall thought for a second and responded. "If I had to meet my God tonight," he said, "I'd rather be an expelled member of this church than to be a leader under its present administration."

Four months later, on appeal by the Southern New York Baptist

Association, the church was ordered to reinstate the membership of Jessie Day. The ruling didn't concern itself with the charges against Moor. Madison could still bar Jessie if they wished, but she would still be considered a member in good standing if she wanted to transfer to another church. Which she did. Their brother Adoniram also wrote into the newspaper and said that he had been completely misquoted in the press about his sisters. His retraction was delivered by a typed letter.

Moor maintained his innocence. "How would I have been able to carry on my work for thirty years if I were capable of doing all these things?" he asked. He told his flock not to worry. "I'm going to stay right here until Hades freezes over," he said.

⚒

A year later, on March 14, 1923, Grace was once again late to court. She was riding a trolley car with her new legal assistant, Marion Lithauer. Hannah Frank had moved on to her own successful practice, as had many of Grace's female assistants. When the car stopped, Grace dropped down from the platform and took a quick look before crossing Third Avenue. A traffic cop was stationed there. He pulled in a breath and blew on his whistle for the crossing traffic, consisting of carriages, streetcars, and automobiles, to stop. Grace started to cross when a small truck pushed through the light and hit her. The driver pulled on the emergency brake and squealed the car to a stop. As he jumped out, Lithauer was kneeling over the fallen body of Grace Humiston.

The cop, W. E. Meier, ran across the intersection and bent down to look at Grace. She was doubled over but still alive. The front wheel of the truck had crushed her ankle. Grace begged the policeman to call a cab, which he did. Lithauer helped Grace into the cab, and they sped off. Meier arrested the driver, a man named William H. Heck.

Grace and Lithauer had the driver take them to New York Orthopaedic Dispensary, but they couldn't find a specialist. Grace had seen too many clients who had relatives go into an emergency ward never to come out. She wanted a specialist. So they drove to Flower Hospital, where Grace was finally admitted. Two specialists from outside of the hospital were called in to consult. Grace was in great pain but still conscious.

Grace suffered a severe compound fracture of the left ankle. But the broken bones that had pierced her skin were the least of her worries. The doctors at Flower were trying their best to prevent blood poisoning, which they knew could cause amputation of the foot or death. They watched her carefully for four days and gave her injections of lockjaw serum with a long silver needle. Grace lay there, still on the white bed, her black hat on the table beside her.

When she was finally out of the woods, the doctors said it would be at least three weeks before she could leave the hospital. And months before she could walk. When Heck appeared before Magistrate Cobb, he said that he was "turning east onto Fifty-ninth Street when the accident happened." Heck said he did "not see Mrs. Humiston in front of his truck, but stopped when he heard her cries."

He was released on $500 bail. Heck also said that the policeman was able to easily see both the truck and Mrs. Humiston, with her sweeping black dress, stepping off the trolley. Heck said the policeman gave him the right of way.

During this time, as Grace recovered, the City of New York faced a new breed of murderer. This hunter didn't lend itself to story or gossip. Its motive was utterly transparent: to sicken and kill anything that breathed. The influenza epidemic that had creeped into Gotham from a Norwegian boat in 1919 had so completely changed the city that, by 1920, the streets looked like an outdoor hospital. Schools were closed. People went to their jobs with cotton masks tied tight around their mouths. Movie theaters staggered their show times so as to spread out their crowds. As the great sickness, which would later be understood as the body's unnecessary overreaction to virus, spread across the boroughs, victims transformed from printed names to empty, place-holding zeroes. Families grieved and cowered behind doors locked to quiet streets. By 1922, the fourth wave of the pandemic was finally ending. Since 1918, over forty thousand New Yorkers had died. The war had taken her sons; the flu had mopped up the rest.

After her accident, Grace stayed out of the public eye, for the most part. She still practiced mostly immigration cases (which were now fewer) and cases of patients with mental illness. She rarely left New York and lived in a series of apartments. When Amelia Earhart completed her solo flight across the Atlantic in 1932, Grace sent her a telegram. It read: "Congratulations."

In her later years, Grace watched her city change even further. New York pushed its way even higher into the sky, turning into almost solid steel, impregnable and stainless. Murders came and went in the news. And yet another war—even greater, if that was even the word for it—began and ended, killing millions across the globe. The public forgot her, and Grace became yet another stylish old lady in a Park Avenue apartment with jars of cold cream and stories gone untold. She became someone whom people wondered about when she clicked her wooden door shut. Her family had always been her cases, and, like any family, they were no longer whole. She had made her work the immense adventure of her life.

On August 1, 1947, Alfredo Cocchi was considered rehabilitated and was released.

On July 16, 1948, Grace was admitted to the French Hospital. Thirty minutes later, she was dead. She had arteriosclerotic heart disease. She was seventy-eight. Her sister Jessie claimed her body, and Grace was buried in Woodlawn Cemetery on July 19, 1948.

Grace and Cocchi never met. But if Grace ever leafed through her old report on Sunny Side in her dark apartment, she would have found, on page 61, a list of people who had thankfully escaped the island.

Grace might have frozen at seeing the name on the upper-right. Her mind might have tried to go back to all those blurry faces. She might try to calculate the math in her head or on a scrap of paper. She

List of the families who escaped from Sunny Side
leaving debts:

Names.

Albonetti Cesare	Santucci Enrice
Pieroni Giovanni	Rocchetti Antonic
Baratti	Cocchi
Pielli Eligio	Pirrini Fernando
Domenicucci Emilio	Rosa Guardino
Contini	Angeletti Giovanni
Ferrara	Socci
Mancini Carlo	Romanelli Enrico
Padroni Enrico	Pacifico Fratesi.
Augusto Fratesi	Frantini Guiseppe
Frantini Luigi	Pantozzi Luciano
Romanelli Cesare	Enrico Santucci
Vincenzo Angeletti	Mrs. Ersille
Laggio Natale	Maggio Carlo

Albonetti Santa.

might look and search for a birth certificate. There was no possible way it could be him. She would look again. She had written this name down, then typed it, all those years ago. Had she run across this man in one of those low cabins? Had she spoken to him? Had he answered? Or was it all in her head? Grace might have gone through the photographs she still had, looking at the black-and-white faces for someone in the back: pale, smiling, and intangible among the tall crops.

In an interview late in life, Grace remembered the first time she met Henry Cruger. Mrs. Felix Adler had introduced them, hoping that Grace would take the case.

"I shall never forget the despair in the face of that man," Grace said. "His eyes were sunken in his head and the last vestige of hope had left him. He sat in a chair in a corner of the office, his head bowed, his eyes unseeing."

"Mr. Cruger thinks you can find his missing daughter," Mrs. Adler said.

"Before I could protest," said Grace, "she reviewed the case for me. She told of the aspersions police had cast upon the girl who was lost; how they had characterized her as 'wayward' when her conduct was unimpeachable. She told of the despair of the Crugers themselves, of the mother in a sickbed frantic with worry, of the sisters and the father himself not knowing which way to turn. Then, when she finished, Mr. Cruger looked up, straight into my eyes."

"Won't you help me find my girl?" asked Henry Cruger.

"Many times since then I have wished that Mrs. Adler had not come to me," Grace admitted. "Many times have I tried to forget the horror of that case, the constant worry and fear, the sickening, disgusting things I saw and experienced." She shook her head.

"I protested at first," she continued. "I told Mrs. Adler and Mr. Cruger that they overestimated me considerably. I told them that there was slight possibility I could uncover more than the police had. Mrs. Adler argued with me. Mr. Cruger sat there with bowed head. And when he raised his eyes and looked at me and said again 'Won't you help me find my girl' I knew that I had lost.

"I am not sorry that I did not turn Mr. Cruger down," said Grace. "I would do it all over again, under the same circumstances."

Epilogue

SENATOR GOLDFOGLE: What do you mean by that statement, that
these things happen all the time in New York City?
GRACE: I mean to say that it is absolutely a system, and it is a
wheel within a wheel. To appreciate the situation, one needs
only to see and hear the whole story.

Hearings Before Committee on Immigration and
Naturalization (1910)

THE CRUGERS

In 1917, during the course of the investigation into his daughter's
disappearance, Henry Cruger withdrew an excess of $9,009.65
from his company with Alfred Brown beyond his regular salary.
After Brown died on October 4, 1918, Henry sued Brown's estate for
$32,000 more.

The Cruger family eventually moved to 2 Cleveland Court in
New Rochelle. Christina did not work, though Helen still did, as a
clerk. In 1936, Christina was driving when she ran into a trolley. No
one was hurt, but she delayed reporting the accident. Henry died on
April 13, 1936, in New Rochelle, without any grandchildren. His
wife died in 1938. Helen died in 1972. Henry and his wife's second
child, Catherine, lived only a year until she died in 1895.

JULIUS J. KRON

After Grace's auto accident, Kron took a trip back home to Hungary in early 1923. Kron, the son of a Hungarian Jew, was born in Hungary, on July 7, 1885, in a house that spoke only Yiddish. His father, Mayer, was now living out on the ragged horizon of old Hungary, part of the newly christened Czechoslovakia.

After the First World War, Hungary was cut into awkward pieces. Count Mihály Károlyi was the liberal pacifist who toppled the house of Hapsburg and took control of Hungary's first republic in November 1918. When Károlyi disbanded the army, Czechoslovakia, Romania, and Yugoslavia all began aggressively expanding their territories into Hungary without fear or reprisal. Károlyi resigned, and the Communist Party of Hungary, led by Béla Kun, filled the void. Kun had a largely Jewish cabinet and enforced his own will through ruthless countrywide acts of violence, known as the Red Terror. Rebel royalists led by Admiral Miklós Horthy made up roving bands of volunteer soldiers who cut through the countryside. Their most feared leader was Pál Prónay, who sadistically hunted, tortured, and killed Hungarian Jews or any perceived Communists that he ran across. If they were women, he would cut off their breasts. In 1919, Horthy assumed control and eventually restored the monarchy as a figurehead. He looked the other way, for quite some time, as Prónay continued his executions across the state. The power in the state was controlled by force, doctored histories, and outright fear. The American papers called them "terrorists."

Kron wrote on his passport that he planned to visit Czechoslovakia, Hungary, Austria, and Serbia "to visit relatives." But he crossed part of that out and instead wrote "Business for the Kron Detective Agency." On the bottom of the passport, the type read that the bearer, in signing, does "solemnly swear that I will support and defend the Constitution of the United States against all enemies, foreign and domestic." Kron sailed on the S.S. *Woodrow Wilson*. He stayed abroad for three months.

By the time Kron returned to America, in the spring of 1925, the exiled pacifist Count Károlyi—still a hero to many—was making a tour of the United States. Though he clearly disapproved of Horthy's brutal regime, now referred to as the White Terror, Károlyi could not voice his thoughts because his visa was contingent on a political gag order. Károlyi, with his dark mustache and eyes, was always thought of as the man who handed Hungary over to the Bolsheviks. So he toured America, smiling and waving, accompanied by his wife, who was widely regarded as one of the most beautiful women in the world.

Newspaper editorials begged the count to voice his opinions, but he would not. By April, the Károlyis were ready to visit Quebec before heading back to Europe. The count had remarked to a reporter that he would like to retire in Canada. He wanted a garden full of vegetables and a fireplace and to spend time with his wife in a narrow valley among the birches and pines. The countess, with her constant smile and high cheekbones, was Continental and adventurous. And as she boarded that boat to Quebec, Julius J. Kron was within fifty yards of her.

Kron and his men had been secretly shadowing the royal couple for nearly the entire spring. Kron even followed them across the border—but was kicked out of Canada after they realized he wasn't a reporter. But he had seen enough. He returned to New York to finish off his report for his client.

On January 18, 1928, Kron's name was again splashed across the front page of a newspaper. But it wasn't the *Evening Sun*, the paper that had been so generous to him in the past. His name was stamped in black on the *Daily Worker.* In a glaring article, the *Worker* ran an exposé with the tantalizing lede NOTORIOUS SPY IN SERVICE OF HORTHY REGIME. The story contended that Kron's detective agency was part of an elaborate spy mission in the United States on behalf of the Hungarian White Terror. The evidence for the argument was a nearly full-size reproduction of a letter from Kron, written on his bold new letterhead:

> *It is with the greatest regret that I must inform you that we are not able to satisfy your claim, for reasons that we ourselves failed to receive the money's advanced by us on the case from the Hungarian Minister, and at a loss to understand his attitude toward us.*
>
> Yours respectfully,
> Julius James Kron.

The addressee, Dr. Jacob Novitsky, was not a doctor. He was a notorious self-proclaimed spy. The *Worker* told a story whereby Kron and Novitsky made forgeries for the Hungarian ambassador to the United States, László Széchenyi, to pass on to Horthy in Hungary, who would use the forgeries as manufactured evidence of his enemies' Communist ties in order to convict and imprison them. Széchenyi was a well-known man around New York City, having married the former Gladys Vanderbilt. They summered on Long Island.

The minister apparently promised Kron one hundred thousand dollars, but he didn't care for the quality of the forgeries, so he refused to pay for them. The *Worker* reproduced one of the forgeries, which indeed looked poor. The *Worker* was by no means an objective newspaper, but the evidence was right there on the front page for all to see. Kron might have hoped it would blow over since nobody trusted the *Daily Worker*. Later that day, a call came into Kron's office. It was the *New York Times*.

Kron admitted to the *Times* that he had been hired by an editor friend of his to trail the Count and Countess Károlyi when they visited the United States. Kron said he knew his friend was also a close friend of László Széchenyi and that this fact was the only truth of the story; there was no forgery scheme. "I do not deny knowing Count Szechenyi or that I worked for him," Kron said. "But not on this case. I deny having received a fee from him." Since the reproduced letter showed that Kron had not been paid at all, his words were true.

Kron said that though Károlyi had met some shadowy people during his trip, he could not link him directly to the Communists. "I wasn't able to find anything detrimental to either the Count or the Countess Karolyi all the time they were here," said Kron. "I don't consider him a Bolshevik, but I do consider him a radical in the European sense." Kron was adamant that he had done this for his friend, and for himself, not for any governmental power. At the same time, Kron didn't disguise his personal views. "Count Karolyi was plotting while he was here to overthrow the present Hungarian Government," Kron told the *Times* reporter. The *Daily Worker* ran three more front pages with photos of letters from Kron complaining about not being paid. The final letter from Kron authorized a Washington lawyer to initiate a lawsuit against the Hungarian prime minister for the lost wages.

Among his many self-proclaimed talents, Novitsky was a forger of some renown. Some wondered if the allegedly forged maps and lists reprinted by the clanky presses of the *Worker* were really his attempts at setting Kron up. There was evidence, but it was untrustworthy. But the next time the beautiful countess applied to enter America, she was denied entrance. The State Department would not say why, only that it had proof that she was engaged in questionable activity, probably of the Communist sort. On the floor of the Senate on February 27, Senator Burton K. Wheeler, of Montana, a left-wing, pro-labor Democrat, was furious about Károlyi's being denied entrance to the States. Wheeler wanted to give the Senate Foreign Relations Committee the secret report of detectives who shadowed the count and his wife. Wheeler said that the report was made by the Julius Kron Detective Agency of New York City.

Jacob Novitsky would return to the national spotlight during the investigation of the missing Lindbergh baby in 1932. Novitsky was suspected of using his skills at forgery to extort thousands from the Lindberghs, much of it never recovered.

Julius J. Kron was admitted to the Joint Disease Hospital in Manhattan on November 16, 1934. He suffered from inflammation of the gall bladder. During an operation to remove it on November 24, 1934, he died on the table. He was forty-nine years old. On his death certificate, his occupation read "Detective."

He was buried in Riverside Cemetery in Saddle Brook, New Jersey, the following day. His death certificate read that he was married to Estelle Kron, who claimed his body. Estelle and their daughters lived in Manhattan at 231 East Eighty-sixth Street. At the same time, Kron had a residence in Brooklyn with a woman named Claire Schwartz, who was first listed in census records as his housekeeper and then later as his wife. They had a son, George, who was sixteen in 1930. Kron's daughters with Estelle were Sylvia, Lilian, and his eldest girl, named Ruth.

FRANK McGEE

Detective Sergeant Frank McGee retired in September 1919 after serving, according to the *Evening World*, "twenty-six years without a blemish on his record." He was, however, "hot under the collar" because he was somehow reduced from the first grade to the second grade with a salary reduction of $2,450 to $1,950 a year. McGee's *New York Times* obituary said that he couldn't devote more time to searching for Ruth because his primary secret assignment was to hunt down German spies. He had a wife, Minnie, and a son, Harold, who was a member of the New York Police Department's homicide squad.

MAYOR MITCHEL

The New York City mayor John Purroy Mitchel, after losing a patriotic, anti-immigrant bid for reelection in 1917 to a farmer turned train conductor (and Tammany man) named John F. Hylan, joined the fledgling air service with hopes of flying in the war. On July 6, 1918, eight months after losing his bid for reelection, Mitchel was flying when his plane turned and went into a steep dive. Mitchel, who had failed to fasten his seat belt, was dislodged from his plane and fell to his death in a Louisiana swamp. Mitchel Air Force Base on Long Island is named for him.

J. J. LYNCH

J. J. Lynch left the city controller's office in 1921 to run in the mayoral primary, but lost. A few years before that, his former partner,

Thomas J. Morris—now his bitter enemy because of business failings—lay critically ill in his home. Without saying a word, Lynch walked to the home of his old friend, lay down beside him, and gave him the full blood transfusion that saved his life. They never spoke again. Lynch died, leaving a wife and four children, on November 24, 1931, Thanksgiving, at age sixty.

LeROY PERCY

Percy was elected as a Democrat to the United States Senate to fill a vacancy and served from 1910 to 1913, before being defeated by James K. Vardaman, who ran on a platform whose major plank was white supremacy. On March 1, 1922, Percy stomped through the streets of his beloved Greenville and straight into a rally of the Ku Klux Klan that was denouncing Jews, blacks, and Catholics. Percy stood in the crowd and heard Klan leader Joseph Camp's speech. Percy ran up to the podium and dismantled every point of Camp's speech to booming applause. "Let this Klan go somewhere else!" Percy bellowed. They left Washington County soon after. Senator Percy died in Greenville, Mississippi, of a heart attack on December 24, 1929. His place of burial is marked by an iron knight holding a great sword.

CHARLES STIELOW

After Charlie Stielow was finally released, he had another son, Edward, named after his father. Charlie died on August 9, 1942, in Orleans County, New York. He was eighty-four. His daughter Ethel, who wrote the letter that may have saved him, lived until 1987, also to the age eighty-four.

THE BLACK HAND

Once they were captured, Black Hand leaders Morello and Lupo were both sentenced to twenty-five years of hard labor in Atlanta. After both had their sentences inexplicably shortened (possibly due to prosecutorial deals), they returned to the streets. Morello was caught again, sent to prison, and, when he got out, was killed by a rival gangster while filing paperwork in 1930. Lupo was stripped of his criminal power and ran a small lottery in Brooklyn. When he died in 1947, very few people knew his name. He was buried in Calvary Cemetery, near Joe Petrosino.

ARTHUR WOODS

Woods became a full colonel in the army and served as assistant director of military aeronautics. In 1920, he was awarded medals from three different countries: the Distinguished Service Medal, the British Order of St. Michael and Saint George C.M.G., and the French Chevalier of the Legion of Honor (France). At the end of the war, he worked under Secretary of War Newton D. Baker to help returning servicemen adjust to home life. He restored historic Williamsburg with John D. Rockefeller and was one of the first to work on national economic programs to help combat the early days of the Great Depression. He died on May 12, 1942, and is buried at Arlington National Cemetery.

JOHN LAGARENNE

After his conviction and fine, Lagarenne immediately applied for a pardon from Governor Smith. A letter on his behalf read that Lagarenne "has an exceptionally fine record for bravery and valor." Lagarenne was reinstated at the level of sergeant. In 1920, he was given a temporary assignment as detective "to duty in office of the District Attorney." He was made a lieutenant in 1921 and a captain in 1929. In 1938, he made full inspector, with acting deputy chief inspector to follow in 1939. In 1942, he became the highest-ranking police official in the Brooklyn West Bureau. He was a member of the Police Honor Legion and the Saint George Society. He died in 1949. His son, Lawrence, became a prominent attorney.

JOHN SNOWDEN

After John Snowden was hanged in 1919 for the death of Lottie Mae Brandon, his story continued to haunt the neighborhood he had lived in. For years, people told of the skies darkening on the day an innocent man was hanged. Snowden's niece Hazel knew about him because of the photograph her father kept alongside a newspaper report of his death. "I would come into my father's room every day and read that story and look at his picture," Hazel Snowden said. "He didn't have to tell me a word. It just burned into me."

Hazel, along with other like-minded Baltimore residents, began a grassroots effort to clear Snowden's name. A private investigator named Tim Turner, his interest piqued by newspaper reports, reexamined the case and concluded that the evidence did not add up to Snowden as the killer. No bloodstains were found anywhere else in the house but on the bed and no murder weapon was ever retrieved. In 2000, after a ten-year crusade, petitioners swayed Maryland Governor Parris Glendening that Snowden's execution had been a "possible miscarriage of justice." After much deliberation, the governor concluded that "while it is impossible at this late date to establish his guilt or innocence, there is substantial doubt that justice was served by his hanging." Governor Glendening granted Snowden clemency. "It's a long time, but it's so good to see justice has been done," said Hazel Snowden. Carlotte Wotring, the seventy-five-year-old niece of Lottie May Brandon, was stunned. "They didn't have DNA back then," she said, "but I'll bet you anything he had lots of scratches on him. My aunt fought for her life." Snowden's grave is now marked by a golden plaque commemorating his clemency.

ANTOINETTE TOLLA

Antoinette Tolla was the last woman New Jersey ever sentenced to die by hanging. Immediately after her commutation, she was removed to the State Prison at Trenton, where she served out her sentence. During that time, she learned English so well that she conversed fluently on the day of her release, when Grace appeared in a car to accompany her home. Antoinette moved to Crystal Street in Brooklyn with her family. She was naturalized in 1927 as a U.S. citizen.

At the time of the commutation, the *Cincinnati Post* offered Grace a bonus of two thousand dollars for her services to Antoinette. Grace instructed the *Post* to place the money in trust for Antoinette. When she was released, a representative of the paper gave her the money. Near the end of her own career, Grace thought of her fondly.

As I look back over thirty years to the naïve world in which Antoinette Tolla's tragedy was enacted, I find the circumstances almost incredible. Here was a poor immigrant woman who had been treated with as little consideration, almost, as a slave before some medieval tribunal. Evidence in her case had been so badly bungled that a gun, and even the autopsy surgeon's report, had failed to be properly included in the record. The woman's testimony in court had been translated poorly beyond recognition.

Antoinette Tolla lives today. After thirty years, in unfailing gratitude and friendship, she still comes to see me occasionally and never forgets to bring some small, hand-made gift. She is a grandmother, for her two daughters have long since married. Obscure though she may be, she is a useful and admirable citizen. I never think of her but with a feeling of gratitude, myself, that it was given me to save this life that would otherwise have been so indifferently lost.

DOCTOR DEVIL

On January 12, 1906, Dr. Emmet Cooper Dent, "Doctor Devil," died suddenly of heart failure, two months after deporting the Romanik family.

SOPHIE IRENE LOEB

Sophie Irene Loeb worked in many arenas of urban reform during the course of her life. In 1917, she served as the first woman strike mediator, settling a complicated taxicab strike in seven hours. During these same years, she worked on a commission to codify child welfare legislation in New York State. She believed that if any child failed to receive proper food and clothing, "the Government must stand in place of his parents." In 1924, she helped to found the Child Welfare Committee of America and coined its motto "Not charity, but a chance for every child." She reported for many years at the *Evening World*, wrote books, and publicly engaged the Palestine question. When she died of cancer on January 18, 1929, at age fifty-two, she was praised as "one of America's most distinguished public servants, an indefatigable worker."

EDWARD SWANN

Edward Swann was district attorney of New York City until 1921. He ran for the New York Supreme Court in 1920 but lost, spurned by Tammany bosses who wanted him out. Swann was later accused of fraud by James A. Delehanty of the Court of General Sessions. Delehanty alleged that Swann had mysteriously dismissed several major indictments of Bowery criminals "without any real investigation of the case and without any witnesses." Swann responded by pointing out that Delehanty was going to be a Republican candidate for DA the following year. Swann died on September 19, 1945. Before he finally left office, Swann summed up his role as district attorney in New York City:

> There is an epidemic of crime. Why? Some say it is due to the war—that the spirit of unrest and consequent disorder always follow wars. Perhaps in part that was the cause for the initiation of a crime wave spreading over the country. It is not the cause for the continuance and increase of crime. The chief cause of the continuance and increase of crime is imitation.

HUMBERTO PIERINI

The onetime worker at Sunny Side who helped Grace expose its practice of bringing Italian immigrants across the Atlantic for contract work later patented a mousetrap. The device would lure its prey across a plank only to drop the mouse into a small container of water to drown. The Pierini trap was patented on June 20, 1922.

JOSEPH GRIGG

Joseph W. Grigg covered much of the news in Europe for United Press and UPI over a nearly fifty-year career. He covered the Blitz in London, saw the Wehrmacht thunder into Poland, had torpedoes shoot at his boat, was taken into custody by the Germans after Pearl Harbor, and had to bang out a story in Algiers as teargas was coming in the window. He met Hitler and Eisenhower, Stalin and Churchill, De Gaulle and Adenauer. He died on October 29, 2000, at the age of ninety.

JOHN DOOLING

John "J.T." Dooling remained a legal advisor for Tammany Hall even after his career as a district attorney ended. He was especially useful when when it came to election year questions and loopholes. Dooling also managed a very successful private practice with his firm Knox & Dooling. He died in 1949 at the age of seventy-eight. When New York Governor William Sulzer was impeached in 1913 for misues of campaign funds, among other things, Dooling was questioned about monies he had given to Sulzer.

HERBERT ROEMMELE

The shy boy who once sketched out a map of Cocchi's basement for Grace, Herbert F. Roemmele, became a beloved professor of mechanical engineering at Cooper Union, where he taught for forty-two years. When introduced at an alumni function years later, some of his students noted that he had "a photographic memory for faces and names." He died in 1983 at age seventy-nine, leaving five children and one great-grandchild.

HENRY STIMSON

Henry Lewis Stimson enjoyed a monumental career in public service. His bloodline reached back to the president of the Continental Congress. As a child, his great-grandmother told him stories of meeting George Washington. At Yale, he was Phi Beta Kappa and was tapped for the mysterious Skull and Bones. After his stint as a U.S. district attorney, Stimson ran for governor of New York in 1910. He lost, badly, and was nicknamed the "human icicle" for his campaign trail demeanor. He served as secretary of war under Taft, where he oversaw the Panama Canal construction and visited the Philippines. On the home front, he was against suffrage. "It is not needed to right any substantial grievance," he said, "and will introduce too many voters who don't know what they're doing devoid of business training and experience. It would certainly tend to throw a disproportionate amount of political influence and power into certain localities and classes of citizens of the state as against other localities and other classes." When the suffragettes marched on Washington, one of them on a horse, Stimson called in the troops.

Stimson served as a lieutenant colonel in the 305th regiment out of Camp Upton. He spent nine months in France. He became secretary of war for a second time, this time under FDR. During the Second World War, Stimson met with generals and commanders, supervised the internment of the Japanese, and yet still found time for vigorous games of deck tennis and quiet evenings at home with his wife.

When President Franklin Delano Roosevelt suddenly died, it was Stimson who briefed President Truman on the existence of the Manhattan Project, of which Stimson was the senior advisor. Once the decision was made, it was Stimson who selected the targets of Hiroshima and Nagasaki. Stimson retired to Highold, his Scotland estate, where he died on October 20, 1950, at age eighty-three.

VAL BRANDON

After his wife's murder, Val Brandon joined the army and fought in France with the 135th machine gun battalion of the Thirty-seventh division. While stationed at Camp Meade, he was reported to have "admitted the crime in a dream." He sued the newspaper that reported it for slander. Once he returned home, Val relocated to California, remarried, and became very active in veterans work. He was elected commander in chief of the California and Nevada divisions of the Veterans of Foreign Wars at its national convention in 1927. He died on August 15, 1968, at seventy-two.

PADDY SOLAN

Paddy worked as the superintendent of building maintenance at Grand Central Terminal until his retirement. He invented the non-slip ramps in the terminal. He retired to West Englewood, New Jersey, where lived with his wife, Sadie, for twenty-three years. He told friends for years that he had solved the Ruth Cruger case.

MARIA COCCHI

By 1944, Maria and her son lived in Brooklyn, at 362 Elton Street. She became a naturalized U.S. citizen.

RUTH

Ruth Cruger skates on cold glass dusted with white snow. There is frost along the edge of her silver skates. She smiles and closes her eyes. She was born on December 8, 1898.

Across the ice, Ruth spots a boy and looks away. Of course, it is more complicated than that. Perhaps she is hot under her heavy coat that she hates or she is angry with her father. Or none of those things at all. That doesn't matter.

Ruth pushes off and cuts across the ice. She feels the cold snow spraying her ankles. People are in coats and mufflers. She catches her skate on an edge and almost pitches forward. She feels her heart in her chest, but stops herself. Everything is fine. She looks at the ice. Like everyone, she wonders what is beneath it. The lake or fishes or just the ground, none of which are that scary, after all.

She laughs and continues on, with an endlessly long afternoon ahead of her. There are no more minutes to even think about. She smiles and is quiet and her cheeks are red and cold. The tips of her fingers sting, but it makes her feel alive. There cannot be skating, after all, without a long dark lake, and skating without one isn't really skating at all. She tips her weight to the right and both skates are on the edge of things now, pushing toward the bright, open space.

GRACE

Grace Winterton was born on September 17, 1869, in Greenwich Village, New York, to Isabella and Adoniram Judson Winterton. Her father, who was named after the famous Baptist missionary, was an insurance claims adjuster. He was not a lawyer, but he very often appeared in high-level court, testifying and providing judgment on claim cases. Grace told reporters that he would sometimes take her to court with him and that she worshipped at his knee. Grace had two sisters, Jessie and Nelly, and a brother, Adoniram Judson Winterton Jr. Their family had deeper claims to fame and history. Grace's grand-uncle was Admiral Hull, who fought on the U.S.S. *Constitution* in the War of 1812. Her grandfather was Henry S. Hull, a brief, one-time partner of the famous abolitionist William Lloyd Garrison.

After primary school, Grace attended Hunter College. In her early twenties, she taught at the Collegiate School, an all-boys school on the Upper West Side. She married Dr. Henry Forest Quackenbos on June 5, 1895, when she was twenty-three. At the turn of the century, Grace enrolled in the night class at NYU law school; she and Henry divorced soon after. In 1906, Grace attended her ex-husband's second wedding as a guest. A gossip magazine later said they split when he was caught engaging in "peephole practices" with his female patients at work.

Grace's mother passed away on June 29, 1903, in Manhattan at the age of sixty-six. Almost a year later, Grace's father died on February 26, 1904, at the age of seventy-one. The cause of death was pneumonia. Soon after, Grace began wearing her signature black wardrobe.

On June 8, 1911, while in Lima, Peru, Grace married Howard Donald Humiston, a Yale lawyer and partner at Humiston, Olcott & Hincks. He had worked with Grace before at the People's Law Firm. Rumors said that when she heard he was in Peru, she followed him and proposed to him directly. She was forty-two. In November 1921, the

Tatler claimed that Grace and Howard were "living apart" and that he was "in a habitat in Greenwich Village." He had also "sought companionship elsewhere." Experts claimed they split because of Howard's alleged excessive drinking. Howard lived most of the year in Provincetown, Massachusetts, on the tip of Cape Cod with friends and acquaintances in a white three-story house. He died in bed of capillary bronchitis on July 21, 1943, at the age of sixty-five. His ashes were interred in Forest Hills Cemetery in Boston. Grace was buried in New York.

Grace's brother, Adoniram, died on December 22, 1929, at Flower Hospital on Fifth Avenue. Grace had previously told reporters that he had died years earlier.

Grace's sister Jessie outlived her, dying on February 27, 1953. Jessie's grandson remembered seeing his auntie Grace when she would come to the apartment on Sundays. He couldn't remember much, other than that she was tall. He was the only person I could find who had actually met her. After our discussion, largely about the grandeur of old New York, he got back in touch with me. He remembered another detail that he was wary of sharing. He remembered overhearing his relatives refer to Grace, behind her back, as "Auntie Disgrace."

On January 15, 1906, Grace wrote a letter to Edward C. Stokes, the governor of New Jersey, as she attempted to sway him about the Antoinette Tolla case.

> I hope you are not influenced by any newspaper notoriety which I seem to have received. It is all so intensely distasteful to me that I have been forced to take a room in Newark where I can escape in the day time from Yellow Journal reporters who are only combing for secusation. I beg you to believe that whatever items of news they have gleaned for their papers, they have not received them from me.

After the Cruger case, the New York Police Department's apparatus for finding missing people went from unofficial assignments in a branch house to an evolving, centralized system of integrated police work that would come to be known as the Bureau of Missing Persons and, later, the Missing Persons Squad. Presently, there is no twenty-four-hour delay after victims are reported. In fact, victims of crimes are acted on immediately. But if the victim is eighteen or older, according to Joseph Giacalone, a former sergeant with the NYPD, "we just file paperwork." In 2014, thirteen thousand people were reported missing in New York City. The year before, eight thousand of that number were children. Before Grace, girls who were labeled "wayward" or "lost" were given a moral and categorical distinction that stopped most people from looking for them. Grace, whose given first name was Mary, felt differently. When she spoke about her career late in life, it was with wisdom gained at great cost: "I want to tell you just a little about my girls," Grace said, "for they are all mine; each and every one of them, of all the thousands I know well, has a particular place in my heart.

"It is the unfortunate truth," Grace said, "that too often the attitude of the official police of the United States is *the girl was bad to begin with.* It is because the search for the missing girl is so often conducted upon the basis of this utterly false possibility that so many cases, in my opinion, are annually dropped from the police department as 'unsolved' and the hopes of so many parents crushed to the ground."

"Ruth was not a willful girl who left her home voluntarily," Grace said, "as every police official connected with the search assured me that she was. They had no proof—none of them had a single fact against her—but they all said that she could not possibly have been abducted. They admitted that a little child might be overpowered and made away with in a store like Cocchi's, situated on a busy street, but a girl eighteen years old—never. They pitied me for my faith in girl nature and, wisely shaking their heads, insisted that she must have gone off of her own will—the old, sad story.

"But I have proved that she didn't leave home that way. I have proved that she was a brave, good girl and that she died in an effort to shield her honor. It was not the 'old, old story' that the police harp on when a girl disappears and detectives fail to trace her. It was a murder.

"It is convenient, or course," Grace continued, "to assemble meager evidence that the girl was seen boarding such and such a train or taking a certain mysterious taxicab in company with a young man, always unknown. This promptly curtails the searching activities. This exceeding proneness to put the entire burden of responsibility upon the shoulders of the missing girl herself is a great evil. Occasional crimes against womanhood by degenerates must always figure as one of the horrible possibilities of community existence. But the wholesale sacrifice of young womanhood upon the altar of ignorance and vicious conspiracy can be checked."

Grace's point, as always, was simple and practical, but it still sounded radical. "Just because girls bob their hair, wear short skirts, dance crazy dances and look a little more sophisticated than girls of the last two generations looked, does not indicate with absolute certainty—as many of our public figures have announced in bold print—that the younger generation is on the road to ruin," she said.

Grace fought many battles in her career, both as a lawyer and as a detective. But her approach never varied when it came to rallying others to the cause at hand. Years earlier, while testifying before Congress on immigration, she said, "This grave question can not be boiled down to mere statistics . . . It is not a question of how much of this you will tolerate before you pass laws which will wipe out the evil. It is a question as to whether you will tolerate it at all."

According to the National Center for Missing and Exploited Children, the FBI investigated 466,949 cases of missing children in 2014. The NCMEC tip line on reported sexual exploitation of children and young adults received 1.1 million reports in 2014. According to the U.S. Department of Justice, 100,000–300,000 children are at risk for entering the U.S. commercial sex trade. According to the U.S. State Department, 600,000–800,000 people are trafficked across international borders every year, of which 80 percent are female and half are children. I wanted to reprint all the people gone missing in the last year here, at the end, but it would not have been "cost effective," they told me, even in the smallest type. So think of one name for me. Maybe it is someone you know. Or someone you saw on a show or a flier once. Or maybe it is your name, or a name you once had. Whoever it is, write that name here: _____. If you don't know anyone, put the name of someone you can't imagine losing. They are the same name.

On May 6, 2013, as I was working on this book, I heard over the radio that three young women in Cleveland, where I live, had been miraculously found alive after being missing for over a decade. Michelle Knight, Gina DeJesus, and Amanda Berry escaped imprisonment in an ordinary-looking house through a combination of self-preservation, quick thinking, and the wild kindness of a stranger named Charles Ramsey, who refused to look the other way. All three women had been considered lost causes by local police and the FBI. All three are alive today.

As I finish this book, the latest name of a young woman that crosses my screen—unsearched, unbidden—is that of Tiffany Sayre, who went missing on May 11, 2015. The search for this mother of two toddlers lasted more than a month, until her body was found, wrapped in a sheet, in a wooded area on June 20. They found her on Father's Day.

"Makes me mad, makes me hurt," Thomas Kuhn, her father, told the local television station. "All I know is we are going to catch you, whoever you are.

"We are coming for you," he said.

Author's Note

I wonder if it won't be the same with the children as it has been with us. No matter how long each one of them lives, won't their lives feel to them unfinished like ours, only just beginning? I wonder how far they will go. And then their children will grow up and it will be the same with them. Unfinished lives. Oh, dearie, what children all of us are.

—Ernest Poole, *His Family* (1917)

On one appropriately hot Tuesday in July 1924, Oscar Zinn burned the collective crimes of New York City all the way down to ashes. During his tenure as the property clerk of the police department, Zinn had checked almost everything imaginable into the evidence lockers at Central. He had handled heavy guns, dirty money, and bloodied knives—so many knives—along with heroin, cocaine, costumes, and even axes and saws. One time, a few years earlier, he even checked in a bar of chocolate that had been turned in by a particularly honest member of the Junior Police Boys. Zinn had inspected all of these things and written them down in his ledger. He then placed them on their shelves to await trial or auction. When they were needed, Zinn would send them back up again and note it in his files. They usually came back. But sometimes things just disappeared. But when they were here, in the evidence room, he knew what was where. But for all the purse guns and stilettos, most of what he had was clothing. There were stacks and stacks of it, left over from crimes and investigations. Dark and brittle with blood, he handled them carefully.

Which made today, July 8, 1924, all the more satisfying. On this day, Oscar Zinn arrived at work early and looked at the tower of material in front of him. One by one, Zinn lifted each bundle and threw it into the central incinerator. Most of it would go up almost instantly. Some of it had been in storage for twenty years. Over the course of the day, Zinn oversaw the burning of twenty-five years of old criminal evidence. In total, five hundred bundles of clothing were consigned to the basement fire.

There was infamous material here. There were the clothes worn by Barnett Baff, the so-called Poultry King who was murdered on Thanksgiving Eve in 1914. There were the clothes of Harry Thaw's victim, shot to death on the roof of Madison Square Garden. There were the terrible pillowcases that Hans Schmidt stuffed the body of Anna Aumuller into, which provided the evidence that sent him to the chair. There were the already-black clothes of Ruth Wheeler, who had been killed and placed in a fireplace by Albert Wolter when she answered his ad for a stenographer. And the little clothes of five-year-old Guiseppe Varota, who had been drowned by kidnappers. All of these real-life cases, all of these true-life people, had ended a long time ago.

And somewhere in the stacks of bound bundles that lifted light and burned fast were the bloodstained clothes found on Ruth Cruger's body. Oscar Zinn tossed the clothes in. All that remained of the case were the records in a file, somewhere upstairs.

A few years later, a young woman looked at those very same files. There were handwritten notes, canvass reports, and even photographs. Her name was Isabel Stephen, and she wanted to be a writer since before you were born. Growing up in Dorchester, Massachusetts, she had a short story published in the *Boston Post*. After that, she began to think it might be possible. She didn't want to be a nurse or teacher. Her story, "Caught by a Human Cat," was a scary tale of mesmerism and a nighttime train ride. She saw her name in print and looked away before looking back again. Within ten years, Isabel was writing newspaper stories for all manner of papers up and down the East Coast. She specialized in women's portraits: the popular small biographies of ladies of society, actresses, or general women of stature (or mischief).

Soon, Isabel was working for the McClure Syndicate and writing for real magazines. She had an office with a typewriter. She also wrote for United Press. Her name was appearing under stories all across the country. She specialized in writing about women. But Isabel also wrote secret things. There was a new type of magazine on the stands these days. Featuring lush painted covers and lots of indiscriminate type, these magazines had covers of wide-eyed women with bright flesh and bared knives. They had names like *Clue, Mystery,* and *True Detective.*

Isabel wrote for the McFadden mags that were long, in-depth summaries of crimes bolstered by photographs, diagrams, and drama. McFadden paid by the word. That was part of their value now. To find stories, Isabel scoured old newspapers. There were stories she remembered, too. Then she would go down to the police station and look at the old records. Then she would try to track down the arresting officer or detective. McFadden insisted on it. This was not fiction. But it was never wholly the truth, either. These were mysteries, after all.

So by the time Isabel Stephen sat in Grace Humiston's apartment, it was with some awe. She knew what this woman had accomplished. Isabel looked down at her notes that all of a sudden had become messy. As Grace spoke, her eye glittering, Isabel was already seeing it come together in her head. She had to start with the facts she could get and try to reconcile them with what the newspapers had said. Isabel could see the basement as she started to think it back into the world. She looked at one of the photos. "A single electric bulb" might work. But Isabel knew her readers wanted justice and vengeance and atmosphere, too. And murder. Maybe that was part of the problem. But Grace's eyes were kind, Isabel thought. Sad, but kind. Isabel then realized that the woman in front of her had actually seen this and lived it. That was a big, impossible difference. Isabel knew she could not capture that eye, but she was still going to try.

Grace told Isabel to look up a man named Julius Kron since he might have some stories for her. The detectives—the great ones—sold their stories, or at least the germ of them, to magazine writers, who would add a little flair to them. Not only to sell magazines, but to add a level of drama that had long since passed from the story itself. Good stories, like people, grew after they ended. Isabel was seeing another reason for that kind of storytelling, too. People needed to listen.

Isabel wrote up this story—"as told to"—for *True Detective Mysteries*. This was a cooperative effort to at least get closer to the truth. And to tell a good story. Or the parody of one. And to sell some mystery magazines. That's what got the story read at all. So Isabel kept writing, using evidence to detect presences and support connections. She wrote a few stories on the exploits of Grace and Kron. Readers ate them up. Then she moved on.

Lois Weber's 1916 film about Charlie Stielow allegedly featured a female detective. But only three reels are known to survive. In 1939, the syndicated newspaper feature "Lessons from Historic Crimes," by Captain Eugene de Beck and Dr. Carleton Simon, featured the Ruth Cruger mystery. Grace was mentioned, but only briefly. The writers gave the moment of the case's solution to Solan. In 1956, a very short syndicated newspaper story titled "The Case of the Frightened Eyes" details the Cruger case but does not mention Grace at all, though it mentions a male detective in passing.

On December 8, 1962, there was no news in New York City. There were births, deaths, sports scores, crimes, and murders, but none of it went reported by the usually endless roll of city newspapers. After weeks of posturing, the International Typographical Union, Local No. 6, ordered all of its members to strike. They were mostly Italian or Irish, second-generation New Yorkers, faced with the onset of new printing technology that they feared would render their workers' skills with a Linotype machine obsolete.

When the strike was finally settled 114 days later, they had reached an agreement, but it only led the way to greater debt. The strike killed papers in a town that in the 1920s had nineteen dailies. By 1970, there was only the *Times,* the *Daily News,* and the *New York Post.* Writers scattered to literary outlets and television. The records of the old papers ended up in libraries and archives, commonly called morgues.

In 1973, the New York Police Department officially closed their central headquarters on 240 Centre Street, moving its operations to the monolithic 1 Police Plaza. Instead of relocating their past records to the new location, the department instead filed fifty years' worth of police records—full of the names of the guilty, the innocent, the lost, and the victimized—directly into the East River. The heavier files sank while the smaller ones fluttered on the surface as they smeared out and floated into nothingness. The old headquarters was later converted into a luxury apartment building.

A book of 1978 student essays designed to use crime to teach the research paper had an entry called "Grace Humiston: The First Woman Detective," by Tim McCarl. There are some great academic articles on Sunny Side by Randolph Boehm and others that have appeared in history publications. Grace's story appeared in an article by Karen Abbott on the Web site for *Smithsonian Magazine* and in a novel, *Grace Humiston and the Vanishing,* by Charles Kelly. I found her by chance when I stumbled onto her 1917 interview in the *New York Sun* while researching the Black Hand.

After an exhaustive search of New York libraries, law schools, and private archives, no concentrated gravity of Grace Humiston's personal papers seems to have survived. Some very early financial records of the People's Law Firm are held at the New York Public Library, and the odd letter or two can be found in archives here and there. Everything else is scattered among stories told by others in newspaper articles, magazines, court records, congressional testimony, and the circular lines of history. There is plenty of dialogue from all of these sources; it is quoted here as it was originally published, left alone in its original state. The reader must, as those of the time had to, consider each individual source. That is part of the story, too. And while the larger events here have been investigated and presented as truth, there are still connections that had to be imagined—small gestures, moments, and emotions—that are laid over an infrastructure of facts. This is a story about real people, not just their vital statistics.

Grace's files might have been taken by the Bureau of Missing Persons (and later destroyed) when she was fired by Woods. Or perhaps she simply had nowhere to store them once her practice was shuttered. Or maybe she had just had enough. Very surprisingly for a lawyer, she also died without a will. Her very small savings was claimed by her sister Jessie. Most of the court records of Alfredo Cocchi's trial in Italy were destroyed in a fire. All that remains is a brief summary of his final trial in a heavy, handwritten book on a dusty shelf in Bologna.

Grace's files as an employee of the U.S. government, as well as those of J. J. Kron, may have also been destroyed in a fire on June 23, 1972. Or they may still exist, though under seal by the Espionage Act of 1917, signed by Woodrow Wilson in order to protect the sensitive work of government agents.

This is the path of evidence that led to this book. The story thus remains, like any story about murder, incomplete in that, although we may hope to understand at least some of the facts and conditions of Ruth's death, we can never completely understand the inconceivability of the very act itself. The only absolute of this story is that Ruth Cruger was murdered. The actions of all the people in this book may then be understood as a collective attempt to reanimate her last days—to communicate with her—in order to find answers, justice, and a hoped-for peace. Or just to say good-bye. Although this is her story, there are an unimaginable number of other cases just as factual as Ruth Cruger's. That is the only truth of crime.

Earlier in her career, when Grace was juggling dozens of immigration cases, she said that "I could go into these cases very fully and show you the sadness which attached to each individual story." That was always her methodology: to find the story of a case in order to

evoke a response from others. Though Poe introduced the full character of the detective in fiction, the word first appears in Dickens's *Bleak
House* to describe a Scotland Yard inspector. The new word, created to
fit a singular character, was an extension of the word "detect," or "to
discover or identify the presence or existence of something." Something behind a veil. Or something we don't understand. Or someone
we have lost—and hope to see again.

NOTES

T he sources of this story extend across newspaper articles, court documents, magazine exposés, government reports, muckraking stories, gossip, deduction, and the connections among them. In the absence of primary sources from Grace Humiston, I have endeavored to tell the story around that space to show how culture and media shape our understanding of her life. It is perhaps not a usual way of telling a story. She was not a usual person.

Sources are documented using unnumbered endnotes organized by chapter. Notes are keyed to the text using signal phrases or descriptions of the topic covered. When a note documents dialogue, the last few words quoted appear in the note as a key, and the reader can assume the citation includes all preceding quotations. Quotations are unaltered unless indicated with square brackets. Dialogue is presented as is from its various sources. In the very few instances where I use imagined dialogue to advance the narrative, it appears without quotes.

In my attempt to convey visual details and turns of phrase that re-create progressive-era New York, I relied on primary sources, including photographs from the New York Public Library and the Library of Congress, rather than secondary accounts of the era.

Newspapers are a major source of this story's power. In most cases, I veer toward the "reputable" New York papers, but at times I use less-well-regarded papers to show how the story spread. Sometimes, I use a wire story in a nonregional paper because it was a better, easier-to-read reproduction. Smaller-market papers were often my source for testimony because they could more easily print the full transcripts. Where discrepancies in coverage of cases exist, I note it so that readers can decide for themselves.

That being said, this is a story about the past. Everyone in this story, save one person, is gone. The center of this story is a still space that cannot be wholly filled. It can only be approached. It can only be told from the perspective of others trying to reach it themselves.

PROLOGUE

The main sources for Doyle's visit to New York are William R. Hunt, *Front-Page Detective*, Bowling Green, OH: Bowling Green State UP, 1990, 201; "Will Be Lynched," *Brooklyn Daily Eagle*, May 27, 1914, 3; Russell Miller, *The Adventures of Arthur Conan Doyle*, New York: Thomas Dunne, 2008.

"from general knowledge" (p. 2): "No Mystery in Crime," *Houston Post*, December 22, 1912, 29.

"sight of New York" (p. 2): "Conan Doyle Fears," *New York Times*, May 31, 1914, 44.

"thunder on their own heads" (p. 3): "Conan Doyle in Gotham," *St. Louis Post-Dispatch*, May 27, 1914, 10.

"arrived in New York" (p. 3): "Sir A. Conan Doyle," *New York Times*, June 1, 1914, 25.

"football at the age of forty-two" (p. 4): Marguerite Mooers Marshall, "A Woman Can Never Get Anything," *New York Evening World*, May 28, 1914, 3.

"place for that" (p. 5): "Sir Arthur Visits Tombs," *New York Evening World*, May 28, 1914, 3.

"they'll bury it" (p. 5): "Two Prophets," *Detroit Free Press*, July 12, 1914, 44.

"never been the same since!" (p. 6): "Pilgrims Greet A. Conan Doyle," *Chicago Daily Tribune*, May 29, 1914, 2.

"Sherlocks over here" (p. 6): William R. Hunt, *Front-Page Detective*, Bowling Green, OH: Bowling Green State UP, 1990, 201. The phrase is also attributed to Joseph Choate: "Pilgrims Ask Doyle": *The New York Sun*, May 29, 1914, 10.

Burns as actor (p. 6): These films were *Universal Animated Weekly No. 117*, June 3, 1914; *Our Mutual Girl: Episode 22*, June 15, 1914; *The $5,000,000 Counterfeiting Plot*, September 1914. Doyle's cameos mostly involve his visit to America. While filming *Our Mutual Girl*, Doyle, "leading man Edward Brennan, and famous humorist Irvin S. Cobb got involved in heated discussion on the number of edible sausage," according to *Moving Picture World*, vol. 20, April–June 1914, 1598.

"First World War had begun" (p. 6): The onset of the First World War is the major historical event that takes place during the events of this book. I have chosen to keep it on the periphery to mirror what happens in terms of personal focus when someone loses a loved one. The world seems unimportant.

son's tragic passing (p. 7): Andrew Lycett, *The Man Who Created Sherlock Holmes*, New York: Free Press, 2007.

"for a sign and a consolation" (p. 7): "There Is No Death," *Indiana Gazette*, November 20, 1918, 2.

"evidence in this world" (p. 7): "War Stimulates Interest," *The Index-Journal*, April 13, 1919, 9.

"only a veil" (p. 7): "There Is No Death," *Indiana Gazette*, November 20, 1918, 2.

1: TRUE DETECTIVE MYSTERIES

The details of this scene are taken from several pulp sources: Julius J. Kron with Isabel Stephen, "The Inside Story of the Ruth Cruger Case," *True Detective*, May 1926; Grace Humiston, "Won't You Help Me Find My Girl?" *Actual Detective*, May 4, 1938; Dick Halvorsen, "The Hidden Grave," *Master Detective*, April 1954.

Call her (p. 10): Grace Humiston with Isabel Stephen, "Won't You Help Me Find My Girl?" *Actual Detective*, May 4, 1938.

2: THE MISSING SKATER

The story of the critical first hours after Ruth's disappearance, including dialogue, is taken from a number of sources, including newspapers, detective magazines, city maps, and weather reports. The majority of the narrative is from Grace Humiston, "Won't You Help Me Find My Girl?" *Actual Detective*, May 4, 1938; Dick Halvorsen, "The Hidden Grave," *Master Detective*, April 1954; "Another Arnold Mystery," *New Castle Herald*, February 15, 1917, 1; "Girl Kidnapped," *New York Evening World*, February 15, 1917, 1; "Pretty Girl Skater," *New York Times*, February 16, 1917, 20; "Cocchi Must Be Returned," *New York Evening World*, June 23, 1917, 2; "Won't Limit Inquiry," *New York Times*, June 24, 1917, 2; "Swann Prepared," *New York Sun*, June 26, 1917, 4; "Police Were Deaf," *New York Times*, June 26, 1917, 8; "Police Graft Bared," *New York Sun*, June 24, 1917, 6. There is some variation on who goes with Helen on her second trip (and how many times she returns), but the accounts are otherwise in agreement.

Helen's shiver (p. 14): "Sister Warned," *New York Evening World*, June 26, 1917, 2.

"looked positively happy" (p. 15): "Missing Schoolgirl," *New York Evening World*, February 15, 1917, 1.

Description of Henry Cruger (p. 16): "Father of Slain Girl," *New York Evening World*, June 25, 1917, 3.

first clue (p. 19): "First Clew," *Brooklyn Daily Eagle*, February 16, 8.

Alfredo Cocchi's disappearance (p. 21): "Man Disappears in Cruger Case," *New-York Tribune*, February 17, 5.

3: THE CORONER'S CABINET

The majority of background information, dialogue, and information about the Antoinette Tolla case comes from Gertrude Klein, "But the State Said She Must Hang," *Actual Detective*, March 23, 1938; *State v. Antoinette Tolla, New Jersey Court of Errors and Appeals*, vol. 375, no. 7, 1906. Government sources: Dept. of State—Sec. of State's office—Miscellaneous Filings (Series III): "Governor Edward C. Stokes Commuted the Death Sentence," March 9, 1906, item 370; "Reprieve of Antoinette Tolla," February 7, 1906, item 371; "Governor Stokes Suspended," January 10, 1906, item 694; Governor Edward C. Stokes—Correspondence, 1904—1908: file 618; Court of Pardons, relating to A. Tolla (7 letters); Death Record for Joseph Sonta, March 4, 1905; New Jersey State Archives Dept. of Institutions and Agencies, New Jersey State Prison at Trenton Inmate Registers, 1894–1975, vol. 21. Thanks to Bette M. Epstein, of the New Jersey State Archives, for her kind help.

"I shot him" (p. 23): Gertrude Klein, "But the State Said She Must Hang," *Actual Detective*, March 23, 1938.

"indict for murder" (p. 24): Ibid.

"For the defense" (p. 26): "Woman Will Help in War," *New York Times*, Sept. 15, 1907, 6.

"it by reason" (p. 26): Leslie J. Tompkins, "Notes and Personals," *American Law School Review*, vol. 4, 1911–12, 176. Ashley was born in Boston on July 4, 1851, and was a Yale graduate.

more than a handful (p. 27): The first woman lawyer in New York, Kate Stoneman, passed the bar in 1886, but only after an arduous battle to change the Code of Civil Procedure to allow women to take it at all. She practiced in Albany, mostly in suffrage cases. Albany now observes "Kate Stoneman Day" and gives out awards; see katestoneman.org and katestonemanproject.org.

Clarice Baright (p. 27): Virginia G. Drachman, *Sisters in Law: Women Lawyers in Modern American History*, Cambridge, MA: Harvard UP, 2001, 133. Baright would go on to become a pioneering attorney nicknamed "The Lady Angel of the Tenement District" for her work with the poor.

Dean Ashley's teaching (p. 28): "Law Schools," *Brooklyn Daily Eagle*, August 15, 1912, 89.

"become a lawyer" (p. 28): Leslie J. Tompkins, "Notes and Personals," *American Law School Review*, Vol. 4, 1911–12, 175. Ashley believed in leaving the bar to law school entry low while making it very difficult "to get out." "He hated sham,

despised pretense, and avoided publicity. Quiet and simple in his tastes, he chose to live his life in the congenial and loving society of his family and intimate friends. A man of firm convictions, he rarely expressed an opinion until he had given the subject thoughtful consideration and when once his mind was made up, took a positive stand and retained it." He died on January 26, 1916, about a year before Ruth Cruger's disappearance. Clarence D. Ashley, *Annual Report: Including Proceedings of the Annual Meeting of the American Bar Association*, vol. 24, 1901, 477. According to Ashley, "There is no question that women are thoroughly able to practice law. They themselves will work out the problem, and they are doing it in New York to-day. Only last year a bright little woman went out of the law school, and the result is that she and her husband are both practicing law successfully together."

Legal Aid Society (p. 29): *Thirtieth Annual Report to the President of the Legal Aid Society for the Year 1905*, New York Public Library Archives. In 1904, they took 20,277 cases and paid out $58,665 to clients. They took on work "no matter how small their claims, nor how helpless or poor the claimants." That year, they spent $22,702. The most popular cases were "Advice," "Complaints Agt. Attorneys," and "Domestic Difficulties."

one thousand female lawyers (p. 29): "Women Lawyers in America," *Evening Star*, February 16, 1906, 8.

"may have it" (p. 30): Gertrude Klein, "But the State Said She Must Hang," *Actual Detective*, March 23, 1938.

"is manifestly fanciful" (p. 30): Ibid.

an incendiary editorial (p. 32): "Mrs. Tolla Granted a Reprieve Today," *Trenton Times*, January 10, 1906, 1.

killed before his arrival (p. 32): "Murder to Save Mrs. Tolla," *Trenton Times*, January 15, 2.

under her lower lip (p. 34): New Jersey State Archives Dept. of Institutions and Agencies, New Jersey State Prison at Trenton Inmate Registers, 1894–1975, vol. 21.

"not do so" (p. 34): "Counsel Retained to Save Mrs. Tolla," *Trenton Sunday Advertiser*, January 7, 1906, 1. Grace heard that Caesar Barra was working with Antoinette's lawyer to ask for a pardon. She thought he had been disbarred ("Lawyer Causes Man's Disbarment," *New York Times*, October 4, 1905, 16). Barra said in the press that he felt confident that the appeal would be granted.

"woman-killing country" (p. 34): "City Priest Would Save Murderesses," *Trenton Times*, January 8, 1906, 6. "Let the Stars and Stripes shine and float all over the world as an emblem of strength. Don't let the other peoples think that beautiful flag is stained with the blood of women."

"assault the woman" (p. 34): "Mrs. Tolla Found Guilty," *Trenton Times,* January 17, 1906, 1.

Antoinette's cell window (p. 36): Gertrude Klein, "But the State Said She Must Hang," *Actual Detective,* March 23, 1938. Afterward, Antoinette cried and talked with Anna Valentine, another death row prisoner. Father Lambert, the prison chaplain, would visit at night and hear these conversations, praying for them both. There is debate whether she actually witnessed the execution.

"is rendered doubtful" (p. 37): *New Jersey v. Tolla, Reports of Cases Argued and Determined Before the New Jersey Supreme Court,* Newark: Soney and Sage, 1906, 523.

about five years (p. 38): Letter, Office of the Sheriff of Bergen County Hackensack to Secretary of State James Mercer, March 10, 1906, Department of State Secretary of State Office miscellaneous filings (series 3), box 370, 1836c–1915.

4: THE HEATHERBLOOM GIRL

"very little of his business" (p. 41): "Man Disappears in Cruger Case," *New-York Tribune,* February 17, 5. All of the dialogue in this beginning section is from this article.

"protection for their children" (p. 42): "Hunt Missing Man," *New York Times,* February 17, 1917, 1. The document was signed by Mrs. Pattinson, Mrs. Gershwin Smith, Mrs. John H. Brown, Mrs. B. M. Oxley, and Miss Grace M. Chamberlain.

How much they loved Ruth Cruger (p. 43): "Students Join Hunt," *Washington Herald,* February 17, 3; "Movies to Present," *New York Times,* February 21, 1917, 20.

"in the newspapers" (p. 43): "Saw Weeping Girl," *New York Evening World,* February 17, 1917, 1.

blind woman (p. 44): Wording taken from Paul Strand, "Print shows woman beggar wearing 'Blind' sign and New York City beggar's permit," *Photograph—New York,* 1917. Library of Congress Prints and Photographs Division, Washington, D.C. Call No. TR1.C5 1916/1917 (case X) [P&P]. I am using this photograph as a representative image of the beggars Henry Cruger would have seen. There is no evidence to prove that he indeed saw this particular woman, though there is no evidence he did not. Throughout this book, I similarly use other contemporary details and situations to fill out cultural and social details. This is a story of creative nonfiction, not an academic history.

become a detective (p. 44): "Lost Cruger Girl," *New York Evening World,* February 19, 1917, 1.

"sent in search of her" (p. 44): "Pretty Girl Skater," *New York Times,* February 16, 1917, 20.

"knew it was she" (p. 45): "Sure Ruth Cruger Rode," *New York Times,* March 2, 1917, 2; "Chauffeur Gives Cruger," *New-York Tribune,* February 20, 1917, 6.

"which [I] did" (p. 46): "Sure Ruth Cruger Rode," *New York Times,* March 2, 1917, 2.

"wide black hat" (p. 46): "Police Graft Bared," *New York Sun,* June 24, 1917, 6.

"had been crying" (p. 46): "Lost Cruger Girl," *New York Evening World*, February 19, 1917, 1.

"for police shirking" (p. 47): "Man Who Last Saw," *New York Evening World*, February 16, 1917, 1.

"with me long ago" (p. 47): Ibid.

"and the children" (p. 47): "Lost Cruger Girl," *New York Evening World*, February 19, 1917, 4.

nothing in-between (p. 48): Ernest Poole, *His Family*, New York: Macmillan, 1917. Poole's book is set in 1913 and tells the story of widower Roger Gale as he tries to understand his three modern daughters who are navigating life in New York City. Known for its inclusion of real-life detail and events into its fictional narrative, the book won the Pulitzer Prize in 1918—the first given to a work of fiction. The work is largely forgotten today. In an attempt to get closer to 1917 language, I have, at several points in this book, consciously reflected some of Poole's brief phrases and images in homage. *His Family* is in the public domain.

"should be done" (p. 49): "Girl Drugged," *New York Times*, February 20, 1917, 20.

"You big fool" (p. 49): "Woods Sworn In," *New-York Tribune*, April 9, 1914, 2. Woods's inauguration day was the same day as the funeral of Detective Joseph Guarnieri. Woods's pals at the Harvard Club had sent roses for his inaguration. Woods supposedly looked at the flowers for a moment and had them sent on to the detective's family instead. For more on Woods, see Arthur Woods, *Policeman and Public*, Ithaca, NY: Cornell UP, 2009 (reprint); Arthur Woods, "Police Administration," *Proceedings of the Academy of Political Science in the City of New York*. New York: City of New York, April 1915, 54–61. *The Arthur Woods Papers, 1884–1938* on microfilm, Washington, D.C.: Library of Congress, shelf no. 19,604.

"to shoot me?" (p. 50): "Corporation Counsel Polk," *Brooklyn Daily Eagle*, April 17, 1914, 1. Mitchel was convinced, in the hours afterward, that it was a larger conspiracy and began brandishing his own pistol in the air.

"none of them did" (p. 50): "Polk Expected," *Harrisburg Daily Independent*, April 18, 1914, 1. Mahoney, after trial, was sent to a mental asylum.

"dealing with strange forces" (p. 50): "Malone Warns Revilers," *Brooklyn Daily Eagle*, April 18, 1914, 2. Attributed to both Mayor Mitchel and here to Dudley Field Malone, collector of the Port of New York.

Barking Squad (p. 51): "Nothing Like a Canine Sherlock Holmes," *New York Times*, September 6, 1908, 46.

long campaign of murder (p. 52): Francesco Maraesciallo Bianco, "The Story of 'Jo' Petrosino," *The Scrap Book*, April 1910; Herbert Asbury, *The Gangs of New York: An Informal History of the New York Underworld*, New York: Knopf, 1928; James Dalessandro, "Petrosino v. The Black Hand," *Playboy*, January 2010; "Old-Time Racketeers,"

Brooklyn Daily Eagle, June 18, 1951, 1. Tom McDonough played for the "Barnstorming All-Americans" and was a .300-hitting third baseman; "Masquerading Sleuth," *Brooklyn Daily Eagle*, June 20, 1951, 5; Anne Romano, "Italian Squad," *Italian Americans in Law Enforcement*, Bloomington, IN: Xlibris, 2010; Bernard Whalen and Jon Whalen, *The NYPD's First Fifty Years*, Lincoln, NE: Potomac, 2015.

Black Tom Island (p. 52): "Munitions Explosions," *New York Times*, July 31, 1916, 1. At 2:08 A.M. on July 30, 1916, German saboteurs set off explosions on Black Tom Island, an ammunitions dump located off Jersey City, causing reverbations that allegedly made the Brooklyn Bridge sway. Less than an hour later, another explosion showered the region with debris. Six people were killed in the aftermath, including a baby.

without its own controversies (p. 52): "School Children Told Life," *Washington Times*, November 2, 1910, 6. An English teacher, Miss Henrietta Rodman, had been disciplined for teaching the work of Victorian novelist George Eliot. It wasn't the choice of novel so much as the details of Eliot's personal life: she had lived openly with George Lewes, who was married to someone else.

"insulted me in the street" (p. 53): "Gang Annoys Schoolgirls," *New York Evening World*, May 1, 1903, 6.

used secret hand signs (p. 53): Ibid.

the people huddled (p. 53): Information on the early days of the New York City subway from *The City Beneath Us*, edited by Vivian Heller, New York: Norton, 2004.

"to go home" (p. 54): "Find Clue," *Washington Times*, February 19, 1917, 2.

Heatherbloom Girl (p. 54): "Moving Signs Along Broadway," *Edison Monthly*, December 1911, 226; Gregory Gilmartin, *Shaping the City*, New York: Clarkson Potter, 1995, 443; James Traub, *The Devil's Playground*, New York: Random House, 2004.

"(Signed), Ruth Cruger" (p. 55): "Girls' 'Prison Note,'" *Washington Herald*, February 22, 1917, 1.

false leads (p. 55): "Cruger Girl May," *Asbury Park Press*, February 19, 1917, 2. A girl named Mildred Van Loan saw a blotter note on the ground while playing near the Hudson River. It was an "S.O.S." message from "Ruth Cruger." Another fragment of the blotter seemed to say "Metropolitan Motorcycles" on it. Mildred showed her father, who took it to police. They dismissed it as having no value. The handwriting was later determined to be different from Ruth's.

tidal wave of clues (p. 55): "Fear Cruger Case," *New York Evening World*, February 22, 1917, 2.

Woods at Scotland Yard (p. 56): "An American Sherlock Holmes," *Deseret Evening News*, September 14, 1907, 14.

"out of the experience" (p. 56): "N.Y. City Sleuths," *Washington Times*, September 11, 1914, 7.

"few such mysteries" (p. 57): "Where Is Ruth Cruger?" *New York Times*, February 28, 1917, 10.

fifty detectives (p. 57): "Fifty Detectives Fail," *New-York Tribune*, February 28, 1917, 5.

"to the bottom" (p. 57): "Fifty More Submarines," *Scranton Republican*, February 22, 1917, 8.

"can be a detective (p. 58):" "Police Trace Two," *New York Evening World*, February 21, 1917, 1.

ice-skating—alone (p. 58): "Ruth Cruger Hunt," *New-York Tribune*, March 6, 1917, 15.

"in my motorcar?" (p. 58): "School Chum," *New York Sun*, March 1, 1917, 8; "Woods Aids Hunt," *New-York Tribune*, February 15, 1917, 3.

"an invitation to dinner" (p. 59): "Seek New Man," *New York Times*, February 25, 1917, 10.

Henry's reward (p. 59): "Reward of $1,000," *New York Evening World*, March 7, 1918, 1. Swann then asked the Board of Aldermen to double it; "$1,000 Reward," *New York Times*, March 8, 1917, 11.

"be a lost girl" (p. 60): "Ruth Cruger Gone," *New York Evening World*, February 23, 3.

5: THESE LITTLE CASES

The physical description of the People's Law Firm is from Katherine Glover, "Justice and Legal Aid," *Brooklyn Daily Eagle*, August 5, 1906, 16.

"to help you" (p. 62): "New Field of Legal Work," *New York Times*, June 11, 1905, 47.

"Portia of the East Side" (p. 63): "Lawyers Vs. Shysters," *Boston Evening Transcript*, December 13, 1905, 18.

"di Modeste Condizioni" (p. 63): "Women Lawyers in America," *Evening Star*, February 16, 8.

"mother" (p. 63): "New Field of Legal Work," *New York Times*, June 11, 1905, 47.

156 Leonard Street in Little Italy (p. 63): *New York Charities Directory*, New York: Charity Organization Society, 1907, 87.

"dominate their hearts" (p. 65): New Field of Legal Work," *New York Times*, June 11, 1905, 47.

Rosie Pasternack (p. 65): Ibid.

"lady pay me" (p. 67): Ibid.

"$5 as for $500" (p. 68): Katherine Glover, "Justice and Legal Aid," *Brooklyn Daily Eagle*, August 5, 1906, 16.

"get my wife!" (p. 68): Ibid.

"have on now" (p. 68): Ibid.

trust-buster cases (p. 68): "Woman Will Help in War Against Trusts," *New York Times*, September 15, 1907, 6. After a long three years in court, Grace won $17,000 to return to twenty-three people in Bath Beach, which was half of what the city assessed on their property, along with the taxes.

"police wouldn't help" (p. 70): "Woman Gets Thieves," *New York Times*, October 3, 1905, 6.

"little cases" (p. 71): "Justice and Legal Aid," *Brooklyn Daily Eagle*, August 5, 1906, 16.

"hurts nobody yet" (p. 71): "Deportation of an American Citizen," *Daily News–Democrat*, October 7, 1905, 10. All of the dialogue in this section is from this article, which was picked up nationally.

Ward's Island (p. 72): Situated off Manhattan between the Harlem and East Rivers, it had over four thousand beds for psychiatric cases in 1905, making it the largest mental institution in the world.

"year after arrival" (p. 72): "Regulation of Immigration," *Report on the Committee on Immigration*, section 11, Act of March 3, 1891, Washington, D.C.: Government Printing Office, 1902, 428.

"of moderate means" (p. 72): "Deportation of an American Citizen," *Daily News–Democrat*, October 7, 1905, 10.

"the devil coming" (p. 73): Nellie Bly, "Ten Days in a Mad-House," *Around the World in Seventy-Two Days and Other Writing*, New York: Penguin, 79; Deborah Noyes, *Ten Days a Madwoman*, New York, 2016; Brooke Kroeger, *Daredevil, Reporter, Feminist*, New York: Three Rivers Press, 1995.

Antonio Vigiani case (p. 76): "Lawyer Causes Man's Disbarment," *New York Times*, October 4, 1905, 16.

Mt. Carmel festival (p. 76): Robert A. Orsi, *The Madonna of 115th Street*, New Haven: Yale UP, 2010.

Michael Cica (p. 78): "Tin Can Blown," *New York Times*, July 20, 1905, 3.

The Black Hand (p. 79): "Police Guard Woman Lawyer," *New York Evening World*, July 20, 1905, 10.

"we have you" (p. 80): "Pay or Beware," *Minneapolis Journal*, September 30, 1905, 3.

"about to die" (p. 81): "Priest and His Church Guarded by Detectives," *Brooklyn Daily Eagle*, August 15, 1907, 14. The church was at 22 Powell Street.

Black Hand in Westchester (p. 82): "Black Hand Terrorizes Westchester," *New York Evening World*, July 7, 1905, 4; "Alleged Queen of Black Handers," *Pittsburgh Press*, March 10, 1918, 42; "Murder Taught by Black Hand," *Richmond Planet*, February 1, 1908, 6.

barrel murders (p. 81): Mike Dash, *The First Family*, London: Pocket, 2009; John Dickie, *Cosa Nostra*, New York: St. Martin's, 2004; "Barrel Murder Mystery," *New York Times*, April 20, 1903, 1; Michael Zarocostas, *The Barrel Murder*, CreateSpace, 2013, fiction.

diaper (p. 81): William J. Flynn, "The Black-Hand Testament," *Lima News*, April 2, 1920, 24.

"keep your mouth shut" (p. 82): William J. Flynn, "Methods of Blackmailing," *Lincoln Evening Journal*, March 30, 1920, 2.

Bennie Wilenski interview (p. 83): Dialogue from "White Slaves in Labor Camp," *New York Sun,* July 28, 1906, 1; "Slaves in Florida," *Minneapolis Journal,* July 16, 1906, 4.

Schwartz arrested (p. 84): "Grand Jury Indicts," *New York Times,* October 21, 1906, 6. The S. S. Schwartz Employment Agency was at 113–115 First Street and 283 Bowery.

Southern Agricultural Colonization Society (p. 85): "White Slaves in Labor Camp," *New York Sun,* July 28, 1906, 1.

Edward Schoch (p. 85): "Another Labor Camp Refugee," *New York Sun,* July 31, 1906, 5.

Bishop Broderick (p. 85): "Southern Peonage Stories," *New York Sun,* August 2, 1906, 4.

"atrocious, bloodthirsty system" (p. 85): Richard Barry, "Slavery in the South Today," *Cosmopolitan,* March 1907, 481–91.

$300 from McClure (p. 85): Robert B. Outland III, *Tapping the Pines,* Baton Rouge: Louisiana UP, 2004, 237.

Jessie Day (p. 86): This information is from a personal interview with her grandson, conducted by the author.

Martha Bensley Bruere (p. 86): dialogue from "The Housewife and the Law," *Buffalo Courier Sunday Magazine,* June 11, 1911, 8. Bruere would write about Prohibition and the Triangle fire. In this account, she urges Grace to take a young journalist she nicknames "The Light" along with her to the South. This person might be Hannah Frank.

"talk about it" (p. 88): "Peonage Inquiry Started by Moody," *New York Times,* October 18, 1906, 5. Another version has her first going to Moody, then Russell.

Henry Stimson (p. 88): "News Briefs," *Washington Evening Star,* November 3, 1906, 6.

Florida pushback (p. 88): "Big Suit Against Mrs. Quackenbos," *Pensacola Journal,* January 23, 1907, 7; "Asks for Information," *Ocala Evening Star,* February 26, 1907, 1; Jerrell H. Shofner, "Mary Grace Quackenbos, a Visitor," *Florida Historical Quarterly,* January, 1980, 273.

"an entire community" (p. 88): "Clark Is Angered," *Washington Herald,* March 5, 1907, 4.

"was entirely untrustworthy" (p. 88): Pete Daniel, *The Shadow of Slavery,* Urbana, IL: U of Illinois P, 1991, 104.

Florida indictments (p. 90): "Peonage Cases in the South," *Atlanta Constitution,* March 18, 1907, 6.

"being rendered gratuitously" (p. 90): "Peonage Cases in the South," *Atlanta Constitution,* March 18, 1907, 6.

Schwartz and other agents (p. 90): "Two Peonage Arrests Here," *New-York Tribune,* March 17, 1907, 7.

Julius J. Kron (p. 90): "Tale of Attempted Bribery," *New York Sun*, April 6, 1907, 10. The restaurant was on 616 Fifth Street. "The Drawing of Jurors," *Indianapolis News*, April 28, 1908, 6. Mr. Bagg later tried to buy the jury; "City Brevities," *New York Times*, June 15, 1907, 2. The trial stalled because the jury couldn't reach a decision.

6: ARMY OF THE VANISHED

Lee's dialogue is taken from "New Ruth Cruger Clue," *New York Times*, February 24, 1917, 16; "Sure Ruth Cruger," *New York Times*, March 2, 1917, 8; "Police Graft Bared," *New York Sun*, June 24, 1917, 6; "Gives New Clue," *New-York Tribune*, February 24, 1917, 6; Dick Halvorsen, "The Hidden Grave," *Master Detective*, April, 1954. Lee had a photographer partner named Edward Beach, who only appears in a few accounts.

"told me everything" (p. 93): "Search Widened in Cruger Case," *New-York Tribune*, February 18, 1917, 13; "Chum of Miss Cruger," *New York Evening World*, March 3, 1917, 3.

"here with Seymour" (p. 94): Ibid.

"Richard Butler" (p. 95): Seymour Many's dialogue reconstructed from "Sure Ruth Cruger," *New York Times*, March 3, 1917, 5; "Chum of Missing Ruth Cruger," *New York Evening World*, March 3, 1917, 3; "Student Quizzed," *New York Evening World*, March 2, 1917, 6.

"Alibi Schedule" (p. 95): "Examines College Students," *New-York Tribune*, March 3, 1917, 8.

"a pretty girl" (p. 90): Ibid.

"very favorable impression" (p. 97): "Cruger Case Still," *New York Sun*, March 3, 1917, 3.

Ruth liked riding (p. 97): "Baffled Police," *New-York Tribune*, March 5, 1917, 9.

"a college student" (p. 98): "Sure Ruth Cruger," *New York Times*, March 3, 1917, 5.

ciphers (p. 98): "Demand for $5,000," *New York Evening World*, March 15, 1917, 3.

Traffic in Souls (p. 99): The film was directed by George Loane Tucker and released by the Independent Moving Pictures Company of America on November 13, 1913. Details of its premiere and reception taken from "At the Sign of the Flaming Arcs," *Moving Picture World*, vol. 18, nos. 8–13, 1964. The film was made at a cost of $5,700 and made $430,000 at the box office.

multiple showings per day (p. 99): Larry Goldsmith, "Gender, Politics, and 'White Slavery' in New York City: Grace Humiston and the Ruth Cruger Mystery of 1917," unpublished article, 5.

"five white slavers" (p. 100): "New York Sees Fight," *Day Book*, February 28, 1917, 14.

"Disappear Yearly in New York" (p. 100): "Ruth Cruger Case," *New York Times*, February 27, 1917, 20. For more background on white slavery, see H. W. Lytle and John

Dillon, *From Dance Hall to White Slavery,* Chicago: Charles C. Thompson, 1912; Ruth
Rosen, *The Lost Sisterhood: Prostitution in America, 1900–1918,* Baltimore: Johns Hop-
kins UP, 1982; Clifford Griffith Roe and B. S. Steadwell, *Horrors of the White
Slave Trade,* 226; "White Slaves Wage," *New York Times,* January 31, 1913, 6. The
Times claimed that white slaves earned a wage of "$57,000,000 a year."

"other place" (p. 101): Ibid.; Larry Goldsmith, "Gender, Politics, and 'White Slavery' in New York City: Grace Humiston and the Ruth Cruger Mystery of 1917,"
unpublished article, 7, notes the similarities between news accounts of white
slavery and American captivity narratives.

"Should be silenced" (p. 101): "Rockefeller Jr. Heads White Slave Inquiry," *San Francisco
Call,* January 5, 1910, 2; "Rockefeller Heads Vice Grand Jury," *New York Times,*
January 4, 1910, 5.

across state lines (p. 101): The Mann Act, passed on June 25, 1910, was also known as
the White-Slave Traffic Act because it made it a felony to traffic "any woman or
girl for the purpose of prostitution or debauchery, or for any other immoral
purpose" across state lines (ch. 395, 36 Stat. 825; as amended at 18 U.S.C.
2421–24).

"For immoral purposes" (p. 101): "White Slave Trade Is Not Organized," *New York Times,*
June 29, 1910, 16.

"less informally associated" (p. 102): Ibid.

"greater the value" (p. 102): "Ruth Cruger Recruit in Army," February 23, 1917, *Evening Public Ledger Night Extra,* 8.

"white slave agent" (p. 103): "Movies to Present," *New York Times,* February 21, 1917, 20.

"to her discovery" (p. 103): "Ruth Cruger Hunt," *New York Evening World,* March 22, 1917,
5; "Sure Ruth Cruger," *New York Times,* March 3, 1917, 5.

"Mrs. Sherlock Holmes" (p. 103): "She's Sherlock of Cruger Case," *Muskogee Times-Democrat,*
June 20, 1917, 1. "She is New York's Sherlock Holmes." This was the first printed
usage of the comparison I could find, though the New York press was quick to
call any newsworthy detective a "Sherlock Holmes."

breaking up the ice (p. 104): "Will Dynamite Ice," *Washington Herald,* March 7, 1917, 3.

Cocchi's black sled (p. 104): "What Happened to Ruth Cruger?" *Milwaukee Journal,* July 2,
1938, 10.

through her own tears (p. 105): "New Cruger Clue," *New York Evening World,* March 16, 1917, 6.

7: THE MYSTERIOUS ISLAND OF SUNNY SIDE

The major details and facts of Sunny Side come from Mary Grace Quackenbos,
Report on Sunnyside Plantation, Arkansas, Department of Justice Straight Numerical

Files, Record Group 60, 100937, September 28, 1907. Other sources include *Arkansas Historical Quarterly*, vol. 50, no. 1, spring, 1991; *Shadows over Sunnyside*, edited by Jeannie M. Whayne, Fayetteville: Univ. of Arkansas Press, 1993, especially the excellent chapter by Randolph H. Boehm, "Mary Grace Quackenbos and the Federal Campaign Against Peonage," which provides the definitive historical analysis of Grace's presence at Sunny Side. For background: James G. Hollandsworth, *Portrait of a Scientific Racist: Alfred Holt Stone of Mississippi*, Baton Rouge: Louisiana State UP, 2008, 152–59. For an index of the U.S. Department of Justice peonage files, see *The Peonage Files of the U.S. Department of Justice, 1901–1945*, edited by Pete Daniel, Bethesda, MD: University Publications of America, 1989. A remarkable source is Elizabeth Olivi Borgognoni, *Italians of Sunnyside 1895–1995*, Lake Village, AK: Our Lady of the Lake Catholic Church, 1995, a self-published history of Sunny Side from the Italian Americans still living in the area. There is a companion cookbook that is also well worth the cost. Both are available at ourladyofthelake.us. I have chosen to spell it Sunny Side only because that is how Grace spelled it in her report and correspondence to Washington, D.C. The more usual spelling is Sunnyside.

"ranges, or hunts" (p. 108): "Justice in South," *Chicago Daily Tribune*, December 31, 1907, 2. The dialogue for this entire exchange is from this article. Another version brings Pettek to Greenville for trial, but most accounts place the shotgun proceedings in Sunny Side. Grace had just received a treasury warrant that may have been how she paid for his release. She made $272.81 a month; Hannah Frank, her assistant, made $54.45, mostly for expenses.

"prosperity of the country" (p. 110): Lee L. Langley, "Italians in the Cotton Fields," *Southern Farm Magazine*, May, 1904.

in the proper amounts (p. 111): James C. Cobb, *The Most Southern Place on Earth*, New York: Oxford UP, 1992, 135.

red water (p. 113): John M. Barry, *Rising Tide: The Great Mississippi Flood of 1927*, New York: Simon and Schuster, 1997; "Increased Brain Iron," *NeuroImage*, March 2011, vol. 55, 32–78.

"conditions the best" (p. 116): Quackenbos, *Report on Sunnyside Plantation, Arkansas*, Department of Justice Straight Numerical Files, Record Group 60, 100937, September 28, 1907.

these black words into the sea (p. 116): Dell'orto gave his travelers a paper to prepare them. It read:

Where is your Final destination? Ans/ Sunny Side, Ark.

Have you a ticket to the final destination? Yes or No

By whom was the fare paid? Ans/ Luigi Riginelli

Are you in possession of money?

You have to tell the amount and in order not to have trouble you have to have in your pocket at least fifty liras.

Grace discovered that the tickets themselves were purchased through Peter McDonnell, who worked at Ellis Island.

"but I will" (p. 117): John M. Barry, *Rising Tide: The Great Mississippi Flood of 1927*, New York: Simon and Schuster, 1997, 112.

for all of those things (p. 118): Mary Grace Quackenbos, *Report on Sunnyside Plantation, Arkansas*, Department of Justice Straight Numerical Files, Record Group 60, 100937, September 28, 1907.

"wrong at Sunny Side" (p. 119): Ibid.

"a complete bankruptcy" (p. 120): Ibid.

"spent in driving Negroes" (p. 120): Ibid. The general manager set aside 140 acres as a wage crop to be harvested, if needed, by black farmers whose wages would be paid by the Italians. This extra layer of peonage was particularly disturbing. According to Grace, "the negro has money and the Italian has no friends." She concludes, "In some ways the negro planter makes terms more advantageous . . . yet the debt sytem is the same and seems even more of an indignity when forced upon the Italian by a negro."

"should be investigated" (p. 121): Ibid.

"directly at stake!" (p. 122): "Make Rivers Navigable," *Boston Evening Transcript*, October 5, 1907, 4. Roosevelt's words were met with cheers, even though his own Army Corps of Engineers was trying to—and would—kill the legislation to carry out his plan.

"ungentlemanly behavior" (p. 122): John M. Barry, *Rising Tide: The Great Mississippi Flood of 1927*, New York: Simon and Schuster, 1997, 115.

"Crittenden arrested for peonage" (p. 124): Mary Grace Quackenbos, *Report on Sunnyside Plantation, Arkansas*, Department of Justice Straight Numerical Files, Record Group 60, 100937, September 28, 1907; Randolph H. Boehm, "Mary Grace Quackenbos and the Federal Campaign Against Peonage," *Shadows over Sunnyside*, edited by Jeannie M. Whayne, Fayetteville: U of Arkansas P, 1993, 61; "Mrs. Quackenbos Charges Peonage," *Daily Arkansas Gazette*, October 31, 1907, 6.

"Slaves on Farm" (p. 124): "Millionaire Has Slaves on Farm," *Oregon Daily Journal*, Oct. 27, 1907, 1.

"a professional woman" (p. 124): "Who Is She?" *Greenville Times,* September 29, 1907.

special assistant appointment (p. 124): "A Woman Is Bonaparte's Aid," *Daily Review,* November 14, 1907, 1; "Women Lawyer Fights," *Washington Times,* September 10, 1907, 9.

louder and higher (p. 125): "Mrs. Quackenbos Is Facing Charges," *Trenton Evening Times,* November 16, 1907, 1.

the president insisted (p. 125): "Bonaparte Can Not Oust Woman Aid," *Daily Review,* November 21, 1907, 1.

disproved and dismissed (p. 125): "Mrs. Quackenbos Is Vindicated," *Niagara Falls Gazette,* November 20, 1907, 9.

"has been verified" (p. 125): Percy, as well as Roosevelt, knew that such a substantial request "might require an investigation from the Department of Commerce and Labor."

"law in New York City" (p. 126): Letter, Teddy Roosevelt to Albert Bushnell Hart, January 13, 1908, Albert Bushnell Hart Papers, Harvard University Archives.

"beneath the bushel" (p. 126): "So Runs the World Away," *Wichita Eagle,* November 23, 1907.

House committee on labor (p. 127): "Congress to Hold," *Indianapolis Star,* February 7, 1908, 5.

"no experience" (p. 127): "Percy Makes a Reply," *Gulfport Daily Herald,* October 14, 1909, 7. Percy responded to Grace's article in like terms. "I saw the article," he said. "It is shallow, sensational, and written to sell."

"dear Manhattan Isle" (p. 127): "Lays Bonaparte in Congress," *New York Evening Telegram,* March 2, 1908, 2.

"tailor to a mine" (p. 127): "Statement of Mrs. Mary Grace Quackenbos," *Hearings Before Committee on Immigration and Naturalization,* House of Representatives, 61st Congress, Washington, D.C.: Government Printing Office, March 29, 1910.

everyone in the room laughed (p. 128): "No Indictment in Big Peonage Case," *Frankfort Roundabout,* February 1, 1908, 3.

"just the contrary" (p. 128): "Peonage Proved," *Chicago Tribune,* February 19, 1908, 1. Grace's whole immigration argument was later printed as "The Answer to the Immigration Problem," *Pearson's,* January 1911, 96, and in a self-published book titled *A Question for the House of Governors,* New York: People's Law Firm, 1909. The thrust of Grace's plan was to move immigrants out of densely populated cities and into the country for job opportunities, to eradicate tuberculosis, and to fight white slavery through a central system of "agents" based on the German plan. Grace also proposed a separate division specifically to help immigrant women.

"spoiled from city life" (p. 129): "Statement of Mrs. Mary Grace Quackenbos," *Hearings Before Committee on Immigration and Naturalization*, House of Representatives, 61st Congress, Washington, D.C.: Government Printing Office, March 29, 1910.

barber story (p. 129): This dialogue is taken directly from "Statement of Mrs. Mary Grace Quackenbos," *Hearings Before Committee on Immigration and Naturalization*, House of Representatives, 61st Congress, Washington, D.C.: Government Printing Office, March 29, 1910. The barber's name was Salvatore Giannangeli. When Grace asked if he could get her workers, he said: "I will get a horse and wagon and go out in the country tomorrow and begin to get the men." "Can you get a whole hundred?" responded Grace. "Yes," he said.

"grow like everything" (p. 133): Martha Bensley Bruere, "The Housewife and the Law," Sunday Magazine, *Buffalo Courier*, June 11, 1911, 8.

8: THE GIANT AND THE CHAIR

I have reconstructed the Charlie Stielow story largely from George H. Bond, "Report by the Special Deputy Attorney," New York: New York State Attorney General's Office, 1917; Frank Marshall, "Where There Are Women There's a Way," *Good Housekeeping*, July 1918, 54; Colin Evans, *Slaughter on a Snowy Morn*, London: Icon, 2010. Descriptions of Sing Sing are from photographs and firsthand accounts: Denis Brian, *Sing Sing: The Inside Story*, Amherst, NY: Prometheus, 2005; Alfred Conyes, *Fifty Years in Sing Sing*, Albany: State U of New York P, 2015.

Mazzella case (p. 135): "Mazella to Die," *Brooklyn Daily Eagle*, June 28, 1915.

"hold of that" (p. 135): "Woman Who Solved Ruth Cruger Mystery," *New York Sun*, June 24, 1917, 42.

Warden Miller (p. 135): Frank Marshall White, "A Function of State," *New Outlook*, October 18, 1916, 389.

"house that night" (p. 136): Linda J. Lumsden, *Inez: The Life and Times of Inez Milholland*, Bloomington: Indiana University Press, 2004, 148. The letter was dated March 31 of that year.

words in the air (p. 136): Colin Evans, *Slaughter on a Snowy Morn*, London: Icon, 2010, 190.

Nelson Green's confession (p. 138): Ibid., 359. Charlie initially denied what his brother-in-law was claiming. He just shook his head. Mrs. Green went to the law firm of Coe & Harcourt to represent the two. "They have got to have someone," she said. But the lawyers turned her case down. "It would cost too much," they said.

guns in the barn (p. 139): Ibid., 128. Jim Fisher, "Courtroom Charlatan," jimfisher .edinboro.edu, 2008. They had been given to Charlie by Raymond Green, another brother-in-law. The guns were in the barn laying on the hay. Once the police started to be interested, the guns were locked in a suitcase. A local crime expert and druggist named Albert H. Hamilton persuasively testified that a microscopic scratch on one of the killing bullets matched one of the .22 guns. He was later exposed as a fraud. Grace didn't put much credence in his theories.

Mazella (p. 139): "Convicts as Pallbearers," *New York Times*, August 15, 1920, 23. Mazella died in prison on August 14, 1920, after being a model prisoner for five years. His relatives could not be located, but "he was so well liked by prison employees and inmates a collection was taken up by the Mutual Welfare League." Inmates served as pallbearers as he was buried in Kensico Cemetery. He died of heart trouble.

Misha Appelbaum (p. 140): "Cult Leader Here," *St. Louis Dispatch*, June 11, 1916, 34; advertisement for Humanitarian Cult, *New York Evening World*, October 2, 1916, 4.

Cult members (p. 140): "Ask Whitman," *Buffalo Courier*, July 28, 1916.

Sophie Irene Loeb (p. 140): "Sophie Irene Loeb," *New York Times*, January 19, 1929, 1; "Sophie Irene Loeb," *New York Times*, January 21, 1929, 4.

complete her housework (p. 141): "What Does It Look Like?" *Winfield Daily Free Press*, Dec. 17, 1913, 2.

"the weaker victim" (p. 144): "Two Women Saved," *Springfield Republican*, August 13, 1916, 3.

"surround the case of Charles Frederick Stielow" (p. 144): Sophie Irene Loeb, "Man Facing Death," *New York Evening World*, July 18, 1916, 8.

"shadow of death!" (p. 145): "Ask Whitman to Spare," *Buffalo Courier*, July 28, 1916, 1.

"to live in" (p. 146): Alice S. Cheyney, "Inez Milholland Boissevain," *Vassar Quarterly*, February 1917, 106.

execution of Becker (p. 146): "Becker Makes Final Plea," *New York Times*, July 21, 1915, 1; "Becker Dies in Chair, *Middletown Times-Press*, July 30, 1915, 1.

"imprisonment instead of death" (p. 147): Colin Evans, *Slaughter on a Snowy Morn*, London: Icon, 2010, 212.

"to see Papa" (p. 147): "Ask Whitman," *Buffalo Courier*, July 28, 1916.

Whitman's decision (p. 148): "Hangs the Murder," *Buffalo Express*, August 12, 1916, 5.

ice-cold strawberry shortcake (p. 148): Colin Evans, *Slaughter on a Snowy Morn*, London: Icon, 2010, 219.

finding O'Connell (p. 149): "Mrs. Humiston's Story," *Buffalo Express*, August 12, 1916, 5.

O'Connell's reputation (p. 149): George H. Bond, "Report by the Special Deputy Attorney," New York: New York State Attorney General's Office, 1917.

Sophie Loeb convinces Justice Guy (p. 150): Frank Marshall, "Where There Are Women There's a Way," *Good Housekeeping*, July 1918, 54.

pursuit of him (p. 154): "Her Chosen Task," *Boston Post*, August 20, 1916, 58.

King's arrest (p. 154): George H. Bond, "Report by the Special Deputy Attorney," New York: New York State Attorney General's Office, 1917; "Text of King's Confession," *New York Evening World*, August 14, 1916, 2.

King's retraction (p. 158): "King Repudiates Confession," *Republican-Journal*, August 15, 1916, 2; "King Freed of Murder Charge," *Times Herald Olean*, August 15, 1916, 6; "Fight for Stielow Goes On," *New York Evening World*, August 16, 1916, 3; "King Now Retracts," *New York Times*, August 15, 1916, 5; "My Confession Is a Lie," *New York Evening World*, August 14, 1916, 1.

second interview (p. 159): "Mr. Humiston Succeeds in Seeing King," *Times Herald Olean*, September 12, 1916, 1.

"this innocent man?" (p. 160): "The Example of Inez Milholland," *New York Evening World*, November 29, 1916, 10.

"for all womanhood" (p. 160): Ibid.

"imprisonment for life" (p. 161): Colin Evans, *Slaughter on a Snowy Morn*, London: Icon, 2010, 288.

"save me from the Chure" (p. 161): Ibid., 282.

final report (p. 162): George H. Bond, "Report by the Special Deputy Attorney," New York: New York State Attorney General's Office, 1917. The final comprehensive report by George Bond was damning. According to a witness, Nelson Green was working on a farm when Detective Newton pulled up alongside a barn and grabbed a length of rope before grabbing Green and "hearing" his confession. Newton placed stool pigeons and hidden Dictaphones in Stielow's jail, but they couldn't get anything off him. One witness overheard Newton saying of Green, "He is the biggest boob I know. I told him to go on and make this confession and blame it all on the other fellow. That he was too good a man to be a farmer all his life and that we would make him a deputy sheriff, and he swallowed it."

commutation of sentence (p. 162): George H. Bond, "Report by the Special Deputy Attorney," New York: New York State Attorney General's Office, 1917.

Stielow film (p. 162): *The People vs. John Doe*, directed by Lois Weber, Universal Pictures, December 2, 1916. Originally titled *The Celebrated Stielow Case*, only twenty-nine minutes of this sixty-minute film have been located. Grace seems to be represented by a female attorney in the film; Shelley Stamp, "Life's Mirror," *Lois Weber in Early Hollywood,* Oakland: University of California Press, 2015, 98.

9: THE MANHUNTER OF HARLEM

The description of the motorcycle shop is largely from photographs in the newspapers and in pulp magazines, especially Grace Humiston with Isabel Stephen, "Won't You Help Me Find My Girl?" *Actual Detective,* May 4, 1938; Dick Halvorsen, "The Hidden Grave," *Master Detective,* April 1954; "Persons and Scenes," *New-York Tribune,* June 17, 1917, 8; "Murder of 18-Year-Old," *Spokesman Review,* June 24, 1917, 30.

"SELLING OUT" (p. 164): "Ruth Cruger's Body," *New-York Tribune,* June 13, 1917, 16.

Julius J. Kron (p. 165): Julius J. Kron with Isabel Stephen, "The Inside Story of the Ruth Cruger Case," *True Detective,* May 1926.

"food will decide the war" (p. 165): menu, Hotel Manhattan, November 13, 1917, New York Public Library. Call No. 1917-0422-wotm.

Kron's dialogue with Cruger and Grace (p. 166): Julius J. Kron with Isabel Stephen, "The Inside Story of the Ruth Cruger Case," *True Detective,* May 1926.

Herbert Roemmele (p. 168): Julius J. Kron with Isabel Stephen, "The Inside Story of the Ruth Cruger Case," *True Detective,* May 1926; "Return of Cocchi," *New-York Tribune,* July 17, 1917, 12. Sometimes spelled "Rameley," Herbert (sometimes Harold), according to Kron's account, "had towwhite hair and blue-gray eyes."

Snyder finds Cocchi (p. 170): "Man Long Sought," *New York Evening World,* May 31, 1917, 1. This is detective work on my part: the article is unsigned, but indicative of Snyder's style. He seems to have already been in Italy as the *World*'s war correspondent. There are differing accounts of who located Cocchi first. S. S. Dumont, United States consul at Florence, reported in a letter received by Swann that Cocchi was in Italy. Yet another story had Cocchi turned in by a relative in Italy; "Bicycle Repair Shop": *Kansas City Star,* June 6, 1917, 10; "Her Maiden Name," *Philadelphia Enquirer,* June 8, 1917, 1. For more on Snyder: Alice Ziska Snyder and Milton Valentine Snyder, *Paris Days and London Nights,* New York: E. P. Dutton, 1921.

"extraordinary about her" (p. 171): "Ruth Cruger Taken Abroad," *New York Sun,* June 7, 1917, 4.

10: THE PALE MAN

extradition (p. 172): "Ask Extradition," *New Castle News*, June 7, 1917, 1; "To Question Cocchi," *New-York Tribune*, June 8, 1917, 14; "To Ask Italy for Cocchi," *New York Times*, June 8, 1917, 9; "Italy Likely to Cut," *New York Evening World*, June 18, 1917, 2.

"sell the shop" (p. 172): "Mother Doubts," *New York Evening World*, June 7, 1917, 12.

"were very lax" (p. 173): "Alfredo Cocchi Is Located," *New York Sun*, June 1, 1917, 6.

"Mrs. Grace Humiston" (p. 173): "Mother Doubts," *New York Evening World*, June 7, 1917, 12.

"near a solution" (p. 173): "To Ask Italy," *New York Times*, June 8, 1917, 1.

"disappearance of Miss Cruger" (p. 173): Ibid.

Grace and Woods (p. 174): Grace Humiston with Isabel Stephen, "Won't You Help Me Find My Girl?" *Actual Detective*, May 4, 1938.

"something on Cocchi" (p. 175): Ibid.

Madame Mureal (p. 176): "Cocchi, Who Evaded," *New York Evening World*, June 20, 1917, 2; "Girl of 16," *New-York Tribune*, June 20, 1917, 16.

Kron's employment (p. 179): Julius J. Kron with Isabel Stephen, "The Inside Story of the Ruth Cruger Case," *True Detective*, May 1926; Dick Halvorsen, "The Hidden Grave," *Master Detective*, April 1954.

"I know you now!" (p. 181): Dick Halvorsen, "The Hidden Grave," *Master Detective*, April 1954.

"taken down there" (p. 182): "Says Cocchi Headed," *Pittsburgh Press*, June 27, 1917, 1.

speak anymore (p. 182): "Arthur Woods Signs," *Amsterdam Evening Recorder*, July 5, 1917, 2.

"will you do that?" (p. 184): Julius J. Kron with Isabel Stephens, "My Encounter with a White-Slave Ring," *Mysterious Crimes*, New York: True Story, 1934.

secret traincar (p. 184): The famous *Mineola* was said to have been able to speed its wealthy passenger from the Belmont Hotel on Forty-second to Belmont Park.

"border-line psychopathic cases" (p. 186): Julius J. Kron with Isabel Stephens, "My Encounter with a White-Slave Ring," *Mysterious Crimes*, New York: True Story, 1934.

"that is her affair" (p. 187): Ibid.

"I'll fire you" (p. 187): "Guy H. Scull Marries," June 9, 1914, 11.

"this over with me" (p. 183): Julius J. Kron with Isabel Stephen, "The Inside Story of the Ruth Cruger Case," *True Detective*, May 1926.

"cup of Tantalus" (p. 188): Ibid.

"snooping around long time" (p. 188): Grace Humiston with Isabel Stephen, "Won't You Help Me Find My Girl?" *Actual Detective*, May 4, 1938.

"give you a couple of men" (p. 189): Julius J. Kron with Isabel Stephen, "The Inside Story of the Ruth Cruger Case," *True Detective*, May 1926.

cup of Tantalus (p. 189): Bruce Yeany, "Hero's Fountain," *If You Build It, They Will Learn*, Arlington, VA: NSTA Press, 2006, 86; Thomas Ewbank, "Tantalus' Cups," *Ewbank's Hydraulics*," New York: Bangs, 1854, 520. Also called a Pythagorean cup, this cup uses hidden chambers to force the drinker to quaff its contents in moderation.

11: A DOOR TO THE UNDERWORLD

"on them all yet" (p. 191): Julius J. Kron with Isabel Stephen, "The Inside Story of the Ruth Cruger Case," *True Detective*, May 1926. All the dialogue from Kron, McGee, and Maria Cocchi is from this source.

through the coal vault (p. 193): "Mrs. Cocchi Forces Cruger Case," *New-York Tribune*, June 15, 1917, 9. Borough sidewalks had vaults: open spaces beneath the sidewalk sometimes covered with metal grates. The main reason for sidewalk access was to make coal deliveries less messy. Some people were known to turn their vaults, often lit by glass sidewalk tiles, into makeshift underground apartments.

"They're crazy" (p. 194): "Ruth Cruger's Body," *New-York Tribune*, June 13, 1917, 16.

"resumed to-morrow" (p. 195): "Mrs. Cocchi Forces Cruger Case," *New-York Tribune*, June 15, 1917, 8.

the opening of the vault (p. 195): "Ruth Cruger's Body," *New-York Tribune*, June 13, 1917, 16.

"for a grave" (p. 196): Julius J. Kron with Isabel Stephen, "The Inside Story of the Ruth Cruger Case," *True Detective*, May 1926.

placed it in his pocket (p. 196): "Dig for Cruger Clues," *New York Times*, June 13, 1917, 22.

"bossing the job" (p. 197): "Bone Unearthed," *New York Sun*, June 13, 1917, 6. "If I could get Cooper's authority," Kron said. "We could go ahead and dig. But I'm hungry and awfully tired."

"trick on you" (p. 197): Ibid.; "Ruth Cruger's Body," *New-York Tribune*, June 13, 1917, 16. Kron took the bone to a dentist he knew at 70 Manhattan Street. Dr. George Butterworth looked at it and said that it was most likely from a cow. Another doctor, Dr. O. C. Rever, said, "[I]t's a hip bone, but I cannot say definitely whether it is from a human being or an animal." The police said they were most likely relics from the days when Cocchi's basement was a butcher's shop.

"hungry and awfully tired" (p. 197): "Bone Unearthed," *New York Sun*, June 13, 1917, 6

won't give up the keys (p. 199): "Blocks Cruger Search," *New York Times*, June 14, 1917, 9.

"investigation in the past" (p. 199): "Mrs. Cocchi Halts," *New-York Tribune*, June 14, 1917, 16.

"manner in New York" (p. 200): "Vital Events That Followed," *New York Evening World*, June 18, 1917, 2.

agreed to help (p. 200): "Cruger Inquiry," *New York Evening World*, June 27, 1917, 2. Solan would later claim—under oath—that this was his idea, but the absence of his name until exactly this point in the story seems to suggest otherwise. He said that Kron and McGee were out on the sidewalk when he made the discovery of Ruth Cruger's body. He was superintendent of Grand Central Terminal and knew Henry, whose office was also located there.

to buy it (p. 202): "Cocchi Is Indicted," *Auburn Citizen*, June 18, 1917, 9; Julius J. Kron with Isabel Stephen, "The Inside Story of the Ruth Cruger Case," *True Detective*, May 1926; "Ruth Cruger's Body," *Brooklyn Daily Eagle*, June 17, 1917, 1. Some accounts have the auctioneers, Mr. Lind and Mr. Greenberg, authorizing entry to the Cocchi shop or even buying it themselves.

"Hurry back here" (p. 202): Grace Humiston with Isabel Stephen, "Won't You Help Me Find My Girl?" *Actual Detective*, May 4, 1938.

"around the neck" (p. 205): "Ruth Cruger's Body," *Brooklyn Daily Eagle*, June 17, 1917, 1.

Cruger family physician (p. 205): "Mrs. Humiston," *New York Evening World*, June 18, 1917, 2.

a material witness (p. 205): "Mrs. Cocchi Is Held," *Ellicottville Post*, June 20, 1917, 7; "Ruth Cruger Was Killed," *Washington Herald*, June 18, 1917, 1.

in the care of neighbors (p. 205): "Ruth Cruger Ripper," *New-York Tribune*, June 18, 1917, 12.

"is a murderer" (p. 206): "U.S. to Bring Pressure," *New-York Tribune*, June 24, 1917, 6.

"HOLD COCCHI" (p. 206): "Ruth Cruger's Body," *Washington Post*, June 17, 1917, 9.

12: A SECOND GUESS

Captain Dan Costigan (p. 207): "Ruth Cruger's Body," *Washington Post*, June 17, 1917, 9.

"under way, will develop" (p. 208): "Police Should Have Found," *New York Evening World*, June 18, 1917, 2.

"Spare no one" (p. 208): "Police to Excavate," *Brooklyn Daily Eagle*, June 20, 1917, 1; "Woods Orders," *New York Evening World*, June 20, 1917, 1.

fled Bologna (p. 208): "Italy Asked to Seize," *New York Sun*, June 19, 1917, 5.

traffic in white slaves (p. 208): "Swann Aids Search," *New York Sun*, March 1, 1917, 8.

Consuelo La Rue (p. 209): "Drugged, Abducted, Enslaved," *New-York Tribune*, July 4, 1917, 12; "Mrs. La Rue Tells of Drug and Kidnappers," *New York Times*, June 26,

1917, 3. "Try to Murder," *Evening News,* June 19, 1917, 1; "Louise La Rue Tells How She Was Trapped," *New York Times,* July 4, 1917, 1; "Beat Informant," *Washington Times,* June 19, 1917, 1.

what I'd done (p. 209): "Girl Charges Men," *New-York Tribune,* June 20, 1917, 16.

had been choked (p. 210): "Woman Whose Tip," *Leavenworth Times,* June 20, 1917, 1.

he found substantiation (p. 210): "Cocchi Attempts to End Life," *New York Sun,* June 25, 1917, 5.

"you to say anything" (p. 210): "Police in Row," *Brooklyn Daily Eagle,* June 19, 1917, 1.

"detective searching for her" (p. 210): "Sensation over Attack," *Kingston Daily Freeman,* June 19, 1917, 6.

ransacked apartment (p. 210): "Try to Murder," *Evening News,* June 19, 1917, 1; "Mayor Defends Woods," *New York Times,* June 22, 1917, 3.

La Rue told police (p. 211): Julius J. Kron with Isabel Stephen, "The Inside Story of the Ruth Cruger Case," *True Detective,* May 1926; "Mrs. La Rue Tells of Drug and Kidnappers," *New York Times,* June 26, 1917, 3. Elements of the Stephens story seem overly imaginative: Kron claims to board the boat to Argentina to follow another of the count's victims. Over the course of a three-week trip to Buenos Aires, Kron recognizes a fellow female detective who helps him stop the slavery operation.

if she tried to escape (p. 211): "Death Threat for Girl," *Pittsburgh Press,* June 21, 1917, 1; "La Rue Mystery Is Likened to Fiction of East," *New York Daily Herald,* August 5, 1917, 3. New Yorkers read this in the paper and thought of Mata Hari, who had just been put on trial for being a German spy after being arrested on February 13, the same night Ruth Cruger disappeared.

"nothing more to say to you" (p. 211): "Police in Row," *Brooklyn Daily Eagle,* June 19, 1917, 1.

against injury or intimidation (p. 211): "Cruger Demands," *New York Times,* June 21, 1917, 1.

on guard at all times (p. 211): "Two Policemen at the Bedside," *New York Herald,* June 21, 1917, 3; "Another Girl Escapes Fate," *Pittsburgh Daily Post,* June 20, 1917, 7; "Mayor Defends Woods," *New York Times,* June 22, 1917, 3.

Camorra ties (p. 212): "Sensation over Attack," *Kingston Daily Freeman,* June 19, 1917, 6.

stuffed in a barrel (p. 212): "Barrel Murder Mystery," *New York Times,* April 20, 1903; David Critchley, *The Origin of Organized Crime,* New York: Routledge, 2009. The Camorra supposedly began at a three-man card game under a tree in Seville. When one of the men lost, badly, he pulled a knife. But one of the other men said that blood must be conserved among brothers, not shed. The men made a pact, kissed and embraced, and went their separate ways. Thus the Camorra was born, under the tree of knowledge.

"two more girls may be killed" (p. 212): "Girl Charges Men," *New-York Tribune,* June 20, 1917, 16.

"have been for nothing" (p. 213): Julius J. Kron with Isabel Stephens, "My Encounter with a White-Slave Ring," *Mysterious Crimes,* New York: True Story, 1934, 147.

"to make things hum" (p. 213): "Personal and Impersonal," *Brooklyn Daily Eagle,* June 20, 1917, 6.

"memorial to Ruth Cruger" (p. 213): "Two Policemen at the Bedside," *New York Herald,* June 21, 1917, 3.

"save her honor" (p. 213): "Popular Fund Urged," *New York Evening World,* June 20, 1917, 1; "His Statue Memorial," *Indiana Gazette,* July 11, 1917, 12; "Cruger Memorial," *New-York Tribune,* June 24, 1917, 6. By July, Onorio Ruotolo, an Italian sculptor, had begun work on a monument to Ruth depicting a figure being threatened by a coiled serpent. "I could not bring the child back to life, but I could make the memorial to show the father that the great bulk of the kindly Italian people feel his suffering," said Ruotolo.

"is steadily improving" (p. 214): "Light on Cocchi's Relations," *New York Evening World,* June 21, 1917.

"passing the buck" (p. 214): "Cruger Record," *New York Sun,* June 28, 1917, 1.

spots of human blood (p. 215): "Blood Stains Convince," *New-York Tribune,* June 22, 1917, 16; "Cocchi Indicted," *New-York Tribune,* June 19, 1917, 14.

"discovered and punished" (p. 215): "Cruger Case Brings Probe," *New-York Tribune,* June 22, 1917, 16.

"report was written on" (p. 215): "Cruger Demands Woods Removal," *New York Times,* June 21, 1917, 1.

"Very truly yours" (p. 216): *New York Times,* June 22, 1917, 3. The mayor to Henry Cruger: "Lamentable as is the failure of the police to succeed in your daughter's case, it is clear that when one considers such a question as the success of a police administration, one must consider its whole history and record."

Ruth's burial (p. 216): "Italy Asked to Seize," *New York Sun,* June 19, 1917, 5; "Italian Indicted," *Durham Morning Herald,* June 19, 1917, 8.

stolen items (p. 217): "Another Mystery in Cruger Case," *Lima News,* June 19, 1917, 1.

13: THE POINTED FINGER

Civic Fame (p. 218): "The Girl Higher Up," *Pittsburgh Press,* March 9, 1913, 53; "The Girl Beneath the Gilding," *New York Times,* December 9, 2007; James Bone, *The Curse of Beauty,* New York: Regan, 2016. Audrey Munson was the real model for this statue and many others.

"no specific orders on it" (p. 220): "Capt. Cooper Details Work of His Staff," *New York Evening World,* June 22, 1917, 2.

premeditated act (p. 221): Inspector Faurot dug up cellars at 227 West Eighty-third

Street, a former store of Cocchi's, from early 1914 to November 1915. The detectives found a cache of old newspapers, including a morning paper dated February 16, 1917, detailing Ruth's disappearance.

"shielded by the police department" (p. 221): "Jealous Woman, Murdered Girl," *Chicago Daily Tribune*, June 20, 1917, 13.

"Take Care of Alfredo Cocchi" (p. 221): "Cooper Admits Bungling," *New-York Tribune*, June 23, 1917, 1.

"not keep away from women" (p. 222): "Wife of Cocchi Will Identify," *New York Evening World*, June 25, 1.

with the Children's Society (p. 222): "Cocchi Indicted," *Democrat and Chronicle*, June 19, 1917, 1.

kind of grafting operation (p. 222): "Cooper Admits Bungling," *New-York Tribune*, June 23, 1917, 1. Once inside the store, victims, through gritted teeth, would have to buy something innocuous, such as a monkey wrench, for an outlandish price. In return, Cocchi would tear up the ticket and share the profits with the cops who gave it in the first place. "These summonses, it appears," said Swann, "were generally served on automobilists. The summoned autoist was directed to go to such-and-such an address, of Cocchi or someone else. When the autoist got there he was shown newspaper clippings quoting Magistrate House on what he expected to do with the next speeders." The summons were written in pencil so that they could be used multiple times.

Cocchi's knife (p. 222): "Cruger Case Brings," *New-York Tribune*, June 22, 1917, 16.

"ripper" (p. 223): "Ripper's Mark Found," *New York Times*, June 18, 1917, 1.

"wise to do so" (p. 223): "Mrs. Humiston to Direct," *New York Evening World*, June 18, 1917, 2.

"cellar by Burns" (p. 224): "Mayor Defends Woods," *New York Times*, June 22, 1917, 3. Burns had an illustrious career and would go on to be the first director of the Bureau of Investigation of the U.S. Department of Justice, the precursor to the FBI. J. Edgar Hoover was his successor. Burns also instituted the first national fingerprinting system.

"off the case" (p. 224): "Cocchi Taken; Mayor Orders Police Probe," *New-York Tribune*, June 22, 1917, 1. Burns Agency detective James Downing also helped in the investigation.

She then got away (p. 224): "Police Shake-Up," *Brooklyn Daily Eagle*, June 22, 1917, 1.

held on charge of murder (p. 224): Ibid.

"return to my babies" (p. 225): "Wife Begs Cocchi," *New York Evening World*, June 26, 1.

baby was ill (p. 225): "More Police Stupidity," *New York Evening World*, June 28, 1917, 2.

Cocchi's imprisonment (p. 225): "Cocchi Now in Dark Dungeon," *New York Evening World,* June 30, 1917, 2.

asked for a physician (p. 225): "Death Threat," *New York Times,* July 3, 1917, 4.

painting of St. Cecilia (p. 226): Antonio Forcellino and Lucinda Byatt, *Raphael: A Passionate Life,* Malden, MA: Polity, 2012, 195–98. The oil painting by Raphael shows Saint Cecilia contemplating the silent music of a choir of singing angels. The work now hangs in the *Pinacoteca Nazionale* in Bologna; Percy Bysshe Shelley, *Letters from Abroad,* London: Edward Moxon, 1845, 116.

"$100 a week" (p. 226): "Cocchi Declares Ruth Cruger," *New York Evening World,* June 25, 1917, 2.

"I didn't mean to" (p. 227): Ibid.

"some vital spot" (p. 227): "Cocchi Declares He Spent," *New York Evening World,* June 26, 1917, 2.

"the ninety-nine cases" (p. 228): "Priest Says Cocchi," *New York Sun,* June 26, 1917, 4.

called him "Al" (p. 228): Ibid.

14: THE MAN WHO LAUGHS

Alfredo Cocchi's interrogation and confession is from "Slayer Committed Crime," *Evening World,* June 23, 1917, 1; "Cocchi Acquits Police," *New York Times,* July 28, 1917, 9; "Cocchi Admits," *New-York Tribune,* June 24, 1917, 1; "Cocchi Tells How," *New York Times,* June 26, 1917, 8. The timeline of when Cocchi said what is unclear, so I have reflected that in the narrative.

"forget my trouble" (p. 229): "Spat with Wife; Wine and Murder," *Wichita Beacon,* July 28, 1917, 4.

"touching a hair of her head" (p. 230): "Cocchi Acquits Police," *New York Times,* July 28, 1917, 9.

"remembered my wife" (p. 230): "Aided, Cocchi Says," *New York Sun,* June 26, 1917, 4.

Cocchi attempts suicide (p. 231): "Cruger Slayer Tries Suicide," *New Castle Herald,* June 25, 1917, 1.

she had been detained (p. 231): "Mrs. Humiston to Direct," *New York Evening World,* June 18, 1917, 2.

"tell everything" (p. 231): "Cooper Admits Bungling," *New-York Tribune,* June 23, 1917, 1.

"to commit it" (p. 232): "Cocchi Tries Suicide," *Washington Post,* June 25, 1917, 3.

"She's so jealous" (p. 232): "Aided, Cocchi Says," *New York Sun,* June 26, 1917, 4.

"privation and fright" (p. 233): "Cocchi a Gay," *Washington Post,* June 26, 1917, 5.

"attacks on children" (p. 233): "Bologna Authorities," *Santa Ana Register,* June 26, 1917, 1.

"ashamed to tell" (p. 233): "Cocchi Confesses to His Kinsman," *Wilmington Dispatch,* July 3, 1917, 1.

"degenerate by heredity" (p. 234): "Cocchi Describes Motor Shop," *Waco Morning News*, June 24, 1917, 1.

"whom I can serve" (p. 234): "Cocchi Confesses," *Lima News*, June 23, 1917, 1.

"I won't see him" (p. 234): "Why Hire a Lawyer?" *Independence Daily Reporter*, June 28, 1917, 1.

"in this uncertainty" (p. 234): "Question Priest," *New York Times*, June 26, 1917, 3.

plead insanity (p. 234): "Insanity the Cocchi Plea," *Middletown Times-Press*, June 27, 1917, 1.

woman slipped into Bologna (p. 234): "Cocchi Makes Full," *Washington Post*, June 24, 1917, 6.

drops of human blood (p. 236): "Ruth Cruger's Murderer," *New-York Tribune*, June 20, 1917, 16.

"the first line" (p. 236): "Slayer Committed Crime," *New York Evening World*, June 23, 1917, 1.

"they had done it" (p. 236): Ruth Cruger's Body," *New York Herald*, July 11, 1917, 2.

"just ordinary 'cock-eye'" (p. 236): *Logansport Pharos-Reporter*, October 11, 1917, 4. The accepted pronunciation seems to be "KOH-Kee."

"I did it just as a joke" (p. 237): Ruth Cruger's Body," *New York Herald*, July 11, 1917, 2.

"scenes of jealousy will end" (p. 237): "Aided, Cocchi Says," *New York Sun*, June 26, 1917, 4.

"my enemies in this country" (p. 238): Ibid.

15: THE SLIDING NUMBER

"strongly suspect you" (p. 240): "Record Is Altered," *New York Sun*, June 28, 1917, 5.

Cocchi's father, while visiting (p. 240): "Cocchi Secreted Here," *New York Sun*, June 28, 1917, 5.

refused to come out (p. 241): "Question Priest on Cocchi's Tale," *New York Times*, June 26, 1917. Grace and Kron said that they hired a woman detective in March to call Father Moretto to arrange an interview. She went to his house, but he wouldn't answer the door; see chapter 11 of St. Raphael Society for Italian Immigrants, *Center for Migration Studies*, 2000, 229. Moretto had a long history of charges levied against him.

"left the prison" (p. 242): "Cocchi Secreted Here," *New York Sun*, June 28, 1917, 5.

testimony of Lagarenne and McGee (pp. 242–43): "Wallstein Starts Police Shake-Up," *New York Sun*, June 27, 1917, 4; "Blame in Cruger Case," *Washington Post*, June 27, 5.

shaking, bleeding boy (p. 243): "Sulzer Graft Witness," *Boston Evening Transcript*, January 21, 1914, 4. Dominick Celibarde, fifteen years old, had recently been released from the Catholic Protectory.

"you are honest" (p. 243): "Gross Negligence," *Greensboro Daily News*, June 29, 1917, 1.

"congregation of the Washington Heights Baptist Church" (p. 244): "Two Witnesses," *New York Sun*, June 30, 1917, 5.

"to help me" (p. 244): "Evasive Answers," *Rochester Democrat and Chronicle,* June 30, 1917, 2.

"has been convicted" (p. 245): "Two Witnesses in Cruger Case," *New York Sun,* June 30, 1917, 5.

deputized him in secret (p. 245): "Cocchi Secreted Here," *New York Sun,* June 28, 1917, 5; "Native Town," *Washington Times,* July 3, 1917, 5; "Death Threat," *New York Times,* July 3, 1917, 4.

Grace's scheduled testimony (p. 245): "Better Detectives," *New York Sun,* July 1, 1917, 5.

Henry Ankenmann (p. 245): "Cruger Demands," *New York Times,* June 21, 1917, 1.

motorcycle license (p. 246): "Cocchi's Boast," *New York Evening World,* July 3, 1917, 1. The records of the Automobile Bureau showed that Cocchi did not have a driving license, either.

Summons were served (p. 246): "Whitman Orders Cruger Case," *San Francisco Chronicle,* July 5, 1917, 4.

it would resume (p. 246): "Scull Is Called," *New York Evening World,* July 5, 1917, 1.

"investigation of police methods" (p. 246): "Mayor Suspends Wallstein," *New York Sun,* July 5, 1917, 4.

"yet to be proved" (p. 247): Ibid.

Talley (p. 247): Ibid. Judge McIntyre instructed the grand jury that "[a] crime is an act or omission forbidden by law."

"this means a long delay" (p. 248): "Death Threat for Cocchi's Pursuer," *New York Times,* July 3, 1917, 1.

"the dreadful electric chair" (p. 249): "Cocchi in a Dungeon," *New York Sun,* June 30, 1917, 5.

"Homicidal" (p. 249): Death Certificate for Ruth Cruger, February 13, 1917, file No. 19448, Department of Health of the City of New York.

stopped at 2:10 P.M. (p. 249): "Cocchi Loses Nerve," *New York Sun,* July 10, 1917, 4.

"it was not difficult" (p. 250): Captain Eugene de Beck and Dr. Carleton Simon, "Lessons from Historic Crimes," *Ottawa Journal,* January 11, 1939, 10.

"they didn't see it" (p. 250): "Her Black Eyes Tempted," *Arkansas Daily Traveler,* June 25, 1917, 1.

if he had done it beforehand (p. 250): "Police Accused" *New York Sun,* July 11, 1917, 1.

"wherever the trail leads" (p. 251): "Cocchi Depicts Fight," *New York Times,* July 12, 1917, 20.

hour each day (p. 251): "Cocchi Made Book," *New York Evening World,* July 7, 1917, 3.

"any man in this city" (p. 251): "Cocchi Must Be Returned," *New York Evening World,* June 23, 1917, 2.

"caused the crime" (p. 252): "Fear of Police," *Topeka Daily Capital,* July 24, 1917, 10.

"to get away" (p. 252): "Cocchi Must Be Returned," *New York Evening World,* June 23, 1917, 2.

16: MRS. SHERLOCK HOLMES

Grace's interview from "Woman Who Solved Ruth Cruger Mystery," *New York Sun*, June 24, 1917, 42; "Mrs. Grace Humiston Tells," *Eau Claire Sunday Leader*, July 8, 1917, 9; "Mrs. Humiston," *Waco Morning News*, July 8, 1917, 9; "Mrs. Grace Humiston Does Not Look Like a Detective," *Brooklyn Daily Eagle*, June 24, 1917, 6; "Mrs. Humiston's Theory," *New-York Tribune*, June 17, 1917, 8.

"at every step" (p. 259): "How I Solved the Ruth Cruger Mystery," *Pittsburgh Press*, June 21, 1917, 1.

"begin the work" (p. 259): "Mrs. Humiston," *Waco Morning News*, July 8, 1917, 9.

"dissuaded by that" (p. 259): "Mrs. Grace Humiston Does Not Look Like a Detective," *Brooklyn Daily Eagle*, June 24, 1917, 6.

"born and bred New Yorker" (p. 260): "Woman Who Solved Ruth Cruger Mystery," *New York Sun*, June 24, 1917, 42.

"missing-girl editor" (p. 260): Larry Goldsmith, "Gender, Politics, and 'White Slavery' in New York City: Grace Humiston and the Ruth Cruger Mystery of 1917," unpublished article, 26.

to only speak to them (p. 260): Guido Bruno, "Commissioner Woods and New York's Missing girls," *Pearson's Magazine*, October, 1917, 166.

"Ay, any change" (p. 261): "Lines to Mrs. Humiston," *New-York Tribune*, July 8, 1917.

petrified near a riverbank (p. 261): "It's Satan Dead, They Say," *Concord Times*, August 2, 1917, 8.

"had been disgraced" (p. 262): "Cocchi Makes Confession," *New Castle News*, June 23, 1917, 2.

Athos's testimony (p. 262): "Belief Grows Stronger," *Courier-Journal*, July 27, 1917, 2. Martin Donnelly, the private detective, also testified that said he saw a filthy Cocchi emerge from his cellar around 11:30 on the night of February 14. Though obviously damning, this was incredibly providential.

"right of privacy" (p. 263): "Mrs. Humiston Wins," *New York Times*, August 11, 1917, 16. The court directed Mrs. Humiston to file a bond of $2,500 to protect the defendants.

"moment of passion" (p. 265): "Ruth Cruger's Finder," *Pittsburgh Post-Gazette*, August 12, 1917, 36.

"7476-Rector" (p. 266): "Detectives," adverstizement, *Evening Telegram*, July 18, 1917.

job offers (p. 266): "Woods Enlists Aid," *New York Times*, July 22, 1917, 9.

Grace's personal bodyguard (p. 266): "Society Women Join the Ranks of War Workers," *Washington Times*, September 30, 1917; photograph, *Evening Independent*, July 7, 1917. Commissioner Woods founded the home Defense League to aid the police: 22,000 volunteered, without pay. Renamed the New York Reserve Police

Force, women volunteers patrolled childrens' areas and were trained in emergency first aid.

"against white-slavers" (p. 266): "Mrs. Humiston, Who Cleared," *New York Evening World*, June 18, 1917, 2. Mrs. Adler: "Those of us who aided Mrs. Humiston in this matter urge that some organization, preferably a women's organization, make it possible for this highly gifted and very capable women to continue the work. Undoubtedly she could find and save many girls."

every major city in the United States (p. 267): "To Protect Women," *Newport Journal*, August 31, 1917, 2.

Morality League (p. 267): "League to Protect Girls," *New-York Tribune*, August 8, 1917, 14.

police special investigator (p. 267): Mark Twain, *Scrapbook*, vol. 39, May 1–September 15, 1917. Twain cut out this article, along with the striking image of Grace's bodyguard, for his scrapbook.

"the control of men" (p. 267): "Woman Who Cleared Cruger Case," *Washington Post*, June 19, 1917, 4.

"with the tides" (p. 267): "Mrs. Humiston Is Hampered," *Lima News*, July 24, 1917, 7.

Code and Ritual (p. 268): Alberto Verrusio Ricci, "Black Hand Exposed," *True Detective*, September 30, 1930, 29; Ibid., October 30, 1930, 50.

La Rue's fiction (p. 268): "Miss LaRue's Tale," *New York Times*, July 24, 1917, 9; "Miss La Rue's Woes Sound Like a Book," *New York Sun*, July 24, 1917, 4.

Mrs. H. T. Clary (p. 269): "Grand Jury Calls," *New York Times*, July 19, 1917, 7.

"had while they last" (p. 269): "Miss La Rue's Woes Sound Like a Book," *New York Sun*, July 24, 1917, 4.

kind of self-hypnosis (p. 269): "Hypnotic Power of Books," *New York Sun*, August 12, 1917, 50.

indicted on blackmail (p. 269): "2 Indicted on Story," *New-York Tribune*, August 21, 1917, 14.

17: THE MARKED NECK

Details from Joseph F. Dougherty and K. S. Daiger, "Behind Drawn Blinds," *True Detective Mysteries*, March 30, 1930; "Arrest of Suspected Man," *Washington Times*, August 10, 1917, 2.

"for all time" (p. 271): "Suspicion Attaches," *Washington Times*, August 10, 1917, 1.

"Human Spirit" (p. 272): *New York Pickets at the White House*, photograph, January 26, 1917, National Woman's Party Records, group II, container II: 276, Library of Congress; *Suffragist with "Kaiser Wilson" Poster*, photograph, record group 165, Records of the War Department General and Special Staff, National Archives and Records Administration.

"entered their doors" (p. 272): Alissa Franc, "A Woman Visits," *Washington Times,* August 10, 1917, 2.

"going to be solved" (p. 272): "Bride Killed," *Washington Times,* August 11, 1917, 1.

"around her waist" (p. 273): Alissa Franc, "Other Man Tale," *Washington Times,* August 11, 1917, 3. "We are unconsciously accustomed to hearing women talk this way. We know that the lives of these women are, and always have been, straight and clean, and that this way of talking is simply an outlet for a little surplus vanity. We feel it does not matter."

"a woman assailant" (p. 273): "Mrs. Humiston Tells," *Washington Times,* August 12, 1917, 1.

"which to work" (p. 273): "Woman Expert," *Washington Times,* August 13, 1917, 2.

playing craps (p. 274): Joseph F. Dougherty and K. S. Daiger, "Behind Drawn Blinds," *True Detective Mysteries,* March 30, 1930, 31.

"unusually black" (p. 274): "Negro Is Held as Annapolis Slayer," *Washington Post,* August 14, 1917, 1.

Snowden's interrogation (p. 274): "Negro Cringes under Grilling," *Washington Times,* August 14, 1917, 2; Jennie H. Ross, "Alleges Brutal Methods Used to Make Snowden Confess Crime," *Afro-American,* February 2, 1918; Stephen Braun, "Clemency for Hanged Man," *Los Angeles Times,* June 2, 2001.

did not confess (p. 274): "Maintains Innocence," *Washington Times,* August 16, 1917, 1.

exhumation of Lottie's body (p. 274): "Believe Woman Was Assaulted," *Washington Herald,* August 15, 1917, 1; "Mrs. Humiston Says," *Washington Times,* August 13, 1917, 1.

"will never rest" (p. 275): "Miss Murray Aids," *Washington Times,* February 21, 1919, 6.

"if you don't" (p. 277): "Delay Inquest," *Washington Herald,* August 16, 1917, 2. A joke later appeared in some Baltimore newspapers about Grace's inability to drive a car; this story might be the genesis of that.

"pause to think" (p. 277): "A Woman Visits," *Washington Times,* August 10, 1917, 2.

Grace visits Snowden (p. 277): "Mrs. Humiston Sees Snowden," *Washington Times,* August 16, 1917, 1.

18: HER LAST BOW

"in regard to the others" (p. 280): "Exposes Social Ills at Camp," *Washington Post,* November 16, 1917, 3.

Bell's iron command (p. 280): "Attention! Officers of the 77th Division," *New York Evening World,* August 28, 1917, 1; Norval Dwyer, "The Camp Upton Story 1917–1921," *Long Island Forum,* February 1970; Roger Batchelder, *Camp Upton,* Boston: Small, Maynard & Co., 1918.

Not until later (p. 280): "No Second Draft Until the Spring," *Breckenridge News*, August 29, 1917, 7.

practical warfare (p. 280): "Turn Camp Upton into a Vast School," *New York Times*, October 15, 1917, 20.

"Hello France" (p. 280): "Good-Bye Broadway, Hello France," composed by Billy Baskette, lyrics by C. Francis Reisner and Benny Davis, New York: Leo Feist, 1917. This song was the most popular tune of 1917.

tank watch and round glasses and *Bell wary of visitors* (p. 280): "Weird Trip to Camp Upton, *Brooklyn Daily Eagle*, September 9, 1917, 5.

"is a fighting man" (p. 281): "Singing Man a Fighting Man," *Indiana Gazette*, August 27, 1917, 6.

"learned to the press" (p. 281): "Bell and Fosdick Deny Vice Charge," *New-York Tribune*, November 17, 4.

"the camp unescorted" (p. 282): "Gen. Bell Denounces Humiston Charges," *New York Times*, November 17, 1917, 9. "Women visitors are conducted to the YWCA hostess houses to await soldier friends and relatives by representatives who meet all trains at the Camp Upton Station."

"put them into effect" (p. 282): "Won't Aid Fosdick," *New York Times*, November 17, 1917, 9.

"you don't mind" (p. 282): "Camp Upton," *Brooklyn Daily Eagle*, September 18, 1917, 3. "Dominick Lannie would very much like to have his folks send him a pound or so of American cheese. He has a pet field mouse that he wants to nurse back to health."

"Signed WOODROW WILSON" (p. 283): "Bibles for our Troops," *Breckenridge News*, August 29, 1917, 7.

"going over the top" (p. 283): "Upton Boys Ready," *New York Sun*, November 25, 1917, 16; "Over the Top," *Popular Science*, June, 1918, 877.

Stimson in Upton (p. 283): Godfrey Hodgson, *The Colonel*, Boston: Northeastern UP, 1992, 57. He was there before October. He was there the whole time.

"he lives forever" (p. 283): "Gen. Bell Stirs Riverhead," *Brooklyn Daily Eagle*, September 12, 1917, 8.

"was on fire" (p. 283): "Harry Lauder," *Evening Star*, July 28, 1917, 9. "The world is on fire. You men, as firemen, must put it out. And you'll do it. When you get to France and put it out, don't leave a wee bit of red smouldering. Put it out clean. You're going to light up civilization. You boys are the lamplighters of the world. You're going to light it up as never before, and . . . it will be very beautiful for your children to be able to say: My dad lit that lamp."

"man and wife" (p. 284): "Bell Accuses Mrs. Humiston," *New York Sun*, November 27, 1917, 3.

"in splendid fashion" (p. 285): "Gen. Bell Denies Humiston Charge," *Brooklyn Daily Eagle*, November 16, 1917, 2.

Grace was seen at Patchogue (p. 285): "Bell Accuses Mrs. Humiston," *New York Sun*, November 27, 1917, 3.

"the proper authorities" (p. 285): "Mrs. Humiston Won't Prove," *New-York Tribune*, November 17, 4. "I will be glad to go to Washington," she said, "if I am asked to do so by the proper authorities. If the government wants me to investigate conditions the only thing that I want is the defrayal of the expenses of my investigations and the assurance that I will be backed up in any prosecutions I may bring."

"armies are clean" (p. 285): "Challenges Lawyer," *Oshkosh Daily Northwestern*, November 16, 1917, 1. Secretary of War Baker reiterated camp policy: "This committee has sent special female agents to all camps, whose sole duty it is to look after the protection of women around camps and to guard against anticipated dangers. It is also the duty of military police to watch such matters carefully and, in addition to this, precautions, it is not advisable to disclose, are taken by all military authorities, using facilities which have been confidentially provided for that purpose."

"I am ready" (p. 286): "Won't Aid Fosdick in Camp Inquiry," *New-York Tribune*, New York 17, 1917, 9. "I believe that something should be done in this matter, for the sake of our young girls. If it is true that the health of the soldiers must be cared for, then I suggest that licensed resorts be established at the camps. Also, I suggest that these fatherless babies who are coming into the world be legitimized or be given the name of the father at any rate, and both mother and child cared for. Remember, these young mothers in New York now have the vote, whether they care for it or not, and remember, also, that they will hate their country if this shame is allowed to remain on their shoulders."

"what conditions are" (p. 286): "Mrs. Humiston Ready," *Washington Times*, November 18, 1917, 1.

"will be sufficient to refute them" (p. 286): "Bell Accuses Mrs. Humiston," *New York Sun*, November 27, 1917, 3.

brides in nearby Patchogue (p. 286): "Three Soldiers Take Brides," *Brooklyn Daily Eagle*, November 22, 1917, 15.

"Uptonia" (p. 286): "Baby Born in Cantonment," *Gazette Times*, November 18, 1917, 14.

trouble in the neighboring towns (p. 287): "Yaphank Vice Story Blasted," *New York Sun*, November 17, 1917, 1.

"mentally and physically" (p. 287): "Officers Urgently Needed," *New-York Tribune*, November 17, 1917, 10.

Upton vice (p. 287): "Finds No Girl Died," *Washington Post*, November 18, 1917, 2; "No

Liquor, No 'Dope' Law," *Brooklyn Daily Eagle*, August 27, 1917, 7; "Hell's Kitchen," *New-York Tribune*, September 21, 1917, 5.

"in our jail" (p. 287): "The 'Limit' Promised to Crooks," *Brooklyn Daily Eagle*, October 13, 1917, 3.

crooks in line (p. 288): "Camp Upton Eager," *New York Sun*, October 1, 1917, 2.

dressed in black (p. 288): "Couple Planted in Hotel," *New-York Tribune*, November 27, 1917, 5.

19: ARMY OF ONE

eyewitnesses who saw them (p. 293): "Bell Accuses Mrs. Humiston," *New York Sun*, November 27, 1917, 3.

"peddling gossip" (p. 293): "Mrs. Humiston Is Peddling Gossip," *New-York Tribune*, November 30, 1917, 5.

"all the boys I am" (p. 293): "Bell Catches," *New York Times* November 19, 10; "Camp Upton Charges," *Army and Navy Register*, December 1, 1917.

"a right, you know" (p. 294): "Mrs. Humiston's Charges," *Middletown Times-Press*, November 19, 1917, 5.

"at least in this locality" (p. 294): Ibid.

hightailed it to the hotel room (p. 294): "Mrs. Humiston Admits," *New York Sun*, November 27, 1917, 3. The *Sun* reporter called Grace Humiston's office for a statement on Bell's findings. Grace admitted that she sent Adkins and a "Miss Francis" to Camp Upton to register at the hotel on the military reservation there as man and wife under an assumed name. She reminded the reporter that they did so successfully. They registered as a married couple, despite their obvious age difference and might have done so without problem if they were not recognized by a soldier.

"shaded in this manner?" (p. 294): "How It Works," *New-York Tribune*, November 28, 1917, 10.

"this disgusting errand" (p. 295): "A Disgraceful Experiment," *Brooklyn Daily Eagle*, November 28, 1917, 6.

"disgusting trick" (p. 295): "Humiston 'Plant' Scored by Baker," *Washington Post*, November 29, 1917, 5.

"of sensation mongers" (p. 296): "Light on Mrs. Humiston," *New-York Tribune*, November 29, 1917, 8.

"things that ain't" (p. 296): "Intimates Mrs. Humiston," *Salina Daily Union*, November 16, 1917, 4.

"scintilla of evidence" (p. 296): "Mrs. Humiston's Charges," *New-York Tribune*, November 29, 1917, 3.

lasted three hours (p. 296): Ibid.

"problems on our hands" (p. 296): "New Charges Made by Mrs. Humiston," *New York Sun,* November 29, 1917, 14.

"thoroughly fumigated" (p. 297): "A Study in Morbid Psychology," *Brooklyn Life,* December 1, 1917, 9.

"remove the smirch" (p. 297): "Rookie Demands That Slur," *Brooklyn Daily Eagle,* December 9, 1917, 45.

"he has set" (p. 298): "Brands Humiston Camptales False," *New York Sun,* December 19, 1917, 4.

"crazy about uniforms" (p. 298): Ibid.

"activities to New York" (p. 299): "Takes Police Power," *New York Times,* December 30, 1917, 23; "Woman Morals Guardian," *Milwaukee Journal,* December 30, 1917, 1; "Mrs. Humiston Is Dropped," *New-York Tribune,* December 30, 1917, 3.

committee disbanded (p. 299): George W. Wickersham, Joseph P. Lincoln, James S. Cushman, Rev. Dr. Charles Parkhurst, Mrs. Felix Adler, Mrs. A. Ladenberg, Evangeline Booth, Harold Content, Mrs. William Curtis Demarest, and Rev. Dr. Charles Slattery all resigned.

Izola Forrester (p. 300): Izola worked with Grace in the Morality League, in her office, and in a variety of other roles. Izola, the granddaughter of John Wilkes Booth, was a secret writer who honed her craft while working on and off with Grace. She went on to have a terrific career as a writer.

"various army camps" (p. 300): "Pair Driven from Camp," *Washington Post,* November 28, 1917, 2.

former New York City policemen (p. 300): Roger Batchelder, *Camp Upton,* Boston: Small, Maynard, 1918. The Upton military police force included 142 former New York policemen, some during its construction phase.

"to Mayor Hylan" (p. 301): "Mrs. Humiston Explains Why," *New-York Tribune,* December 31, 1917, 5.

a little hollow (p. 301): "Mrs. Humiston Is Dropped," *New-York Tribune,* December 30, 1917, 7. "Commissioner Woods asked for my resignation on December 11, after I had refused to give the committee of which George W. Wickersham is chairman the evidence I possess as to evils in camp areas."

20: THE ASSASSIN STRIKES

The details of the attack come from "Threatens Mrs. Humiston's Life," *New-York Tribune,* January 20, 1918, 8; "Boy Threatens Mrs. Humiston," *Times Herald,* January 22, 1918, 5.

"quite as easily" (p. 304): "Mrs. Sherlock Holmes," *Cromwell Argus*, December 2, 1918, 6.

"sense of suffocation" (p. 304): "Women of Middle Age," *Times Herald*, April 5, 1921, 12.

rule 39 (p. 304): There were still several points of inquiry that didn't seem to fit. One was that Martin Donnelly had seen Cocchi covered in dirt. Another told a story that two employees of the Consolidated Gas Company had been refused entrance to Cocchi's cellar on February 14 and 15.

decision to Justice Goff (p. 305): "Lagarenne Guilty," *New York Times*, Februry 22, 1918; "Detective Is Convicted," *Bridgeport Telegram*, February 23, 1918, 20.

"with the unearthing of it" (p. 305): "Gives Lagarenne Credit," *New York Evening World*, February 18, 1918, 3.

signature on some reports (p. 305): "Convicted Detective Witness," *New York Evening World*, February 26, 1918, 2.

"best of me in court" (p. 306): "Osborne Aims Blow," *New York Times*, February 28, 1918, 9.

dismissed the indictment (p. 306): "Captain Cooper Discharged," *Brooklyn Daily Eagle*, February 28, 1918, 1; "Acquitted in Cruger Case," *New York Times*, March 1, 7.

Lagarenne's sentence (p. 306): "Cruger Case Sleuth Fined," *New York Evening World*, April 19, 1918, 2.

court costs (p. 306): "Special Expenses in Connection with the Murder of Ruth Cruger," *City Record*, City of New York, February 28, 1921.

Snowden verdict (p. 306): "Jury Quickly Finds," *Washington Times*, February 1, 1918, 3; "Find Snowden Guilty," *Washington Post*, February 1, 1918, 2.

"she was doing" (p. 307): Court of Appeals (Records and Briefs), John Snowden, October term 1918, case no. 95, vols. 1–2; "Ask New Trial," *Washington Herald*, December 6, 1918, 2.

Val Brandon testimony (p. 307): John Snowden v. State of Maryland, Court of Appeals (Records and Briefs), October Term 1918, case no. 95.

crowd at execution (p. 308): "Cards Issued for Snowden," *Washington Times*, Februrary 27, 1919, 1.

band played gospel (p. 308): "Our Legacy: The Last Hanging," *Capital Gazette*, February 3, 2015.

Murray was there (p. 308): "Mrs. Murray Aids," *Washington Times*, February 21, 1919, 6.

"I will not interfere" (p. 308): "Will Not Interfere," *Evening Capital*, February 25, 1919, 3.

meekly and quietly (p. 309): "Cards Issued for Snowden," *Washington Times*, Februrary 27, 1919, 1. Attorney Theodore Brady said, "I have never in all my experience seen a man like Snowden."

"unsealed if necessary" (p. 309): Ibid.

"Humiston back to Annapolis" (p. 309): "Mrs. Murray Out in Statement Regarding Part," *Evening Capital*, February 27, 1919.

"sweatbox in Baltimore" (p. 309): Hannah Jopling, *Life in a Black Community*, London: Lexington, 2015, 71.

"with a lie in my mouth" (p. 310): Excerpt from the last statement of John Snowden, February 27, 1919.

"God will bring things right some day" (p. 310): "Anonymous Letter," *Evening Capital*, March 3, 1919.

21: THE INVISIBLE PLACES

"it seems to fall" (p. 311): Dante Alighieri, *Divine Comedy of Dante Alighieri*, Trans. Robert M. Durling, New York: Oxford University Press, 1996, 136–38; canto 21.

reservist in the Italian army (p. 311): "Cocchi's Immunity," *New York Sun*, July 7, 1917, 4.

provide food from outside (p. 312): "Cocchi Fights Return," *Washington Post*, June 23, 1917, 5.

Mayor of Bologna (p. 312): "Cocchi Shames Bologna," *New York Times*, July 3, 1917, 4.

Cocchi's testimony (p. 312): "Full Story of Cruger," *Asheville Citizen-Times*, July 28, 1917, 1. Most papers printed a version of the testimony; this paper printed the entire transcript—which is one advantage of a smaller-market paper.

"playing for delay" (p. 314): "Italian Court," *San Francisco Chronicle*, August 10, 1919, 4.

letter from Lynch (pp. 314–16): Criminal Trial Transcripts of the County of New York, 1883–1927, trial 2766, February 13, 1920; microfilm reel 338. Lynch's full letter lists names of people he considers part of the slave trade. They include doctors, candy store owners, and, unfortunately, his daughter's mother, Celia, whom J. J. calls a "friend of Slavers." He particularly lays the blame on a woman named "Black Nellie," whom he accuses of treating girls for abortions.

"ridiculous and preposterous" (pp. 315–17): "Story of Murder," *Wichita Daily Eagle*, June 26, 1919, 1.

"shift the blame" (p. 317): "Court Suspends," *New York Evening World*, June 26, 1919, 12.

trial to resume (p. 317): A note from the Ministry for Foreign Affairs dated August 29, 1919, to Peter A. Jay said that although "there was no evidence of any description tending to connect this woman with the murder," the judge "considered further investigation advisable."

ice plant on Atlantic Avenue (p. 317): "Held on Girl's Charge," *Brooklyn Daily Eagle*, August 24, 1917, 11.

appear in the papers (p. 317): On his own, Kron still attracted sensational cases, even when he wasn't trying to. When Reverend Edward Wheeler Hall of New Jersey was killed—along with his forbidden mistress, a married woman and choir singer named Eleanor Mills—Kron did some side work on the case by finding and corroborating the story of a confidante. Paul F. B. Hamborszky said that Reverend Hall had confessed to him that he was in love with Mrs. Mills and that he had been threatened by her husband. The suspects who went to trial were the reverend's wife, Frances Stevens, and her two brothers. But even with Kron's confession and semi-eyewitness testimony from a woman named Jane Gibson, the suspects were cleared of all charges. Kron also dabbled in real estate; he was the director of the Ricoro Realty Company for the Bronx in 1923.

Ralph Woods (p. 318): "Found Wife in Apartment," *Milwaukee Sentinel*, August 28, 1930, 1.

Gargan busts the Be Kind Club (p. 318): "Captain Turns on Mrs. Humiston," *New York Times*, June 26, 1919, 15. Grace was arraigned on June 25.

Gargan's precinct (p. 319): "Clears Mrs. Humiston," *New York Times*, July 16, 1919, 13. The charges were dismissed in First District Court on July 16, 1919, by the magistrate, George W. Simpson.

"Police Headquarters to stop it" (p. 319): Richard Spillane, "Another Police Scandal," *Commerce and Finance*, July 23, 1919, 970.

the Castle (p. 319): "No Working Girls," *Brooklyn Daily Eagle*, August 26, 1917, 53.

22: THE WITNESSES' REVENGE

All the dialogue in this chapter, unless otherwise noted, is taken directly from Criminal Trial Transcripts of the County of New York, 1883–1927, trial 2766, February 13, 1920; microfilm reel 338.

"something about that ancient crime" (p. 322): *Salina Evening Journal*, October 29, 1920, 10.

"administration of justice" (p. 322): Edward Swann, "Crime of Perjury," *New York Evening News*, July 18, 1916, 12.

Georgette, was dead (p. 331): death certificate for Georgette Cocchi, December 6, 1918, file no. 41436, Department of Health of the City of New York. Georgette was admitted to St. Luke's Hospital very early on December 6; the physician, Dr. Scott, saw her alive, but she died at 6:15 that morning. The diagnosis during her last illness was acute bronchial obstructive syndrome ("ABOS") pneumonia lasting three days. She was buried at St. Michael's Cemetery on December 9. The Cocchis were living at 37 Old Broadway at the time of her death.

conviction (p. 331): "Alfredo Cocchi," Convictions Register, Court of Appeals, Bologna, Italy, 1920. There is a gap in the Archivio di Stato records in Bologna from 1917 to 1920, but the Convictions Register detailing Cocchi's sentencing survives. The most important fact in these pages was Cocchi's eventual fate, but in the background information, we learn that Cocchi was kept out of the Italian army because of "shortcomings," though there are no specifics. A heartfelt thanks to Cesarina Casanova, professor at the Università di Bologna, for her kind help. Thanks also to Dr. Barbara Burgess-Van Aken for her skilled translation of these findings.

Athos was doing well (p. 331): "Weakens Cocchi's Defense," *New York Times*, October 27, 1920, 13.

Cocchi's sentence (p. 332): "Alfredo Cocchi," Convictions Register, Court of Appeals, Bologna, Italy, 1920.

hunger strike (p. 332): "Murderer Cocchi on Hunger Strike," *New York Evening World*, Nov. 1, 1920, 26.

23: HER DARK SHEPHERD

New Justice magazine (p. 333): "New Justice," Catalog of Copyright Entries, Washington D.C.: Government Printing Office, 1920, 153. Advertised as 32 pages for $1.50 a year. Volume I was dated January 1, 1919.

"incidental verbal explanation" (p. 334): *Humiston v. Universal Manufacturing Co.* 189 N.Y.S. App. Div. 467, at 470–71.

Smiling and bowing (p. 334): "Universal to Fight Humiston Suit," *Motography*, July 14, 1917, 64.

as popular as she had been (p. 334): Goldsmith believes that Grace's popularity was a direct result of her political usefulness for others and that that reservoir had been simply used up by the Upton affair. Larry Goldsmith, "Gender, Politics, and 'White Slavery' in New York City: Grace Humiston and the Ruth Cruger Mystery of 1917," unpublished article, 42.

sent her packing (p. 334): "Bittle Refuses Woman Lawyer's Aid," *Buffalo Courier*, June 10, 1926, 11.

"best of both men and women" (p. 335): "Should Women Smoke?" *Syracuse Herald*, January 16, 1921, 10. "I do not think that smoking lowers the morals of a woman for nothing," Grace said, "but I believe that in the eyes of men, women who smoke are considered to be of weaker morale—in fact, I am sure that this is so. Of course, if a woman wants to smoke she has a perfect right to do so."

sixteen years old (p. 336): "Mystery of Our Missing Girls," *Charlotte News*, November 5, 1922, 25.

"Who is the girl" (p. 336): "What Becomes of Our Missing Girls?" *Detroit Free Press*, January 1, 1922, 56.

"blackout parties" (p. 336): "Mystery of Our Missing Girls," *Charlotte News*, November 19, 1922, 28.

"is an endless search" (p. 336): "The Real Reasons Why Girls Leave Home," *Atlanta Constitution*, January 29, 1922, 24.

Church in America (p. 337): Author, interview with Day grandson. In the 1930s, Jessie and two lady friends traveled by auto across the country with her chauffeur in a Packard limousine. The entire trip took almost four weeks.

Moor, who had come (p. 337): "Baptist Temple to Welcome," *Brooklyn Daily Eagle*, August 14, 1914, 12; "Hits Rockefeller at Flag Service," *Brooklyn Daily Eagle*, December 17, 1917, 5. He was also unafraid of controversy. When John D. Rockefeller began to assume the Baptists were behind him, Moor said that "If John D. Rockefeller knew as much about the Bible as he does about the Standard Oil Company, he might talk more intelligently in front of new servicemen."

destroyed by fire (p. 337): "Dr. Moor Stops Sermon," *Brooklyn Daily Eagle*, March 19, 1917, 3; "Dr. Moor Returns," *Brooklyn Daily Eagle*, August 4, 1917, 7.

"Throne of God" (p. 338): "Dr. Moor Stirs Audience," *Brooklyn Daily Eagle*, March 13, 1916, 26.

doors were locked shut (p. 338): "Madison Av. Church," *New York Times*, February 16, 1922, 1; "Church Ousts Third," *New York Times*, February 28, 1922, 3.

"Feeling Gray" (p. 339): "Sift Moor Charges," *New York Times*, February 19, 1922, 14. After Jessie Day was expelled, she turned the incriminating evidence over to the chairman and the board of trustees.

"to embarrass her" (p. 339): "Dr. Straton to Lay," *Brooklyn Daily Eagle*, February 21, 1922, 3.

"its present administration" (p. 339): "Minister Expelled," *New York Times*, February 21, 1922, 5. Dr. John Roach Straton of Calvary Baptist was called in to help mediate.

ordered to reinstate (p. 340): "Baptists Reinstate," *New York Times*, June 11, 1922, 21.

"Hades freezes over" (p. 340): "Minister Expelled," *New York Times*, February 21, 1922, 5.

"heard her cries" (p. 341): "Grace Humiston Run Over," *New York Times*, March 15, 1923, 21.

flu epidemic (p. 341): John M. Barry, *The Great Influenza*, New York: Penguin, 2005.

telegram to Amelia Earhart (p. 342): Telegram, May 23, 1932, New York, to Amelia Earhart, London, George Palmer Putnam Collection, Purdue University Archives and Special Collections.

Cocchi's release (p. 342): "Alfredo Cocchi," Convictions Register, Court of Appeals, Bologna, Italy, 1920; Author, personal interview with Renato Cocchi. Velotopica Cocchi is a bicycle store in Switzerland run by Renato Cocchi, who built and sold his own, very successful, "Cocchi" brand of cycle in 1997. His father was born in Piumazzo, Italy. That is "about 50 kilometers distant from Bologna," Renato said, "so who knows?"

Grace's death (p. 342): Death Certificate for Grace Humiston, July 16, 1948, file no. 16210, Department of Health of the City of New York.

Sunny Side report (p. 342): Mary Grace Quackenbos, *Report on Sunnyside Plantation, Arkansas*, Department of Justice Straight Numerical Files, Record Group 60, 100937, September 28, 1907.

intangible (p. 343): Grace would know that it was most likely not the same person. Or that it might be a common enough name. Or that the numbers didn't fit. But she couldn't know for sure. She might have wondered if it was a relative, or just the same name, or just a reminder that for all the people she had saved, there were many more who were lost, in one way or another.

"the same circumstances" (p. 344): Grace Humiston with Isabel Stephen, "Won't You Help Me Find My Girl?" *Actual Detective*, May 4, 1938.

EPILOGUE

"Estate for $32,000" (p. 345): "Matter of Alfred M. Brown," Surrogates Court, New York County, September, 1921, vol. 116, 485.

"reporting the accident" (p. 345): "Delays Report of Accident," *Pelham Sun*, August 27, 1936.

Kron (p. 346): passport application, Julius J. Kron, U.S. Passport Applications, 1795–1925, Ancestry.com.

Hungary (p. 346): Thomas Sakmyster, *Miklos Horthy: Hungary's Admiral on Horseback*, New York: Columbia UP, 2000; Bela Bodo, "Paramilitary Violence in Hungary After the First World War," *East European Quarterly*, June 22, 2004.

Daily Worker (p. 347): A digital archive of issues is available at onlinebooks.library.upenn.edu. The *Worker* was founded in Cleveland in 1924.

"present Hungarian Government" (p. 349): "Admits Shadowing the Karolyis," *New York Times*, February 27, 1926, 7. The Károlyis would apply to be let into the United States numerous times, but except for a few lecture visits by the count, they would be rejected for any long-term stay. The countess admitted to wanting to retire in America for good, but the State Department refused. "Dangerous," they said.

occupation read "Detective" (p. 349): death certificate for Julius J. Kron, November 24, 1934, file no. 25497, Department of Health of the City of New York. The doctor notes that bronchial pneumonia also contributed to his death. He is buried in Riverside Cemetery in Roselle Park, New Jersey.

McGee's salary (p. 350): "Detective M'Gee Retired," *New York Evening World*, September 18, 1919, 18.

hunt down German spies (p. 350): "Francis B. M'Gee, 67," *New York Times,* July 20, 1939, 25.

death of Mitchel (p. 350): "Belt Unfastened," *New York Times,* July 7, 1918.

death of J. J. Lynch (p. 351): "J. J. Lynch Dead in Yonkers," November 25, 1931, 17.

death of Percy (p. 351): Bertram Wyatt-Brown, *The House of Percy,* New York, Oxford UP, 1994, 3. Five years later, during the great Mississippi flood of 1927, Percy sent his son, William Alexander Percy, to direct the work of thousands of black laborers on the levees near Greenville. He prevented them from being evacuated when the levee was breached. They were forced to work without pay to unload Red Cross relief supplies, which required the work of volunteers. Both father and son were criticized for these actions.

death of Stielow (p. 351): "Charles Stielow," *Medina Daily Journal,* August 10, 1942, 1.

Lupo and Morello (p. 351): Thomas Reppetto, *American Mafia,* New York: Henry Holt, 2004.

death of Woods (p. 352): "Arthur Woods," *New York Times,* May 13, 1942, 19.

"office of the District Attorney" (p. 352): "Police Department Orders," *New York Sun,* January 23, 1920, 10.

John Lagarenne (p. 352): "J.L. Lagarenne, Ex-Deputy," *Brooklyn Daily Eagle,* June 19, 1949, 19.

"burned into me" (p. 353): Stephen Braun, "Clemency for Hanged Man," *Los Angeles Times,* June 2, 2001; Susan Sontag, *On Photography,* New York: Farrar, Straus and Giroux, 1977. "All photographs are memento mori. To take a photograph is to participate in another person's (or thing's) mortality, vulnerability, mutability. Precisely by slicing out this moment and freezing it, all photographs testify to time's relentless melt."

"fought for her life" (p. 353): Ibid.

"so indifferently lost" (p. 354): Gertrude Klein, "But the State Said She Must Hang," *Actual Detective,* March 23, 1938, 52.

death of Dent (p. 354): "Dr. Dent," *Charities and the Commons: A Weekly Journal of Philanthropy,* vol. 15, October 1905–March 1906, 513.

death of Sophie Loeb (p. 355): "Sophie Irene Loeb," *Democrat and Chronicle,* January 19, 1929, 2.

"crime is imitation" (p. 355): Edward Swann, "What Do District Attorneys Say," *Brooklyn Daily Eagle,* June 26, 1921, 64.

Pierini's mousetrap (p. 355): "Still Another Mouse-Trap," *Popular Science,* October, 1919, 76; Brodie Crump, "Tidbits from the Phone Book," *Delta Democrat-Times,* November 22, 1972, 4.

Churchill, De Gaulle and Adenauer (p. 356): Richard Roy, "Joe Grigg's WWII Experiences," downhold.org/lowry/griggs.html.

death of Dooling (p. 356): "J.T. Dooling Dies," *New York Times*, November 16, 1949, 29.

monies he had given to Sulzer (p. 356): *Documents of the Assembly of the State of New York*, 136th Session, Albany: J.B. Lyon, 1913, 129.

death of Herbert Roemmele (p. 356): "Herbert Roemmele," *New York Times*, August 16, 1983. At the time of his death, he had one great-grandchild.

"and other classes" (p. 357): "Suffrage Not a Natural Right," *New York Times*, May 24, 1915, 10.

death of Stimson (p. 357): "Henry L. Stimson," *New York Times*, October 21, 1950.

"admitted the crime in a dream" (p. 357): "Dead Girl's Spouse," *Washington Times*, April 9, 1919, 1.

national convention in 1927 (p. 358): "Past Supreme Commanders," *Military Order of the Cootie*, Program Book 2011–2012, 22.

Solan (p. 358): "Grand Central Terminal Says Farewell," *New York Times*, July 1, 1948, 25.

Maria Cocchi (p. 358): "Maria Cocchi," National Archives and Records Administration (NARA), Washington, D.C.; Index to Naturalization Petitions of the United States District Court for the Eastern District of New York, 1865–1957; microfilm serial M1164; microfilm roll 44.

Grace's background (p. 359): "Mrs. Grace Humiston Tells," *Eau Claire Sunday Leader*, July 8, 1917.

"sought companionship elsewhere" (p. 360): "I Hear—," *Tatler*, November, 1921, 6.

excessive drinking (p. 360): Author's personal conversation with Randall Boehm.

Forest Hills Cemetery in Boston (p. 360): death certificate for Howard Humiston, July 21, 1943, registered no. 33, Office of the Secretary Division of Vital Statistics of the Commonwealth of Massachusetts.

"Auntie Disgrace" (p. 360): Author's personal interview with Day grandson.

"not received them from me" (p. 360): Letter, Grace Quackenbos to Edward C. Stokes, January 15, 1906. New Jersey State Archives, R. Group: Governor Edward Caspar Stokes (1860–1942) Series: Correspondence, 1904–08, files 618–21, box 6.

"we just file paperwork" (p. 361): Kanyakrit Vongkiatkajorn, "NYPD: How the Police Handles Missing Person," themissingny.nycitynewsservice.com, 2015.

"place in my heart" (p. 361): "Is It Safe for a Woman Ever to Tell All?" *San Francisco Chronicle*, April 18, 1920, 3.

"can be checked" (p. 362): "Disappearing Girls and White Slaves," *Urologic and Cutaneous Review*, vol. 21, October, 1917, 594.

"road to ruin" (p. 362): "Mystery of Our Missing Girls," *Charlotte News*, December 3, 1922, 27.

"you will tolerate it at all" (p. 362): "Statement of Mrs. Mary Grace Quackenbos," *Hearings Before Committee on Immigration and Naturalization*. House of Representatives, 61st Congress. Washington, D.C.: Government Printing Office, March 29, 1910, 438.

NCMEC (p. 362): missingkids.org. The site walkfree.org also provides worldwide statistics and resources.

State Department (p. 362): "Trafficking in Persons Report," U.S. Department of State, July 2015, http://www.state.gov/j/tip/rls/tiprpt/.

Cleveland girls (p. 363): John Glatt, *The Lost Girls,* New York: St. Martin's Press, 2015.

"coming for you" (p. 363): Meghan Keneally, "Small Ohio Town," ABC News, June 24, 2015. http://abcnews.go.com/US/fbi-now-helping-search-killer-string-murders -ohio/story?id=32006473.

AUTHOR'S NOTE

Ruth's clothing (p. 366): "Can Now Forget," *San Bernadino County Sun,* July 9, 1924, 20.

"Frightened Eyes" (p. 368): "Case of the Frightened Eyes,"*Daily Herald,* July 8, 1956, 43.

morgues (p. 369): Scott Sherman, "The Long Good-Bye, *Vanity Fair,* November 30, 2012.

Grace Humiston (p. 369): Karen Abbott, "Mrs. Sherlock Holmes," *Smithsonian*.com, August 23, 2011; Charles Kelly, *The Crime Lawyer,* Kindle ed., 2002, and *Grace Humiston and the Vanishing,* Self-published, 2012, fiction; Tim McCarl, "The First Woman Detective," *Murder, Mischief and Mayhem: A Process for Creative Research Papers,* Urbana, IL: NCTE, 1978.

work of government agents (p. 370): FOIa request 1301332-000, October 6, 2014.

"to each individual story" (p. 370): "Statement of Mrs. Mary Grace Quackenbos," *Hearings Before Committee on Immigration and Naturalization. House of Representatives,* 61st Congress. Washington, D.C.: Government Printing Office, March 29, 1910, 433.

BIBLIOGRAPHY

MAJOR WORKS

The majority of sources for this book are the newspaper articles or periodicals that are cited in the notes. This list includes the major textual sources on Grace Humiston and some of the subjects of this book. The shortness of this list reflects how little has been written about her.

Abbott, Karen. "Mrs. Sherlock Holmes." *Smithsonian*.com. August 23, 2011.

Boehm, Randolph. "Mary Grace Quackenbos and the Federal Campaign Against Peonage." *Shadows over Sunnyside*. Fayetteville: U of Arkansas P, 1993.

Bond, George H. "Report by the Special Deputy Attorney." New York: New York State Attorney General's Office, 1917.

Borgognoni, Elizabeth Olivi. *Italians of Sunnyside 1895–1995*, Lake Village, AK: Our Lady of the Lake Catholic Church, 1995.

Daniel, Pete, ed. *The Peonage Files of the U.S. Department of Justice, 1901–1945*. Bethesda, MD: University Publications of America, 1989.

Dougherty, Joseph F., and K. S. Daiger. "Behind Drawn Blinds." *True Detective Mysteries*, March 30, 1930.

Evans, Colin. *Slaughter on a Snowy Morn*. London: Icon, 2010.

Halvorsen, Dick. "The Hidden Grave." *Master Detective*, April 1954.

Humiston, Grace, with Isabel Stephen. "Won't You Help Me Find My Girl?" *Actual Detective* May 4, 1938.

Hunt, William R. *Front-Page Detective*. Bowling Green, OH: Bowling Green State UP, 1990.

Kelly, Charles. *The Crime Lawyer*. Amazon Kindle ed., 2002.

———. *Grace Humiston and the Vanishing*. Self-published, 2012.

Klein, Gertrude. "But the State Said She Must Hang." *Actual Detective*, March 23, 1938.

Kron, Julius J., with Isabel Stephen. "The Inside Story of the Ruth Cruger Case." *True Detective*, May 1926.

———. "My Encounter with a White-Slave Ring." *Mysterious Crimes*. New York: True Story, 1934.

Marshall, Frank. "Where There Are Women There's a Way." *Good Housekeeping*, July 1918.

McCarl, Tim. "The First Woman Detective." *Murder, Mischief and Mayhem: A Process for Creative Research Papers*. Urbana, IL: NCTE, 1978.

New Jersey v. Tolla. *Reports of Cases Argued and Determined Before the New Jersey Supreme Court*, Newark: Soney and Sage, 1906.

Outland, Robert B., III. *Tapping the Pines*. Baton Rouge: Louisiana UP, 2004.

Poole, Ernest. *His Family*. New York: Macmillan, 1917.

Quackenbos, Mary Grace. *A Question for the House of Governors*. New York: People's Law Firm, 1909.

———. *Report on Sunnyside Plantation, Arkansas*. Department of Justice Straight Numerical Files, Record Group 60, 100937, September 28, 1907.

"Statement of Mrs. Mary Grace Quackenbos." *Hearings Before Committee on Immigration and Naturalization*. House of Representatives, 61st Congress. Washington, D.C.: Government Printing Office, March 29, 1910.

RESOURCES

National Center for Missing and Exploited Children:
www.missingkids.org
1-800-THE-LOST (1-800-843-5678)

FBI Kidnappings and Missing Persons
www.fbi.gov/wanted/kidnap

The Polly Klaas Foundation
www.pollyklaas.org

U.S. Department of Justice
National Missing and Unidentified Persons System
www.namus.gov

Project Jason
www.projectjason.org

The Wayne Foundation
www.waynefdn.org

I.C.E. Child Exploitation Investigations Unit
https://www.ice.gov/predator

RAINN

www.rainn.org

National Suicide Prevention Hotline

1 (800) 273-8255

Walk Free

www.walkfree.org

ACKNOWLEDGMENTS

Thank you, reader, for buying, downloading, or borrowing—and reading—this book.

The two people who deserve the most thanks are my editor, Michael Homler, and my agent, Scott Mendel. They saw right through the infinite previous ideas that came before this one. They instead pushed me to write something different and unsafe in the genre I dislike the most. This was not the book I set out to write, but in all the ways that count, it absolutely is. I am very grateful that even when they doubted my ideas, they never doubted me.

Because so little evidence exists of Grace Humiston's life, I relied on the important work of great librarians and archivists from all over the world. In no particular order or affiliation, they are David Gary, Margaret Chisholm, John Nann, Maurice Klapwald, Christina Violeta Jones, Rebecca L. Collier, Michael Foight, Gregory J. Plunges, Esperanza Lopez, Suzan Tell, Robert Ellis, Tal Nadan, Lisa Darms, Celeste Leigh Brewer, Gregory J. Plunges, Rosalba Varallo Recchia, Tammy Kiter, Julio Hernandez-Delgado, Linnea Anderson, Landis McEachin, David P. Sobonya, Lisa Darms, and Celeste Brewer.

Other people who helped or offered their expertise include Patterson Smith, Doug Willete, Larry Goldsmith, Joni Balter, Jeff Trexler, Barbara Burgess Van-Aken, and Cesarina Casanova in Italy. Special thanks to Randy Boehm, who knows more about Grace than anyone alive and whose work on Sunny Side is the gold standard. He welcomed me into the "Grace Club" with open arms. I very much look forward to his own book on her.

Personally, for advice, support, or encouragement along the way, thanks to Gary Lee Stonum, David Giffels, the Cleveland Arts Prize, Stephanie Michaels and David Weaver of the Ohioana Library, George Bilgere, Cyrus Taylor, Jim Calder, the NEOMFA, Henry Adams, Peter Whiting, Michael Clune, Grafton Nunes, Robert Maschke, Matt Martin, Dave Lucas, Lance Parkin, Heidi MacDonald, Gerard Jones, Nathan Greno, Lisa Nielson, Bob Pruyn, Renato Cocchi, Lee Chilcote, Alenka Banco, Mike Householder, Shelley Costa, Tom Batiuk, Anne Trubek, Ted Sikora and Milo Miller, and the great Rosa Ransom and Suzanne DeGaetano of macsbacks.com. And Shelley and Paul Servodio, who are my friends. And to everyone I thanked in *Super Boys*. Thanks as well to the good people at St. Martin's Press, especially John Morrone, Lauren Jablonski, Amelie Littell, and Angela Gibson, who all made this a better book.

A very heartfelt thanks to President Barbara K. Snyder, of Case Western Reserve University, for instituting a family leave plan, letting me work on this book in guerrilla fashion between changing diapers and playtime with my son.

Thanks to Eric Dicken, also of Case Western Reserve University, who asked me to introduce my favorite author, Neil Gaiman, at a reading there. Though it was a great experience, it was Eric's act of somehow remembering that I was a fan—and then asking me to do it—that was even better than the event itself (no offense, Neil). Thanks, pal.

Thanks to my family—everywhere and everywhen—for putting up with me when I made charts and taped photos to the walls and rushed through dinner and never slept. You are the best—I love you all. Thanks to Caroline, for always being the best mystery. And to James and his new brother or sister—I don't know your name yet, or who or what you are, but we're all waiting for you.

See you soon.

INDEX